INTRODUCTION TO THE THEORIES AND VARIETIES OF MODERN CRIME IN FINANCIAL MARKETS

INTRODUCTION TO THE THEORIES AND VARIETIES OF MODERN CRIME IN FINANCIAL MARKETS

FIRST EDITION

Edited by

MARIUS-CHRISTIAN FRUNZA

ELSEVIER

AMSTERDAM • BOSTON • HEIDELBERG • LONDON
NEW YORK • OXFORD • PARIS • SAN DIEGO
SAN FRANCISCO • SINGAPORE • SYDNEY • TOKYO
Academic Press is an imprint of Elsevier

Academic Press is an imprint of Elsevier
225 Wyman Street, Waltham, MA 02451, USA
The Boulevard, Langford Lane, Kidlington, Oxford OX5 1GB, UK

Library of Congress Cataloging-in-Publication Data
A catalog record for this book is available from the Library of Congress

British Library Cataloguing in Publication Data
A catalogue record for this book is available from the British Library

ISBN: 978-0-12-801221-5

For information on all Academic Press publications visit our website at http://store.elsevier.com/

Typeset by SPi Global, India
Printed in USA

Contents

III

TYPOLOGIES OF CRIME ON FINANCIAL MARKETS

3A. Insider Trading

3B. Ponzi Schemes

3C. Pump and Dump—Market Manipulation

3D. Rogue Trading

3E. Initial Public Offerings

3F. Mis-Selling

3G. Money Laundering in Financial Markets

IV

MODERN FINANCIAL CRIME

4A. Hedge Funds

4B. Emerging Markets and Financial Crime

4C. From Terrorism Financing to Terror's Economy

4D. Cybercrime

Preface

Following my previous book *The Carbon Connection* about the fraud on carbon markets [1], I decided to pursue the review of crime typologies in financial markets and to use the experience gathered in analyzing the missing trader fraud to other investment clusters and crimes.

In the aftermath of the financial crisis a series of crimes and misdemeanors were revealed by regulators and investigators. All these white-collar offenses are small pieces of a bigger puzzle depicting a vulnerable state of financial markets to internal and external threats.

Some quantitative methods and exploratory methods are introduced along with various examples of crimes. The book aims to present a balance between qualitative and quantitative analysis described in a language accessible to an average red person in both areas of financial crime and statistics. Beyond the technicalities introduced in the textbook it should be noticed that data mining and statistical analysis alone cannot tackle the full complexity of crime on financial markets. They need to be accompanied by comprehensive knowledge of the criminal phenomena along with all elements involved in an offense.

The book covers a number of geographical regions starting with the United Kingdom, and proceeding to Continental Europe, Central Asia, Turkey and the Russian Federation on both sides of the Urals, Central and South East Asia, and the United States. A number of people were interviewed including financial regulators, investigators, and individuals with knowledge about the world of organized crime.

The research process involved two major challenges. One the one hand, gathering sufficient intelligence relating to various crimes and trying to interact with persons involved as offenders, whistleblowers, investigators or victims in financial offenses was difficult due to the reluctance of these people to talk about crime in the context of the financial industry. One the other hand, finding the right balance between the qualitative descriptions of offenses in financial markets and introducing the more technical aspects of the investment industry was another challenge to meet.

Prologue

The perception in certain circles of financial crime as a softer non-violent crime creates a false impression. White-collar crime as opposed to blue-collar crime introduces a bias in the way financial offenses are analyzed.

Firstly, both white- and blue-collar crimes are highly interconnected, with each generating externality in the other category. On one hand, fraud on the markets such as the manipulation in agricultural commodities prices can create social unrest in certain regions of the globe, thereby increasing the chances of physical assaults or robberies. On the other hand, blue-collar crimes like smuggling of illegal items during the Prohibition era can lead to a large accumulation of liquidity which if transferred to markets can create or worsen a financial crisis.

Secondly, financial crime is no different from a psycho-emotional point of view from committing any other type of offense. There is a level of conscience where manipulating a stock or creating a network for money laundering is no different from smuggling goods or holding up a bank. The psychological and emotional triggers have many similarities.

Over the past decades traditional organized crime migrated slowly toward more sophisticated areas of white-collar crime. Therefore the factors involved in the typology of financial crime are very heterogeneous and include various social backgrounds and psychological profiles. The common theory of a positive correlation between poor education, low income per capita and crime does not hold true in this scenario.

Thus the knowledge of criminal phenomena from a purely process-oriented perspective is absolutely necessary. When constructing a framework that explains the offense it is first necessary to understand the behavioral and psychological mechanisms that underlie an offender or a criminal enterprise.

Acknowledgments to the First Edition

The author would like to gratefully and sincerely thank Didier Marteau, Michel Mouren, Derek Cunningham, Evgueny Kurinin, Piotr Ryzenkov, and Cristian Martiniuc for their support.

Special thanks are due to Leslie Pitts for the late night shuttles in London, but also to *Chazz*, the most charming presence from the "Marquis of Cornwallis," and Pop Nelson Simone (Nelson Mondialu) for their inspiring personalities and stories.

The author is also grateful for the academic contribution, inputs and support of the following:

- The Laboratory of Excellence for Financial Regulation in Paris (LABEX—ReFi) represented by Prof. Didier Marteau, Prof. Dr Christian de Boissieu and Francois Gilles Letheule for providing access to the databases (IODS, Barclays Hedge, Bankscope, Financial Times, Bloomberg).
- Prof. Dr Evgueny Shurmanov from the Ural State University for continuous support and scientific collaboration.
- Prof. Dr Aurora Castro Teixeira from the University of Porto for her efforts in organizing the most cutting-edge conference in financial crime to the Interdisciplinary Insights on Fraud and Corruption (I2FC).
- Prof. Dr Gunther Capelle-Blancard from Paris I Sorbonne University for his guidance.
- Prof. Dr Pascal Morand, from the Chamber of Industries in Paris, for his support.
- Dr Zsolt Pataki and Dr Joseph Dunne, heads of research at the European Parliament in Brussels.

The author is very grateful to Nick Leeson for agreeing to be interviewed, and to Europol and Olivier Fouque from the French customs for their ideas. The author is grateful to Tom Heineman for the opportunity to make his debut in the cinema world in *Carbon Crooks* (http://carboncrooks.tv/). Special recognition is due to the Press Office of the Istituto per le Opere di Religione for their time and for providing much useful information, and to Trafigura for their bibliographic assistance.

The author is grateful to Scott Bentley for making this project happen and to Susan Ikeda for her continuous support and patience.

Mr X Anonymous Interview

May 2014

BIOGRAPHY

This interview took place in May 2014. Mr X is working for the investment banking division of a major global bank.

Marius Christian Frunza (MCF): *Has the business model of investment banks changed over the last decade, and what is the future of the investment bank in the current context?*

X: I think that the model has not changed, but it should change, that is to say that the regulatory constraints that are imposed on banks should lead to a greater simplification of business, with a significant reduction of market activities or activities involving the balance sheet, and in return, a move to simpler operations—I have given two interviews on the return to simplicity, to commercial sales models in which the banks sell, take deposits, lend, and confer very simple hedging tools. I think this is the kind of evolution that the sales models for finance and investment must undergo because the regulatory constraints will push them to simplify, on the one hand because the balance sheet will be more constrained, producing less ability to achieve leverage on operations, and on the other because the regulators are rightly increasing the working capital risk threshold. So, in my opinion, this trend toward simplicity and a return to traditional banking, as in the 1980s or 1970s, will take place in the next five to ten years.

MCF: *In this context, in terms of strategic products, should there be a reduction in complexity?*

X: We have to get back to the business of traditional commercial banking, taking deposits and giving loans, transaction banking, that is to say, cash management and everything connected with credit, and then opening up to capital markets, through the offer of market capital in bonds or investments in bonds issued by companies or shares, and a small hedge of interest rate changes, something much simpler than what banks can do today. Very complex derivatives, etc., must disappear.

MCF: *In this context, is there room for innovation?*

X: No, but we do not expect banks to innovate. They are expected to provide credit to their clients, and to give investors the opportunity to invest their balance sheet items. Business clients need relatively simple banking services at the end of the day, and investor clients need to invest in simple products they understand. I think financial innovation will now become very marginal.

MCF: *Nevertheless, there are still a lot of changes in terms of market structure. Indeed, it is clear from the arrival of high-frequency trading, algorithmic trading, that the markets…*

X: Yes, but it will all go away again.

MCF: *So broadly speaking, we will see a return to fundamentals in the markets?*

X: Yes, and all these complex activities, which are proprietary activities, are going to disappear. Quite rightly, the regulators are restricting them. So it is normal for them to disappear. High frequency trading contributes nothing to the clients that we serve, whether corporate borrowers or investors actually investing. Maybe we will still have some hedge funds, but within clear regulatory constraints so that they do not have a competitive advantage over other investors in terms of market access.

MCF: *In this context, the role of hedge funds will change. Will they resume what they were doing previously in the future…?*

X: No, they cannot really resume it, because they need leverage, and the banks will give them less of it. Indeed, if banks give leverage to hedge funds, it means that they are taking the leverage on their balance sheets, which will happen less and less. In addition, behind this, hedge funds will take risks, but not necessarily high-frequency, but rather straight credit risks or underwriting risks which the banks will not necessarily take: Guaranteeing subordinated loan tranches, positioning on specific capital investments that banks cannot take on their own accounts, or perhaps underwriting or co-underwriting transactions that banks cannot fully take on their lines.

MCF: *The next subject for discussion concerns disputes and practices of mis-selling, rogue finance and rogue trading. I will start with structured products and then the complex products that have led since 2009 to numerous disputes in the markets between various entities about everything to do with rogue finance, mis-selling, etc., especially everything to do with interest rate derivatives, toxic loans, etc.: what is your view of that?*

X: I believe that the regulator is right to have a very disciplined approach to all these issues, first of all to ensure that products sold to clients are understandable for them—the product must be simple—and secondly to ensure that banks cannot possibly take advantage of market shifts on special fixings—as we have seen with commodities, FX and interest rates—which can create a disadvantage for the clients. So all in all, I think that a much more disciplined approach to a number of factors can only be beneficial to the market in the future, but anyway I think that this must all form part of a major simplification of the product range. Of course, these processes must be adjusted to be more in line with the client's interest and to avoid special arbitration areas, but on the other hand I think that they will be resolved by themselves because the products will also become much simpler.

MCF: *But can we say that complexity created these problems? Are they the result of complexity? Are they a lever?*

X: No, they are partly due to the complexity of the entire product offering and to misunderstanding, since the products were complex, by the end clients of some of the mechanics. There was misunderstanding of some of the mechanics by the managers in the banks themselves. This is obvious from the Libor fixing problems, for example, for managers of banks, when you look at what has been said about the banks that are now in the spotlight of the courts or journalists, that management did not really understand what the traders were doing because neither the clients nor the management understood that there could be areas where there could be operations which were not in the client's interest but in the interest of the bank.

MCF: *If we look back to the 1980s, to the case of Michael Milken, and then back to today with the Libor case, can we say that there is a procyclicality factor in everything to do with rogue finance? Does it depends a little on the trend?*

X: I do not think that it is the fact that there is a bull market or a bear market that is important, but rather the fact that when there is a more active market—which is essentially the case when there is a bull market—with greater liquidity and volumes, this can lead to the development of more products, and possibly arbitrage that might not be done in the client's interest. But I think that the regulation has also evolved, that is to say, what today might be seen as an action that is not in the client's interest was not necessarily seen a few years ago as something that could perhaps be against the regulations. The regulations have rightly become stricter. I think that we are now in something that is simpler in terms of environment. I believe that bull markets often bring more liquidity and therefore a more dynamic market: we meet new people who join banks and are perhaps not well supervised. There is more hiring, and so there may be a little less direct supervision, and the risks are certainly higher in bull markets than in bear markets where the banks rein in their activities more.

MCF: *What happens next depends on slightly controversial decisions of the courts, in particular the French traders Kerviel and Picano-Nacci, who went down last year and a few days ago. It is clear, indeed, that there is still a part of this business for which the banks are held liable; so, the liability is somewhat shared between the environment and the individual. Do you agree with that? And in this type of case, what is the role of the institution and the environment, and what is the role of the individual?*

X: If a burglar breaks into a house, is it the fault of the police or of the burglar? That is to say, is it the fault of the police because there were no policemen in front of the house? With the banks, it is the same thing. Depending on how you look at it, the liability is not just that of the individual committing the fraud, but further back, whatever the principles or the number of locks you put on a door, the burglar can get through the basement window. Depending on the culture of the country, you can take more or less immediate measures, or you can have a different approach. So I think it is very much a cultural matter.

MCF: *There has been discussion of whether it is the fault of the police or the burglar, but it is true that the recent crisis is something that recurs in financial services and that there is an asymmetry between risk managers and operators. Sometimes public opinion thinks that the capacity of risk managers has been reduced…in terms of organization, process, resources, training, etc. Is that something which…?*

X: I do not believe that. I think we should go back to the analogy of the burglar and the police: if you put a policeman in front of every house, it will be less likely they are burgled. They might still be, but at some point, it is not the amount of resources that proves that the establishment of whatever kind (a bank, an insurance fund, etc.) is more or less protected. I think that, behind that, it is much more the nature of the risks that will dictate the resources and processes that need to be implemented. In banking, front office activities have decreased a lot in terms of resources and number of operators, whereas control activities have increased quite a bit. So we have had contrasting developments in terms of resources. The fact that today we have more investment in everything connected with risks versus a reduced front office means that the initial situation was too unbalanced, there were not enough resources for the number of operators. I think it all depends on the level of refinement of those involved. Major risks for banks are IT risks, for example, in which you can have computer attacks from hackers: these risks were much less likely a few years ago; today many more resources are deployed because hacking techniques have improved, and the exposure of banks is much greater. So I am sure the marginal action in risk resources will definitely decrease after a certain time, and today what is more important is to decide not to do a range of things rather than to do something and then need additional risk resources. There are a number of segments where either the bank has no particular competitive advantage, or there is no local presence; so it is better for the bank to stay away, rather than expand, with all the additional costs that involves. Take the example of European banks that are growing in Asia: there are lots of banks that have strategic visions, but the competitive advantage of European banks in Asia is very limited—no local presence of domestic banks, no in-depth knowledge of the markets, no hiring of networks of locals, etc. All in all, I think that this development can only lead to a number of operational market, credit and regulatory risks. I think that rather than saying, "We will expand in Asia, we will invest heavily in the Middle East," the best thing is to say, "We are not going to expand in Asia, we will just stick with the markets we know." When we look at the problems of credit risk, which is a very common issue, a European bank that is expanding in Asia today, in order to take credit decisions on clients, will have a very limited reading of the credit risk of Asian clients and the movements in credits. It will have a much more limited sense of them, since the bank's management structures are in Europe, and when you do not have that sense then, inevitably, mistakes will be made which local banks will not make. Do you have to have several local credit analysts to try to compensate for this, so that ultimately credit functions or investment strategies will be taken over by management? If management has a poor understanding of the case, I do not think that hiring additional credit analysts will compensate for this lack. All in all, I think the best way to manage these risks is to decide on the one hand to simplify your business and on the other to be positioned in sectors that you understand—when I say that you understand them well that means that you have a particular competitive advantage.

MCF: *When it comes to bank losses due to unauthorized trading problems or anything that revolves around what may be called financial crimes, it is clear that the focus is still on the pretty big losses at the heart of distribution or on the profits that can occur due to bad decisions.*

X: I think that the greatest losses of banks still relate to the provisions that are part of their traditional business. Of course, when you lend money to clients, there is a certain probability of default, so that banks have to make provisions. But then, what are the loss levels compared to the initial expected loss, and what is the offset, positive or negative? There is less focus or analysis on what has happened than on the more dramatic losses. When we look at the huge bank losses, it is still about the provisions and their relationship to the expected loss, that is, the projected loss. I think the key factors today are to simplify the models so as to limit the probability of distribution losses alone due to unauthorized actions on an operator account, but I think a very big focus should also be the use of credit portfolios, the targets that are given to the bankers who grant credits, and how these bankers are assessed and evaluated so as to be sure that there is consistency between the targets and the behavior in order to optimize and better manage the loan portfolios. These days, we too readily forget that banks must first of all lend money, and that it is in terms of credit that they lose market share. I am not sure that researchers or journalists are focusing much on that, but it is the heart of the business.

MCF: *You talk a lot about credit as an activity. Should we expect that the classical players on Wall Street or the big Anglo-Saxon investment banks will change course at some point?*

X: If the Anglo-Saxon investment banks remain pure investment banks, they will not make loans, but will certainly offer consultancy. As for the European banks, which are banks with a global offering, that is, retail as well as business, you must remember that each of the largest European banks lends between 250 and 300 billion euros in Europe to European clients. That is still a lot of loans, and an error of credit assessment can lead to significant losses compared to the average expected loss. I think the first thing to do is to clean and regularize the management of these loan portfolios: that is the first task of a bank; market activity, etc. is a secondary activity.

MCF: *In terms of risk management, it is true that the classical framework tends to focus on rare events. Do you think that today it is necessary to understand rather the entire P&L of activity, the structure, the drivers…?*

X: You have to look at how business leaders manage their work. If I start with market activities, it is necessary to ensure the robustness of the processes, because they are defined, but then applied by people who, inevitably, can make mistakes—the person who has never made mistakes does not exist. So it is necessary to have different levels of control and to ensure that they are effective. This is a process approach that is relatively conventional and the various events of the past mean that the levels of control and sensitivity are well developed in banks, although the process requires a commitment which must never stop: when processes are set up, it is crucial to ensure that they are applied, which is difficult but necessary. When you do this, you avoid losses on credits, but you do not avoid market losses in an adverse market—that depends on sound activity, management costs, and other factors, and that is a matter of limits or risk appetite. On credit, it is something else: it involves the need for approaches that can be to very granular credits, rather more statistical approaches—anything that has to do with the financing of consumer credit, for example, or credit to individuals, etc.—or much more specific approaches—when granting credit to corporations, you are perhaps a bit between the two extremes in terms of approach: there, credit analysis, risk allocation and concentration risk must be the focus. In addition to these credit risks, you have everything to do with the targets and nature of the targets given to the bankers, the traders: if you set a credit volume target to bankers, like the classical target given in banks about 15 years ago, the rational banker will lend to riskier clients because he can charge them higher finance fees. If the target volume is risk-adjusted, that is to say, if you look at the amount of interest less the loss from client defaults, you then have an approach on which the operators try rather to achieve a distribution of their risk such that the actual loss will be very close to the expected loss, and prevent the actual loss being well above the expected loss, which is the task of true credit portfolio management: converging on the expected loss and not going over it. I think that credit approaches and targets depend on the understanding of the latter but also on the development principles of the assessments and targets defined, and in my opinion that is still not well understood, either by the managers of banks or by the regulators.

MCF: *If I can digress for a moment on credit, before introducing a measure such as volume adjusted by risk, you need a credit risk modeling system that is marginal, that can be...*

X: As regard risk-adjusted volume, or risk-adjusted revenue, every client should have a rating in a bank that is basic. A rating indicates the expected loss. Is the rating model of a bank correct? There may be differences between the various banks, when they have an advanced rating model which they define themselves, but they all more or less converge on the same models. So I think that rating clients on the one hand is not very complicated to do and on the other is relatively standard between banks, and it will become even more so with the review that the European Central Bank is currently carrying out, to ensure that there is comparability of banks between European clients. The European Central Bank is in the process of taking over supervision. So I think it really depends on the targets: you set credit risk-adjusted targets for your banking teams—I know this is not necessarily the case in other banks; on the other hand, there must be other ways to manage risk, and simply setting a risk-adjusted target will not in itself achieve that. Afterwards, you have to look at how the credits are clustered, how you are going to manage concentrations. I can set a risk-adjusted target for a banker who has one credit in his portfolio that will meet my target; if another has a thousand credits in his portfolio for the same nominal amount, he is more likely to hit his expected loss because his exposure is much more granular, while the one who has only one credit will be either very good or very bad. So, a risk-adjusted target alone is not sufficient; on top of that, you have to look at the concentration target, the distribution of exposures, etc. This is what is most important today, in my opinion.

MCF: *In that context, if you generalize this to all activities, does the modeling risk play a more important role than before?*

X: I think the modeling risk plays a more important role than before because banks have more models. In the past, they had no modeling risks because there were no models, but that does not mean they had no risk—this approach is perhaps a little too unsophisticated. Today, there is a modeling risk which, because of the greater use of models, means that the sensitivity to modeling error is larger. That is tautological in a way. Then, the key point for me is not so much the modeling risk, but knowing what the reins are for a commonsense approach. To try to illustrate this point, the major ongoing debate is about the bank leverage ratio versus capital consumption, the latter being calculated by the banks on the basis of models, so that you can have a capital adequacy ratio of 9% or 8%. Some regulators say that beyond the capital amounts required for a bank to seem to be safe, there must also be a ratio to the leverage ratio, that is, the capital size to the balance sheet size, the size of the balance sheet not adjusted for risk under Basel, better known as Basel III. I think that that is not at all stupid because the calculation of capital under Basel III is done by models, and models can create inconsistencies or very high risk concentrations: there are some models that have virtually no risk when working with AAA, that is, very high, ratings. So, you can build up huge risk concentrations for very low capital commitments. This can be on sovereign debt and, behind that, if you do not have the rein of common sense, which is the nominal exposure or leverage ratio, the balance sheet size in capital against the specific balance sheet size, you will not know the adequacy of the situation. I give you an example: the largest German bank has a capital adequacy ratio of 8% or 9%, so beyond the regulatory constraints, and capital to balance sheet size ratio of 3%: is a balance sheet protected by 3% of the capital reassuring? Probably not, and being protected by 4% of capital will probably not be much more reassuring. What is the right exposure in terms of leverage that a bank must have? That is for everyone to judge. And I think that a "mark to model" approach, without returning to a nominal approach, that is, the nominal concentration of risk after assessment on a particular asset against the balance sheet total, for a sector: this does not enable you to manage these risks. So simply trusting the model is actually to make the bank very exposed, and you always have to have a return to the nominal exposure. If there is one lesson to learn from the crisis it is that.

MCF: *You are talking about credits. Do you think the role of the major rating agencies will change?*

X: No, I do not think so, because banks do not use the rating agencies. You do not give out credit on the basis of the agency rating. You do your own credit analysis, and the rating given is not used for your own analysis or in the rating used for defining regulatory capital. I think that in the crisis the rating agencies showed that they were far behind the evolution of credit, not that they do a bad job, but that they are a lag indicator rather than a lead indicator, which is understandable for reasons of structures or indeed the calculations of potential risks they can make. Today you have three major rating agencies, not that many. Should you have more? Do the rating agencies give fairly transparent information to users, etc.? I do not know, but I think that investors should rely less on credit rating agencies. A good investor must take credit decisions on his own assessment of the credit, not on something that he has been given by a rating agency.

MCF: *Going back to market risks, two terms that are making a lot of noise today—even if you say that they are likely to become rather less used—are high-frequency trading and dark polls. Aside from the flash crash, which happened a few years ago, could there be a wave of rogue finance in this context?*

X: Finance being based on the concentration of financial markets on large amounts invested, I think there will always be risks of rogue finance or incorrect behavior, but certainly not where you expect it. High-frequency trading is basically an operational risk—for example, a computer that you can no longer control, or poorly defined price because of a badly reassessed parameter—rather than a matter of market risks, since, by their nature, positions are closed every night. So I think the risks are more operational than anything else. Future fraud risks in banks will come from places that are not being scrutinized enough today. Huge amounts of controls have now been put in place for market activities after certain events that may have taken place. On the other hand, as I mentioned earlier, the real risk is in fact at the IT level. We have not yet seen a major fraud because hackers have broken into a bank and transferred billions of euros by converting the second decimal place to cents on all transfers, or making transfers below sensitivity thresholds. It is possible to transfer billions without people necessarily noticing. For me, the real risk is there rather than in market activity risks, to which considerable attention is devoted *a priori*, even if frauds have recently occurred in major Swiss banks, etc. This is something that will continue to happen, but I think it will decline because of control methods. The risks will come from elsewhere, and I am thinking in particular of IT.

MCF: *If you are talking about the IT side, is this where the term Big Data comes in?*

X: That is a different subject. Banks have access by their nature to a huge amount of information about clients, because we know everything they buy and everything they sell, and we know all of their financial flows. This information could certainly be used better by banks to understand the behavior of their clients better, and possibly offer them product deals, if the clients agree of course—there is a notion of confidentiality about client transactions. This could certainly be very useful, like what Amazon or eBay are doing already, by analyzing what their clients are buying, given that a bank holds much more data because it knows everything that the client spends. However, banks are not exploiting this information. So I do not see any link between this information and rogue trading, etc.

MCF: *Yes, but there could be IT fraud, etc.*

X: IT fraud is mainly about access to client accounts and making transfers. There, on the other hand, the risks are huge. I think the next really big problem could be, for example, just the computer system of a bank that crashes because of the actions of hackers or even States. It seems that a particular State may have introduced viruses into the nuclear processing plant of another State, in the Middle East. If you can do that in a closed system, you can certainly introduce viruses which reduce the system of a bank. If the system of a bank crashes, it is a real problem both for itself and its clients. What keeps me awake at night these days is basically that, because there are very major risks involved. Anyone can put a USB key in a PC, or click on a false document attached to an email, and expose the system to viruses, despite the safety systems in place.

MCF: *So at the moment there are no real defenses against that risk at the regulatory level?*

X: No, and I think that at the moment the regulators are tending to focus on market risk and distribution risk rather than on IT risks, but that is just my opinion, I could be wrong. And I think that IT risks are now greater than the distribution risk, in terms of consequences.

I gave a presentation to the finance graduates at a reputed university. They work part time in banks, so I asked them what they were doing. They said: "I am working in the structured derivatives department of big banks etc." I told them they had made a bad choice by working in derivatives because derivatives are on the way out. They said, "Yes, but it is important. Can you create, have creativity in derivatives, innovation?" I explained to them that it has been clear for a long time that innovation is useless. And I think when you look basically at the medium term, the overdevelopment of financial products or derivatives or too complex products is on the way out. I said that the "new derivatives" are cash management and trade finance, which are quite important sectors where, by being a little smarter, the bank can be quite profitable, with a very good risk profile. And when you lend money and perform cash management, you cover your cost of capital in general. The market values the activity at a multiple of book value, which is not the case for trading or derivatives activities. So when you look at where you want to put the capital in a bank, you put it into loans for cash management rather than derivative activities. That is why I think that there are quite profound changes going on, but I am not sure they are well understood today, and in any case it takes time for universities to adjust their programs because they are still working on the capital markets and derivatives. As I said earlier, the model is one thing, but getting back to reality is another. All the nonsense that has happened in banks or regulators has happened because they have the right model, whereas in fact people were looking back to the nominal—to avoid problems, you have to follow the nominal. When I say follow the nominal I mean follow the nominal in the balance sheet. It is not very exciting when you put it like that, but I think it is part of the way things are going.

Nick Leeson: Interview

London, United Kingdom, February, 2014

BIOGRAPHY

In the early 1980s, Nick Leeson landed a job as a clerk with royal bank Coutts, followed by a string of jobs with other banks, before moving to Barings, where he quickly made an impression and was promoted to the trading floor.

Before long, he was appointed manager of a new operation in futures markets on the Singapore Monetary Exchange (SIMEX) and was soon making millions for Barings by betting on the future direction of the Nikkei Index. His bosses back in London, who viewed with glee his large profits, trusted the whizzkid. Leeson and his wife Lisa seemed to have everything: a salary of £50,000 with bonuses of up to £150,000, weekends in exotic places, a smart apartment and frequent parties, and to top it all they even seemed to be very much in love.

Barings believed that it wasn't exposed to any losses because Leeson claimed that he was executing purchase orders on behalf of a client. What the company did not realize is that it was responsible for error account 88888 where Leeson hid his losses. This account had been set up to cover up a mistake made by an inexperienced team member, which led to a loss of £20,000 Leeson now used this account to cover his own mounting losses.

As the losses grew, Leeson requested extra funds to continue trading, hoping to extricate himself from the mess by doing more deals. Over three months he bought more than 20,000 futures contracts worth about $180,000 each in a vain attempt to move the market. Some three quarters of the $1.3 billion he lost Barings resulted from these trades. When Barings executives discovered what had happened, they informed the Bank of England that Barings was effectively bankrupt. In his wake Nick Leeson had wiped out the 233-year-old Baring Investment Bank, who proudly counted HM The Queen as a client. The $1.3 billion dollars of liabilities he had run up exceeded the entire capital and reserves of the bank.

Eventually arrested in Frankfurt, Germany, Nick spent a few fraught months trying to escape extradition to Singapore. He failed and in December 1995 a court in Singapore sentenced him to six and a half years in prison. His wife Lisa got a job as an airhostess to be able to visit him regularly. At first, their marriage survived the strain of being apart, but she eventually divorced him. Within months, Leeson was diagnosed as suffering from cancer of the colon. His weight plummeted and most of his hair fell out from chemotherapy.

Finally released in 1999, and despite his return to the UK bringing the realization that the high life had been swept away—he was effectively homeless and without a job—Nick enjoyed a fairly hedonistic first year seeing friends and family but also continuing his cancer treatment.

Nick Leeson has proved his resilience and has been able to capitalize on his experiences. He was paid a substantial fee for the newspaper serialization of his book in the *Daily Mail*. The story was then turned into a film, *Rogue Trader*, starring Ewan McGregor. In 2001, he completed a psychology degree and Nick now spends much of his time presenting talks to companies on Risk

Management and making after-dinner and conference speeches based on his life experiences.

With a psychology degree and a second marriage to Irish beautician Leona Tormay (with her own children Kirsty and Alex) after trying for a baby they were delighted when, in 2004, Leona gave birth to a baby boy. Nick comments: "I'm of the mindset that cancer must not take you over and control your life. I do believe that the more positive you are, the greater your chance of survival." His advice to others is never to bottle up stress as he himself did: "You need to talk and express yourself as I now do to Leona. With cancer as with other problems, it's amazing how adaptable human beings are, and you will be able to cope provided you keep a strong frame of mind."

In April 2005, Nick was appointed Commercial Manager of Galway United Football Club, rising to the position of General Manager in late November 2005. The same year Nick published his second book *Back from the Brink, Coping with Stress* co-written with psychologist Ivan Tyrell. July 2007 saw him appointed as CEO of the football club and he remained in this position until his resignation in February 2011.

Marius Christian Frunza (MCF): *Hello Mr Leeson. It is a great honor to finally meet you. Many people I know in the financial industry that I know read your first book so I think it is probably more popular than a lot of classic financial books.*

Nick Leeson (NL): It should be a cautionary tale for anybody.

MCF: *The financial world had passed through some major events and crises over the past 20 years. From your perspective has the banking (investment banking) industry kept its elitist "culture" or has it evolved into something different?*

NL: I think what you see is wherever risk is, there are different ways people deal with it. Where there is risk, there is always opportunity for something to go wrong, be that by deliberate fraud, be that unintentionally or by mistake in the beginning. If you look at the large number of scandals that happened over the last number of year, I think at their embryonic stage if you like a lot of them were characterized by people bending the rules as much as they could. And I think this is a culture that always existed in investment banking. It is a culture which is extremely competitive as you know. There is competition between individuals, there is competition between desks, there is competition between firms and there is competition even between financial markets, all trying to do better than the others.

Ultimately it is presented more so in volume and in profit and I think they are the main metrics people are looking for to measure success. I do not think that has changed materially over the years, I think that is still the same if you speak to any investment broker, salesman, or trader they are still measuring themselves by how much profit they make, that's what the financial markets understand and if you work for a French equity trading desk or if you work for a South East Asian trading desk again it is the amount of profit that has been made by that desk that is the metric that is measured. It is not about how ethical you are or how compliant you are or how safe your business is, the measurement is still how much money you are making. And I think that adds to the competition. For me I often described it as a modern day amphitheater, where the gladiators go into battle and the best, the strongest, the most successful survive and the rest of the people don't. And I think within that sort of environment you are looking for people that are very disciplined and follow the rules in order for the risk you take to be qualified and to be safe and you are looking for certain type of individuals and I wasn't that during that period; I wasn't particularly risk averse and I was particularly quite stubborn and undisciplined in terms of the trading that I was doing and that from a psychological perspective is not the type of person you want exhibiting that risk for you.

But if you look at how the culture changed over the years some people would suggest that with the LIBOR rate fixing the culture is getting worse. And with the quantity of the losses it would be fair to suggest that the culture is getting worse as well, because there are larger sums of money involved. A large part of that would also be the type of trading that's done now: it is high frequency, it is far more computer orientated and algorithmic orientated and the volume and the frequency of the trading have just increased at such a level that it defies the understanding of the average person. I was with a friend of mine in Dubai recently and I think he managed to make 37 trades in less than 1 microsecond. And that in itself presents huge risk to the market place.

A culture doesn't change unless it is changed. The tone is set from the top within the organization and all from the top within a regulatory body. The thing that was very apparent over the past 20 years, post the collapse of Barings is that there has never been an adequate deterrent to people doing wrong within the market place. When you are in a risk-taking environment and the deterrent and the control are not strong and in place, I think there is the tendency to push those boundaries all the time and that's certainly what I did from an individual perspective and you see that with most of the episodes that continued from that time as well.

MCF: *This amphitheater with gladiators that you mention has grown more and more over the past years. The financial/investment industry grew significantly in the Western world over the past decades representing in some countries the main economic driver. If we make a parallel with the car industry, do you think the "core business model" of the "amphitheater" is today fully understood by governments/politicians or decision makers? What impact can this have on the global economy?*

NL: I don't and if you look at regulators and if you look at governments around the world they do differ by location. For instance in Germany in particular the regulator has a very different approach to the regulator in the United Kingdom. I think it is difficult to generalize too much, but my opinion would be that the regulators, the governments, and the central banks don't really understand enough and have enough experience to really drill down into detail and the word I often use they don't really challenge what is going on within the business or within the industry, because they don't have the necessary degree of understanding and knowledge to do so. And if you look typically to a government, every government is different; I live in Ireland now and the government is populated with a lot of school teachers, people that you would not associate with being in any way involved in the financial markets and trying to control it and that's why the situation in Ireland got so bad as it did as quickly as it did, the people in place to ask those difficult questions they just were not adequate in terms of the level of their knowledge and their experience.

MCF: *Do those people in charge within regulators or governments at least understand that there is a problem in order to get the right skills or counsel for dealing with it?*

NL: The market is continually moving and changing and adapting. Financial markets are based on speed and complexity and making money. Banks, investment banks, and speculators are always looking for new ways of making money, and making that money in the most efficient way they possibly can. The target is always moving, and whenever you see new regulations and new controls they become dated very quickly. People talk about reactive and proactive risk management, but it needs to be active all of the time, because that target is continually moving and that needs a lot of investment and a lot of quality from a personnel perspective and I think that the two have always been lacking and they have probably been lacking for hundreds of years. And you will never catch that moving target unless you up your game and you get closer to it. I don't think responsibility is solely with governments, clearly it is with central banks and regulators, but they are equally as not up to the game as the governments are.

MCF: *Technology reshaped structurally the investment/financial world. From exchanges to* *control systems and trading platforms, technology is present everywhere. Is the arrival of big data, social networks, etc. an asset for regulators or can it go against the tendency of increasing market surveillance?*

NL: I think it should be an asset, but it is only an asset if it is used correctly. I speak to a lot of different audiences, very financial oriented and a lot of firms are looking to use all data available out there. In my day it was a simple market rumor between two people talking or three people talking and asking what Barings is really doing, whereas now you have all social media that exists, where people probably are exchanging views on what is happening on the market and any concerns that they may have and I think there is an awful lot of data that you can use, but like any data that you are using for any business you have to work out which are the best indicators and which are the most efficient in terms of what they are showing. I think within the organizations there are so many clever ways people can use the information at their disposal. I am a firm believer that whenever there is a financial crisis the information is always there. You are maybe not accessing the information. People are right now looking at, if you are a trader, what part of the business you are accessing, what account, what time of day you access, how many times you access it, what time you come into the office, what time you leave the office, do you need to be there during that time and piecing all that information together it would definitely highlight whenever somebody is doing something wrong. But you need to do it in a real-time environment.

MCF: *"Wall Street" started hiring over the past decade the so-called "rocket scientists," achievers in fundamental sciences like maths, physics, statistics, etc., but with less or no "real-world business experience." Has the required profile of a trader changed?*

NL: I think it changes. There are still some traders in the true traditional sense, but they are very limited in number in these times. And that is an educational thing. As much you grow up with an open market, there are a certain set of attributes for succeeding in that market. They tend to be more visual and more obvious than if you are trading behind a screen. The catalyst would have been when we started to trade after hours on LIFFE or other markets. Traders traditional traders had to adapt to see if they could work well with the screens. Few people had succeeded for a while, there were few people that continued to succeed. I know personally one or two of them. But very few people adapted for that change from the traditional trading floor environment, be that on LIFFE or SIMEX or other stock exchanges. There are one or two that exist in Chicago and New York and you see more of what we described as traditional traders in that environment and a number of traditional traders who survived to the present day and continue to thrive and trade because they adapted to the new world of algorithmic, high frequency trading, and the person I mentioned in Dubai is one of those. He would have been a traditional Eurobond Interest rate-type trader and is now market making in gold and oil. But only because he managed to adapt and master the new technology. He would employ people as well in order to achieve this. His typical employee would be a double physics graduate from "Oxbridge" or new universities like Guangdong in China or from one of the Indian universities. Thus you have a mix of people that are very hungry, have a very strong desire to succeed, have a great work ethic and are supremely intelligent at the same time as well. If in the UK it is more of an Oxbridge mentality, for somebody that comes from that traditional trading environment that moved into the modern-day trading he would attribute a lot to the hunger of the person and I do not want to typecast anybody but from an Oxbridge environment they might not be quite so much hunger. If you have a fairly decent life already you may not have that urgent desire to achieve.

When you read my book you'll have seen that we have had a basic squawk box that would go to the trading floor or to the execution area in Osaka and I would shout my orders through that squawk box and somebody would execute the order in Osaka. One of the people that executed my orders in Osaka was a person called Mike Lurch and he is now one of the biggest arbitrage traders in the world. He has an office in Honolulu, he has a very successful trading business called Tora Trading, and he was the subject of the book *Ugly Americans* by Ben Mezerick, a book more in the style of *Wolf of Wall Street* than an analytical work about what is going on in markets. Mike would have come from my history and would have been my order filler and he would move singly, it seems, from the trading order environment to the screen trading environment. Bet very few have done it. If you have a look at the trading floor in LIFFE 20 years ago and how many people from there are still trading that would be a handful of people because they were not able to adapt to the way that it changed.

MCF: *Does the word "trader" still properly define the role of dealing financial instruments or should it be replaced with "numerologist," "(smooth) data operator," or "quant merchant"? We witness not only the increasing use of numerical models and numerical systems in the investment world, but also decision making based exclusively on models. Numbers are explained with other numbers. What is your view on this point?*

NL: The traditional definition of a trader is of somebody seeing an opportunity and benefitting from that opportunity; whereas now you key a number of metrics into a box and the box triggers when necessary and human interference is minimal now; in the past it would be the main part of it and that presents positives and negatives. The negatives are that the volumes and the direction of the trading can vary one way or the other very quickly, and that's why it needs to be controlled.

MCF: *With all the models, systems and thousands of academics dedicated to financial topics nobody picked up in 2007 that a many banks were long on mortgages of unemployed people in the United States. Is this a paradox?*

NL: I think it goes back to channeling down into the detail and challenging what happens. And somebody should have a good enough overview. And that overview has to be somebody in a central bank, regulation or in government. Because somebody should put all the pieces together to test if this will happen. It is like many of the Merrill Lynch alpha funds lost a lot of money overnight, a good few years ago (10-15 years ago), because one of the criteria that they set to measure risk was missed. There is a lot of human error and we spoke a little earlier about technology and I've always believed that technology has a huge part to play in the financial market.

The difficulty in bringing some of the technology into the market is that it costs. Boards have always resisted that and banks have resisted that to a certain degree over the years because it is a an opportunity cost as opposed to what they could use to make money. It is something that should be encouraged.

MCF: *Is this resistance only because of cost or also because if systems are there the probability of having everything tracked and recorded is higher and that would reduce some freedom that exists right now, with manual things etc.?*

NL: If you look to any financial scandal, where the oversight breaks down is with the human. That has always been the case. Thus any argument toward freedom and interpretation is one that can be quickly rejected. Everything is about mitigating risk. If technology can mitigate that on the basis that you don't want a scientist taking all of the data and not coming out with any results. It has to be streamlined, it has to be proven to work and it has to be beneficial.

Trawling through everybody's Facebook account to come up with one remote item that really had no impact on what was going on within the business is not a meaningful use of your time. So it is how you streamline and how you bring it to the people's attention. So I think if you look to my own activity during that time with Barings it would be manual.

There were many psychological and behavioral things that were highlighting something is going wrong: the way I look, the way that I changed, the time I was arriving, the time I was leaving, and how that changed over the period. If you look to Adoboli or Kerviel, it would be the same as well: part of the firm they were accessing, how often they were in different parts of the business, influencing what was going on over there, the time they were accessing data, all of those things would have indicated that something was going wrong. But the only part that you are interested in is of course if there's an exception.

MCF: *It was mentioned in the Socgen report that Kerviel didn't have any holidays for a few years, he was trying to be on the floor as much as possible.*

NL: This is something that nobody allows any more or hopefully it doesn't. In my case, during a period of three years, for the first year I was the first person in the office and the last one to leave and sometimes I was leaving at 2-3 in the morning because there was always work and toward the end I was the last to come in the office and I was the first one to leave. So I completely flipped around. And there was obviously something that premeditated that. I went from one extreme to the other throughout that three-year period. Physically my health deteriorated throughout that period and just physically looking at me from the beginning to the end there were considerable changes and stress was very evident in the way that I looked. I manipulated the trade data and that could have been documented and seen by somebody in technology in terms of data that arrived from the exchanges and how it went through the accounts. There were so many simple things that you can always think of one more thing that you could predict, and it is about streaming which one works and taking it from there.

MCF: *Do you think that "The Market" is determined/controlled by the investors or are investors controlled by "The Market." In other words is there a likelihood that banks created something they do not have control of?*

NL: I was in India a few years ago and somebody from Deutsche Bank explained to me that the traditional way to invest from a market would be: you got a phone call from a sales person that would normally be very accommodating and looking after you and taking you out for dinner; and as years go by the relationship was often key with a decent bit of research behind it as well and a company that was renowned for that research. The sales people are now almost in a sales support unit. Because if a client has a problem with a box you sold, you help them out and explain it better. It's gone from what I would describe as a traditional sales type of environment to selling the bigger important costumers boxes and they are doing the algorithmic trading on their own. The whole market changed not only traders, but also the way the sales work in the organization.

You are now in a situation where there is a lot of noise and people are trying to work out what that noise means and they base their decision on how they interpret that noise and that noise is a lot of different things that happened in the market place, the volume that had been traded, the way the price is moving, how quickly it is moving and a machine somewhere is deciphering all these things from the details you are giving and instructing a trade. There are still traditional investors. I met one of them recently who asked me what I think about RBS shares. By the time you as an inexperienced individual react to price movement the prices have already moved 40%. The chances of you timing the entry and exit absolutely correctly to generate the best response are pretty much zero so it is difficult to do but there are still traditional investors though they are a very small part of the market these days.

MCF: *The recent crisis brought forth a lot of cases of unauthorized trading (rogue trading cases): Kerviel (SocGen), Adobolis (UBS), Iskil (JP), Picano Nacci (CNCE-France). Why is unauthorized trading always revealed relative to losses? In theory there is* *a chance of making gains on these trades, so what happens with unauthorized gains?*

NL: There are a number of reasons. If somebody makes a profit it would be deemed to be a good trade, whereas when those losses are exposed they tend to be consolidated over a period of time. I don't think it is ever an isolated trade that is reported, it is a period of irregular activity rather than an isolated case, so the loss you are looking at is magnified to a certain degree.

Somebody told me I was in down to number 14 in terms of all-time losses. And that's a sign that when you are looking back at a culture of risk, people are talking but the message is not getting through. The only conclusion for me is that the deterrent for people to do that action is not sufficient. If I had ever realized I would spend three and a half years in prison, I would like to think I would have reacted differently. Anybody who wants to work in financial markets does not ever expect to spend a day in prison. You typically look to reasonably educated people for whom prison is not a potential outcome. Something happens and you freeze and do not deal with the situation and not being able to deal with it ultimately results in prison sentences.

There are some important things to bring into consideration. I hate the word criminal as much as anybody else. And I spent three and a half years in prison so I am incriminated by the dictionary definition. But the one difference that I try to make is that there is no criminal intent. And we can think of financial scandals where there is deliberate intent. I think that is the distinction that needs to be drawn. Everybody should go to jail who is involved in anything which is criminal. Perhaps there is a difference as Madoff went to prison for the rest of his life because there was deliberate intent; my case is borne out of error, mistake and pretty poor decision making. My sentence was six and a half years. And there are a lot of people with sentences around that length. I think a distinction is necessary. It all comes under the banner of white-collar crime. But there should be a distinction between intent and lack of intent. In my case, it is fair to say it was not premeditated. That premeditated aspect of it is an aspect that should be looked at.

There is a stage where it starts as an error, and you try to cover it up as best as you can for a while and you develop a method that gives you some success in covering up. How much of that is premeditated? You have worked out a way to hide things and you continued to do it, is that premeditated? For me it was not the plan before. Some of the speculation that existed at that time is that I saw flaws in the systems and I tried to take advantage of them. It actually happened the other way around. It was money lost and then I saw flaws in the system that enabled me to conceal for longer. Because if it was me taking advantage of a flaw to make a profit then the intention would be to make money myself. It is semantics to a certain degree and I totally accept that, but we have to be honest about the way that it happened and it's important to spell it out.

MCF: *Some analyst claim that the Kobe earthquake played a crucial role in your losses.*

NL: It is a theory that it is often put forward. At that stage I was out of control, whether that was a combination of ego, being very stubborn and stupid, and a greedy type of mentality. I am not sure. When I look back at it, the bank was running out of money. Kobe didn't have a huge impact on how much money the bank had. Barclays and Citi were the principal lenders and they were withdrawing the credit line and I still needed money. Kobe certainly played a part, but the position was so critical by then, there was no way of really managing it, as we went through certain levels in the market there were other factors that were depressing the market a little bit further and this is my honest take on it; by the end of 1994 the position just became unmanageable, not that I ever manage it greatly, but it was very much controlling me by then and I had given up hope.

MCF: *How do you see the LIBOR case?*

NL: I have always pinned my colors to the mast on that one. It is false accounting and therefore is a crime. False accounting exists in every country and is a crime. The other reason I would consider it a crime is because it was premeditated, it was coordinated and was consolidated over a period of time. For all those reasons it is a crime. The amount of benefit can be argued and I accept that some people would argue that LIBOR is not as widely used as it used to be.

It was pretty much the Holy Grail of how markets were based, and whether you paid *x* percent above LIBOR it has impacted somebody and if you have manipulated that rate it is false accounting. I am categorical about that and therefore a crime has been committed. It is like in Ireland at the moment, different jurisdictions moved at different paces and that's not good. Post global financial crisis in the United States there has been a number of insider trading trials, rogue trading trials, lots of different trials where people were brought to justice quite quickly and they have got big sentences. Bernie Madoff is obviously one of the bigger ones, but Raj Rajaratnam and all of those guys as well.

In Ireland, the country most affected by the global financial crisis, the issues of the banking guarantees happened in 2008 and up to 2014 nobody had been brought to trial. The trial starts this week for the Anglo-Irish executives. With passing time there is less and less appetite to bring people to justice. If there's going to be criminal charges brought against LIBOR traders you would think they would be there now. And it goes back to the whole deterrent angle I talked about earlier. If you fix LIBOR for a number of years and you used to work for Deutsche Bank and you lose your job and go a couple of doors down the road to work for a big fund manager that's not sending a good signal. From a behavioral and from a psychological perspective, we can look at as if this is everyday thinking that the worst that is going to happen is that you will lose your job.

I give a simple analogy from my period looking back chronologically and I am simplifying this to the maximum degree. I had done very well at Barings for a while. If somebody had exposed my illegal trading in year 1, I would have been given a slap on the wrist. If this had happened in year 2, I would have lost my job. Having the mentality to think like that you will not stop because you have more time. If it had been clear that I would go to jail at any time during that period, I would not have taken the risk because it was not only the operational risk of the banks it was also the personal risk I was undertaking as well; and that was not clear to me and was never made clear to me, and there were not many episodes that were really clear during that period either. But you would like to think, as I said earlier, that nobody wants to spend time in prison and if people understood that was the consequence then hopefully they would not make the same decision.

Then you have Kerviel and Adobolis. Adobolis is a strange case anyway, because he was doing a lot of stuff personally outside of it, where he was borrowing from payday lenders doing spread betting on top of losing all that money at UBS. Of all the cases I heard of, he was probably the most out of control and perhaps worse. I go to a lot of events which are risk management orientated and I've got a couple of observations on that: Working for Detica or BA systems all of these people coming up with new risk management modules these days, you only hear about the losses, but you don't hear about all the losses. There is a rogue trading episode every week pretty much. UBS had another one recently, Credit Suisse had another one recently but they are of a magnitude that isn't reported. But you are seeing this at the moment in the industry. A friend of mine that used to work with me on the trading floor on LIFFE is now the head of trading risk at KPMG; KPMG didn't have a department like that in the previous 15 years. There is a lot more focus on trying to work on prevention. I still see it as the main thing and for me the risk is the bit between the hare and the tortoise.

MCF: *Despite regulation it seems that there has been little progress in dealing with all these issues.*

NL: Wherever you see new regulation or new legislation is becoming dated very quickly, it goes back to risk management and how risk management should evolve. Risk management is something that should be active all the time, it is not something you wait till the end of the trading day and you look at what people have done, it should be continual, and there should be alerts or anomalies detected if something is going wrong; it is like having a camera behind the trader and watching what he is doing all of the time. That is the kind of environment that you want to get to; it does not have to be physically a camera above the trader, but you need to have enough control of what he is doing and how it is being done. I do not think it should go as far as looking how one is pressing the button on the screen if we get that far.

If traders think that they are constantly surveyed and monitored and people have that close control of what they are doing, I don't think there will be much appetite for operating outside of the rules. It is when they think they can push a little bit more which I think is human nature anyway. If you have a rule as you grow up as a kid you push you parents further and further and you see how much you can push them. Financial markets are at that point; certainly when I was working at Barings and Morgan Stanley prior to Barings, a lot of money was spent on working out how we could push those rules a little bit further. Do I ever see that changing drastically, unfortunately I do not.

MCF: *Nevertheless it seems that despite more means, more tools and methods risk managers are behind in the race with traders in terms of both business comprehension and salaries. Things haven't changed so much over the years. Is there a problem regarding the position of the trader in the company, compared to the risk managers who seem less valued, lower paid and sometimes with an embarrassing role?*

NL: It does have a role. And that is fairly standard across the industry. Even today I speak to risk managers who do have this issue. There is a case you can look at, Jonathan Sugarman, who had a problem with Unicredit which is based in Dublin at the moment. He was a risk manager and he brought his concerns to the CEO of Unicredit in Dublin about what the capital adequacy looked like and he was told that he had got his calculation wrong. A few more days passed and he was still concerned over the level of capital adequacy within the organization so again he took his concerns to the CEO and he was told that he was wrong. Eventually he went to the Central Bank and reported Unicredit to the Central Bank. Unicredit found out about this and Central Bank questioned Unicredit who told them everything was OK, and eventually Jonathan Sugarman had to resign because his position was untenable. Now he cannot get another job in the industry, he has never been employed in financial circles because he went against the grain, and reported something that he saw and you look to some of the other whistleblowers that have existed, be they with HBOS, tend not to be reemployed in the industry. It is almost as if there is an *omerta* or a hidden law against speaking out in the world of finance.

MCF: *On one hand, Hollywood productions and media in general present investment bankers as having a very "flash" behavioral pattern. On the other hand, the traditional view of bankers is as very conservative and prudent people. Is there inside the financial world a specific behavioral pattern that encourages risk-taking activities? What generates this behavior? Why do 25-year-old math graduates change in behavior overnight and try to act like reality-show celebrities?*

NL: The answer is simple for me and it is money and the power of money. If you look at any other industry, I can give you a couple of examples in professional sport. If you look to any American footballer post-retirement they either lose all their money or they are drug addicts. It is quite strange. They had all that money for a while and it is taken away from them. If you look at Premiership footballers, they have a lot of money at a young age. Footballers are often typecast as stupid which is unfair, because there a lot of educated footballers, but they have that money very early in their life. Bankers are no different. You get very aroused, very early in your carrier, and my statement would be you are not necessarily mature enough to deal with that and it is too much money too soon. And this is why some of the behavior manifests itself and some very loud, gregarious extroverted individuals in banking would be like that anyway. But like you say the double physics graduate who lives with his mom until 24, what is the trigger that when he starts to work in a bank that sends him psychopathic almost in terms of his previous behavior. It is too much too soon. It is like Premiership footballers who start betting on horses and rather than betting 20 pounds on horses they bet thousands and money loses it value. And you look at the way some Premiership footballers behave and some of the things they have been involved in, it is similar to what happens in a lot of banks. *The Wolf of Wall Street* is on current release.

If you look back on my story I was 25 years of age when I was in Singapore and I was 28 when everything started to fall apart. I wasn't mature enough from a business perspective to cope with everything that happened in that period and that's a phrase I used in the book. When an immature person has status, they will do anything, absolutely anything to protect it.

Bankers have status, a successful banker has status among other bankers, footballers have status, they are idolized on a daily basis and both places you get paid a lot of money. I was never really in that sphere, I was always quiet and introverted, but I had my moments, from an ostentatious point of view. My friend who is the trader in Dubai who is still very successful was the most out there of the people working in financial markets at the time. It is not nice when you look back on some things, but it happens.

MCF: *Can limits on gifts and entertainment play a role in these issues? Are they as prevalent as before?*

It is definitely still in, because it is still a way people get more business. If you are going after somebody whether you are selling them a box or an investment I still believe that a lot of people still believe that the defining point is the degree or the level of attention you give that person. I was at a conference in Mumbai a few years ago, a lot of the high profile inventors and firms from India were in attendance. It was a two-day conference and it was a not for profit organization and all the big banks were there and the key decision at the end of was which party you were going to. Deutsche Bank would employ or invite all of the Bollywood actors or actresses. Everybody went there because those people wanted to meet the stars of the screen in India. I cannot remember what were the other options but Deutsche Bank won.

MCF: *This question is linked to psychology/stress pathology. Investment banking work is obviously stress related for various reasons. A very specific stress is linked mainly to psychological factors. What is the role of stress in the behavior of a banker?*

I think it comes down to the way you cope with that stress and again that's a certain amount of education for coping strategies that people use. There are coping strategies that are good and there are coping strategies that are obviously very disruptive. There's a great need for HR departments and things like that to continuously teach people from an ethical behavior point of view about how you are coping with things. That never existed at that time with Barings. It was: Here you are, here is your trading, there is your desk, tell us how much you make at the end of day. There was no real support around the person and that was entirely necessary. So the coping strategies I would use would be sticking my head in the sand and just ignoring what was going on and not talking to anybody about was what happening. There is a definite need to encourage people to talk about what is happening to them or about what is their experience in the work place, to see if there are any concerns not to the extent they became a whistleblower, because I don't think that's ever really worked over the years. In fact it's not about what people do, they tend to pick up the thing they know the best and use it. For me that was alcohol.

Alcohol postpones and blocks out a lot of stuff on what's happening and we know there is a lot of alcohol that surrounds financial markets, be that from the level of entertainment or the perspective of ending a tough day and a lot of people are having three or four beers after work; and not dealing with the reality of the situation. So it is about encouraging better coping strategies; mine were very disruptive, I never touched drugs or got involved with anything like that, even if there were a lot of drugs, that was never my thing. There were many days when I was just completely blocked out through getting to a stage where you couldn't remember what you'd done the day before. And that is very disruptive. And if stress manifests itself you don't exercise as much, you don't eat as well as you should, take care of yourself and it's a very fast-paced life and is very difficult sometimes to take your foot off the accelerator and say: Look can I have a day for me now and try to look after myself rather than being very work and profit oriented and where are we going to generate the profit.

MCF: *This stress in the long term can generate somatic-physiologic changes in the human organism. Do these things become visible in human behavior? Can this lead to a metamorphosis in the behavioral patter of a person? What is your experience on this?*

NL: I think they do because if you are abusing alcohol over a long period of time, certainly your reactions change, your thought process changes, the behavior changes as well. If you are stressed about something, you become aggressive with people and it does manifest itself in many different ways. There are a number of manifestations that you could characterize for everybody, but individual ones as well. I spent three and a half years in prison and I had to dissect a lot of what I did and the way I reacted to certain things and the way I was in certain relationships and you don't like the way you were, but the way you were was part of what you were experiencing at that time and that was the stress combined with way too much alcohol, not enough alcohol, not dealing with the situation and all of that combined with a poor relationship with my wife and a lot of activities I shouldn't have got involved in across the broking and banking scene. They were quite regular in Singapore at the time. And you wouldn't think anything was wrong with it but it was manifestly wrong, but is a component of what you've been through. I remember when I have been in Singapore and it has been the case recently as well, you did see young kids making very bad decisions that may not have been entirely work related. There was a case of a 23- or 24-year-old trader who jumped out the window because his girlfriend split up with him. If he was thinking rationally and was not under pressure from the work place his thinking process might have been very different, or maybe not be I cannot say. You do react in very strange ways when you are under that degree of pressure to perform all the time because if you are not performing you have no job.

MCF: *There is no major institution in the investment world that hasn't been hit by a scandal with criminal allegations. To paraphrase Adam Smith can we say that there is an "invisible evil hand" in the financial world that moves legitimate organizations and business into a "darker" criminal zone?*

NL: I think that everything that's deliberately permitted is wrong. If you look at the subprime crisis, and it goes back to a comment about the amphitheater type of environment, for every profit there has to be a loss. Every bank is trying to achieve that profit and any market you are going to is not just banking related but involves many businesses, there are times when margins are big and quickly erode until there is no margin. So banks try to find an innovative way to create a derivative of that business and make more profit and that is the problem. You get back into a situation where you have some statisticians or mathematicians who are defining these new vehicles or new methods through which the bank will make a lot of money. And sometimes they get it wrong and if you do get it wrong the backstop should be that compliance staff and board of directors pick it up. Over the years they failed spectacularly at doing that. The focus is on making money, and it can implode, be that CDS or anything else in recent years. And this is the way it will always be. Banks will always continue to bring new products to the market.

MCF: *With the recent crisis the ethical aspect of investment banking has often been discussed. Few advocated the idea that banks give a free option on risk to their employees in order to generate profits. Is "moral hazard" a consequence or a business model?*

NL: It is profit motivated regardless of what banks may say. Obviously they try to mitigate the risk as much as they can. I think it is more than new vehicles, as that edge goes out on one particular market place and people look to the next avenue in which they will make money be that a new method of trading or a complete new market. It tends to be those that spiral out of control; you don't see too many huge losses coming out of plain vanilla equity markets, because they are fairly consistent and fairly well understood. It is how derivatives and certain types of derivative are impacting on the business and CDS is another good example and of course the subprime market as well. The traditional investment vehicle that has been around for years tends not to offer too much exposure to risk.

MCF: *Since 2007 we saw bank failures, bailouts, indictments, manipulation scandals and also people making huge profits. Why did we need a crisis to observe these things?*

NL: I think the crisis happened and people were scrutinized more, and if you tend to look things come in clusters. If you look to my episode in 1995 which resulted in the collapse of the Bank and there was no way of hiding, very quickly you had Hanamaka on copper, Iguchi with Daiwa. Iguchi is an interesting case in itself. Daiwa refused to take that case to the regulator and only because a whistleblower brought it to Daiwa's attention, that actually made the media. Sumitomo on copper had the biggest loss, 2.2 billion, Iguchi was 1.4 and mine was 1.3 or 1.2 billion dollars. So they all happened in a cluster; it is not surprising to me anyway that all this happened in the cluster around the global financial crisis. The magnitude of those losses was in billions but some of the ones that happened recently were all below 10 million dollars so therefore you don't hear about them and you will never hear about them. In the environment post-financial crisis, everybody knew that so much more scrutiny was going to be on the industry with a lot of impact on the industry, so people either exposed what was going on or implicated themselves.

MCF: *There is a tendency to blame financial crimes on a single person. Nevertheless when these crimes emanate from an organization or a department, this tendency disappears. Do we still need a "Public Enemy" character?*

NL: What happens is from a bank's loss recovery perspective the easiest thing is to point the finger at an individual and to personalize it to that degree and that is right to a certain degree because it's the individual who carried out the illegal activity, of which the consequence were the losses. But from the banks' perspective it takes the spotlight away from them and as much as you blame the individual you should really be highlighting the banks' insufficient controls. And it is buying a bit of time putting all the attention on the individual and then when eventually people turn around asking questions about your own bank and your own controls you make changes. Regardless of what financial scandal you look at that pattern is evident each time: target the individual, get the attention away from us so we can put our house in order. It doesn't even need to be an individual. During the global financial crisis it was easy to blame bonuses for what happened. Half of the population thinks that this is why it happened and half may not but it gives us something to target.

MCF: *Despite the introduction of electronic and IT controls and surveillance, it appears that cases of financial crimes are increasing in number and frequency. Compared to the time when trading orders were written on paper the number of public cases of unauthorized and insider trading has increased. Is the technology something that is helpful for controls or can it be used against the system?*

NL: You definitely can be too sophisticated I haven't seen too many business that are too sophisticated. You tend to find that it's a hard sell to bring too much technology, from the opportunity cost perspective. I believe that technology mitigates risk and takes away some of the risk if it's used correctly.

MCF: *More and more regulation is being applied in the investment industry. Can regulation lead and generate solutions for the many problems in the financial industry? Will the number of white-collar crimes diminish?*

NL: The quality of the regulation particularly over the past 20 or 30 years has been poor, as much as you can drill down to the detail in terms of your own individual organization. I have been with the Bank of England and they are obviously looking at all the controls and policies at the moment and at that event they admitted that the technology they use is dated, is unsophisticated and needs to be improved drastically and this is quite a shocking statement of where the regulators in this country are. It tends to rely on self-regulation and that's not sufficient either, because global financial collapse is everybody having a problem at the same time and that's down to an overall regulator and not Goldman's or RBS's knowing that they are OK, it comes down to an overall regulator knowing how different parts of the global financial market or the countries' financial markets affect each other.

A basic example is when I was in Singapore and I was trading on the Singapore International Monetary Exchange and I was very long on the futures market on the Nikkei 225 and Singapore had a process of nondisclosure and so they didn't disclose any information at the end of the day, but Osaka did; and in Osaka I was extra long on market as well. Internally at Barings somebody should've been looking at these two long positions. At Barings they perceived them to be hedged, so either the regulators in Singapore couldn't have seen the true position on SIMEX in addition to the trading positions in Osaka and I was only on one side and I was risking many multiples the size of the banks. I don't think they get it then, I don't think they got it know. They've obviously improved, I'm not suggesting they haven't, but the market place is keeping its distance.

MCF: *What role would the arrival of dark pools and dark liquidity play in better execution?*

NL: There are always new issues and there always will be new issues in the future because of the innovation and the complexity, that will never change. And it is pursuit of perfection, pursuit of vehicles that are always going to generate profit, and don't think anybody is ever going to get there, it is always moving to the next stage and other banks are quick to catch up and margin erodes and you move on to the next thing, and somebody comes up with a new degree of complexity or speed or innovation and regulators don't keep pace.

MCF: *We see that a lot of the old investment banking business has been incorporated into the "hedge fund" industry. Will this lead to a new type of issues (i.e., trading losses and bankruptcies)?*

NL: It depends on which country you are in. Certainly in the UK there are some banks that are too big now. RBS and Lloyds are probably the two that split the market and they represent far too much of the retail space in the UK, and they should be split up. RBS is still being supported by taxpayers. That will make the market place safer for individuals from commercial or retail customers' perspective and there will be those investment banking arms that will continue to trade the way they did in the past, but they will not have the balance sheet they had in the past. There's been a lot of deleveraging but the economic situation makes it difficult for the banks to make as much money as they have in the past. The Volcker Rule and things like that have limited the number of products as well. A very quick analogy is when I used to work years ago, Morgan Stanley and Barings had huge teams of lawyers and IT experts continually working out ways that the rules could be bent, so more profit could be made, that it could be made more efficient, if whatever booking vehicle that could reduce tax or provide a situation that could benefit the company. There was always bending and pushing the rules as far as you possibly could and we will see that again.

MCF: *Recently banks developed methods for understanding the P&L of trading activities and mining the track-record of traders and funds managers. Can this provide more information about the behavioral pattern of a trader?*

NL: People have to work out quickly what are the best indicators and I think some would look to things like proprietary trading which is as behavioral as anything else, because as we talked about, this fosters stress. Any trader has a certain degree of stress; but if you do something illegal your stress level will go up very quickly and excessively and that may manifest itself in the way you are trying to hide what's going on and you access parts of the business that you would not normally, the P&L reports being the way the trade files are sent through and authorized before they go on their very way, or maybe as simple as the hours you are spending in the office and something changes dramatically over time, the fact you don't take a holiday in three months. From a very rogue trading perspective it is more behavioral than anything else. There are accounting formulae and metrics by which you should be able to highlight something is wrong, but the lead indicators would be the behavioral changes. It is a complement of both quantitative and subjective in terms of the way people are looking and anybody can see profit and loss, these are very visual but it's the way you behave in the office environment that may highlight that something has changed.

MCF: *Can the information available on the web or social networks be used for prevention of financial fraud?*

NL: I did some stuff with IBM in Australia some years ago and they were suggesting that there are ways to bring that sort of information in. In my day people would go for a coffee; in Tokyo some traders would meet up and discuss what was going on, on volatility, on Barings' position, etc. And it was far more laborious. I have a Twitter account and somebody helps me with the Twitter account, I don't know how much detail is in there, but I have seen banks that believe that there is a way to use that information. You could certainly influence opinion, like years ago if somebody was talking about something, it could have an effect on other people's strategies.

When you talk about profit and making money, rightful and wrongful actions come in order to be successful. Success was very much a motivating factor for me through everything that happened during that period. And you counter that with a huge fear of failure and that really colored a lot of what I did once I got into that bad situation that I was in. I couldn't tell anybody what was going on. I was not a great talker at that time, I kept things to myself and I expected to be able to cope and ultimately couldn't. There are vehicles by which people are able to share their opinions, their views, their concerns in an open and honest manner, things that should always be encouraged within banks. The idea of a whistleblower is a good idea, but psychological pressure within the organization dictates that it doesn't really work, because nobody wants to be the one who is fingered as the one telling tales. I suppose that one thing that occurred to me in the last year in a debate on ethics that I was at in South Africa, my ethical responsibility, my ethical and moral compass never really extend past the very few people that worked for me in Singapore. I wasn't very worried about shareholders' value or about how things affected other people and that colored a lot of the decisions I made as well. I was very focused on getting bonuses for the six or seven people that worked for me and for that reason kept propagating the 88888 accounts and continued the trading through it, but I was blinkered as to how that affected other people.

MCF: *Can people from the criminal world look at financial markets in order to take advantage of its weaknesses?*

NL: They have to have some very good people. To expose weaknesses in the system from outside, I think is very difficult. As negative as I have been about some of the controls that are in place, it is still quite a sophisticated market, so you are looking for somebody with the requisite skills, perhaps involving placing moles within an organization. Those are very genuine threats that I think banks feel, but again the task would be to highlight those behaviors within it and again it is behavioral, it is analytical and using as much analytical evidence as you can of wrongdoing would be a change in behavior if a mole came into an organization and acted one way and it changes and acts in another. That should be something that would be able to be seen and to be evidenced through analyzing the data that is there. I totally get the idea that people can be infiltrated into an organization and anybody can be infiltrated into any organization.

If you have a mature market it's very difficult to do, but if you have a new developing market or are in a country which has inferior regulation or restriction the possibility increases. From a developed banking type of perspective it would be like looking at some of the Eastern European countries. The first concern would be a fast developing economy/economies, because it means that something could be wrong and everybody is looking in a particular direction. Take, for example, Iceland. In a developing economy or developing market, you tend to find the skills set the professional needs for controls is not there, so they should bring in outside help. We see in Russia that good risk managers, good compliance officers are not in that country naturally, so they need to be brought. Iceland was a perfect case. They had no real risk managers, no compliance officers. The economy was booming, the stock market was going crazy and lending was all over the place and ultimately the day came when everything collapsed and criminal charges were brought. Dubai was another case of something similar happening and now slowly coming back. Economies overheating or starting to overheat and enjoy fantastic growth for me is always a cause for concern because it tends to suggest that is too one directional.

MCF: *Can the flashy lifestyle and frequentation of bankers lead to inappropriate contact with underworld elements that could exploit this link?*

NL: This is something that I never encountered or heard spoken about and I do not know if it is realistic. People in governments are found to have given secrets to people in bed and there have been examples of spies who worked for both sides. It is impossible to say: No one can say it never happens. It is difficult to work out and I can understand the motivation for trying to do it if profit is involved.

For example, I was trading on the Nikkei 225 in Singapore, the lead market was in Osaka and it was a Nikkei 225 future contract in Chicago which was very irregularly traded and it might be a couple of people trading and there were very few people hedging overnight, but a little business went through Chicago. But if anything I was doing was premeditated and I was looking to steal money it would have been very easy for trades to be hedged in Osaka and Singapore, losses on trades to be posted in Chicago, and if somebody in Chicago had an account and if we traded between ourselves overnight, I would lose money in Singapore and he would make money in Chicago. If that was the intention I could've done, but it didn't occur to me until afterwards.

When I first flew back to Singapore there was a guy called Daniel. Danny was a broker with a different firm, I was transacting the biggest volumes of Nikkei 225 by far and everybody was aware of that and were watching what I was doing and they thought I was extremely successful (but they were wrong). But I also did some JGB (Japanese Government Bonds) trades. The way I was doing the JGB trades was that I was getting Danny to transact them in Tokyo and then he would sell to me in Singapore. He would do the transaction over the phone and I would ask where the market was; he would make the bid at six and I would buy at six, because he would already have bought it before at five in Tokyo. In fact I was giving him a tick for very trade, and I was trading quite a lot with him like that. When I went back to Singapore toward the end 1995, the Singapore authorities kept the passport of two people: one was Danny and the other was James Backses, who was CEO of Barings. And they wanted to arrest them both and they wanted me to give evidence against them. When they looked at Danny's trading record, he was very short in Singapore. In their view, he made 280 million pounds but what they hadn't seen is that he was long in Japan, so perfectly hedged. I explained that to them but they kept Danny's passport for 9 months but eventually let him go.

After I was released from prison in 1999 the liquidator sat me down and they brought up all the trading stats from that period and I had a guy who was doing the orders filling for me called George. He was an order filler; he was not working for any bank but for many banks. They looked to all trading patterns and they saw trades with another guy having the initials TKE. George traded an extraordinary amount of times with TKE. The question from liquidator was if based on this information could there have been collaboration between the two fillers. Based on what they were showing me I cannot rule out if there was collaboration Do I think there was any collaboration? I think the answer is no.

It is just the two biggest order fillers on the floor trading with each other during the day; at that time I wouldn't have dreamt of it, but based on the way the evidence was presented there's no way you could've possibly said it was chance.

There's a possibility that things like that can happen. It arises from being within the market then trying to infiltrate it. On the culture side the big thing for me is that the deterrent is very important. If people don't think there are consequences, then the deterrent doesn't work. If you have a rule that says if you do this you get fined 1 million pounds, if it is never imposed and never implemented then you might as well not have the rule. There are many rules which are in the end a waste of paper. There is a need for a case where things are enforced. LIBOR is a great example of what needs to be done, because it sent that huge message to the market and to new entrants in the market. With culture the tone is set from the top, but culture often occurs from what you see happening within the organization. For me as a young lad working and seeing the life of a trader and things that were going on, I regularly saw trades going to an error account and those trades were coming out after a few minutes, hours, or days later. When I was in the situation where I could put something in an error account it wasn't a big deal, everybody was doing it. But it was wrong, for everybody. But if you see things like this happening you find it easier to do them yourself. There are countless examples, one being that of a trader in Barings in Hong Kong who was trading regularly outside his limits, and he would often manipulate the mark to market, so that it would present his trades in a more favorable light. He did a bit of other stuff, like manipulating arbitrages. He was a similar age to me and they caught him in Hong Kong, prior to my being exposed in Singapore. He did lose his job, but he could have been prosecuted and he went to work for another bank in Singapore and there was no real consequence to his actions. This fosters a belief in yourself that if you manage to get part of the losses back it's not a big deal. He is still in Singapore and he is one of the biggest volatility traders in the world. He was taught a lesson that helped him on this pattern forward. He was discovered and he became far more disciplined and far more compliant than in the past and excelled because of it.

Morgan Stanley was fined recently for the Mortgage Backed Securities case and that defines what they have done. JPMorgan were fined 13 billion dollars last year, the "whale" being part of it and MBS were part of it. The 13 billion dollars fine will be tax deductible, and the money will go to the regulator anyway. It doesn't have the impact on the business that you perceive it would have. Fines do not work, banks are too big to fail. They shouldn't be allowed to get to the size where they are too big to fail. We shouldn't let banks get to that stage but many are almost there. What they didn't realize when they let Lehman's go was that Lehman Brothers was pretty much implicated in every trade which existed around the world and therefore that affected everything, especially CDS.

PART I

SHORT HISTORY OF FINANCIAL MARKETS

CHAPTER

1A

Historic Perspective of Financial Markets

OUTLINE

1 BACKGROUND

In the realm of public opinion the financial markets started to be an important factor in the real economy only over the last few decades. But when taking a closer look, one should go back in the times of Ancient Rome or to the trails of the Silk Road to study the origins of financial markets. Markets have three main conceptual features that are critical in understanding how they began and how they work: value, transferability, and time-dynamic. Certainly value is a fundamental feature. Perceiving value as an abstract, intrinsic, rationale, and measurable concept of an item leads naturally to the *raison d'être* of markets. In the Old Testament Cain's crops seemed less appreciated or less "valuable" than Abel's cattle in the view of a supreme being. The abstract dimension of value personified through the views of a divine being creates antagonism in human nature. In Max Weber's Protestant Ethic, the accumulation of value is perceived to have a close relationship to the *communis providentia* and ultimate salvation. Metaphorically speaking a financial crime aiming to distort the value of an asset would have the same mechanism as Cain's fratricide.

Transferability is a concept that is *sine qua non* in the existence of markets. Once value exists as a rational ubiquitous attribute, one would be able to transfer a property if value is rationally agreed between two parties.

Time is the third dimension necessary for markets to exist. If the value of an asset is not stationary the time-worthiness accounts for the cost that results from the variation. The idea of time worthiness is clearly described by Benjamin Franklin [2] who pointed out the relationship between time and the capacity of an individual to earn:

> Remember, that time is money. He that can earn ten shillings a day by his labour, and goes abroad, or sits idle, one half of that day, though he spends but sixpence during his diversion or idleness, ought not to reckon that the only expense; he has really spent, or rather thrown away, five shillings besides.
> ***Benjamin Franklin [2]***

It would be a very difficult, abstract and subjective exercise to go back to the genesis of the first financial transactions and to try and

http://dx.doi.org/10.1016/B978-0-12-801221-5.00016-6

recreate the origin of these three concepts: value, transfer, and time. Historians believe that the origin of markets as we now perceive them was in early sixteenth century. Amsterdam, but a series of recent monographs revealed the existence of financial markets during ancient times. Most likely finance as we know it today did not exist in ancient and medieval times, but we can claim based on historians' findings that the financial physiology was similar in many ways to what is observed today. Going back to the texts of Ancient Babylon, Greek democracy, and the Roman Empire, we observe that not only do we find the same functions as in today's financial world but also the same pathology. Speculation and fraud seem to have always existed, the only difference being that electronic platforms have taken the place of the forum in Ancient Rome.

2 ANTIQUITY

Historians trace banking activities to ancient civilizations, where individuals or institutions gave loans to farmers and traders in the form of spot commodities (i.e., grains). Archeological research identified credit-type institutions in 2000 BC in Assyria and Babylonia, ancient Greece, China, India, and the Roman Empire.

The origin of financial markets cannot be specified exactly in space and time, historians giving many different views. If one assumes that the concept of markets as well as the concept of banking are strictly related to the existence of a method and a system able to represent, confine and record transactions then one could point the beginning of markets to the times writing was invented. Writing was a necessity mainly in urban areas for systemizing, organizing, and controlling a society. Taxation and population censuses are examples of areas where writing is critical. In the ancient period urban development was directly linked to the trade of goods and commodities. The oldest records of commodity trading are in ancient Sumer around 4500 BC. The trading was recorded via clay tokens, three-dimensional geometric representations that are thought to be the precursor of cuneiform writing. Clay tokens sealed in a clay vessel represented information like the volume of commodities promised to be delivered. Later in history, cuneiform tablets replaced the tokens and thus made possible the appearance of a more complex monetary system.

One of the most prominent cities in the Sumerian Era was the city of Uruk, ruled once by the mythical Gilgamesh around the twenty-seventh century BC. The city peaked in importance in the third millennium BC and started to decline after 2000 BC. The archeological findings in this city are a rich source of information for financial historians. Tokens and tablets describing the first financial trading were discovered that were the origin of the first financial markets.

Van de Mieroop [3] reproduced the content of a tablet describing the trade between a supplier of wood, named Akshak-Shemi, and a client, called Damqanum. The contract was written in the nineteenth century BC.

> Thirty wooden [planks], ten of 3.5 meters each, twenty of 4 meters each, in the month Magrattum Akshak-shemi will give to Damqanum. Before six witnesses (their names are listed). The year that the golden throne of Sin of Warhum was made.
> *Van de Mieroop [3]*

Weber [4] analyzed this fragment in depth and considered that this is more than a simple trade and is in fact the first example of a forward trade. The trade was to be settled at a future date and was thus an ancient version of a forward contract. If we compare this excerpt with a section of a standard ISDA[1] Master agreement for a coal transaction it can be observed that the main points (buyer, seller, delivery point, quantity, etc.) are similar to those used 4000 years ago.

[1]International Swap and Derivatives Associations that aim to insure safe and efficient derivatives markets to facilitate effective risk management for all users of derivative products.

> Seller's and Buyer's Obligations: With respect to each Coal Transaction, and subject to the terms and conditions of this Agreement, (A) Seller shall sell and make available or deliver, or cause to be delivered, the Contract Quantity to the Delivery Point during the Term (in the case of U.S. Coal) or each Delivery Period (in the case of International Coal) and (B) Buyer shall purchase and receive, or cause to be received, the Contract Quantity at the Delivery Point during the Term (in the case of U.S. Coal) or each Delivery Period (in the case of International Coal) and shall pay Seller the Contract Price. With respect to Coal Transactions that are physically settled options, the obligations set forth in the preceding sentence shall only arise if the option is exercised in accordance with its terms. ISDA Master agreement.

Commodities like grain were obviously at that time the main financial measure and also the currency of trade. On a transcription of a Mesopotamian tablet dated around 1700, Swan [5] depicts a transaction in which two farmers received from the King's daughter a quantity of barley, that they will use as planting seed and which had to be returned at harvest time.

> Three kurru of barley, in the seah-measure of Shamash, the mesheque measure, in storage, Anum-pisha and Namran-sharur, the sons of Siniddianam, have received from the Naditu priestess Iltani, the King's daughter. At harvest time they will return the three gur of barley in the seah-measure of Shamash, the mesheque measure, to the storage container from which they took it. Before (two witnesses whose names are listed). Month Ulul, 19th day, year in which King Abieshuh completed the statue of Entemena as god. ***Swan [5]***

This type of transaction that could be considered as a loan or even repo agreement was very common in those days so we could easily consider it as a primal type of market that could involve a certain degree of complexity, involving auctions or secondary markets.

These forward deals were also accompanied by credits, thereby making them precursors of the first structured products.

If the trades involving grains and other agricultural assets are linked to the basic demand of the urban population, a further degree of sophistication occurred with the use of metals (mainly precious metals) as an exchange currency. As indicated in Zarlenga [6] agricultural and metallic commodities (mainly barley and silver) by weight served as the primitive monetary system in these societies. The occurrence of interest rates on grains or livestock currency is somehow obvious as the biological stock can multiply over time through plantation or animal multiplication. The archeological discoveries from Mesopotamia revealed a crucial innovation in the economic system, that allowed interest rates to be perceived on transactions or loans having noble metals as assets, and requiring metal interest payment. This concept was later extended to all monetary mass and financial transactions. There is obviously a difference between the interest perceived for a grain transaction and the interest on a metal loan, due to the fact that grains can generate a natural surplus while metal will at best remain constant in volume. The opinion was later developed on the commodities markets as "convenience yield" which represents the opportunity cost of having the financial asset (the metal) and not the physical asset (the grains).

> Six shekels silver as a su-la loan, Abuwaqar, the son of Ibqu-Erra, received from Balnumamhe. In the sixth month he will repay it with sesame according to the going rate. Before seven witnesses. These are the witnesses to the seal. In month eleven of the year when king Rim-Sin defeated the armies of Uruk, Isin, Babylon, Rapiqum and Sutium and Irdanene, king of Uruk. ***Van de Mieroop [3]***

The tablet excerpt from the previous paragraph dated around 1809 BC shows that a Mesopotamian merchant borrowed silver, engaging to repay it with sesame grains based on a floating interest rate after six months. The transaction could be perceived in a basic way as a barter agreement but if we consider the time factor it is more like a loan and a forward sale of grains or a silver repo and a commodities (silver vs grains) swap.

It seems that these transactions from the Sumerian time would be classified today as over-the-counter transactions with an important counterparty risk. To lessen the risk of disputes the transactions were written on the tablets and agreed in the presence of witnesses. This did not reduce the risk of the counterparty breaching its duty at the delivery date and thus the need for some form of trade code or financial regulation appeared. Trading and annex activities were essentially done in the cities, harbors, crossroads of commercial roads, and religious sites like temples. Kummer and Pauletto [7] underlined the role of temples in ancient Mesopotamia as privileged places for establishing and recording financial transactions. Economic literacy and mathematical knowledge was at the time a characteristic of priests, thereby facilitating the transcription and the interpretation of the trades in the cuneiform language. Engaging in forward contracts or loans relied on the good faith of the merchant, thereby making the spiritual-ethic role of the religious sites critical. The bookkeeping of various trades that involved long-term or long-distance trading made these temples primitive versions of clearing houses and public forums ancient versions of trading floors.

The Code of Hammurabi from ancient Mesopotamia dated around the year 1772 BC is not only the oldest written codex but also a very rich source for the history of finance. It provides contractual examples of trades but also covers almost all the aspects of commercial laws of that time that show how trading should be done. In the light of the transactions presented previously it can also be considered as the first example of "financial" regulation. The following passage of text is the 48th law of 282 contained in the Code of Hammurabi, a precursor of what would be called today a structured note. The debt is paid in grains after the harvest, but if the climatic conditions are adverse no debt is incurred. One could perceive the products as climatic/cat-nat insurance or as a structured note with an interest cap indexed on the weather conditions.

> If any one owe a debt for a loan, and a storm prostrates the grain, or the harvest fail, or the grain does not grow for lack of water; in that year he need not give his creditor any grain, he washes his debt-tablet in water and pays no rent for the year.

As pointed out by Weber [4] the most interesting feature of this tablet is its portable transferability. The cuneiform tablet gave the trader the option to pay the bearer of the tablet. This suggests that the holder of the tablet could transfer the contract to a third party.

Wasendorf and Stahl [8] recall that around the same period, 2000 BC, in ancient China rice producers bargained with merchants to deliver specified quantifies of rice at a future date for a given price. These contracts were typically closed before the rice was planted in order to guarantee the merchant a specific quantity of rice at a predetermined price and assure the rice producer a market for the crop.

Cuneiform writing was widespread in the ancient world before the Phoenician alphabet started to be used. Records of long-distance trading contracted through cuneiform tables have been revealed by archeologists across the Oriental world. Returns based on nonagricultural commodities like metals have often been found throughout the ancient history of the Orient from Sumer to Egypt. The oriental financial system was crystallized around the central authority of the royal house who was among other things the biggest trader of commodities, the biggest lender and also the regulator. Thus the economic, fiscal, and financial policies were driven by the will of one person or a small group of persons.

The oldest recollection of commodity market prices comes from ancient Babylon and was put together by Slotsky [9], as shown in Figure 1. Temin [10] showed that the Babylonian prices of agricultural commodities followed a random pattern. They rose sharply after the death of Alexander the Great in 323 BCE and more gradually toward the end of the period.

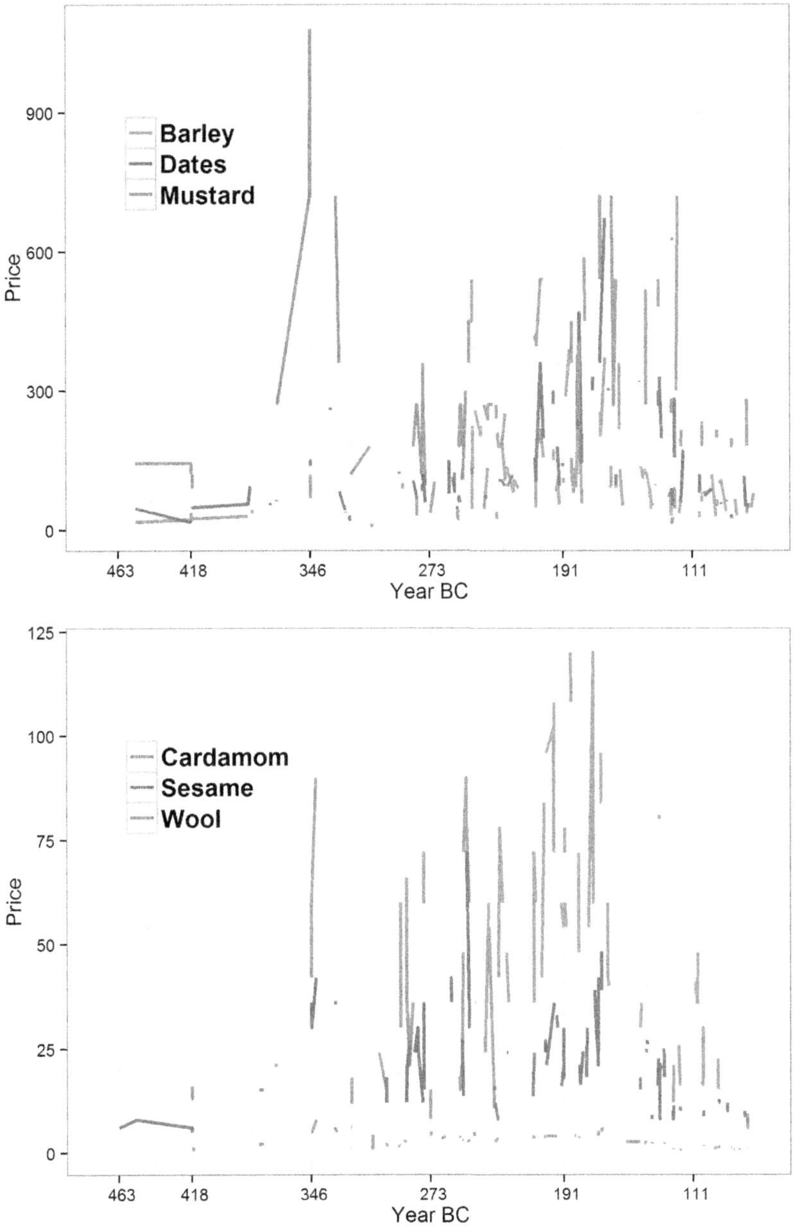

FIGURE 1 Evolution of commodity prices in Babylon between 460 and 100 BC. The prices of agricultural commodities varied in random fashion. They rose sharply after the death of Alexander the Great in 323 BCE and more gradually toward the end of the period [10].

The Greek civilization had a considerable influence on the Oriental influx of knowledge that came from the economic relationships of Greece with the territories of Asia Minor.

As mentioned previously, in Ancient Mesopotamia the basic banking services (deposit taking and provision of loans) were found in temples and priests acted as bookkeepers and bankers. The authoritarian type of state organization was linked very closely with state power, religion, trade, and wealth around a unique axis from the monarchy down to the temple. Greek democracy secularized, liberalized, and modernized the financial services. Financial transactions were undertaken by private individuals as well as public organizations (this was later incorporated by the Romans as societas). Nevertheless the role of temples remained dominant and thus Delphi, as well as being an important center of divination, also became a reference point in the Greek financial world. With increased migration into Asia Minor, Greeks also exported the banking system developed in the temples. With the rise of the Athenian fleet in the Mediterranean and Black Sea, the financial services followed this trend and Athens became a prototype financial center [11]. The Athenian system increased the influence of finance on commerce. Thus shipping and shipped goods were financed though loans and the cargo of the ships was used as a form of collateral for loans. Insurance was also underwritten for ships that may have sank in adverse weather conditions. The loans charged interest and the debts could be transferred from one financier to another. By introducing interest on loans private Athenian financiers were able to innovate compared to the classic temple-based services and to remunerate deposits and thus to create a business model that is still used today. Most importantly, in Athens the concept of value, or more precisely fair value, began to take hold. Various trades, financial services, and instruments had value in gold or silver and traders were able to assess the value of different items or services in terms of precious metal value. The money market was essentially made up of loans between various banks or traders. Around 600 BC, despite a flourishing economy, Greek cities encountered a bigger problem: a debt crisis followed by a profound structural and social crisis. In the absence of central banks and regulation, there was a rapid increase in usury in Greek cities.

Solon, one of the first Athenian statesmen, introduced measures that were controversial at the time. Athenian society had a massive rural population with high levels of debt and few opportunities to trade. Many commodities were scarce and the monetary system was highly unregulated. These facts, juxtaposed with increasing interest rates, made possible the development of the practice of usury and loan sharks. Individual debt was marked on a Horoi which was a boundary marker, usually made from a slab of marble or limestone, a few feet high. Horois were a symbolic and legal bondage of one person to its debt and denoted the obligation of payment. As slavery was common in the Polisa and no law of bankruptcy existed, people who could not repay their debts became the collateral for that debt and became slaves to their debts. In 594 BC Solon abolished this practice, destroyed the Horois and canceled the slave-link notes by emancipating slaves and attempting to regulate the monetary and fiscal system. These measures increased trade and exchanges with other regions of the world. Solon's reforms and the debt relief were considered by many as the basis of Greek prosperity over the following centuries.

Going back to the time of the Macedonian expansion under Alexander the Great, another reference to forward trading appeared in the Arthashasthra, an ancient Indian book on statecraft, economic policy and military strategy, written in Sanskrit. It identified its author by the names *Kautilya* and *Vishnugupta*, both names that are traditionally identified with Chanakya (c. 350-283 BC). Nayan Kabra et al. [12] claim that Kautilya affirmed in the book that prices should be fixed taking into account the investment, the quantity to be delivered, duty, interest, rent, and other expenses. The phrase in Arthasasthra that is thought to refer to future trading is "desakalantaritanam."

Greek culture was taken over by the Roman Republic after the Macedonian phalanx was defeated by the Roman legions at Pydna in 168 BC. Romans also incorporated the banking system. Despite becoming a Roman province Greek banks continued to exist within the Roman domain on Delos, where there were both temple and private banks [13]. Interestingly despite the turmoil the Greek banks continued to operate over time with great stability, taking deposits and making loans and mortgages. Greek banks could thus be considered the precursors of commercial and retail banks.

The most developed financial system in the ancient world was without any doubt in Ancient Rome. Rome's strength as a military and economic power started to grow during the last centuries of the Republic. Probably the main comparative advantage over other ancient civilizations was not the power of its military but the development of its culture. Roman law is still today the basis of the modern legal system and the decimal numeric system predominated until the development of the binary-based computer. A robust and convenient numerical system together with a good legal framework acted as the main drivers of progress of Rome. These two features together allowed merchants to have an accurate way of encrypting the contractual information while closing the deals. On top of that Rome understood that encrypting the information is necessary but not sufficient for economic development. Dissemination of information across the republic and subsequently during the Empire was enabled by a comprehensive network of roads, many of which were used long after the fall of the Empire. Another useful point for further analysis is the fact that Ancient Rome saw the introduction of the first corporations with legitimate shareholders [14, 15]. During the Republic, Rome used to subcontract many of its functions to groups of individuals *(publican)* organized in the *societates publicanorum*. From temple maintenance, army supplies, tax collection, road building, and mining activities, Rome used contractors to provide a wide and varied range of services. The bidders were organized in *societas* had a structured governance and appropriate financial records. *Societas publicanorum* played a very important role during the republic and lost their power during the Empire. *Societas* also had an ownership type similar to that of modern shareholders. It is considered that the main features of the modern corporation thus seem to have been granted to the *societas publicanorum*. The existence of the *societas publicanorum* did not depend on the individuals involved; a representative could act for the company, ownership was fungible, traded in the form of shares, and separated from the control of the company [14, 15].

3 MEDIEVAL PERIOD

After the fall of Rome and the restructuring of the defunct Empire around the Byzantium, Western Europe suffered many upheavals, not only from the political social perspective. Christian principles and the later Catholic dogma reshaped the economy of the post Roman world. As a general trend financial gains were not welcome in "De Civitate Dei" and did not bring salvation [6]. The view of the Scholastics (1100-1500 AD) was that money is a measure, and should just be a means to an end that enables items to be bought and sold. In the thirteenth century, the Vatican condemned usury and banned interest on money, with the execution of dividends on shares in the Roman inherited Societas and rent from property.

In the early fourteenth century after the third crusade Venice was the main economic force in the Mediterranean sea and the Venetian banks were active lenders to governments and also traded in securities, acting in many ways like modern brokers [6]. In 1351, the Venetian Government outlawed the information-based manipulation of government securities arising from rumors about the price of government funds. Other Italian cities including Pisa, Verona, Genoa, and Florence also began to have flourishing banking activities and traded in government securities. Italian companies financed by those banks were also the first to issue shares, which were later leveraged by the low countries in the first stock exchange.

In post Carolingian France the inflow of trades from the Orient under the influence of new Crusader states gave some power to banks and a dense network of "courretiers de change" was established in the country to mediate the relationship with the banks.

In late thirteenth century in Bruges commodity traders gathered in the same building owned by Van der Beurze, which was the precursor of the trading floor. In 1409 that informal meeting became institutionalized and the "Bruges Beurse" across Flanders. In 1351 the Venetian Government outlawed the spreading of rumors intended to lower the price of government funds. Bankers in Pisa, Verona, Genoa, and Florence also began trading in government securities during the fourteenth century. This was only possible because these were independent city states not ruled by a duke but by a council of influential citizens. Italian companies were also the first to issue shares. Companies in England and the low countries followed in the sixteenth century.

Meanwhile in imperial China during the Song Dynasty (960-1279 AD), Hou [16] mentions that the revolutionary minister Wang An-Shih (1021-1086 AD) promulgated a system resembling a "futures" market that allowed the state to collect and resell goods (grain or tribute) and use the funds at its disposal to procure goods at the most convenient time and place [8].

Flanders saw the birth of the first stock exchange as far back as 1531, in Antwerp. Brokers and moneylenders would meet there to deal mainly in government bonds.

The 1600s were a period of substantial colonial expansion by the Netherlands, England, and France. The Dutch East India Company founded in 1602 was the first joint-stock company to get a fixed capital stock and, as a result, continuous trade in company stock occurred on the Amsterdam Exchange. The South Sea bubble was the first major speculative bubble in stock markets that arose in the wake of colonial expansion.

The Netherlands was also one of the countries to issue derivatives in Europe, with tulips being the first asset traded forward. The Tulip bubble is remembered in history as the first commodity with speculatively inflated prices and also the first crash on the futures market.

In parallel in Japan during the Edo era in the early 1700s a rice futures market appeared in Osaka with a mechanism similar to modern clearing with margin mechanism and settlement.

4 MODERN ERA

The Battle of Waterloo undoubtedly had more socio-political than financial impact. Nevertheless the era of the Napoleonic wars emphasized the role and the power of bankers and financial markets in European history. The role of banks in the global economy continued to increase along with the capital markets.

A historic time series of American stocks from the early 1800s to the present day using data from the works of Schwert [17] and Siegel [18] is shown in Figure 2. The dataset is adjusted for inflation and corrected for survivorship bias. It can be seen that $1 invested in 1802 in the US equity markets would result two centuries later in a value of $400,000. The annual average return is 6% and is statistically positive at the 95% confidence level. The empirical annualized volatility is 14.3%.

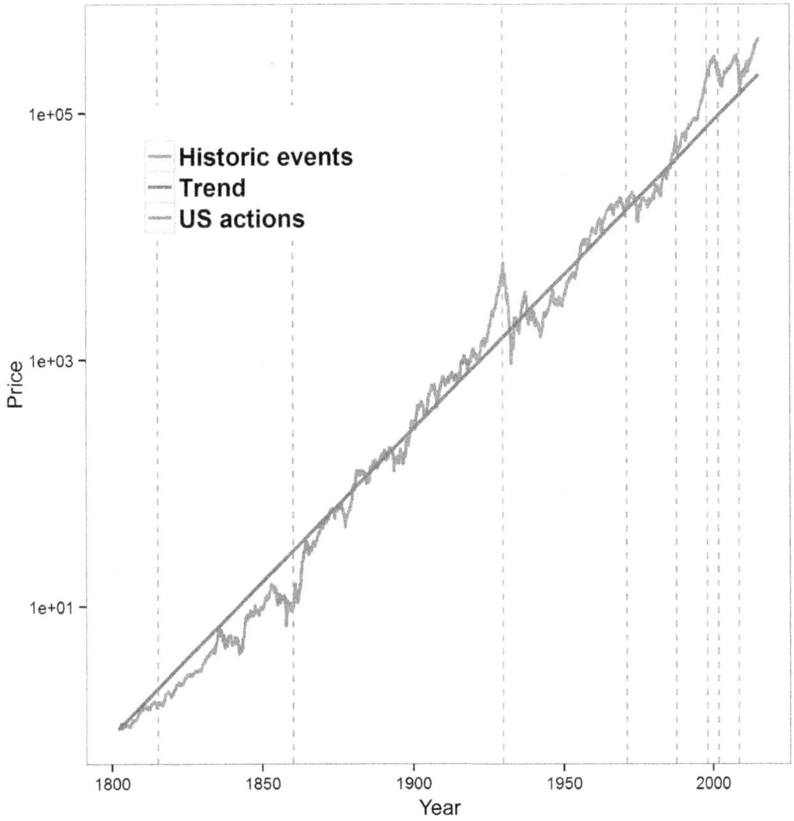

FIGURE 2 US Stock Index 1802-2015: The historic time series of American stocks from the early 1800s to the present day was compiled using data from the works of Schwert [17], Siegel [18], and the Dow Jones Index. The main historical events are indicated: Battle of Waterloo, Secession War, Great Depression followed by World War II, 1970 oil crisis, 1987 market crash, 1998 Russian default, 9/11, Lehman Brothers default.

Figure 3 shows the distribution the monthly returns of the US equity index and Table 1 the main statistical features.

The first conclusion is that the US stock market shows a positive long-term growth trend confirmed over the past two centuries. The periods of long depression are followed by periods of strong growth.

In order to assess the robustness of the hypothesis of the long-term trend in the stock market a scenario analysis is employed. Thus based on a bootstrap procedure from the initial set of monthly returns, market scenarios for a buy and hold strategy are built with various horizons from 5 to 35 years. For a large number of samples (5000 samples) the average performance and the worst-case scenarios at 90%, 95%, and 99% confidence levels are calculated. The results are shown in Figure 4. The average performance of 6% is quasi-constant for all investment horizons. Nevertheless the worst-case scenario indicates a strong negative performance for shorter holding periods. For a 5-year investment horizon for the centenary scenario a −10% return can be observed. For investment horizons longer than 25 years the expected return is positive. These findings were confirmed by other similar studies in the literature [19].

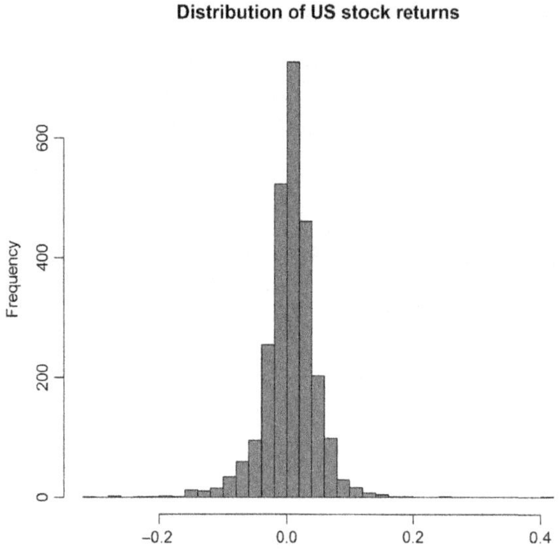

FIGURE 3 Histogram of the monthly returns of the US equity index.

TABLE 1 Statistical Features of the US Stock Index

Metric	Estimate
Mean (yearly)	0.060
Std. deviation (annualized)	0.143
Skewness	−0.489
Kurtosis	8.91

The second conclusion is that the hypothesis of stock market growth holds even assuming a crisis scenario with the condition that the holding period is long enough. Market analysis methodologies have more sophisticated tools, but the basic assumption when investing in financial markets of long-term positive growth. Many of the institutions involved in the investment industry try to adopt the prospect of long-term growth into short-term gains, which inevitably leads to massive losses for many investors.

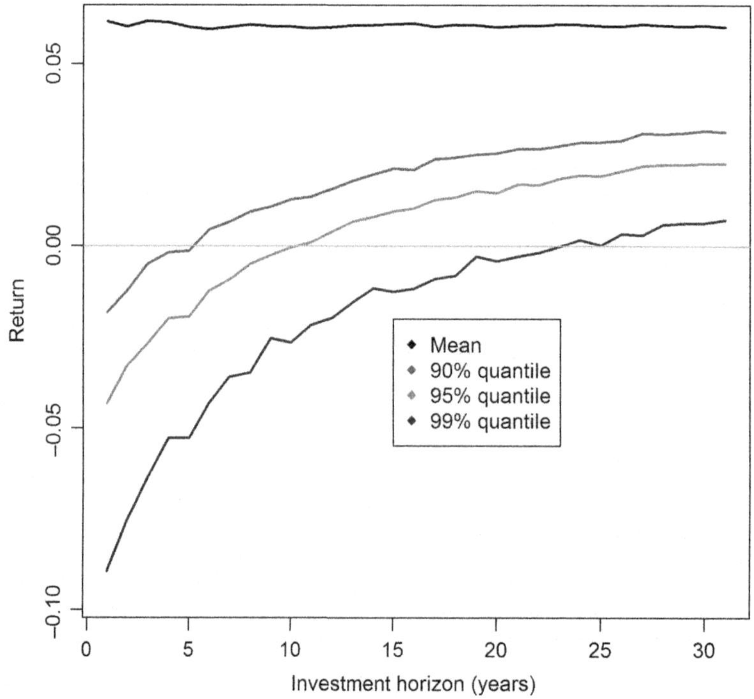

FIGURE 4 US holding period.

CHAPTER

1B

A History of (Non)violence

OUTLINE

1 BACKGROUND

The term *financial crime* covers a broad range of actions that are currently classified as offenses across various jurisdictions. Its sense and scope have evolved throughout history depending of the regulations and the increasing sophistication of financial instruments. A more formal definition[1] points to any kind of criminal conduct relating to money or to financial services or markets, including any offense involving: fraud or dishonesty, misconduct in, or misuse of information relating to, a financial market, handling the proceeds of crime, or the financing of terrorism. If the allegations toward money laundering and terrorism have more recent history, the role of information with regard to financial transactions is without doubt the key point in distinguishing criminal from legitimate actions.

Following the timeline presented in the previous chapter and exploring a flashback to the Sumerian era, it is important to dissect conceptually the central figure of the trader in an Ancient City. The monarchy provided the city with monetary assets in the form of coinage or other commodities, which were used as support of exchange for the transactions taking place in temples. The traders and/or the priests were buying and selling various merchandise in order to fulfill the consumption needs of the City or for overseas trades. Similar to modern times two types of traders could be identified: the primal producer/consumers and the intermediaries who were trading for *speculative* reasons. The former class is referred to as "hedgers" in the modern era when talking about traders of financial instruments. From the recollection of ancient documents quoted by historians it is easy to assume that the role of speculators was significant. In addition the development of credit markets brought about usury as an additional element in the picture. Speculation and usury are two main areas targeted by the various

[1] FCA Handbook 2013, glossary, https://fshandbook.info/FS/glossary-html/handbook/Glossary/F?definition=G416.

http://dx.doi.org/10.1016/B978-0-12-801221-5.00017-8

regulation from ancient to modern times, from Hammurabi code and Solon's law to modern regulation for the separation of trading activities and commercial banks (Glass-Steagall Act).

Financial theory argues that the role of speculators in financial instruments and also in physical trading is to provide liquidity. Since ancient times speculators have been able to act as wholesalers and to collect physical goods from smaller suppliers and to distribute these products to larger markets, thereby providing liquidity. During those times as well as today it is argued that speculators play a very important role in the market by providing liquidity and timing to markets. A market with only producers and end consumers would not be very practical and the match of offer and demand would be very inefficient.

2 ANCIENT TIMES

Usury was without doubt one of the first types of misconduct in financial transactions in order to increase artificially the profits from loans. With the development of commerce especially in the Greek cities and Roman period, financing played a crucial role and brought doubtful practices in terms of loans. The Athenian debt crisis during Solon's reign showed the systemic use of usury in Greek society, which almost led to its collapse.

The first description of a scheme analogous to market manipulation was described by Aristotle concerning the Greek philosopher Thales of Miletus in the sixth century BC. Thales predicted that the next olive harvest would be better than expected and put down a deposit in order to buy the usage of oil presses for the following harvest. The olive production was abundant as Thales predicted and consequently the demand for presses increased, the philosopher being able to sell his rights at a higher price. In fact Thales was *cornering*[2] the market controlling a large share of the supply.

Another type of crime relating to financial transactions occurred in 360 BC, when two Greek armorers Xenothemis and Hegestratos intentionally sank one of their empty ships in order to claim the premium of the "insurance." Shipping being very risky during that period the buyer would take the full risk and pay in advance the shipment independently whether or not the ship arrived at its destination. Xenothemis and Hegestratos were supposed to ship a load of corn from Syracuse to Athens and they planned to sink the empty ship in the middle of the sea. Nevertheless their scam failed and they were brought to justice.

3 DUTCH PERIOD

The early medieval period did not produce many significant developments in financial markets or in financial crimes. With the rise of the stock market in Amsterdam in the early seventeenth century, new developments occurred in the financial misconduct area. In 1668 Joseph de la Vega wrote a book *Confusion of Confusions* [20], which is the earliest detailed recollection describing the operations of the modern stock market and the mechanism of bubbles, crashes, and misconduct. The various mechanisms involved which included margin trading, short selling, and manipulation were presented as a dialog between a merchant, a shareholder, and a philosopher [21]. De la Vega's book was written between two episodes that marked the early financial markets: the *tulip mania* and the South Sea Company bubble.

[2]Cornering a market consists of buying enough stock (or securities), or to hold a significant long commodity position which would allow the holder to manipulate its price.

The tulip market in the Netherlands along with the rice market in Dojima were the first futures markets. Tulips were brought in Holland in the late sixteenth century and the tulip bulbs were traded in the main Dutch cities. With a shortage in supply due to a disease that affected the tulips the price started to increase and tulip mania erupted and peaked during the winter of 1636-1637, when some bulbs were reportedly higher in value than precious metals. In February 1637, tulip bulb contract prices collapsed and the trade stopped, generating massive losses for many of the speculators.

The South Sea Company had a small trading business since the early 1700s with Spanish colonies. When the war between Spain and Holland started in 1718, the company developed a scheme which converted government debt into South Sea stock, thereby reducing the Dutch government's debt. At that moment a bubble kicked off and the South Sea created many investment vehicles and in parallel many companies became listed in order to profit from the bubble. Thus more than 50 companies rose by 100% to 800% in less than a year and then lost nearly all of their gains within two months [22]. Directors of the South Sea Company used illegal methods like bribery and misrepresentation in order to inflate the stock. The bubble was also fertile ground for many other stock frauds. In September 1720, the bubble burst and prices fell dramatically in only a few days, thereby exposing the fraud behind the South Sea Company. Figure 1 shows the evolution of the stock price for the South Sea Company and other associated vehicles as well as its influence on other stock

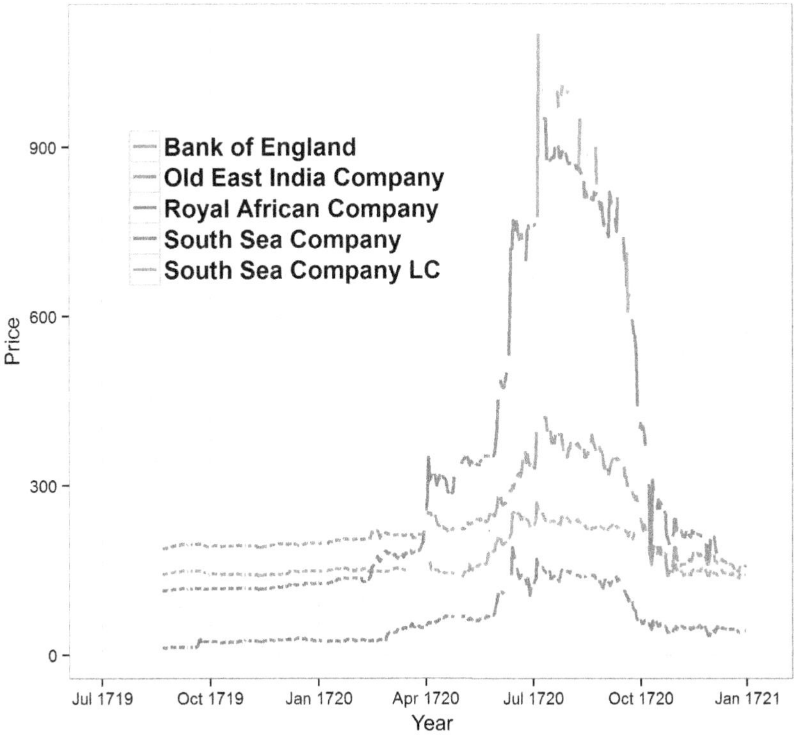

FIGURE 1 South Sea bubble: evolution of the stock price of the South Sea Company and other associated vehicles as well as its influence on other stock prices like the Old East India Company and Bank of England. *Source: Frehen et al. [22].*

TABLE 1 List of the Main Episodes of Fraud and Misconduct on Financial Markets in the Early Modern Period

Year	Name/company	Synopsis
1637	Tulip mania	The tulip mania was the first case in history of irrational behavior of investors
Early 1700	Sir Henry Furnese	While serving as Director of the Bank of England, Sir Henry Furnese was involved in securities price manipulation
1720	South Sea Company	First bubble in Amsterdam stock markets, related to the South Sea Company, which used bribery and fraud among other things to boost the price
1720	Mississippi scheme	Mississippi Company having privileges on French colonial trades was listed though the Compagnie d'Occident, a French bank backed by the Orleans Family. A bubble that begun in 1719 burst as the company had no real assets in the colonial areas
1814	Thomas Cochrane & Charles de Bérenger	Great Stock Exchange Fraud was the result of false news that Napoleon had been defeated by the royalists
1815	Nathan Meyer de Rothschild	The legend claims that the English banker made a fortune due to the fact that he knew in advance the outcome of the Battle of Waterloo
1822	Gregor MacGregor	Sold bond backed by a quasi-imaginary territory: Poyais situated in Honduras

prices like the Old East India Company and Bank of England.

Table 1 shows some representative episodes of misconduct or which would be qualified as misconduct in the modern era. With the exception of the South Sea Company many of the events had at the center charismatic figures who were bankers or financiers. In the early 1800s with the development of stock markets in many European countries, securities frauds were frequent due to the lack of reliable information and efficiency. *The Count of Monte Cristo* [23], an all-time best seller published in 1844, includes some cases of early fraud on stock exchanges.

4 EARLY SECURITIES FRAUD

The modern era of financial markets witnessed the development of stock markets in parallel with the industrial revolution. The growth of industrial output, the technological progress of the Victorian period as well as expansion toward the West of the United States boosted stock markets on both sides of the Atlantic. Securities frauds in the modern era were ignited by the desire of many Indus trail tycoons to take over companies. Therefore, a high number of corners of short-squeezes occurred on various shares (i.e., Hudson and Harlem railroads corners [24]).

The early 1900s and especially the roaring 1920s that preceded the Great Depression were prolific for the securities investors and the stock market rush attracted a high number of offenses and frauds. Following the 1929 crash the United States adopted the first major federal law regarding the sale of securities: The Securities Act of 1933. The Act aimed to bring more transparency in financial statements of firms as insurance for investors and to tackle the misrepresentation and fraudulent activities in the securities markets.

Table 2 presents some relevant events during the modern era. Among the many stock

TABLE 2 List of the Main Episodes of Fraud and Misconduct on Financial Markets in the Modern Era

Year	Name/company	Synopsis
1863	Cornelius Vanderbilt	Vanderbilt cornered the market, allowing him to take control of the Hudson River Railroad
1868	Cornelius Vanderbilt v. Jay Gould	Vanderbilt tried to corner the Erie Railroad stock, starting a financial war with Jay Gould. Finally his ploy failed as he was not able to push prices up
1920	Allan Ryan	Ryan was an investor in Stutz Motor, a well-known car company. He successfully short squeezed the market but in the end due to intervention of the NYSE which suspended the shares, he plunged the firm into default
1920	Charles Ponzi	Charles Ponzi developed a scheme that is still referred to today, promising huge returns to investors
1922	Clarence Saunders	Saunders, the founder of the grocery network Piggly Wiggly, tried to corner the stock of his own company based on a huge loan. The corner failed and the company defaulted
1929	Clarence Hatry	Before the crash of the London Stock Exchange, Hatry, a reputed financier, was indicted for fraud as he issued fraudulent stocks

market-related examples is the original Ponzi scheme, orchestrated by Charles Ponzi in 1920.

5 REVOLUTION IN CRIME

The post World War II era brought an increase in the frequency, severity, and typologies of crimes on financial markets. This revolution in crime took place at three different levels: organizations, financial instruments, and technology.

First the organizations and mainly the financial institutions became not only targets for crimes but also cradles of misconduct. In the previous periods fraud and misconduct were generally orchestrated by very rich and powerful individuals with a strong influence on the markets. Similarly to the modern era, financial crime on securities markets were generally phenomena which grew around individuals like Michael Milkin or Ivan Boetsky who acted within their own private investment firms. Subsequently, individual misbehavior was found within big banks. The 1990s class of rogue traders including Leeson and Hamanaka is an example of how bank employees developed illegal schemes within organizations that led to huge losses and even bankruptcy for their employers. In more recent history organizations themselves were involved in structural misconduct like the LIBOR and FX rigging. These frauds involved reputed financial institutions organized in cartel-like groups attempting to manipulate the markets.

Second the financial instruments created new opportunities not only for investment business but also created new avenues for crime. Securing with huge loans to corner stock markets was one sophisticated scheme of the early 1900s. A century later sophisticated instruments with price determined with complex computation became vehicles for misconduct. The Goldman Sachs Abacus case speaks for itself despite the fact that the Wall Street giant did not face criminal charges. The same situation in relation to the toxic structured credit sold to municipalities unable to understand and assess the risk of those products represents another example in this sense. Instruments not only became complex from a pure financial point of view, but also in the legal sense. Structured products are harbored by so-called Special Purpose Vehicles often incorporated in tax heavens (i.e., Bermuda, the Cayman Islands).

Finally, the introduction of technology in financial markets and more broadly in the financial industry reshaped financial crime. Market manipulation and spread of misleading information accelerated with the move of stockbrokers and market researcher online. Thus boiling room and microcap stocks fraud are today much easier and cheaper to implement compared to the time when everything was done over the phone.

If in the early 1980s money laundering cases like the Banco Amrbosiano case were done though traditional instruments like loans and cash transfers, the relatively recent example of Liberty Reserve shows how the Internet enhanced the money laundering industry. Bitcoin and crypto-currency add a new layer of speed to the influx of technology in the world of crime.

Table 3 presents a selected list of financial crimes of various kinds which occurred over the past three decades.

GOLDMAN SACHS & CO.: THE ABACUS DEAL[a]

Synopsis

Paulson & Co., a New York-based hedge fund, felt in early 2006 that the subprime market was fragile and asked Goldman Sachs to create a product based on residential mortgage-backed securities (RMBS). Goldman built a product called ABACUS which was a Collateralized Debt Obligation (CDO), a security whose value and payments are derived from a portfolio of RMBS. CDOs have various tranches from senior (low yield) to junior (high yield). An asset manager ACA Management selected the pool of assets to enter in the ABACUS deal. Goldman market also a Credit Default Swap, which was a protection against the default of the mortgage-backed securities. Paulson & Co. bought the CDS and bet against the fall of the ABACUS. IKB Deutsche Industriebank, a German bank along with ACA Management, were the main investors in the ABACUS product. When the subprime crisis reached its peak, IKB lost $150 million, ACA $900 million, and Paulson made almost $1 billion.

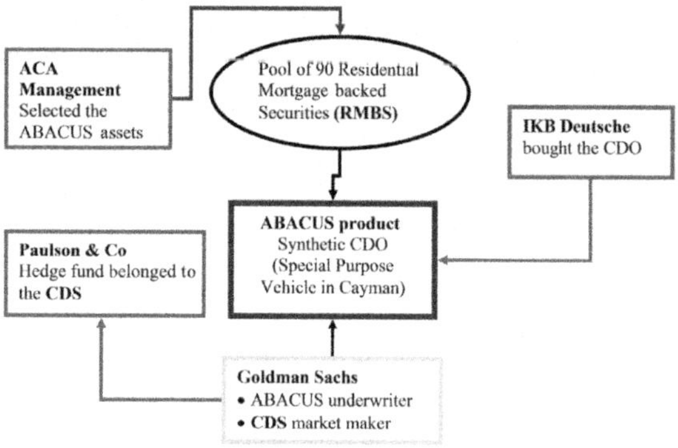

Aftermath

When the Security Exchange Commission (SEC) investigation started in 2010 one of the persons deemed responsible was Fabrice Toure, Goldman's trader in charge of the product. He was dismissed by the banks which settled for a total of $500 million.

[a]SEC vs Goldman Sachs, http://sevenpillarsinstitute.org/case-studies/goldman-sachs-and-the-abacus-deal.

6 OUTLOOK

> What really matters is an awareness of how greed and fear can drive rational people to behave in strange ways when they gather in the marketplace. ***Joseph de la Vega, Confusion of Confusions [20]***

It is said that history repeats itself. Crime in the financial market in the current environment involves both criminal organizations as well as traditional reputed financial institutions. The common factors that reunite these worlds are greed and fear. With the current lack of sustainable growth at a global level and the continuous

TABLE 3 Milestones of Fraud Typologies on the Financial Market in the Modern Era

Year	Event	Synopsis
1982	Banca Ambrosiano	The bank with links to the Vatican and the controversial banker Michele Sindona operated suspicious transactions involving organized crime
1986	Ivan Boetsky	Conducted an extensive insider trading operation on stock markets being charged by the SEC with $100 million
1989	Mickael Milkin	Milkin, one of the biggest players in junk bonds, was indicted for racketeering and fraud and banned for life from markets
1980-1990	Yakuza on Japanese stocks	Japan's markets were infiltrated by organized crime which had a large influence on firms
1995	Nick Leeson	One of the first big rogue traders who caused the bankruptcy of Barings bank
1995	Yasuo Hamanaka	A Sumitomo metal trader, he manipulated (cornered) the copper market for almost a decade
1995-2000	Mob on Wall Street	The New York five families on Wall Street were involved in securities fraud
2000	Stocks fraud	The Internet and later social media were used as a vehicle for stock manipulation
2002	Enron default	Enron default due to a series of misconduct including cooking the books, manipulation, conspiracy with the auditors
2006	Brain Hunter	Amaranth, a reputable hedge fund, lost $6 billion in a few weeks on the gas market. Hunter tried to manipulate gas prices
2008	Madoff	The biggest Ponzi scheme led to losses of almost $60 billion
2008	Goldman Sachs's ABACUS	A subprime product is recommended to a client (Bank) while another client (hedge fund) is helped to play the market
2009	Dexia toxic credit	The Belgian bank mis-sold huge amounts of structured debt to European municipalities
2009	Carbon permits fraud	A huge fraud with participation of global organized crime occurs in the carbon emission market
2010	Liberty Reserve	One of the biggest online platforms for money laundering is shut down
2012	LIBOR manipulation	The reference for interest rates was manipulated by a consortium of banks
2014	FX manipulation	The main FX markets were manipulated by the major banks
2014	Betting market	Sport betting markets were allegedly linked to match rigging
2014	High-frequency trading	Media quoted the first allegation of market manipulation in relation to HFT
2014	Bitcoin	The main Bitcoin exchange MgTox closes following a cyber-attack, suffering massive losses

innovation in markets, financial crime can only expand in size and scope. The only turning point that can be foreseen at this point is a drift in the role of financial institutions. Currently banks have a monopoly on financial transactions and they are the unique providers of *banking services*. With the foreseeable increase of misconduct in financial markets the monopoly might be reconsidered, thereby creating a strategic reorientation of the financial sector.

CHAPTER

1C

Financial Markets in the Technology Era

OUTLINE

1 THE SECOND INDUSTRIAL REVOLUTION

The New Age of finance started with the technological revolution and the development of systems able to stock, analyze, and transform information. For many young bankers working in fields like algorithmic trading the concept of financial markets is *sine qua non* to technology. No one would be able to imagine, markets without technology. Computers are a recent development, however, if we consider the time scale of financial market history. The difference in the way grains were negotiated on the Chicago Mercantile Exchange in the early 1970s was probably similar to the way Greeks were trading in the Forum during the reign of emperor Hadrian. Yet today one is able to design and write a dozen lines of commands in the unspoken language of a machine that can place thousands of orders in a second on the same Chicago Mercantile Exchange and to correlate this information with the stock market from another exchange.

Despite the current revolution taking place in large data storage and mining, one of the most used tools today in financial institutions is the Excel spreadsheet. The ancestors of the Excel spreadsheet were some applications (Lotus 1-2-3, VisCal, Multiplan) that saw the light in the early 1980s, which allowed unsophisticated analysis of data and basic computations. The use of Excel in financial services represented a major milestone in the financial world. The use of computers and spreadsheet applications clearly increased the data analysis capacity, but also reshaped the investment banking and the financial sector in general from an anthropological point of view.

Prior to the 1980s, professionals in the financial sector were part of an inner circle, which did not divulge its secretes to *neophytes* or unauthorized personnel. From simple operations like the pricing of a mortgage to more complicated merger valuation or trading strategies, the details were kept within a small and elite circle of people. For instance partners of the big investment firms would calculate the valuation of a firm or hedge fund using a pen on the page of a newspaper [25]. It would take some time for a new employee to understand how this type of calculation was done.

http://dx.doi.org/10.1016/B978-0-12-801221-5.00018-X

The introduction of technology and the use of computers and spreadsheets made it possible to carry out computations in real time; this democratized financial techniques. With computers and the use of spreadsheets these techniques became accessible to an increasing number of people. With time this became a new discipline studied today in many universities: computational finance. One of the first educational programs in computation finance was introduced at Carnegie Mellon University in 1994.[1]

Technology is today the core of the investment world and part of the day-to-day life of bankers at all levels. From client data storage to valuation and from order transmission to Back Office confirmation all operations involve information technology. Over the past decades banks have attempted to minimize the role of manual operations and to automate processes as much as possible. This tendency reshaped the trading activities in banks and led to new instruments and products. In the financial markets technology also became a focus of competition, investment firms vying with each other not only for clients but also to perform transactions quickly, with high computation and data storage capacities.

As shown in Table 1 the Internet represented a second milestone in the development of the investment industry. If Excel and other applications were able to spread financial knowledge to a larger mass of people, the World Wide Web made financial information available to anyone. Thus until the late 1990s market prices were available to the public via the media (newspapers, radio, TV) or on demand if a person asked their broker for a quote. Today the web can provide anyone with access to many financial information suppliers. More than that a lot of the information is available at no cost, like end of day closing prices from instruments listed on major exchanges. Internet-based technology not only brought information to the wider public, but also made market investment available to a larger number of potential investors. With the Internet bubble in 2000 brokerage business moved online and private individuals were able to open accounts to access real-time information and make investments. Retail customers and small and medium enterprises became a significant target clientele for the major investment banks, which started to propose tailored products. Not only did stock, bonds and trackers become available via online platforms, but also derivatives instruments on commodities, foreign exchanges, etc. The sector of individual traders (day-traders) is one of the fastest growing sectors in the brokerage houses.

Computers and the Internet provided the techniques, the information and access to markets for a larger number of investors. As mentioned technology is not only a tool but also a competitive weapon for obtaining better and faster information and analyzing high volumes of data. Technology changed structurally the investment world. Until very recently investment and generally banks were seen as a business, where social and human qualities prevailed. Many bankers came from a liberal arts background; banks and bankers were supposed to be people with impeccable reputations in society and were judged by their clients and peers through a very qualitative framework, which was in line with the elitist closed circle image. Technology was to finance what the steam engine was for manufacturing in the Victorian period. In the same way that during the industrial revolution physical labor was replaced by the use of engines, technology replaced the esoteric image of the investment world with financial engineering. With the use of technology, investment banking started to witness a strong inflow of practices from engineering and from the industrial world. Thus Wall Street witnessed more employees with a science and technology background.

[1]Center for Computational Finance, http://www.math.cmu.edu/CCF/index.html.

TABLE 1 Milestones in the Evolution of Technology and Their Impact on the Financial Industry

Year	Technological innovation	Impact on the financial industry
1957	Fortran	One of the first programming languages used in much financial software. Even now, some applications run in Fortran
≈1960	Commercial computers	First generation of computers enters the field of banking
≈1960	Computers are used by investors	Fund managers begin using computers for testing strategies
1970	Computers are introduced in exchanges	Major exchanges use computers for flow management (NYSE, NASDAQ)
1971	SAS (Statistical Analysis System)	SAS is one of the main providers of analytical tools for the financial industry
1973	SWIFT	Protocol of interbank communication that allows the international transfer of funds
1975	First personal computer	Banks start to provide their employees with computers
1978	Matlab	Leading software for modeling in the automotive and aerospace industries that was introduced in banks' analytical departments
1979	dBASE	One of the first databases that was a commercial success in the financial industry
1984	C language programming	One of the biggest revolutions in programming, which is used in investment banks for building in-house models
1982	Internet protocol	The Internet revolution reshaped financial markets with traders moving from trading floors to sit at desks with computers
1983	C++ language programming	Object-oriented version of C, very popular with quantitative analysts in investment banks
1983	First mobile phone	Communication between traders, brokers, and clients gained a new level of speed
1983	Lotus 1-2-3	One of the first spreadsheet applications
1987	Microsoft Excel for Windows	Currently the most popular spreadsheet-based application
1992	Optic fiber with amplification	Internet communication speed increases greatly
1992	Electronic trading platforms	Automated trading algorithms became possible
1994	First online brokers	Investors can buy and sell securities online
1995	Online banking service	Banks provide services to customers via the Internet
1997	R	Open source statistical tool which has one of the biggest communities of contributors
2002	Blackberry	Mobile device popular in the financial industry, allowing users to access financial information (Reuters, Bloomberg)
2004	Facebook	Social network which redefines the human interaction and the way people establish relationships
2007	iPhone	Smartphones allow users to place trades on markets in just a few clicks
2008	Cloud computing	Changes of paradigm in storing data with technology shared resources
2009	Bitcoin	New crypto-currency that revolutionizes payments and markets

Banks' governance started to be similar to that of a an industrial plant, including transverse functions, matrix type organization, support functions and emergency teams. The trend was not only organizational but also in terms of methods and techniques used for making investment decisions. One area where many banks failed was in their dependency on a small number of people. Thus engineering concepts from sectors like aerospace began to be applied in the investment world. Optimal control is an example of this, used on a large scale in the aerospace industry for various tasks of aircraft design, like optimal computing trajectories or programming automatic pilots. When engineers started to be hired in the investment industry many of these optimization techniques from the aerospace industry were adapted to real-time data processing. Signal and image analysis was leveraged to market data analysis that resulted further in algorithmic trading. Furthermore the technology relating to signal transmission was use to develop high-frequency trading. Machine learning techniques like the support vector machine, neural networks, or genetic algorithms used first in image processing were used to develop sophisticated trading strategies in hedge funds.

2 OUTLOOK

"With the growing number of physics graduates working in banking I start to worry for the security of nuclear plants" Head of operational risk in leading institutions, 2006

Despite the massive influx of physics graduates on Wall Street, those who didn't take that avenue and remained in academia managed to push forward the fundamental sciences. In terms of the impact of technology, two areas seem to have momentum.

First, two areas of quantum physics that could make an impact are quantum teleportation and quantum cryptography. Quantum teleportation, introduced in the early 1990s by Bennett et al. [26], could revolutionize the computing universe with the quantum computer which would have much more power than the current ones. Similarly a quantum Internet would allow transfer of data with new speed level, not depending on distance between emitter and receptor and with fewer issues in terms of security. Financial transactions on markets would be executed at much higher speed than today and.

A by-product of the quantum teleportation research is that quantum cryptography used appropriately could solve the issues of electronic security of financial transfers and transactions. However, the quantum cryptography could also be a source of additional risk as hackers could potentially be able to breach the networks and servers easier than can be done today. Cryptocurrencies would also bring in a new era of quantum cryptography that would be used instead of the current hash algorithms.

A second field of interest is DNA computing introduced by Adleman [27], which aims to use molecules of DNA as a medium for computation. This technology would most likely enhance the computing memory by imitating the human brain with the ability to handle millions of operations in parallel [28].

PART II

ORIGIN OF CRIME ON WALL STREET

CHAPTER

2A

From Error to Fraud, Misconduct, and Crime

Despite the massive changes in the investment industry over the past decades some things remained unchanged. Mainly the belief that this industry can generate profits for both its agents and investors has remained unchanged over the years. If in the 1970s the proportion of the financial services in the economies of industrialized countries like the United Kingdom or United States was less than 6%, in recent years this share has increased to almost 10% or to almost 25% if one accounts for the underlying services. In recent years, the share of the financial industry not only increased but reached a critical size thereby creating an imbalance in the developed economies. The Lehman default pushed the US economy into a structural crisis, that needed aggressive measures in order to boost growth. The sovereign and financial crisis in peripheral European states pushed the European Union into a scenario of long-term economic depression. Figure 1 presents a comparison between the impact of the crisis on the economies of the United States and European Union. During the financial crisis the US plunged further down toward the bottom of the credit cycle than the European Union, but started to recover faster after 2012. Nevertheless the debt to gross domestic product (GDP) ratio increased more quickly for the United States, which managed to tackle the financial crisis through this strategy.

How are these findings related to finance? If the industry was able to satisfy investors' high expectations in terms of returns when the influence of finance was limited, the scalability of the returns with size is not apparent from an economic perspective. Using the financial crisis as a risk-revelation event, Moussu [29] shows a very strong negative effect of precrisis Return over Equity (ROE) of banks on shareholders' returns, controlling for numerous bank characteristics associated with the risk to shareholders. The results indicate that ROE was a clear aggravating factor in the financial crisis, as it provided incentives for managers to develop excessive risk-taking strategies. Tests performed on a subsample of banks reveal that incentive compensation is highly related to the level of ROE, which tends to prove that monetary incentives were directly associated with the maximization of this metric. The incentives to maximize the ROE could also have resulted from the fact that references to ROE are prevalent everywhere, within and across banks.

After 2008 the myth of the 15% ROE became a distant memory. The banking industry entered into a low ROE environment and the reinforcement of bank capital requirements pushed the

http://dx.doi.org/10.1016/B978-0-12-801221-5.00001-4

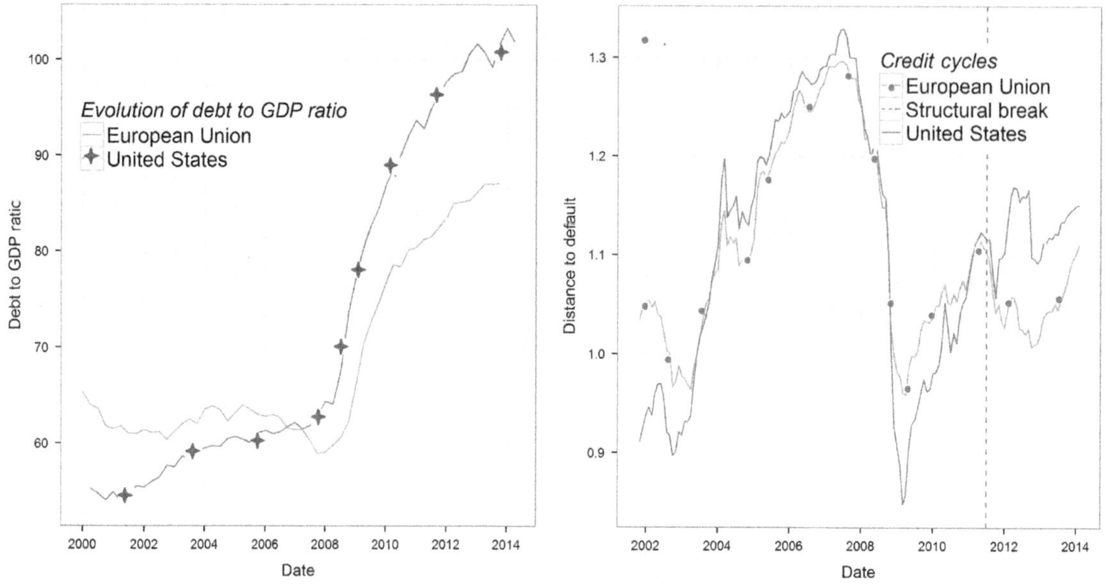

FIGURE 1 Comparison between the impact of the crisis on the economies of the United States and European Union: during the financial crisis the US plunged deeper toward the bottom of the credit cycle than the European Union, but started to recover more quickly after 2012. Nevertheless the debt to GDP ratio increased more quickly for the United States, which managed to tackle the financial crisis through this strategy.

banks into a phase where they were more keen on "economizing" equity than on increasing the returns. In the case of the United States financial industry [30] peaked in terms of share in the national GDP just before the Great Depression, when the stock market mesmerized a huge part of the population with the illusion of high profits (Figure 2). The question is whether an oversized financial industry is able to provide the same level of above average profitability.

This phenomenon, known as the financialization of the economy, brought about some irreversible mutation in the banking sector. From being an elitist inner circle milieu, banking rescaled to a fully fledged high-scale industry. Many countries saw this as a critical point for the macro-stability of their economies. From a behavioral point of view, managers and operators within financial institutions looked to keep their wage levels, despite being in a industry that was larger, with a higher number of employees.

As mentioned in the first chapter the work culture and ethic in the financial industry changed massively with the democratization of financial techniques. Many people from a blue-collar background entered the industry, attracted by the high salaries and social position that came with it. The new blood infused into the system brought more aggressive practices manifested through more greedy and aggressive dealings with clients and within the firm. The old gentry was slowly eclipsed by hungrier newcomers. These social qualitative changes juxtaposed with an increase in the sophistication of the financial products led to many collateral effects, many of them negatively affecting the reputation of the sector. The cultural drift of the industrialization of banking and the increase in speed of the transactions led naturally to the occurrence of human error in financial transaction. It is not implied here that the financial services were bulletproof before, but its increasing weight in economies

FIGURE 2 Share of the financial industry in the US economy. The share of the financial industry peaked before the Great Depression and also after the credit crisis. Since the end of the World War II the ratio increased from almost 2% to 8% in 2013.

made these errors visible. One of the most common errors in banking are those generated by manual operations. For instance when doing simple trades an operator can input by mistake a wrong number or a wrong instrument or a wrong currency. Obviously in recent years with the decrease of human intervention in the process the frequency decreased but human presence is still needed on trading floors or dealing rooms, etc.

"Fat finger" errors are one category of mistakes that can occur on a desk when a trader hits a wrong input on the keyboard. For instance around October 2014 a Japanese bank avoided the biggest of all "fat finger" meltdowns when an unidentified large stockbroker managed to cancel wrongful trades.[1] Orders for shares in 42 companies worth 67.78 trillion yen (500 billion dollars) were canceled in Tokyo. If the orders had gone through the hapless dealer would have traded more than half the shares of Toyota, the world's biggest car maker, for 12.7 trillion yen. Trades were also scrapped for other big Japanese names such as Sony, Honda, and Nomura. In this case, a huge order was stopped due most likely to controls of the brokerage house. Nevertheless many of the rogue trading cases that lead to big losses or bankruptcies started from simple errors which were hidden or dealt with by the trader through different approaches like fictive trades or manipulating the accounts or forging the confirmation to the back office. In theory, the occurrence of an error of significant size should be priced into the cost of the transaction. And yet it is a common perception that operators try to dissemble operational losses using all kinds of shenanigans. If these kinds of behavior remain undiscovered the operator might use these techniques or dissemble other unauthorized transactions. That was effectively the case of Leeson with the famous "88888" account. It is crucial to underline here an important point in the ontology of a "crime." Errors can reveal weaknesses in the system that could be used to cover up other activities. Thus an unintended error could easily push an operator to committing further

[1]Japanese broker makes £380b "fat finger" trade, http://www.theguardian.com/business/2014/oct/01/japanese-trader-380bn-pounds-fat-finger.

bigger intentional mistakes. Under this scenario it is assumed that there is no intention of severing or damaging the institution and the client. At this point the proposal has the weakness of maximizing its own utility within the institution.

The next phase of the process toward a fully fledged analysis of financial crimes is the intention of developing a criminal enterprise in order to squeeze profits from an organization or clients in the sole interest of a person or a group of people. If a specific process exploiting the weakness of a system is put together than we are dealing with a continuous financial crime enterprise. LIBOR manipulation is a very good example in this sense. The rigging started prior to the crisis with infinitesimal twists of the rate offering a limited advantage to an organization in a relationship with a counterparty and evolving to a systemic offense consisting of systemically rigging the rate, much below its real level. Again in this case the fear element, the fear of so-called amplification of a crisis was exhibited as a motivation for such an act.

An offense that became a product to a certain extent was the "Sokuoka" of the Japanese "antisocial groups". It was justified at the time by the fear of the board of losing control over the shareholder assembly, thereby justifying the presence of the Yakuza in shareholders voting meetings. From error to sin or from fear to crime the journey can sometimes be very short and abrupt.

The few mentioned cases depicting the error-crime issue clearly reveal another topic long discussed by the financial literature: the agent-principal problem. This issue is built around the asymmetry of information between *the principal* and *the agent*. This asymmetry can degenerate into abnormal behaviors and patterns of corporate evolution. Going back to the case of the fat finger error, in an ideal world the operator is supposed to report the issues to management then leading on to *the principal* in order to offer a better view of the challenges of managing the business. Thus *the principal* would be aware if the structure of the company was robust enough and if a bigger error could be handled with the amount of capital currently held. If the operator tried to "deal" with the error alone then we enter into the world of information asymmetry, with a very clear-cut case. The information asymmetry resides not only in the knowledge about an error which is a straightforward case but in issues which are more difficult to categorize. Controls, policy, and regulators are always one step behind the operator in testing the limits of the system, for obvious reasons. The operators (i.e., front office) are dealing with the business continuously and they test the limits on an ongoing proactive basis. The control function assesses these limits only with hindsight and they try to find the flaws in the system. In regard to the forward curve of the ability to tackle a system limit, the operators are in a "backwardation" position while the controllers are in a "contango".

Banks do make contingencies for the likelihood of losses incurred from inadequate or failed internal processes, people and systems, or from external events, corresponding to the operational risk which accounts on average for almost 15% of banks' total regulatory capital. When modeling these losses the scenarios of error are assumed to be correlated to the fraud scenarios. This assumption works well for high-frequency low severity losses like those encountered in payment or credit cards. But when dealing with rare events of high severity and low frequency like those corresponding to rogue trading or market manipulation, the scenarios of error and frauds occurring simultaneously are underestimated, thereby catching many banks unawares when faced with such events (i.e., Barings).

Human error is one of the elements that can lead to white-collar crime through a mix of behavioral, economic, and psychological circumstances. Another starting point for financial crime within an organization is the policy arbitrages. Policy can be internal when linked to an organization's own standards and external when imposed by regulation. A whole debate about the role of regulation in the financial industry can be developed in relation to this topic, and it will be addressed in a later chapter. Conditioned by a set of polices both internal and external an operator will try to find a number of ways to slalom between the red flags imposed by each.

Policy arbitrage takes many shapes, shades, and flavors. It can include the geographical relocation of an activity where the regulatory burden is less constraining, like the drift toward Asia of investment banking. Another type of policy arbitrage is the creation of special entities which do not fall under the scope of a certain regulation, a method used in the selling of subprime mortgages in the year prior to the last crisis. Finding breaches in a regulation or a policy is the most prevalent case, the financial industry having large teams in their legal departments. Policy arbitrage can lead easily to misconduct when employed on an industrial scale. A good example of this is the toxic debts sold by major investment banks to municipalities across Europe which generated many cases of litigation. Misconduct happening in a continuous enterprise involving more than one institution can easily develop into financial crime. Misconduct risk has become a serious problem for financial institutions. From a conceptual point of view misconduct is a general term that encompasses violations of law, regulation of internal policy and the expectation of doing business ethically. The underlying idea of ethical business is difficult to assess even in the light of the opinions of Max Weber and Benjamin Franklin. Each new product or business brings new ethical challenges which are increasing in sophistication and can depend on various perspectives, cultures, etc.

OUTLOOK

In March 2014, the Bank of England[2] launched a proposal to require all firms entering under the scrutiny of the British financial regulators to tailor their employment contracts in order to ensure that bonuses awarded could be reclaimed from individuals where necessary. The British financial authority already had powers to require firms to stop payment of deferred bonuses, called malus. The conditions in which vested remuneration would be reclaimed are explained as follows:

- there is reasonable evidence of employee misbehavior or material error;
- the firm or the relevant business unit suffers a material downturn in its financial performance; or
- the firm or the relevant business unit suffers a material failure of risk management.

This approach is still in the test phase and would be one of the first such measures. Applying financial deterrents to organizations and their employees that fall under the umbrella of misconduct would certainly reduce the chances of errors developing into fraud and of arbitrages leading to misconduct and crime. As any law infringing a penalty to an agent it is crucial not only to announce such a policy but also to apply it, thereby increasing awareness among organizations.

[2]Clawback on bonus awards, http://www.bankofengland.co.uk/pra/Documents/publications/policy/2014/clawbackcp6-14.pdf.

CHAPTER

2B

Moral Hazard and Financial Crime

OUTLINE

1 BACKGROUND

Since the unprecedented consequences of the recent financial crisis the term *moral hazard* appeared frequently in the context of finance and more specifically investment banking. Adam Smith explained over two centuries ago in his book *The Wealth of Nations, Part II, Economic Policy* [31] that the interests of agents are never perfectly aligned with those of their principals, creating a persistent challenge to ethical standards. Based on this assumption, Smith was highly skeptical of the corporate form of economic organization and thought that it would be the partnership form that would predominate, due to the fact that the former places more responsibility on agents.

> It has long been recognized that a problem of moral hazard may arise when individuals engage in risk sharing under conditions such that their privately taken actions affect the probability distribution of the outcome. *Adam Smith*

In the current definition introduced by Krugman [32] moral hazard is described as a situation in which one agent makes the decision about how much risk to take, while someone else bears the cost of the undertaken risk. For instance one trader can expose a bank to massive risk exposures in order to maximize his potential bonus indexed on the performance, without bearing the eventual losses generated by the trade. Moral hazard and its effects are changing the environment where it arises. Therefore, a technical definition or a clear-cut scope are impossible to give. Nevertheless moral hazard can be depicted as an option to take risks which is given to agents. In the light of this analogy, examples of moral hazard include:

- *Account managers in retail and commercial banking*: In the quest for more market share and more turnover operators in traditional banking could increase the revolving/credit lines for their clients. The moral hazard

http://dx.doi.org/10.1016/B978-0-12-801221-5.00002-6

manifests in the form of an option indexed on the debt exposure. The higher the exposure the higher the short-term remuneration.

- *Credit analysts*: When analyzing commercial credits credit analysts have a free option on the credit spread of that company. The higher the spread the higher their expected fees would be and implicitly the variable part of their salaries.
- *Brokers*: Brokers are in a perpetual competition for volume and market clients. In this competition for best prices and best execution they have free daily (short-term) options to give to clients prices out of the market. Their performance is based on the volume of transactions, thereby not accounting for the risk to which they expose the firm.
- *Traders*: Traders in investment banking with high turnover proprietary trading have a free option on volatility. The higher the volatility exposure, the higher the expected positive profit and implicitly their bonus.
- *Structuring*: Structures proposing sophisticated products have a free option on the weight of unobservable parameters needed for pricing those products. More unobservable variables are used in a valuation, easier it is to enter into an asymmetric relationship with client.
- *Fund managers*: Asset managers are judged by their capacity to generate returns. Therefore, in this quest they have an option to deviate from the base strategy and to operate more tactically in order to generate additional performance.
- *Risk managers*: Risk managers have an indirect free option in terms of exceeding risk limits. If they cut all the positions and activities with risk higher than normal that activity might become obsolete and implicitly their role in the organization would be threatened.
- *Auditors*: Auditors are paid by the audited company therefore they rarely use their full power when they discover anomalies in accounting. Enron-Arthur Andersen is a typical case for this issue.
- *Anti-money laundering*: An institution might be tempted to make only a superficial KYC check on a potential client that would generate high commissions, but that might also raise suspicions.
- *Regulators*: In many cases regulators do not apply the maximum penalties or inflict the appropriate deterrents to a misconducting organization. This type of action might put the organization in a distressed situation. Without regulated entities there would be no regulators.
- *Governmental institutions*: Governments of countries where the financial industry has a critical share of the gross domestic product have a free option to accept risky behavior in order to satisfy the upper and middle classes that work in these institutions which are involved in the socio-political life of the country.

Before the credit crisis marked by Lehman Brothers bankruptcy the phrase "Too big to fail" defined one of the "empirical" practices in dealing with counterparty risk. When establishing a trade an agent would ignore the exposure in condition in cases of default if the counterparty was a "big" name. When assessing this practice an institution would enter into risky deals or business thinking that if there was a major loss the institution would be too important for the system to allow it to fail. The bailout of major institutions (AIG, RBS, Dexia, and Bankia) is a bespoken example of this feature. Thus the agent-principal problem becomes a central authority-agent-principal problem. The fall of a "too big to fail" corporation would generate turmoil in the global economic picture of a country, thereby forcing the hand of the central authority to cover the losses of a major economic agent. The potential bankruptcy of an insurer like AIG would have produced a real earthquake not only in the insurance world but over the whole spectrum of economic activities through a contagion effect.

Thus the status of an institution as being too important to be allowed to fail gave a free option to principals or/and to agents to undertake high-risk business in order to achieve high returns. If the opposite happened, taxpayers had to cover the loss through the auspices of a central authority (government or central bank). This almost amounts to a "license to steal". The concept of moral hazard could be easily extrapolated to a whole sector like the financial sector. In countries of the Western world where the financial sector represents between 10% and 25% of the economy, authorities find it hard to regulate or to tax the institution generating systematic risk. Threats of relocation to more benevolent environments or fear of even higher rates of unemployment represent serious arguments for the financial industry in order to impose its views. In conclusion moral hazard can apply to one person inside a company, to one company, or to one system. The massive losses on capital markets over the last 20 years are very good examples of how moral hazard works. Nick Lesson was the first rogue trader to become known to the wider public in 1995 for generating losses of 1.3 billion dollars that lead to the bankruptcy of England's oldest and most exclusive bank. Barings was one of the banks used by the British royal family, but this counted for nothing when a consensus for a bailout of the bank was not reached by its peers and the Bank of England. It seemed back than that Adam Smith's theory of auto regulation was also working in financial enterprises. Some years later with the bankruptcy of Long Term Capital Management (LTCM), a reputed American hedge fund, public opinion started to be aware of the systemic impact that a default of a major institution could have. With Kerviel's rogue trading announced in January 2008 it was obvious that one person can not only bring down a major institution but also can have a devastating impact on the financial markets. As Kerviel was so prominent in European indexes, when the bank cut the positions the markets dropped a few percent in a few hours in all the major trading centers. Adobolis and London Whale provoked similar disasters for UBS and JPMorgan, respectively.

2 WAGE STRUCTURE IN THE FINANCIAL SERVICES

Many sources pointed the finger at the origins of moral hazard, but a consensus has been established that the remuneration structure of this sector is the biggest part of the problem. Banking professionals as well as association football or American football players are considered to be the most overpaid jobs compared to their marginal utility to the economy.[1] Figure 1 depicts the evolution of bonuses on Wall Street. In less than two decades the total amount of bonuses increased more than 15 times. The average bonus grew almost ten times over the same period. The LTCM default in 1998, the Internet bubble and the last credit crunch in 2008 led to a decrease in bonus packages. In the year 2008 when many of the investment banks were bailed out or saved through mergers, the total bonus packages amounted to 17.5 billion dollars which represents the yearly salary of almost 350,000 manufacturing workers.

The level of bonuses depends the financial cycle but have not been seriously affected despite the recent crisis. It is almost like the variable wage is almost guaranteed at a certain level,

[1]Jacques Attali (French economist): "Il y a deux métiers trop payés: trader et footballeur" (December 11, 2008).

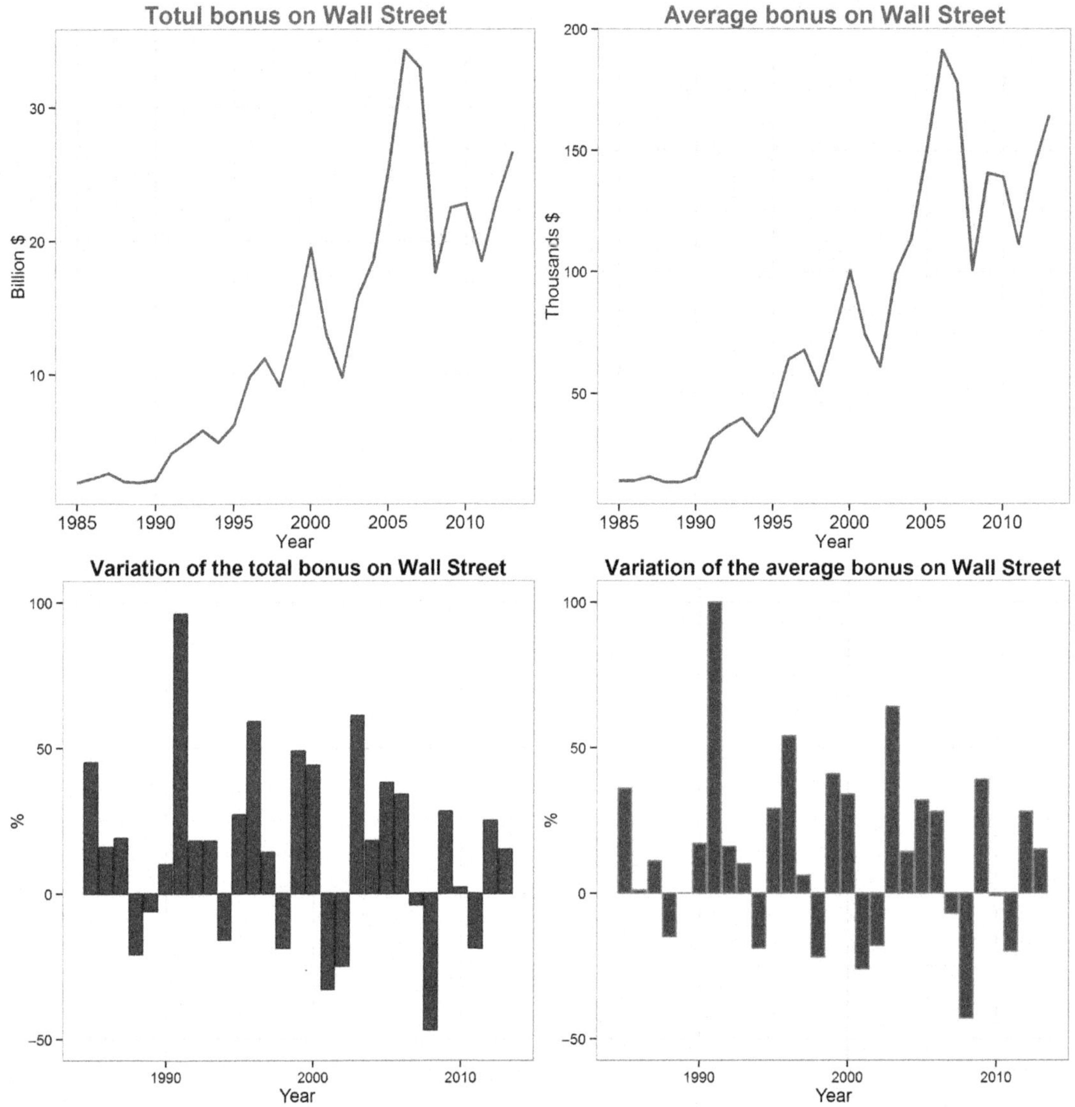

FIGURE 1 Evolution of bonuses on Wall Street: in less than two decades the total amount of bonuses increased more than 15 times. The average bonus grew almost 10 times over the same period. The Long Term Capital Management default in 1998, the Internet bubble and the last credit crunch in 2008 led to a decrease in bonus packages.

the organization having a sort of obligation toward a certain category of its employees. Paying bonuses in crisis times and in many cases using funds from government bailouts exceeds the scope of moral hazard and probably should be classified as *immoral hazard*. In a mathematical representation given a time-varying profit and loss function $\Im_{P\&L}(t, A_t, \sigma_t)$ depending on the exposure to an asset A_t and the volatility σ_t the bonus is proportional to the expected value of the strictly positive cumulated profit and loss profile over a time horizon t.

$$\begin{aligned}\text{Bonus}_t &= \mathbf{E}\left(\kappa \cdot \max\left(\left(\int_0^t \Im_{\text{P\&L}}(t, A_t, \sigma_t)\, \mathrm{d}t, 0\right)\right| F_t\right) \\ &= \mathbf{E}\left(\kappa \cdot \int_0^t \Im_{\text{P\&L}}(t, A_t, \sigma_t)\, \mathrm{d}t \right| F_t\left.\right) - \mathbf{E}\left(\kappa \cdot \min\left(\left(\int_0^t \Im_{\text{P\&L}}(t, A_t, \sigma_t)\, \mathrm{d}t, 0\right)\right| F_t\right)\end{aligned}$$

Further the bonus can be written as the difference between the expedited cumulated profit and loss and the expected value of the negative cumulated profile over a time horizon t. In the long term, the first term tends toward the income generated by the risk-free rate on a bond equal to the exposure. The second term represents the free option given by an organization or a system to its agents as their income depends on the positive tail of their performance. The more volatile trading the agent undertakes the more valuable is the second term. The first term cannot provide much upside so the only way to increase the exacted variable wage is to make the organization accept more risk.

The amount of risk in such an economy can be expressed as quantile of cumulated profit and loss distribution at confidence interval α depending on the organization's aversion to risk. Commonly α is around 99.9%.

$$\text{Risk}_t = \Re \left| \mathbf{P}\left(\left(\int_0^t \Im_{\text{P\&L}}(t, A_t, \sigma_t)\, \mathrm{d}t < \Re \right| F_t\right) < 1 - \alpha \right. \tag{1}$$

Figure 2 shows the result of an experiment comparing the evolution of bonus and risk on a relative scale. A profit and loss pattern was simulated over a one-year time horizon assuming plain long position on an asset following a Gaussian distribution with a drift equal to the risk-free rate and the volatility σ. Trajectories for the asset were simulated though a Monte Carlo approach and the Bonus and Risk profiles calculated accordingly. The Risk profile

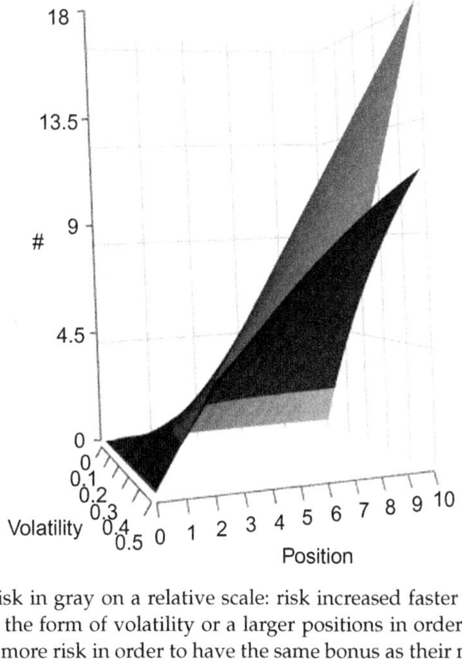

FIGURE 2 Bonus in black and Risk in gray on a relative scale: risk increased faster compared to variable remuneration. Operators need to take more risk in the form of volatility or a larger positions in order to generate a more marginal bonus. Thus newer employees need to take more risk in order to have the same bonus as their more experienced peers.

increased faster compared to the variable remuneration. Operators need to take more risks in the form of volatility or a larger positions in order to generate a more marginal bonus. Thus newer employees or newer activities within an organization need to take more risk in order to have the same bonus as their more experienced peers.

This way of assessing performance ignoring all forms of deterrent would continue to pay an average bonus whatever the level of risk and would compel agents to take more risks for the same marginal increase in bonuses.

3 EFFECT OF EXTERNALITIES

The consequences of acts generated by moral hazard not only have consequences for the organization where they occur but also on other organizations and other sectors of economy. These effects, widely studied in environmental research, pollution, and carbon emissions are known as externalities, more precisely negative externalities. In the 1920s, a British economist, Arthur Pigou [33] introduced the concept of externality and showed that externalities when they are negative can be reduced though a Pigovingian tax.

Externalities constitute a very abstract idea and one definition given by Samuelson and Nordhaus [34] states that: "Externalities or 'spillover effects' occur when firms or people impose costs or benefits on others outside the marketplace." Begg et al. [35] explain the concept as follows: "An externality exists when the production or consumption of a good directly affects businesses or consumers not involved in buying and selling it and when those spillover effects are not fully reflected in market prices."

Pollution and environment-related issues are an obvious example of externalities are generally negative. As a consequence the industries generating those negative externalities make profits with part of the cost being supported mainly by society. In the absence of specific regulations or dedicated markets (no exchange through supply and demand for the right to pollute) and market prices for volumes of pollution or for the damage to the environment negative, externalities generated by industries represent a common burden for society. In a similar way banks taking overwhelming amounts of risks affect through contagion the whole economy, thereby producing negative externalities, similar to industries that pollute the environment. One way to reduce the effect of these externalities is via taxation but its rate and the scope are hard to establish. A Tobin tax was often cited in the aftermath of the crisis but was also criticized for its implementation challenges and the fact it would confer a comparative advantage to countries not implementing it. In the following paragraphs, some relevant examples of sources of negative externalities are described.

Early in 2012[2] Fred Goodwin, the former Royal Bank of Scotland chief executive, had his knighthood removed by the British crown. Previous to these events only convicted criminals or people struck off professional bodies have had knighthoods taken away.

RBS went through turmoil in 2008 when it needed the intervention of the British government in order to be bailed out for an amount of almost 65 billion dollars (Figure 3). The bank's CEO, who had been knighted in the times when RBS became Exchequer's first bank, was heavily criticized over his role in the bank's near-collapse. In the years that preceded the shock RBS was involved in many ventures that revealed themselves to be black holes including the multi-billion-pound deal to buy Dutch rival ABN AMRO at the height of the financial crisis in 2007. In addition RBS became involved in many

[2]Former RBS boss Fred Goodwin stripped of knighthood, http://www.bbc.co.uk/news/uk-politics-16821650.

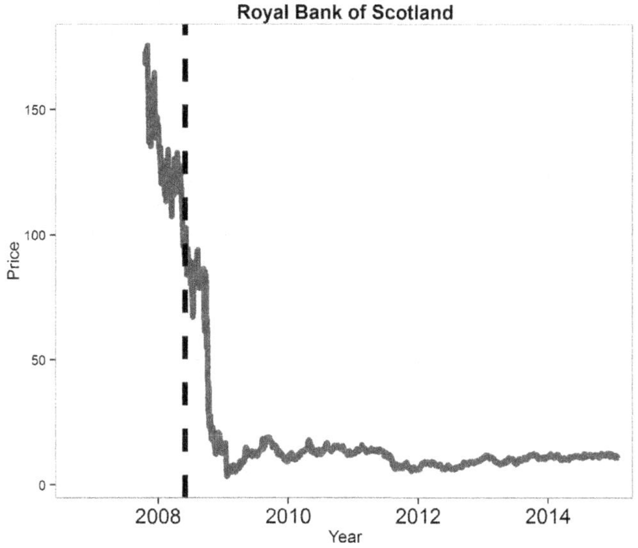

FIGURE 3 Stock price of the Royal Bank of Scotland.

risky ventures such as exotic products trading and structured notes for local municipalities in Europe. The sum of those poor decisions coupled with Goodwin's ambition led the bank toward an unprecedented ordeal. Not only was the English economy affected and thousands of people lost their jobs but also the Dutch financial system was effectively deprived of their premier bank ABN AMRO.

In 2012 the former president of Bankia, Rodrigo Rato,[3] and 32 former members of the failed bank's board were investigated on charges of falsifying accounts, dishonest administration, price manipulation, and improper appropriation. Bankia was nationalized in May 2011 at a cost of 23 billion euros (30 billion dollars) to the public purse after its share price fell by 75% in less than a year (Figure 4). The investigation comes in response to demands from the small Union Progresso y Democracia party, whose leader Rosa Doez accused Bankia of carrying out "a massive fraud" on its small investors because, in her opinion, its stock market launch was based on the falsification of data. The Audiencia Nacional, the court that deals with serious crime, decided to investigate after the anti-corruption prosecutor's office said it believed there was a case to answer. The judge has also summoned the former governor of the Bank of Spain, the president of Stock Market National Commission, the Deloitte partner who worked for Bankia and the legal representative of the Fondo de Reestructuracion Ordenada Bancaria (FROB) to testify. The national assembly (Audiencia Nacional) has also demanded from the savings banks that comprise the BFA-Bankia group details of all credits, loans, and guarantees made since 2008 in favor of the board and executives and their families, as well as political parties. Rato was the Spanish finance minister from 1996 to 2004. After his popular party lost the election in 2004 he went on to head the International Monetary Fund. Another of the accused, Angel Acebes, was interior minister in the same administration.

[3]Bankia board faces investigation over corruption claims, http://www.theguardian.com/business/2012/jul/04/bankia-board-investigation-corruption-claims.

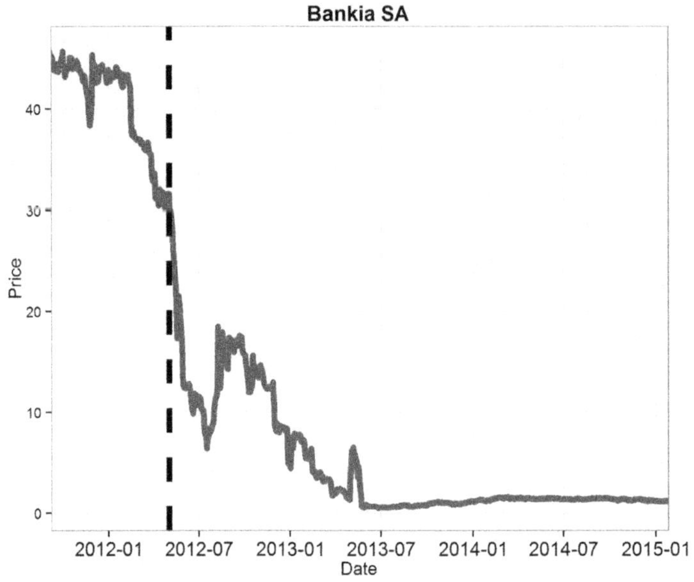

FIGURE 4 Stock price of Bankia SA.

It is interesting that the market anticipated the existence of the London whale and some institutions made a profit from it. The cases of RBS, AIG, Dexia (Figure 5), or Fortis showed that inappropriate management and the possibility of potential economic disaster are not considered as crimes. The Bankia case is the exception as criminal prosecutions followed after the Spanish banks suffered the consequences.

Based on the stock prices of RBS, Bankia, and Dexia before and after the fall, the implied default probabilities were calculated as shown in Table 1. The probabilities of default are determined through a Merton [36] approach based on the market behavior of the stock. The one-year probability of default for a company characterized by a value of assets S and a liabilities level K is:

$$\mathrm{PD} = \Phi\left(-\frac{\ln(S/K) + (r - \sigma_0^2/2)}{\sigma_0}\right) \tag{2}$$

where σ_0 is the volatility of the stock, r is the risk-free rate under a risk neutral assumption, and Φ is the cumulative normal distribution.

The banks appeared to have low default probabilities before the shock, less than 0.5% for RBS and Dexia and 1.5% for Bankia. After the shock the implied rate jumped to almost 50% placing them *de facto* in default. Only the intervention of the governments under debatable circumstances kept those entities solvent.

Derivative portfolios constitute another important source of negative externalities, mainly through the parts which are valued through *mark to model* relying on unobservable variables. These portfolios are classified as Level III assets and represent in the case of investment banks almost 10% of the total securities portfolios amounting to tens of billions of dollars. The underlying parameters used for the mark to model are not observable on the market and generally they are established on the management's opinion of a change of a few basis points in volatility or a correlation assumption that can change significantly the valuation of a portfolio with tens of millions representing the average of the quarterly bonuses in an investment bank. Thus the mark to model becomes in these cases *mark to myself*.

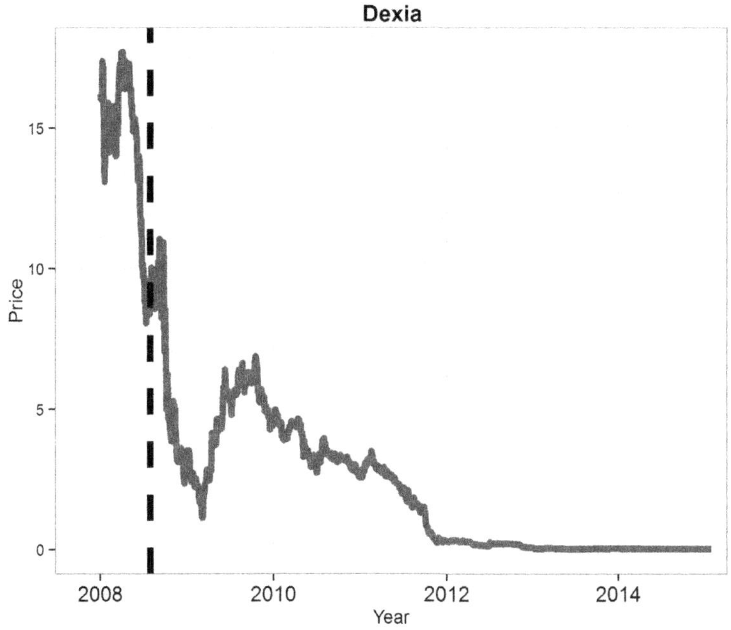

FIGURE 5 Stock price of Dexia.

TABLE 1 PD for Banks

Bank name	Price before the collapse	Price after the collapse	PD before the collapse	PD after the collapse
RBS	150	11	0.0025	0.46
Bankia	37	4.9	0.012	0.43
Dexia	15	3.32	0.0034	0.36

The variation in valuation of the derivatives portfolio is therefore not realized, being only an accounting effect. Structured credit products that made headlines during the financial crisis were part of this category of assets.

4 FROM MORAL HAZARD TO FINANCIAL CRIME

Criminal behavior and moral hazard are different and yet they have similarities. Both scammers and rogue operators look for personal benefit with the risk of damaging the surrounding environment. In other words if we use the terms of the first chapter, moral hazard and crime are both negative externalities and the line of separation between both phenomena is nearly invisible in a case like the fraud on carbon markets. Moral hazard has nevertheless a feature that crime does not. A breach of the law will always be classified as crime if detected. A moral hazard issue could easily become a strategic profit if the situation becomes favorable and no loss is suffered. On capital markets for instance the inception of moral hazard issues is represented by a series of "hidden" actions supposed to be at or beyond the limits of risk. The hazardous operator chooses some circumstances which are favorable to hide her actions. A leveraged situation appears and the institution is exposed to a higher amount of risk. This position could result in a higher return if the conditions are favorable. If a perturbation in the exogenous conditions appears, the position could generate massive losses, thereby becoming visible. In this case, a loss occurs that is classified by the institutions as an exceptional loss and does not affect the operating profit. But if the position generates a gain, it is to the advantage of the operator and profits are accounted as part of the revenues from continuous operations. Moral hazard issues proliferate during periods of turmoil and market instability, when the outlying positions necessitate extra funding and they are tracked by the senior management of the institution or by the regulators. If the loss is too high for the organization the by-product of the moral hazard is considered as fraud or white-collar crime. The operator which carried out the operation is incriminated for misconduct. The fascination for the image of a public enemy may help to deal with the problem in the short term, but the effects of moral hazard are increasing. Organizations tend to favor an individual bearing the guilt of an externality instead of conducting an investigation into their practices. Again the moral hazard in the institution agency relationship is entering another phase. If the externality becomes critical the organization has the option to consider the agents as responsible. Some cases that have been seen in the financial professional community in recent years are perfect examples of this. If the moral hazard gives an incentive to exceed the risk tolerance of a system, once the limit has been passed, it could easily progress to financial crime. The use of inside information, financial shenanigans in pre-initial public offering statements and benchmark manipulations sound more like the cases described in the following chapter dedicated to organized crime. But these recent cases prove that citizens with a regular background, educated at top-level institutions, show organized crime behaviors developing in continuing fraudulent enterprises.

5 OUTLOOK

Moral hazard is a syntagma that represents more than the sum of the two terms: moral and hazard. The phenomena can occur at employee level, division level, or corporate level. If an agent can take as much risk as he wants without incurring any penalty in the case of an adverse event, he has a free option to try and make more money by taking more risks. Psychologically this free option revokes all the conscious and subconscious barriers or adversity toward risk. This mechanism is the very same as that which pushes an individual from legitimate action toward crime. Therefore, wherever there is moral hazard, misconduct, and financial offenses will follow.

Addressing the issue of moral hazard in the financial sector cannot provide any answers in the short term. There is a need to change the psychology of organizations that believe they are indispensable parts of the economic system. Regulation is a solution that aims to cure the symptoms but not the cause. The banking systems have become too big and immune to any action from government. Therefore, the solution is to encourage a moral hazard-free financial system. Economies should have a multitude of sources of finance and Wall Street or the City of London should be one of them. In such a competitive environment with no selective bailouts or preferential treatments the concepts "too big to fail" or "too important to fail" would have less momentum.

CHAPTER

2C

Model Risk

OUTLINE

1 BACKGROUND

The arrival of scientists and engineers in the banking sector in the late 1980s changed significantly the global dynamic of the industry. Human subjective judgment and financial recipes "à la carte" were replaced over time by quantitative models implemented in complex systems aiming to provide a better understanding and more efficient decision making in the risk/return profile of the client and in transactions. Thus a new type of risk arose related to the quality of methodologies employed in banks. Model risk is a type of risk that occurs when a financial model used to measure a firm's risks or value transactions does not perform the tasks or capture the risks it was built for. In terms of regulation, model risk is considered a subset of operational risk, as model risk mostly affects the firm that creates and uses the model. Traders or other investors who use the model may not completely understand its assumptions, scope, inputs, and limitations,

Introduction to the Theories and Varieties of Modern Crime in Financial Markets, Vol. 1
http://dx.doi.org/10.1016/B978-0-12-801221-5.00003-8

which affects the usefulness and applicability of the model itself.

The Board of Governors of the Federal Reserve System [37] emphasized that the use of models invariably presents model risk, which is the potential for adverse consequences from decisions based on incorrect or misused model outputs and reports. Model risk can lead to financial loss, poor business and strategic decision making, or damage to a bank's reputation.

With the increased sophistication in the products being offered and the greater use of technology, the financial industry needed to automate and quantify many of its processes. From valuation to risk management, from decision making to customer service, financial institutions rely more and more on mathematical models built on the top of a growing technical infrastructure. Thus the use of models has become very prevalent in the past two decades, in parallel with progress in computing power and software applications and financial innovation.

Many crucial processes within organizations are supplied or managed by models, thereby generating a double-edged effect. On one hand, the use of models for leveraging existing data reduces significantly the human error and the risk involved in human intervention. Thus many flaws in controls and processes were tackled with the introduction of models. For instance many issues regarding risk and performance allocation across portfolios or traders were addressed through models.

On the other hand, the heavy model and technology-oriented process creates other potential weakness within the organization due to the likelihood of a model being wrongly built, misused, or built on false premises. For example, the Long Term Capital Management default was attributed among other things to model risk. A small error in the fund's option pricing models based on the assumption that volatility was mean reverting was amplified by several orders of magnitude because of the highly leveraged strategy.

The most fundamental of risks is that modeling is just not applicable [38]. For example, it is possible that predicting currency rates or oil price movements is more like forecasting political occurrences than like projecting stochastic processes, with psychological and behavioral aspects being more relevant than mathematics. There is always a temptation to think that complex mathematics has an applicability of its own, but a vision of how things work and interconnect is needed before using mathematics to represent it.

It is necessary to highlight these aspects in the perspective of misconduct and white-collar crime within organizations. The relevance can be easily be emphasized using a parallel with the use of accounting systems. Thus it was that errors or flaws in the accounting process were used in many cases to carry out illegal or unauthorized activities. In the same way, one could use limitations of model risk to enter into gray-zone illegal operations. If in the case of accounting systems the development of these flaws seems straightforward, in the case of model risk there is less margin for error for nonexperts and it is debatable whether such activities can be considered illegal or criminal. Many previous unauthorized trading cases were related to the use of error accounts, where traders manually manipulated accounts in the systems or forged the numbers. From this point of view altering or manipulating a model is a much easier task inside an institution. Accounting is a more straightforward discipline than financial modeling and banks have more means of verifying, tracking, and auditing accounts than they have for models. In many organizations, models tend to be very sophisticated, thereby making them less accessible for anyone who has less knowledge of that model than the person who created it. This asymmetry in regard to models, hidden behind a thick curtain of an apparently intellectual expertise, generates real control issues especially for those businesses relying heavily on models, like exotic derivatives and market making.

2 ORIGIN OF MODEL RISK

Generally speaking a model is a simplified version of reality, and with any simplification there is the risk that something will fail to be accounted for. Figure 1 depicts the basic flowchart of a modeling process. A model is built to address a set of assessments, constituting the model's scope. Model inputs are represented by datasets and generally all the information that is entered into a computation. The model algorithm represents the set of transformations and computations applied to the inputs. This step includes a method which structures the mathematical concepts used in the model kinetics and a system which involves the technological implementation of the method. Model outputs are the set of results obtained from the model, which are used for purposes defined by the model's scope. Errors in modes can occur at any point from design through implementation.

In regard to model risk the following issues can be exploited in developing abnormal behavior and ultimately leading to misconduct within organizations:

- A model may be correct, but the data behind it (rates, volatilities, correlations, spreads, and so on) may be inconsistently estimated or "reverse-engineered" in order to obtain the desired result.
- A model may be appropriate for one type of product, but does not work for another type of product, even they are similar in principle. In this case, the use of the model is not consistent with its initial scope. Even a fundamentally sound model producing accurate outputs consistent with the objective of the model may exhibit high model risk if it is misapplied or misused. Organizations tend to intentionally apply existing models to new products or markets, for reasons of cost efficiency.
- A model might use assumptions which are not compatible with the product or the market for which the model is used. A bank might keep using the same model inadvertently as market conditions or customer profiles change.
- If a number of models are available to address one topic (i.e., a risk measure) the user may cherry-pick the model that gives the results which are in line with its expectations.
- When dealing with sophisticated structures a model might generate an output which

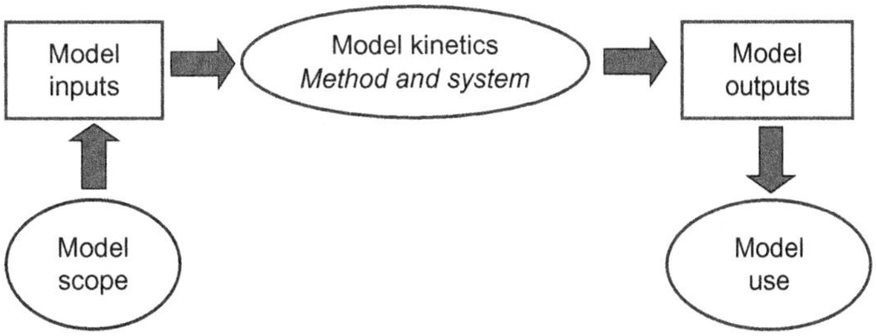

FIGURE 1 Main components of a model: *Model inputs* represents the datasets and generally all the information is used entries in the computation. *Model kinetics* represents the set of transformations and computations applied to the inputs. This step includes a method which structures the mathematic concepts used in the model kinetics and a system which involves the technological implementation of the method. *Model outputs* involves the set of results obtained from the model.

cannot be verified by any means. For example, the prices of a structured derivative cannot be verified by the market due to illiquidity or by disposing of other assets, since the market is incomplete. For the particular case of exotic derivatives, Rebonato [39] defines model risk as the risk of occurrence of a significant difference between the mark-to-model value of a complex and/or illiquid instrument, and the price at which the same instrument is revealed to have traded in the market.

- A model by its very nature is a simplification of reality, and real-world events may make these simplifications inappropriate. Model risk is also a consequence of the assumptions underlying a model that may restrict its scope to a limited set of specific circumstances and situations. A good example is the use of Gaussian dependency for aggregating the default events in the structured credit products that were at the core of the credit crisis.
- A model can include many shortcuts, simplifications, or approximations and this can compromise the integrity and reliability of the results of those calculations, especially when the users of the model are not aware of those approximations and the limitations that come with them.

3 DERIVATIVE VALUATION AS AN EXPECTATION

In the derivatives markets, traders consider the volatility of the pricing process as different from the historical volatility of the underlying asset. This occurs because market players will set state prices to reflect their aggregate preferences and views about market expectations at a certain moment. Hence even the classic [40] pricing model distinguishes between historical and market volatility, calibrated on traded options prices. The theoretical passage of the economy from the physical measure **P** to the *business measure* **Q** is insured by Girsanov's theorem, but in order to apply it options should be liquid and the market should be complete.

In the case of markets with efficiency issues and low liquidity it appears impossible to calibrate the pricing process directly on option prices. Thus we are dealing with a discrete time market that is well known as being in general incomplete. Thus, the *business measure* **Q** is not unique and there exist a multiplicity of economic situations that are compatible with the observed prices. For this scenario the explicit probabilistic approaches described by Black and Scholes [40] and Gerber and Shiu [41] through the Esscher transform, Eberlein and Prause [42] for generalized hyperbolic processes, or Heston and Nandi [43] for GARCH models are valid. Recent research mitigated the pricing issues outside the classic Gaussian risk neutral framework by introducing leptokurtic and skewed distributions and extending Bollerslev's GARCH process. The problem of pricing under market completeness challenges was largely described by the literature through different approaches, mainly focusing on the Stochastic Discount Factor [44–46] or developing empirical approaches [46–50] for instance. Yet all the cited studies have been tested on assets like equities or fixed incomes, which by nature are the closest to the classic framework of financial markets. Changing volatility in real markets makes the perfect replication argument in the sense of Black and Scholes invalid. Markets are then incomplete in the sense that perfect replication of contingent claims using only the underlying asset and a riskless bond is impossible. Of course markets become complete if a sufficient (possibly infinite) number of contingent claims are available and in this case a well-defined pricing density exists. When dealing with new, incomplete, low liquidity options it appears necessary to build new pricing frameworks. The payoff Θ_t is defined as:

$$\Theta_t = E_Q[\Theta_T e^{-r(T-t)}|\phi_t]$$
$$= e^{-r(T-t)} \int_0^\infty \Theta_T(S_T) q_{t,T}(S_T)\, dS_T \quad (1)$$

$$\Theta_t = E_P[\Theta_T(S_T) M_{t,T}|\phi_t]$$
$$= \int_0^\infty \Theta_T(S_T) M_{t,T}(S_T) p_{t,T}(S_T)\, dS_T \quad (2)$$

where t is the time of valuation, T is the option horizon, $q_{t,T}$ is the SDF (the Probability Distribution Function (PDF) under the business (risk neutral) measure **Q**), $p_{t,T}$ is the probability distribution function under the physical measure **P**, and $M_{t,T}$ is the rotation operator, given for the classic Gaussian case by the Radon-Nicodym derivative.

We assume that the returns of S_t follow a Brownian stochastic process characterized by:

$$dS_t = \mu(S_t, t)\, dt + \sigma_P(S_t, t)\, dB_t^Q \quad (3)$$

We note that $\Theta = \Theta_t(S_t, t)$ can be differentiated using Ito theorems as:

$$d\Theta_t(S_t, t) = \left(\frac{\partial \Theta}{\partial t} + \mu(S_t, t)\frac{\partial \Theta}{\partial X} + 0.5 \cdot \sigma^2(S_t, t)\right)$$
$$dt + \left(\sigma(S_t, t)\frac{\partial \Theta}{\partial X}\right) dB_t \quad (4)$$

$$\frac{\partial \Theta}{\partial t} + \mu(S_t, t)\frac{\partial \Theta}{\partial X} + 0.5 \cdot \sigma^2(S_t, t) - r_t\Theta_t(S_t, t) = 0 \quad (5)$$

$$\Theta_t(S_t, t) = \mathbf{E}^{\mathbf{Q}}\left(e^{-\int_t^T r_u du}\Theta_T(S_T, T)|F_t\right) \quad (6)$$

A digital cash or nothing option pays the amount X if the value of the asset is higher than a certain strike K at time T, $S_T > K$:

$$\mathbf{C}_T = \begin{cases} X & S_T - K > 0 \\ 0 & \text{otherwise} \end{cases} \quad (7)$$

If σ_Q is the volatility under the risk neutral measure and ϕ is the normal cumulative distribution function:

$$\mathbf{C}_0 = e^{-rT} E_Q[X\mathbf{1}(S_T - K)_+]$$
$$= Xe^{-rT}\phi\left(\frac{\ln\left(\frac{S}{K} + (r - \sigma^2 T)\right)}{\sigma_Q\sqrt{T}}\right) \quad (8)$$

Without going into the details of the mathematical aspects we understand immediately that the closed-form solution relies heavily on three main aspects:

- First, we assume for all option types that a Gaussian framework is applied. This hypothesis might hold for plain vanilla European options but if we deal with payoffs exhibiting massive changes around a certain strike (like the digital or barrier options), the model might provide distorted results if the market shows abnormal behavior exhibiting, for instance, jumps in prices. Jumps around the strike level involve the payoff going suddenly from zero to a positive value, thereby challenging the Gaussian framework.
- Second, the model depends on input assumptions like interest rates and volatilities.
- Third is the risk neutrality assumption, which in simple terms states that no agent can beat the risk-free rate on a given portfolio in the long term. Here it can be remarked that the hypothesis relies on an abstract term, the risk-free rate, which can have very unusual connotations in certain circumstances.

Last but not least is the framework that evaluates a given instrument as an expectation of its future outcomes, without really incorporating the profile of those outcomes. The debate around the price of an instrument as an expectation

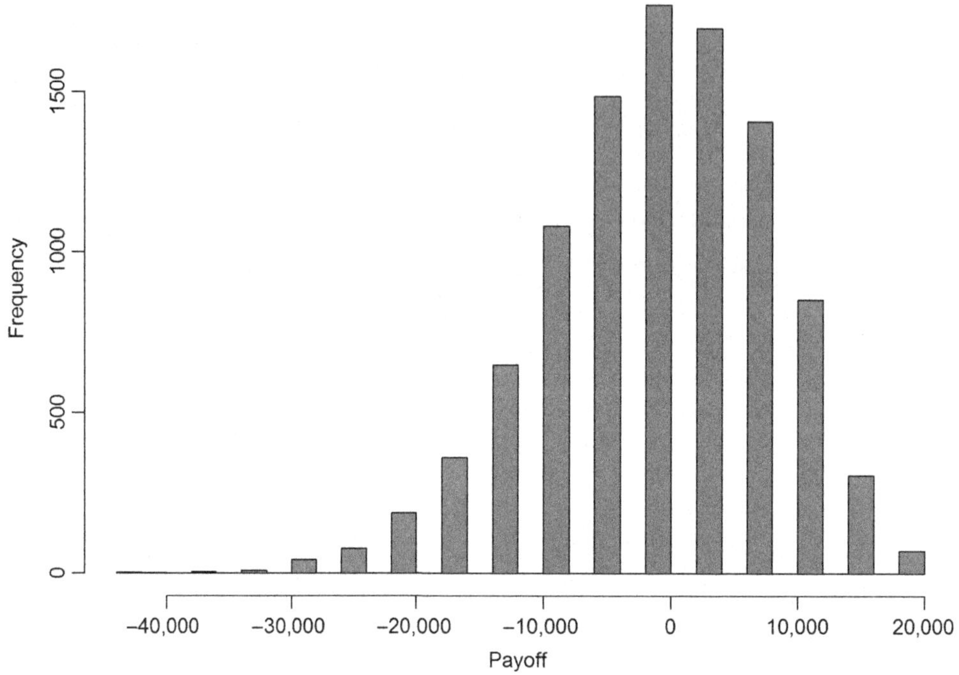

FIGURE 2 Payoff profile.

arise mainly when the profile of the outcomes is highly asymmetric. For example, an instrument **A** indexed on the dice game that pays 6 dollars for each correct prediction of outcome would be normally valued at 1 dollar, as the expected value of the possible payoffs. Here we obviously assume that the dice rolls generate a uniformly random variable. Obviously in this case any investor would consider the price of the instrument as "fair." Now if we consider for an instrument instrument **B** that pays 5 dollars 999 out of 1000 times and receives 3995 dollars once every 1000 trials the price based on the expected value of the outcome would be obviously one. One could ask if anyone would invest in such an instrument that pays almost constantly 5 dollars. To exemplify these aspects, Figure 2 depicts the distribution of the payoff for instrument **B** and shows the distribution of the payoff for instrument **A**.

We can write the following pricing equation:

$$\Theta_B(0) = \mathbf{E}^{\mathbf{Q}}\left(e^{-\int_t^T r_u \, du} \Theta_T | F_t\right) = e^{-rT}[(1 - \exp(\lambda)) \cdot G + \exp(\lambda) \cdot L] \quad (9)$$

where G is the gain and L is the loss occurring with a probability $\exp(\lambda)$.

Figure 4 shows the price of the product **B** depending on the parameter λ.

The value of a derivative and generally of an asset is defined mathematically under the generic form of an expectation. If this fundamental assumption holds for strongly efficient and complete markets, it can be easily challenged in incomplete or low liquidity markets (Figure 5).

As shown in the literature [51] instruments with skewed payoff profiles exhibit the following features:

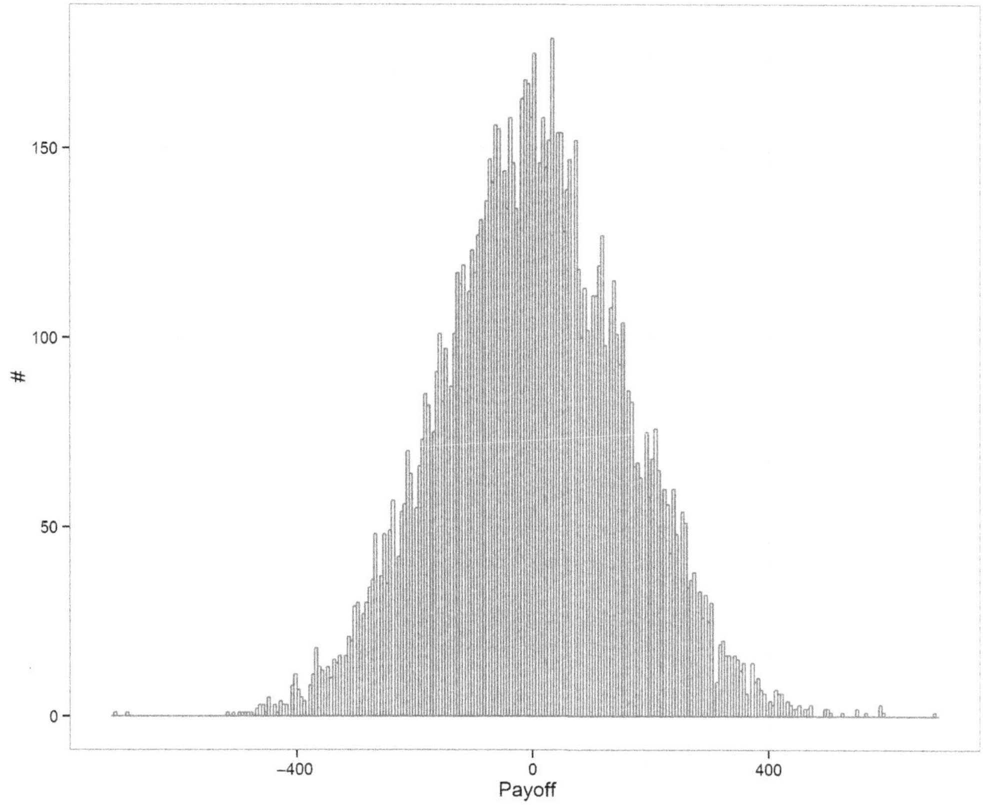

FIGURE 3 Payoff profile an instrument indexed on the dice game that pays 6 dollars for each correct prediction of outcome and a 1 dollar bet.

1. *Distortion of the gain profile.* The true mean of the payoff is different from the median. It is consequently easier for an investor to be attracted by the true mean, particularly if he observes the returns without a clear idea about the nature of the process. The variance will be most of the time lower than the true value.
2. *Market premium.* An investor has a decent performance most of the time, until a crash occurs. But after the shock and before the next shock the investor has a good performance.
3. *Sudden death effect.* It takes a considerably longer time to observe the properties under a skewed process than otherwise. For example, consider a bet with 99% probability of making a profit **G** and 1% probability of a loss **L**. In the case of an asymmetric payoff the true properties of the underlying process will reveal much rarely when compared to a traditional symmetric payoff product.

Certainly the points presented above can increase for a good reason the appetite of many investors for skewed payoff products. Nevertheless if the investor is an incorrectly informed[1] counterparty the investment can easily become

[1]The term informed counterparty denotes a counterparty with the capacity to valuate and assess a product independently.

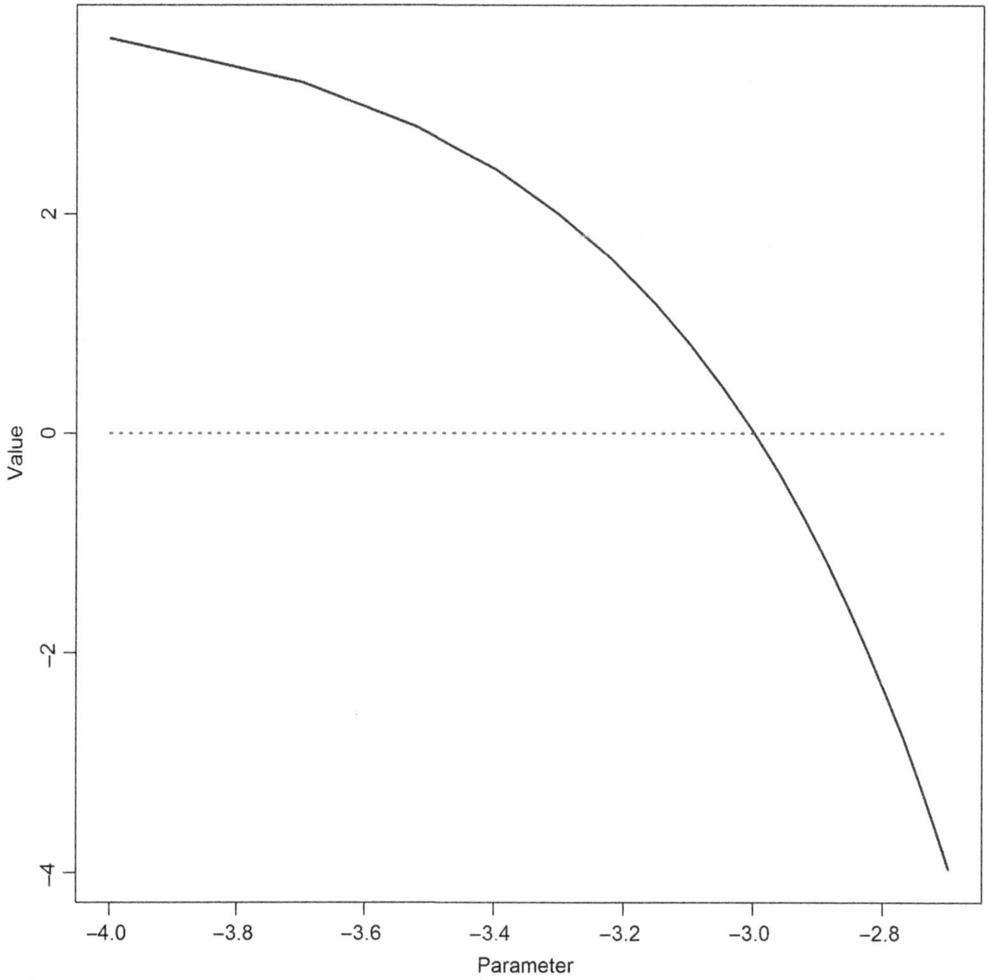

FIGURE 4 Dependence of valuation on the parameter.

a carambolesque lottery-type. Many cases of misconduct or unauthorized trading are based on dissimulating the real nature of the strategy through metrics that do not fully disclose the reality. Clients, regulators, and risk managers review portfolios or traders' books based on a certain number of quantitative assessments supposed to depict accurately the nature of the business.

Proposition: It can be assumed here that for a given control metric and a given investment strategy there is a nonunique way to distort the investment in such a way that the control is respected but the real degree of risk is increased.

For example, from a purely accounting perspective a company that owns the two products **A** and **B**, respectively, would book on its

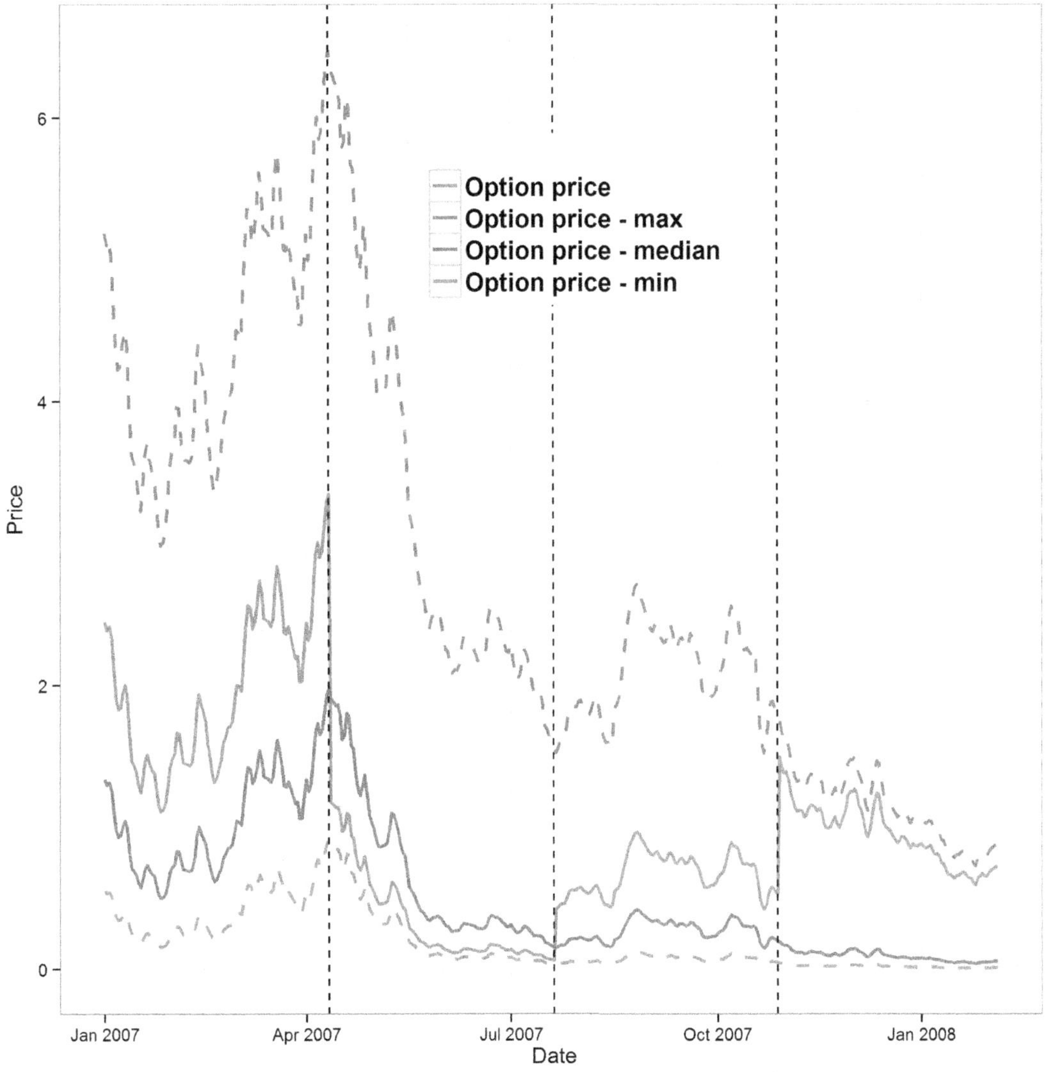

FIGURE 5 Digital option pricing.

balance sheet the same value for each given their mark-to-model. Nevertheless the risk profile of both products is significantly different, a fact which is not reflected because the *fair value* is based on expectation. The accounting regulation International Financial Reporting Standards (IFRS) and to a certain extent the US GAAP imposed guidelines regarding financial instruments. On one hand, fair value is supposed to be accounted for on the balance sheet in order to reflect the true exposure of a company, thereby reducing the issues involving the off-balance sheet products. On the other hand, fair value is based in many cases on one output from the pricing models, which does not fully reflect the risks.

Certainly companies and financial institutions are supposed to hold capital according to their risk measures. But in many cases risk measures do not capture the full-fledged risk profile of a product. We assume that two traders have on their books products **A** and **B**, respectively, that are assessed thorough a historical Value at Risk (VaR) at 95% confidence interval. The risk managers could indicate that the product **A** has a higher risk than the product **B**, due to the fact that the historical scenarios do not yet include the adverse cases when **B** loses 4000 dollars. Thus even the risk metrics could give biased information about an exposure if they are not well adapted to the type of product and risk that they address.

The other fundamental issue of so-called "mark to myth" is that it is highly dependent on the input parameters, thereby introducing additional variability to the balance sheet. This fact is illustrated in Figure 4, emphasizing that the pricing of product **B** depends heavily on parameter λ. A small variation of the parameter can make the price vary from negative to positive values. From an accounting point of view small changes in λ can change the nature of **B** from an asset to a liability.

4 MODEL FAILURES IN INCOMPLETE MARKETS: FOCUS ON CORRELATION

4.1 The Formula That Killed Wall Street

The credit crisis emphasized structural weakness of the investment process across the globe. The fundamental question any economist would ask is why the default in mortgages payments for some facilities of lower classes in the United States generated enormous losses for thousands of investors worldwide. The amount lost was many times higher than the size of the physical losses from defaults. The explanation for this effect resides in the use of credit derivatives, the weapons of mass destruction as Warren Buffet called them in 2002. The subprime mortgage market was nonetheless limited in volume, but investment banks sold derivatives indexed on those credits in massive volumes. In a similar way in the betting markets there are cases, shown in a separate chapter, where the size of the bets on a soccer match is higher than the wages of the footballers. The core question is how reputed investors like the Norwegian Pension Fund lost billions of dollars, despite the fact the investments were in instruments rated as AAA by the rating agencies.

Part of the answer starts with the seminal paper published by Li [52], which provides an elegant solution for pricing derivatives depending on the occurrence of some defaults. The method specifies the aggregation of risks across assets with a Gaussian dependency function. As summarized later in the section this function or copula in scientific terms does not attach a lot of weight to the simultaneity of extreme events. In simple terms let us assume two mortgages which are underwritten to two neighbors living in a suburb of Chicago. If one of them faces financial distress and the payment of his mortgages enter into default there is a high likelihood that his neighbor carrying the other loan would face the same issues. Nevertheless in Li's model the probability of the two neighbors going bust at the same time was near zero. This is why many people consider that the Gaussian copula is the formula that killed Wall Street.[2]

[2]Recipe for disaster: the formula that killed Wall Street, http://archive.wired.com/techbiz/it/magazine/17-03/wp_quant?currentPage=all. For 5 years, Li's formula, known as a Gaussian copula function, looked like an unambiguously positive breakthrough, a piece of financial technology that allowed hugely complex risks to be modeled with more ease and accuracy than ever before. With his brilliant spark of mathematical legerdemain, Li made it possible for traders to sell vast quantities of new securities, expanding financial markets to unimaginable levels. His method was adopted by everybody from bond investors and Wall Street banks to

The second part of the answer is linked to rating agencies which fulfilled both roles of underwriters and credit assessments of those credit products. Obviously there was no incentive to give a low rating to a product for which they were also underwriters.

The role of the dependency model in the financial industry grew with the complexity of the products and is part of the model risk firmament, thereby needing a special focus.

4.2 Focus on Dependency Measures

The basic assessment of the dependency between two variables X and Y with finite first and second moments ($\mathbf{E}(X) < \infty$ and $\mathbf{E}(X^2) < \infty$) is the Pearson's correlation defined as:

$$\rho = \frac{\mathrm{Cov}(X,Y)}{\sqrt{\mathrm{Var}(X)\mathrm{Var}(Y)}} \quad (10)$$

The Pearson's correlation has many limitations in regard to the aggregation of the two distributions. The notion of copula is based on the concept of joined distributions of variables. In a seminal paper, Embrechts et al. [53] revisit the dependency framework for various type of copulas. Without detailing the full extent of the copula theory a short review is needed to further the discussions.

Let X_1, X_2, X_3, ..., X_N be random variables characterizing the returns of N financial assets with continuous distributions $F_1, \ldots, F_n$ and the joint distribution F:

$$F(x) = \mathbf{P}(X_1 \leq x_1, X_2 \leq x_2, \ldots, X_N \leq x_N) \quad (11)$$

As for the copula framework, let us denote an N-dimensional copula, defined on $I^N = [0,1] \times [0,1] \times \cdots \times [0,1]$, as $C(z_1, z_2, \ldots, z_N)$:

- the Gaussian copula:

$$F(Y) = C^{\mathrm{Gaussian}}(z_1, z_2, \ldots, z_N) = \Phi_R(\Phi^{-1}(F_1(x_1)), \ldots, \Phi^{-1}(F_N(x_N))) \quad (12)$$

- the t-Student copula:

$$F(Y) = C^t(z_1, z_2, \ldots, z_N) = t_{R,\nu}(t_\nu^{-1}(F_1(x_1)), t_\nu^{-1}(F_2(x_2)), \ldots, t_\nu^{-1}(F_N(t))) \quad (13)$$

We implemented the following copula:

- the Gumbel copula:

$$F(Y) = C^{\mathrm{Gumbel}}(z_1, z_2, \ldots, z_N) = \exp(-(-\ln(F_1(x_1))^\theta + \cdots + (-\ln(F_n(x_n))^\theta))^{1/\theta}) \quad (14)$$

Following de Kort [54] for two random variables X and Y characterized by the distribution functions F_X and F_Y with copula C, the coefficients of dependency for the lower and upper tails, respectively, are:

$$\lambda_L = \underbrace{\lim}_{z \to 0} P(F_X(X) < z | F_Y(Y) < z) = \underbrace{\lim}_{z \to 0} \frac{C(z,z)}{z} \quad (15)$$

$$\lambda_U = \underbrace{\lim}_{z \to 1} P(F_X(X) > z | F_Y(Y) > z) = \underbrace{\lim}_{z \to 1} \frac{1 - 2z - C(z,z)}{1 - z} \quad (16)$$

ratings agencies and regulators. And it became so deeply entrenched and was making people so much money that warnings about its limitations were largely ignored. Then the model fell apart. Cracks started appearing early on, when financial markets began behaving in ways that users of Li's formula had not expected. The cracks became full-fledged canyons in 2008 when ruptures in the financial system's foundations swallowed up trillions of dollars and put the survival of the global banking system in serious peril.

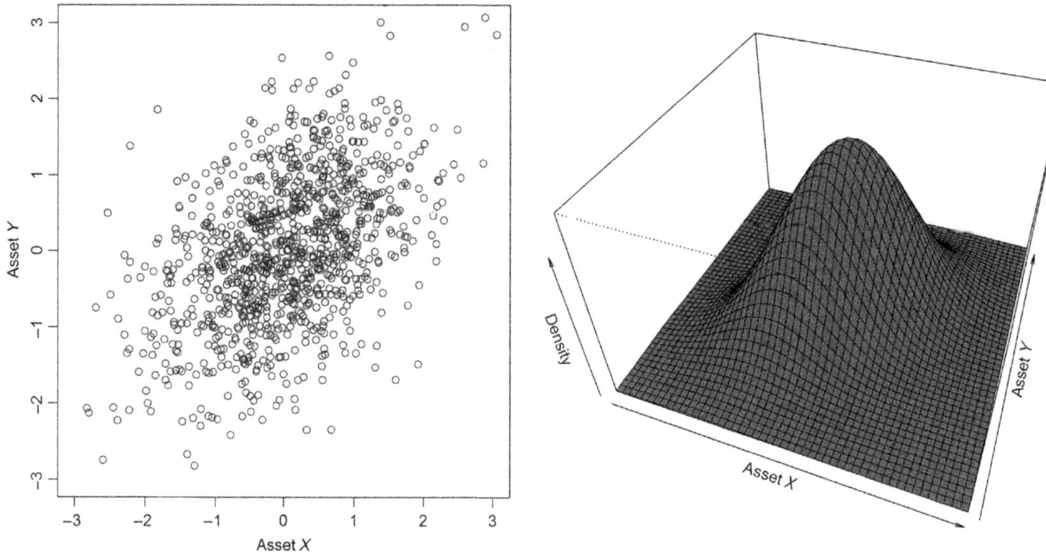

FIGURE 6 *Dependency profile* of the bivariate Gaussian copula. The tails event in assets A and B are not interdependent.

The (X, Y) joint structure is said to have lower (upper) tail dependence if $\lambda_L \neq 0, \lambda_U \neq 0$. For the case of the bivariate Gaussian copula represented spatially in Figure 6, $C^{\text{Gaussian}}(z_x, z_y)$ is defined as:

$$C^{\text{Gaussian}}(z_x, z_y) = \int_{-\infty}^{\Phi^{-1}(z_x)} \int_{-\infty}^{\Phi^{-1}(z_y)} \frac{1}{2\pi\sqrt{1-\rho^2}} \exp\left\{-\frac{x^2+y^2-2\rho xy}{2(1-\rho^2)}\right\} dx\, dy \tag{17}$$

$$\begin{aligned}
\lambda_U &= \underbrace{\lim}_{z \to 1} \frac{1-2z+C(z,z)}{1-z} \\
&= \left| \frac{2z-1-dC(1-z)}{dz} \right|_{z=0} \\
&= 2 \underbrace{\lim}_{z \to 0} P(X > z | Y = z) \\
&= 2 \underbrace{\lim}_{x \to -\infty} P(\Phi^{-1}(X) > x | \Phi^{-1}(Y) = x) \\
&= 2 \underbrace{\lim}_{x \to -\infty} \Phi\left(x\sqrt{\frac{1-\rho}{1+\rho}}\right)
\end{aligned}$$

$$\lambda_U = 0 \quad \text{for } \rho < 1$$

where ρ is the correlation and Φ is the cumulative normal distribution. Thus Gaussian copulas have zero tail dependency for $\rho < 1$. The above equation is regarded by some as the formula that killed Wall Street. It would be more correct to say that its misuse in pricing structured products provoked the subprime turmoil.

Another type of copula with more dependency in the tail events is the *t*-Student copula, which for the bivariate case is expressed as:

$$\lambda_U = \lambda_L = 2t_{\nu+1}\left(-\sqrt{\nu+1}\sqrt{\frac{1-\rho}{1+\rho}}\right)$$

$$\lambda_U > 0 \quad \text{for } \nu > 1$$

$$\lambda_U \to 0 \quad \text{for } \nu \to \infty$$

where ρ is the correlation and ν is the number of degrees of freedom of the t distribution. It can be observed that the tail dependency decreases with the number of degrees of freedom.

For the case of the bivariate Gumbel copula, the dependency has more weight on the upper tail:

$$C^{\text{Gumbel}}(z_x, z_y) = \exp(-(-\ln(z_x)^{\theta} + (-\ln(z_y)^{\theta}))^{1/\theta}) \tag{18}$$

where θ is the parameter of the copula with the form for $z_x = z_y = z$:

$$C^{\text{Gumbel}}(z, z) = u^{2/\theta} \tag{19}$$

which implies that

$$\lambda_L = \underbrace{\lim}_{z\to 0} \frac{C(z,z)}{z} = \left|\frac{dC(z)}{dz}\right|_{z=0} = 0$$

$$\begin{aligned}\lambda_U &= \underbrace{\lim}_{z\to 1} \frac{1 - 2z + C(z,z)}{1-z} \\ &= \left|\frac{2z - 1 - dC(1-z)}{dz}\right|_{z=0} \\ &= \left|\frac{d(2z - 1 + (1-z)^{2^{1/\theta}})}{dz}\right|_{z=0} = 2 - 2^{1/\theta}\end{aligned}$$

For the case of the bivariate Clayton copula for $\theta > 0$ the spatial distribution is shown in Figure 7 and is given as:

$$C^{\text{Clayton}}(z_x, z_y) = ({z_x}^{-\theta} + {z_y}^{-\theta} - 1)^{-1/\theta} \tag{20}$$

with diagonal form:

$$C^{\text{Clayton}}(z, z) = (2z^{-\theta} - 1)^{-1/\theta} \tag{21}$$

$$\lambda_L = \underbrace{\lim}_{z\to 0} \frac{C(z,z)}{z} = \left|\frac{dC(z)}{dz}\right|_{z=0} = 2^{-1/\theta} \tag{22}$$

$$\begin{aligned}\lambda_U &= \underbrace{\lim}_{z\to 1} \frac{1 - 2z + C(z,z)}{1-z} \\ &= \left|\frac{2z - 1 - dC(1-z)}{dz}\right|_{z=0} \\ &= 2 - \frac{d((2(1-z)^{-\theta} - 1)^{-1/\theta})}{dz} = 0\end{aligned} \tag{23}$$

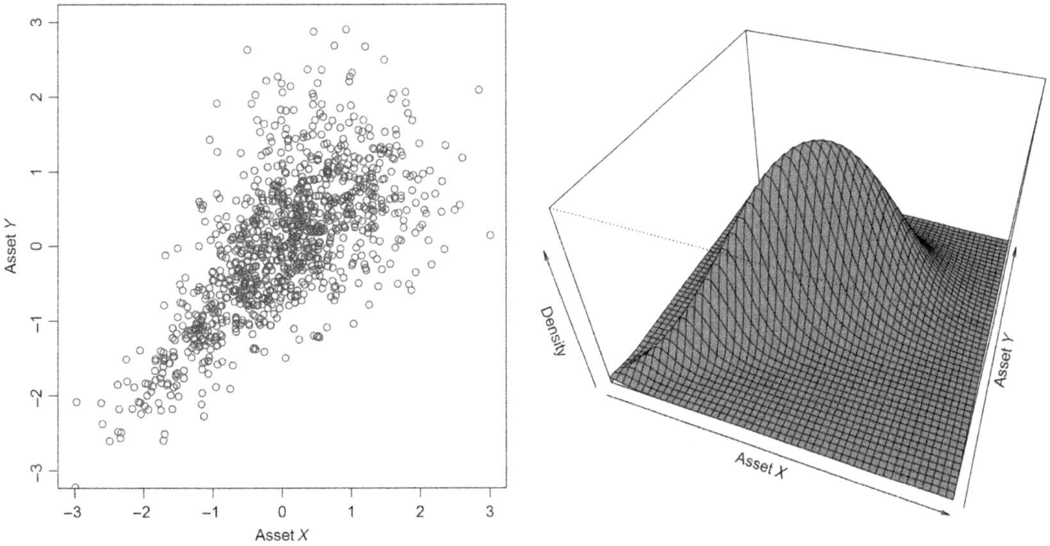

FIGURE 7 Dependency profile of the bivariate Clayton copula. The left tail events in assets A and B are interdependent.

TABLE 1 Copulas

Copulas	$C_\theta(z_x, z_y)$	λ_L	λ_U
Gaussian	$\int_{-\infty}^{\Phi^{-1}(z_x)} \int_{-\infty}^{\Phi^{-1}(z_y)} \frac{1}{2\pi\sqrt{1-\rho^2}} \exp\left\{-\frac{x^2+y^2-2\rho xy}{2(1-\rho^2)}\right\} dx\, dy$	$2 \underbrace{\lim}_{x\to-\infty} \Phi\left(x\sqrt{\frac{1-\rho}{1+\rho}}\right)$	$2 \underbrace{\lim}_{x\to-\infty} \Phi\left(x\sqrt{\frac{1-\rho}{1+\rho}}\right)$
t	$\int_{-\infty}^{\Phi^{-1}(z_x)} \int_{-\infty}^{\Phi^{-1}(z_y)} \frac{1}{2\pi\sqrt{1-\rho^2}} \left\{1+\frac{x^2+y^2-2\rho xy}{\nu(1-\rho^2)}\right\}^{-0.5\nu-1} dx\, dy$	$2t_{\nu+1}\left(-\sqrt{\nu+1}\sqrt{\frac{1-\rho}{1+\rho}}\right)$	$2t_{\nu+1}\left(-\sqrt{\nu+1}\sqrt{\frac{1-\rho}{1+\rho}}\right)$
Gumbel	$\exp(-(-\ln(z_x)^\theta + (-\ln(z_y)^\theta))^{1/\theta})$	0	$2 - 2^{1/\theta}$
Clayton	$(z_x{}^{-\theta} + z_y{}^{-\theta} - 1)^{-1/\theta}$	$2^{-1/\theta}$	0

The features of the few copula types presented above as well as their tail dependency are summarized in Table 1.

4.3 Dependency and Pricing

Going back to the example of the digital option let us consider a double digital cash or nothing call option with respective strikes K_1, K_2, written on the assets S_1, S_2 having copula $\mathbf{C}$. The underlying markets for the two assets are considered the USD-Ruble exchange rate and the oil price. The option will pay the amount X at the maturity T if both assets are higher than the respective strikes:

$$\mathbf{C}_{dd}(T) = \begin{cases} X & S_{1,T} - K_1 < 0 \quad \text{and } S_{2,T} - K_2 < 0 \\ 0 & \text{otherwise} \end{cases} \tag{24}$$

The price of a double digital call option[3] can be written as:

$$\begin{aligned} \mathbf{C}_0 &= e^{-rT} E_Q[X\mathbf{1}(-S_{1,T} + K_1)_+ \mathbf{1}(-S_{2,T} + K_2)_+] \\ &= Xe^{-rT}\mathbf{C}_{dd}(C_1, C_2) \end{aligned} \tag{25}$$

where C_1 and C_2 are the prices of single digital options.

Figure 8 summarizes the price of a two-asset digital option and its driving factors. The price depends in a significant manner on the level of correlation. For a correlation range between a minimum of 35% and a maximum value of 70% the option price exhibits a high variability, especially when the option is out of the money. The variability of the price as a function of correlation disappears when the option is deep in the money. The same observation holds for the price depending on the copula used in modeling. The non-Gaussian copula models generate higher prices, an effect attenuated when the option is in the money.

[3] For the current example $K_1 = 50$, the strike for the USD-Ruble rate, and $K_2 = \$50$ for the oil price.

5 MODEL-RELATED BEHAVIOR

Model behavior and performance are naturally assessed through model outputs. Analyzing model outputs depends on the scope of the model, and whether it is a risk model, a pricing or forecasting model. Risk models differ conceptually from pricing models, because by nature they are target extreme events, while valuation targets the core scenarios of a distribution. Analyzing and benchmarking models raise particular challenges which can lead to inappropriate model selection if the problem is not correctly specified.

5.1 Risk Measures

Rockafellar and Uryasev [55] distinguish four main approaches to the measurement of risk:

- *Risk measures*: The role of a measure of risk, R, is to assign to a random variable X, standing for an uncertain "loss," a numerical value $R(X)$ representing the overall loss.

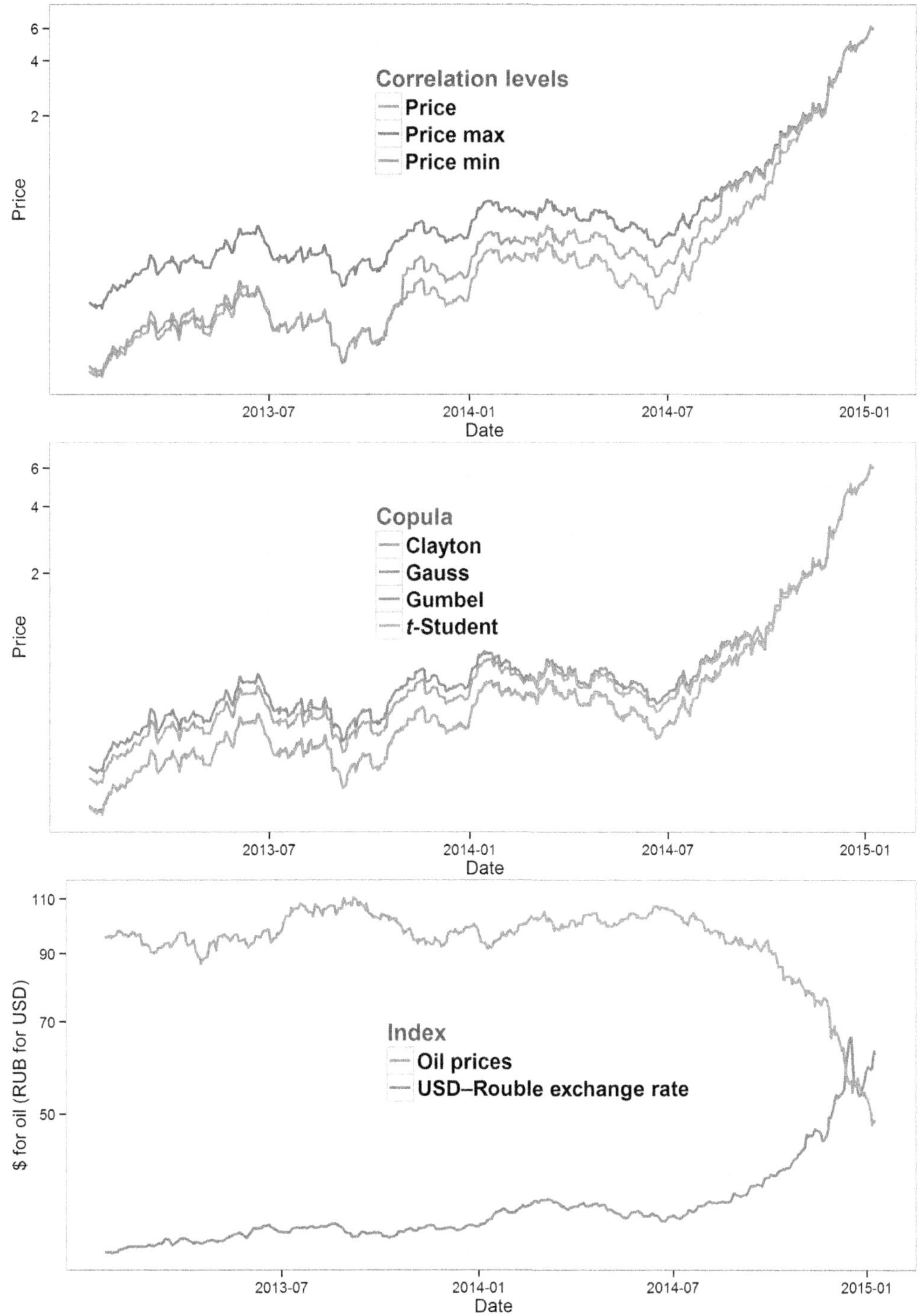

FIGURE 8 Pricing a two-asset digital options: *Top*: evolution of price ranges depending on the correlation; *Middle*: evolution of price range depending on the copula model; *Bottom*: evolution of the oil price and USD-Ruble exchange rate over the past 2 years.

- *Deviation measures*: These measure deviations from benchmarks or targets $D(X) = R(X) - \mathbf{E}(X)$, $\mathbf{E}(X)$ being the expected value of X.
- *Measures of regret*: The role of a measure of regret is to quantify the displeasure associated with the mixture of potential positive, 0, and negative outcomes of a random variable X that represents an uncertain loss.
- *Error measures*: The measure of error is a positive function which quantifies the nonzeroness in a random variable X, for example if X is the absolute difference between the realized and forecasted value of a stock.

Two common risk measures are the VaR and the Expected Shortfall (ES). The VaR at confidence level α defined below is the maximum loss of the variable X which is overpassed with a probability $1 - \alpha$:

$$P[X > \text{VaR}_\alpha(X)] \leq 1 - \alpha \tag{26}$$

The ES is the average loss of the variable X above the confidence level α:

$$\text{ES}_\alpha(X) = \frac{1}{1-\alpha} \int_\alpha^1 q_u(X)\, du \tag{27}$$

For a trading position consisting of a two-asset digital option like that studied in the previous section the two risk measures VaR and ES are shown in Figure 9. As predicted in the above equation the simulation confirms the fact that ES is higher than the VaR, $\text{ES}_\alpha(X) > \text{VaR}_\alpha(X)$. The measure depends on the assumption of dependence between the two assets; therefore, the estimations based on non-Gaussian copulas are more conservative, as they assume a higher dependence of the tail events.

Risk measures are assessed through a number of criteria which include coherence, robustness, and elicitability. Artzner et al. [56] introduced the class of coherent measures of risk that have the following properties:

- Homogeneity: $R(\alpha X) = \alpha R(X)$
- Subadditivity: $R(X_1 + X_2) \leq R(X_1) + R(X_2)$
- Monotonicity: $X_1 \leq X_2 \Rightarrow R(X_1) \leq R(X_2)$
- Translation invariance: $R(X - a) = R(X) - a$ if a is a constant.

In addition to these fundamental coherence properties, risk measures can be:

- comonotonically additive if there exist a real-valued random variable X (the common risk factor) and nondecreasing functions f_1 and f_2 such that $R(f_1(X)) + R(f_2(X)) = R(f_1(X) + f_2(X))$; and
- law-invariance $P(X_1 \leq x) = P(X_2 \leq x) x \in \mathbf{R} \Rightarrow R(X_1) = R(X_2)$.

Coherence properties guarantee that the measure makes sense from an economic perspective and can be used for solvency assessment and capital requirements.

A risk measure for a variable X is said to be *robust* if small variations in the variable distribution resulting either from estimation or misspecification pitfalls result in small variations in the measure.

The capacity to rely on a given model or class of models is assessed within an organization by a phase called model validation. Model validation involves a certain number of tests, mainly focused around *backtesting*. Thus for market risk the model generating the VaR is backtested on the actual portfolio. For credit risk the forecasted default probability of a portfolio is backtested on the actual observed hazard rate. Full-fledged predictive risk measures need to be statistically estimated from past data; roughly speaking, a methodology is robust if it is insensitive to outliers or pitfalls in the data. The choice of the backtesting method should depend on the type of forecast [57], which can be classified as:

- *Point forecasts* for the value of a variable; they are usually represented as the expectation of

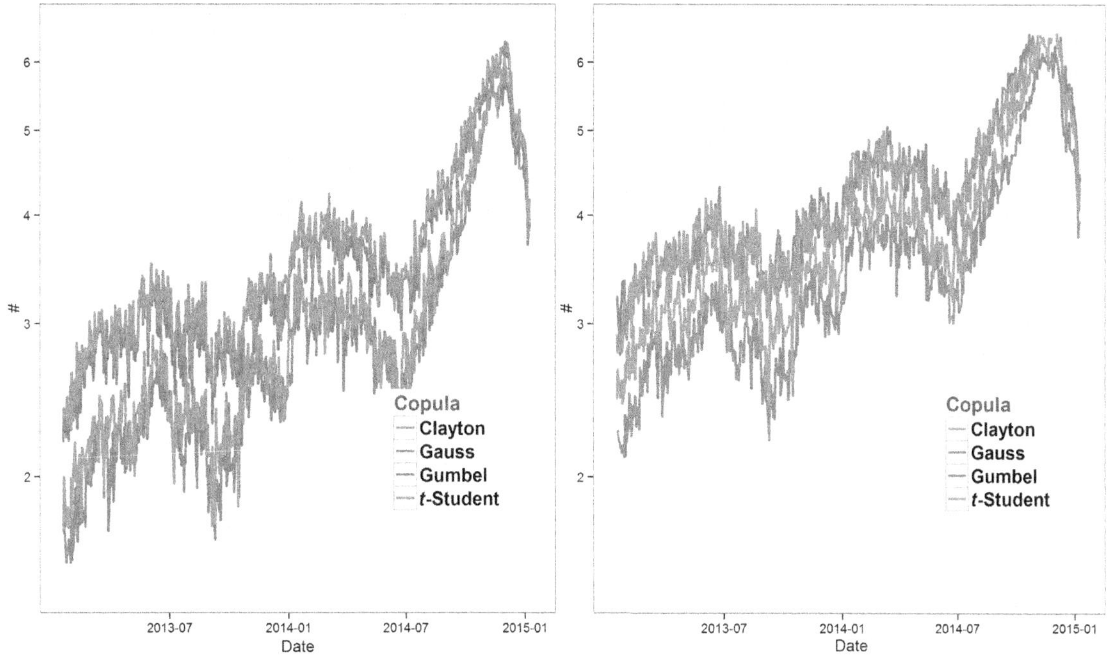

FIGURE 9 Evolution of the VaR and ES for a position consisting of a two-asset digital option. The ES is higher than the VaR. The estimations based on non-Gaussian copulas are more conservative, as they assume a higher dependence of the tail events.

the variable X_{t+1}, conditional to the value of X_t given all the information available at time t. Prediction models for a variable fall generally in this category.

- *Probability range forecasts* that project an interval in which the forecast value is expected to lie with a certain probability. Backtesting for VaR has been well developed, due to the interest of the financial industry, as the main prudential metric for market risk. Two tests are employed:
  - The Christoffersen [58] independence test is a likelihood ratio test that looks for unusually frequent consecutive violations of the VaR boundary.
  - The Kupiec [59] test attempts to determine whether the observed frequency of exceptions is consistent with the frequency of expected exceptions according to the VaR model and chosen confidence interval. Under the null hypothesis that the model is "correct," the number of exceptions follows a binomial distribution.
- *Density forecasts* that project the uncertainty associated with a prediction, by comparison with the point forecast which does not contain any indication such an uncertainty.

A scoring function [60] aims to assign a numerical score to a single valued point forecast based on the predictive point and realization that assigns a numerical score based on the predictive distribution, F, and the realizing observation, y, $S(F, y)$. A proper scoring rule satisfies the following inequality:

$$\mathbf{E}_G(S(G,y)) \leq \mathbf{E}_G(S(F,y))$$
$$\int S(G,y)\,\mathrm{d}G \leq \int S(F,y)\,\mathrm{d}G \quad \forall F,G$$

Table 2 shows the common scores used in the literature [60] for comparing and assessing model performance.

Let us consider a risk measure or function $T(F)$ of the predictive distribution, F, such as the mean or a quantile, then a score S is said to be a consistent scoring function for the functional T if the following condition is fulfilled:

$$\mathbf{E}_G(S(T(G),y)) \leq \mathbf{E}_G(S(x)) \tag{28}$$

for all predictive distributions F and all $x \in R$.

A risk measure or function $T(F)$ is said to be *elicitable* if the above property of consistency is satisfied. This property is fundamental for risk measurement along with coherence and robustness. Elicitability means in simple terms that the risk measures can be backtested and tests can be applied in order to decide if the measure is appropriate.

Table 3 summarizes the main properties of the risk measure currently used in risk management. The introduction in 2013 of the ES as a regulatory alternative to the traditional VaR brought many challenges for financial institutions not only in the implementation but also in the use of this metric. The VaR is not coherent, while the ES is not elicitable (cannot be backtested), thereby raising a lot of issues around its applicability within organizations as a prudential metric.

TABLE 2 Scores Commonly Used for Comparing and Assessing Model Performance

Score	Definition
Square error	$S(x,y) = \lvert x-y \rvert$
Absolute error	$S(x,y) = (x-y)^2$
Absolute percentage error	$S(x,y) = \lvert x-y \rvert / x$
Relative error	$S(x,y) = \lvert x-y \rvert / y$

TABLE 3 Risk Measure Properties: The VaR Is Not Coherent, While the ES Is Not Elicitable (Cannot Be Backtested)

Metric	Coherent	Robust	Elicitable
Mean	Yes	No	Yes
Value at risk	No	Yes	Yes
Expected shortfall	Yes	No	No

Concerning the ES's nonelicitability, Emmer et al. [57] proposed an approximation of this metric as a sum of quantiles which are elicitable, thereby implying that they can be backtested:

$$\begin{aligned}
\mathrm{ES}_\alpha(X) &= \frac{1}{1-\alpha}\int_\alpha^1 q_u(X)\,\mathrm{d}u \\
&= E(X|X \geq q_\alpha(X)) + (E(X|X \geq q_\alpha(X)) \\
&\quad - q_\alpha(X))\left(\frac{P(X > q_\alpha(X))}{1-\alpha} - 1\right) \\
&\approx \frac{1}{4}(q_\alpha(X) + q_{0.75\alpha+0.25}(X) \\
&\quad + q_{0.5\alpha+0.5}(X) + q_{0.25\alpha+0.75}(X)) \\
&= \mathbf{H}(\alpha, X)
\end{aligned}$$

This proposal is useful as it provides a quick solution to a practical problem, but it raises a fundamental issue. If $\mathbf{H}(\alpha, X)$ denotes the above approximation, for any desired level ES^* of ES there is an implied confidence interval α^* for a given variable X such that:

$$\alpha^* = \mathbf{H}^{-1}(\mathrm{ES}^*, X) \tag{29}$$

The bottom line of these findings is that the level of the value of the ES can easily be "reverse engineered" through the parameter α which is not always stipulated by the regulators like it was in the case of the VaR [61]. Thus a trader or bank can choose for the alleged purpose of backtesting the confidence interval that fits the desired level of capital.

5.2 Inconsistent Model Testing

A very good example of inconsistent measures applied to a testing model which can provide counterintuitive and wrongful results is provided by Gneiting [62]. We assume a discrete stochastic process $G_t = \zeta_t^2$, where ζ_t is normally distributed, $\zeta_t \propto N(0, h_t)$, and the variance h_t follows a GARCH process:

$$h_t = \omega + \alpha h_{t-1} + \beta \zeta_{t-1}^2 \quad (30)$$

In the simulation below, $\omega = 0.1, \alpha = 0.4$, and $\beta = 0.45$. Three competing forecast models for the process G_t are backtested with the scores given in Table 2. A first forecast is built under the assumptions that the true process is known, thereby following a GARCH process with the above parameters. The second and third forecasts assume a flat value for the minimum and maximum of G_t, respectively. For practical reasons the maximum and minimum forecasts are $G_t = 4$ and $G_t = 0.1$, respectively. The results of the three forecasts are listed in Table 4 and surprisingly with the exception of the square error all the other scores give flat forecasts as better than the model-based forecasts. This effect is a good example of using an inconsistent measure for benchmarking models. Gneiting [62] discussed this example after he set up appropriate measures in order to avoid this type of bias. Nevertheless this example reflects in a very straightforward manner the pitfalls of model testing and the sources of model risk.

TABLE 4 Benchmark of the Model Tests: With the Exception of the Square Error All the Other Scores Give the Flat Forecast as Better Than the Model-Based Forecasts

Score	Max.	Min.	Model
Square error	13.49	0.75	0.61
Absolute error	3.62	0.37	0.44
Absolute percentage error	11,550	288	2304
Relative error	0.91	3.73	5.69

When the above model test is used as a benchmarking pricing derivatives model, the results can again lead to a biased conclusion. Let us assume that the above forecasts are used to provide the volatility parameter in a contingency valuation model. The prices of derivatives[4] calculated using the true GARCH model and the maximum and minimum flat volatilities are summarized in Table 5. As observed in the forecasting example the flat volatilities provide a better performance when benchmarked with the true GARCH model. This is a classic example of model risk, when inconsistent scores are used to compare models.

Another illustration of the inconsistent model benchmarking is the pricing of derivatives with mean reversion volatility. For this purpose let us assume that the real implied volatility follows a mean reversion patterns:

$$\frac{d\sigma_t}{\sigma_t} = \kappa(\sigma_m - \sigma_t) + \sigma_\sigma \, dB \quad (31)$$

TABLE 5 Benchmarking Pricing Models for a Set of Digital Calls: The Flat Volatilities Outperform the True GARCH Model

Score	Max.	Min.	Model
Square error	122.1	50.77	57.63
Absolute error	9.64	4.53	6.03
Absolute percentage error	4,735,459	94,663	2,424,366
Relative error	0.69	159.03	19,982

[4]For this simulation a digital call with $S = 90, X = 100, K = 10$ is considered.

where σ_t is the stochastic volatility, κ is the parameter for the force of the mean reversion, σ_m is the volatility tendency, σ_σ is the volatility of the process (volvol), and dB is the Brownian process.

Assuming that one analyst constructs the "good model" knowing the real nature of the volatility pattern with the real parameters and another analyst constructs a "wrong model" which is still mean reversion but with different parameters. The patterns of true volatility, good model volatility and wrong model volatility are shown in Figure 10.

Employing both the "good" and the "wrong" models, Table 6 shows the performance of pricing a series of cash-or-nothing digital options. Surprisingly all scores are close in value for both models with a small advantage for the "wrong model." Indeed the parameters of both models outlined in Table 7 are similar in value, but the use of backtesting scores for comparing these models gives counter-intuitive results. In fact the series of tested options are at-the-money and the price is obviously not model sensitive.

TABLE 6 Benchmarking Pricing Models: For At-the-Money Digital Options the Two Models Have Similar Performance

Score	Wrong model	Good model
Square error	1.11	1.14
Absolute error	2.04	2.13
Absolute percentage error	0.041	0.042
Relative error	0.04	0.044

Note: The "Wrong model" seems to be slightly better.

TABLE 7 Parameters of the "Good" and "Wrong" Models: The "Good Model" Follows the True Volatility Process

Parameter	True process/good model	Wrong model
κ	0.15	0.25
σ_m	0.3	0.33
σ_σ	0.04	0.04

TABLE 8 Benchmarking Pricing Models: For Out-of-the-Money Digital Options the Good Model Shows Better Performance

Score	Wrong model	Good model
Square error	0.38	0.36
Absolute error	0.29	0.27
Absolute percentage error	3.62	2.41
Relative error	0.54	0.90

Note: The absolute percentage error, which is the most often used benchmarking score, clearly differentiates the two models.

If a series of out-of-the-money options is considered[5] the good model should provide better results, a fact confirmed by the numerical results in Table 8.

This type of inference often appears in the academic literature and professional works which justify new models based on performance benchmarks like those presented in the previous tables. This can and does lead to model risk if the compared advantage of a model is not well understood and assessed. A common example is the use of models that include leptokurtotic behavior for pricing plain vanilla derivatives. These models would give more clear-cut results for barrier options, more sensitive to jumps in prices.

From backtesting risk measures like VaR to assessing the hedge fund strategies the model tests play a crucial role in the financial industry. The above examples are simple proof that models can be chosen on an inappropriate basis and model testing can be easily manipulated

[5]For this simulation a digital call with $S = 60, X = 100, K = 10$ is considered.

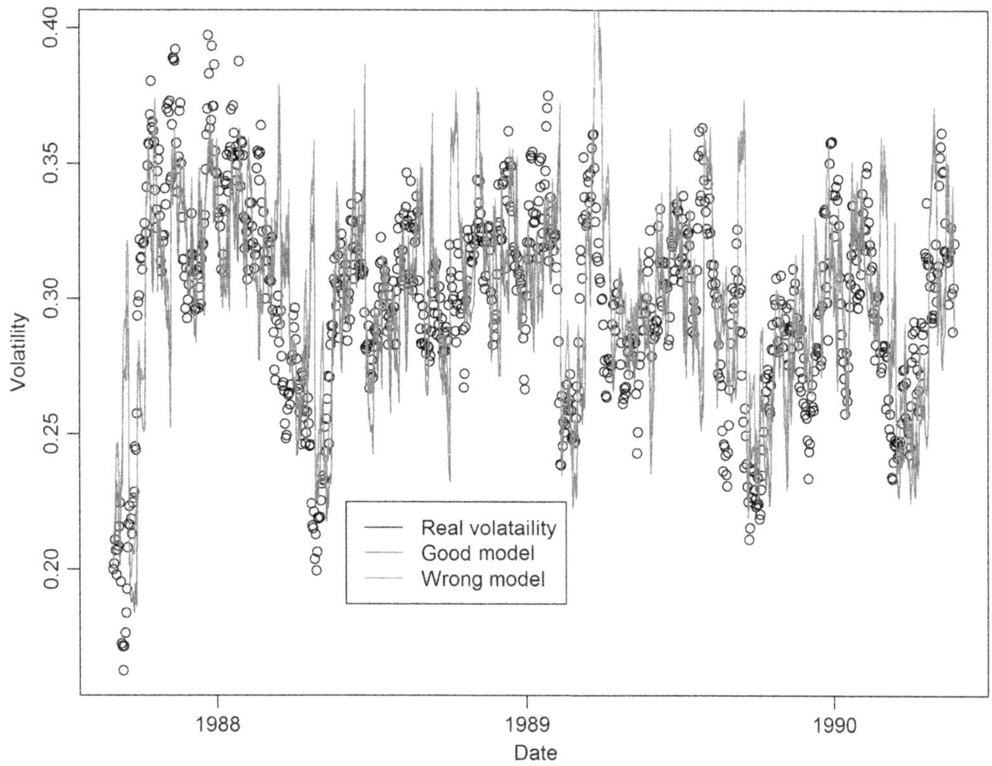

FIGURE 10 Volatility mean reversion model: benchmark of the good and wrong models.

or recommended to an investor or a regulator through the use of inconsistent testing measures.

6 MODEL RISK, MISCONDUCT, AND FINANCIAL CRIME

As already mentioned within financial organizations modeling is seen as important in accounting for ill-intentioned individuals, who aim to take part in illegal activities. A short review of the relationship and implication of model risk in misconduct and white-collar crime is necessary.

The first typology of model-based misconduct is related to structured products. A simplified example is the instrument **B** with the payoff described in the first section and valued with the framework in Equation 9. Assuming that an investment bank sells this product to an investor or embeds it in a note, the following issues can occur.

6.1 Mis-Selling of the Product

The pricing model for a structured product can be a vector for mis-selling, by misleading the investor about the performance of that instrument. When the parameters of the model (λ in our case) are not directly observable this can be used as leverage by the banker in order to *hard sell* the product through embellishing its foreseeable outcome. When the model is too complicated, or the structure of the payoff is too sophisticated and is difficult to assess through a diligence process, asymmetry between the buyer and the seller is created. This can represent a high risk for misconduct or even white-collar crime. Classic examples include the cases of "toxic credits" sold by investment banks to municipalities across Europe mainly in France, Germany, and Italy, which caused serious problems during the Eurozone crisis. Banks created the appearance of very exquisite high-quality products, and the financial planners of those towns, countries, or municipalities did not have any means to understand what was really behind those models used for pricing.

6.2 Misrepresenting the Risk

Another negative externality of the models is the possibility of misrepresenting the risk involved in an investment. Continuing the above example, an analyst can dissimulate the likelihood that the product **B** can generate a negative payoff for the investor, represented by the probability e^{λ}. The analyst can easily manipulate this number, especially when historical testing is used to indicate that the possibility of a big negative payoff is in fact theoretical and in reality can never occur. The investor might be persuaded and think that the product is a win-win deal.

The European countries and municipalities that took structured credit with asymmetric payoffs, indexed, for example, on the difference between long rates in Japan and the United Kingdom, were persuaded that the adverse cases when their interest rate can be very high are almost impossible to realize, and those products were in fact "free lunches" which would provide them with low interest rate credit. When the Lehman collapse occurred and markets became irrational that low probability event did take place and the municipalities had to pay higher than ever interest rates and finally asked for help from countries' state finances.

6.3 Overpricing

When selling a product to an investor the investment bank remunerates itself through the so-called "mark-up,"[6] which is an add-on to one of the pricing model parameters that would generate a higher price. For a plain option the mark-up is on volatility and therefore if the risk neutral value of a plain option is, say, 20%, the bank will earn profit by selling it for a price corresponding to 25% of volatility, which represents a 5% mark-up.

If the pricing employs a complex model with parameters which are not observable it is easier to overprice the investment, thereby requiring a higher premium to be paid by the investor. In the case of the previous example the bank will not ask for a higher premium, because the client will not consent to pay a higher fee, but instead will manipulate the size of the payoffs in such a way that the product would have a much lower value. Thus instead of gaining 5 dollars 999 times out of 1000, the bank can propose a payoff of 4 dollars 998.8 times out of 1000, thereby making the value of the product lower than the value under the initial setup.

6.4 Distorting the Mark to Model

Once a product like that discussed above is sold to the investor at agreed intervals of time the product is revalued based on the mark to model. The new value can change the payoffs for the new period or can be based on a margin call. If the investor does not have the means to price the product or the parameters are provided by the bank there is clearly an asymmetric

[6]In sport betting the equivalent notion is the "vig" or the overround, or even more semantically, "the juice" in street language like in sport betting.

relationship. As long as it is the only source of valuation the bank can communicate the values which suit it best. Mark to model or mark to myth are easy to manipulate, especially when there is only one valuation source. Independent valuation firms have started to provide third-party assessments in the past year, but this does not resolve these issues as these firms can obtain the price only through a model and cannot test it on the market.

The second type of misconduct in regard to model risk deals with the derivative markets. This corresponds to the *Fraud on the market* scenario for derivatives, which can be manipulated easier than stocks or FX.

6.5 Manipulating the "Parameters"

When one of the parameters of a product is not observable like λ in the above example or correlations and volatilities in some cases, investment firms have the opportunity to create a market for instruments which can imply the value for those parameters. This would be similar to the creation of a plain vanilla market for a stock which would generate observable input for the risk neutral volatility. A new market brings with it many opportunities and new threats.

The challenge for a new market is to gain liquidity. If traded on thin liquidity a new market can be easily manipulated. The idea behind this manipulation is not always to gain from the market itself but to make an artificial profit on the underlying business. If the market is manipulated the implied parameter resulting from this manipulation will not have a fair value. The banks manipulating this market might make losses on these trades but can make gains on the product which needs the parameter λ in their pricing model.

This scenario can be developed further if some banks organize a market with some market makers that sell and buy the product in a small circle and thus generate a "market" price, without having any fundamental need for λ.

6.6 Selling Sunglasses and Buying Umbrellas

When products on the market involve asymmetry in information partly as a consequence of model risk the party with more genuine information has a comparative advantage. For example, an institution can recommend the sale of product **B** to its clients advising them that it is a good investment but at the same time buying protection or hedging against an adverse outcome directly or through a related vehicle.

The "selling sunglasses and buying umbrellas" effect occurred during the subprime crisis when some institutions advised their clients to be long on subprimes while they were shorting the market.

6.7 Packaging the Unknown

If a bank has a portfolio of products **B** with a potentially high-risk profile one way of reducing the risk exposure while making a profit is to package those products in various risk tranches and to sell them to other investors. Aggregating packages of instruments **B** in various risk tranches introduces another unknown factor, the dependency on the instrument's payoff profile. The banks can price the tranches with a model assuming a Gaussian copula dependency, where the probability of having negative payoffs simultaneously is very low. Therefore, the investors are exposed to two unknowns: the true value of parameter λ and the dependency. The tranches would have a very good risk/return profile. But as happened during the subprime crisis the negative payoff can occur at the same time and thus generate losses in the tranches.

6.8 Manipulation of New Derivative Products—Painting the Tape

When the product **B** is traded directly or through an index even with a thin liquidity the next step is to create a new derivative having as an asset that index or instrument. On one hand, this new product would bring more completeness to the markets, but on the other hand, it would be a market highly inefficient with no obvious fundamentals. A plain simplification would be to imagine an option market having as an asset a very illiquid stock traded on Pink Sheets. This market with few active traders would be a very easy target and vehicle for any type of misconduct and fraud.

This misconduct can be created by such a market for an illegal purpose like the mis-selling of a product or its manipulation. The pricing of such a product would depend on models and assumptions that are easy to distort in order to create a misperception about its value. By its very nature this type of fraud is very difficult to detect.

The third axis of model risk-related misconduct consists of supplying the risk control function with sham information. When a misconduct or a fraud occurs it is not only essential to hide or dissimulate the facts, the ultimate goal of fraudsters is to create a parallel reality or a new "truth," in which is illegal acts become normal. Models and mathematical tools are the perfect instruments for creating this alternative truth.

6.9 Hiding Unauthorized Trading Positions

Until the recent crisis Front Office and Back Office had different levels of information and resources for completing their tasks. Therefore, the Back Office was involved in a permanent struggle to apprehend and analyze the information from the Front Office. This inequality is growing with the degree of complexity of trading activity.

The unauthorized trading positions can be hidden through the use of models, especially on exotic products. Risk controls and auditors verify the trading activities through the evolution of mark to markets and the P&L profiles. When rogue traders take authorized positions they can justify or hide their trades by changing some parameters in the model in such a way as to make it fit with their desired outcome.

In addition model "cherry-picking" can be another alternative for hiding positions. The trader can pick from a set of models that which is able to best explain his position and to create the appearance that all his positions are disclosed and appropriate to the strategy.

The arrival of new regulations and controls involved in market and counterparty risk introduced a new dimension into the game. Respecting the counterparty risk limits as well as the market risk limits is a real challenge for a trader. The risk models for both market and counterparty risk are not always 100% independent from the model used by the Front Office. In most organizations risk managers rely heavily on the Front Office valuation models to establish their risk profile. In some organizations, the trading and the control functions have completely separate methods and systems. Therefore, the model risk in this case is that the risk manager does not use the right models or uses them in an inconsistent way, thereby allowing traders to dissemble their investment strategies.

6.10 Backtesting Risk and Performance

One of the major drawbacks of model use is their testing procedure as shown in the previous section. Backtesting interval forecasts of risk measurement can provide biased conclusions if conducted in an inconsistent manner. Therefore, the risk metrics can be presented as satisfying the prudential norms when in reality they do not. A simple observation of a bank's financial statement shows that the VaR for trading operations is of the order of millions of dollars while the trading profits are of the order of billions of dollars.

Another relevant issue is related to the backtesting of point forecast models, often used in the funds industry. Fund management strategies like those employed by hedge funds are validated or pitched to investors based on backtesting.

As shown in the example in the previous section these backtests can come to misleading conclusions when improperly applied.

7 OUTLOOK: MEASURING AND LIMITING MODEL RISK

The new regulations relating to misconduct and model risk organization have begun to deploy resources for model auditing and model risk assessment. The costs of this strategy are directly proportional to the number of models, which have increased over time with new products and new risk regulations. Again we have a case of a regulatory fallacy where the controls are one step behind the market and law enforcement officers have less expensive cars than the offenders (with the exception of the *Miami Vice* series).

Dealing with the symptoms does not cure the illness. Organizations have been given the green light to develop all kinds of products tested by whatever model they find appropriate. In the aerospace or pharmaceutical industries, new products need to pass extensive tests and checks before commercialization. For instance in the United States, new medicines are approved by the Food and Drug Administration before going into prescriptions. Similarly the banking regulators could widen their scope to assess tests and approve new products and new models used for valuation and risk before these products go on the market. Thus the likelihood of banks garnering negative externalities is diminished significantly.

In past regulatory waves, banks have been assumed to implement a high number of regulatory metrics but have the freedom to use their internal models, which obviously vary from institution to institution. This intellectual freedom creates a high variability in the banks' capitalization and can result in systemic risk as was revealed by the last Eurozone crisis. Regulators should not only impose norms but also precise and detailed guidelines for measuring those metrics in order to avoid variability in risk charges and to prevent cherry-picking in terms of model use.

Model monitoring and auditing should incorporate a benchmarking function in order to be able to identify the strength and the weakness of each methodology. On a set of competitive models M used for measuring the variable V the model depth $\text{MD}_{M,V}$ conditional to a given set of parameters θ is defined as the ratio between the spread of the maximum and the minimum of V on a set of models M and the usage value V^*:

$$\text{MD}_{M,V|\theta} = \frac{\underbrace{\max}_{M}(V) - \underbrace{\min}_{M}(V)}{V^*} \tag{32}$$

For example, concerning a correlation product the model depth would be able to assess the impact of various dependency copulas in terms of the valuation based on the same parameters. The higher the value of the model depth $\text{MD}_{M,V}$ the higher the risk of inappropriate use of a model. This ratio can be extended to assess the impact of parameters' variability on the output of the model.

For the range of a set of parameters θ used for measuring the variable V, the model depth $\text{MD}_{V,\theta}$ conditional to model M is defined as the ratio between the spread of the maximum and the minimum of V over the range of parameters θ and the usage value V^*.

$$\text{MD}_{\theta,V|M} = \frac{\underbrace{\max}_{\theta}(V) - \underbrace{\min}_{\theta}(V)}{V^*} \tag{33}$$

This measure could be a sound indicator for the pricing of exotic products that depend on unobservable parameters which rely on management opinion. For a multi-asset financial product the correlation is based on subjective views, due to thin liquidity in the respective markets, and the model depth would reflect the impact on the value of the product.

With respect to misconduct and financial crime it is crucial to underline that models have within organizations at least the same impact as accounting. If accounting misrepresentation, manipulation and forging are a real concern for fraud and crime risk, there is not yet the same awareness for models. Behind the appearance of intellectual sophistication misconduct and fraud can easily develop.

Like all other risks financial and nonfinancial model risk can be a source for moral hazard, also due to the fact that it is more difficult to assess and to allocate the resulting losses. By their very nature models are rarely wrong; very often they are misused or supplied with wrong inputs. Misconduct and crime scenarios should also incorporate model risk assessment, in order to get a better apprehension of the pitfalls and weaknesses in organizations.

CHAPTER

2D

Criminal Organizations

OUTLINE

1 BACKGROUND

Traditionally the main activities of criminal organizations have centered on extortion, gambling, human trafficking, and narcotics. The focus on white-collar crime developed later in their history. The first markets for futures trading originated at the start of the eighteenth century in Japan during a period corresponding to the second half of the Edo period. At that time an important role in rice trading was played by the samurai clans. Nevertheless the shogunate and the samurai had long considered the rice futures trade no better than merchant gambling, which contradicted Confucian ideals [63]. The wages of the samurais were paid in rice at the market price. Around the time of the futures trading in Osaka two phenomena occurred concomitantly in the social structure of Japan. First, since 1710 the nominal income of the lower status samurais had fallen by nearly 50%, and their real income had also decreased significantly. Second, the demilitarization of Japan compared to the beginning of the Edo left many samurais in a difficult economic situation. Many joined an emerging criminal group that grew from the ashes of Japan's long civil wars: the Yakuza. During the time of the Dojima futures trading many samurais took debt from brokers of rice bills and entered indirectly into speculative activity. It would not be unreasonable to think that some of

http://dx.doi.org/10.1016/B978-0-12-801221-5.00004-X

the samurais with a troubled financial situation with high debt would have joined the Yakuza while continuing to menace the merchants on the Dojima market. This scenario which is not improbable would constitute the first interaction of organized crime with the financial derivatives markets.

Over the last 20 years criminal organizations have not only carried out activities such as racketeering, gambling, drug, and human trafficking, but they have also had a major impact on the country's economic system itself, through financial activities involving capital markets. The profits from traditional criminal activities involving "street-type" gangster crimes shrank significantly and attracted a lot of attention from both media and investigators. After the World War II the economies of developed countries migrated gradually from a predominant manufacturing type to services oriented. The manufacturing-type economies have some characteristics that allowed organized crime to flourish. The presence of a blue-collar population segment with low wages, the massive use of cash transactions, and the strong dependency on material facilities and infrastructure (building, factories, and transportation) were fertile conditions for illegal activities like racketeering, loan sharking, gambling, or unions' greasing. The migration toward services oriented economies with a major financial industry lessened the power and influence of the old generation of career criminals and brought on to the scene the new "faces of Gommorah."

The "street type" of organized crime is still around in emerging economies like ex-Soviet Union countries, South America, and China, but has lost ground in developed countries like the United States, the European Union, and Japan. The economies of the developed countries have changed structurally over the past two decades and become more concentrated around services and tertiary activities with a delocalization of physical industries to emerging countries. This reality forced the criminal syndicates from developed countries to reorient their operations from classic crime implying various levels of violence toward services oriented white-collar, business-type crimes. The classic image of the gangster was gradually replaced by the image of the businessman and crime gravitated from physical violence toward "gray matter."

The very nature of organized crime makes its operations correlated to the economic activities of civil society. While small-time crooks exploit local failures or breaches in security or surveillance systems, organized criminal activities are based on structural anomalies of civil society. Obviously a local failure in the risk management system of an economic process (i.e., security of a factory stock, or a safe deposit) can be easily repaired, thereby making the crime linked to this failure temporary. A structural dysfunction of the legal economic system is much more difficult to adjust and thus transforms the underlying illegal activities in continuous enterprises, hence the continuity of the big criminal syndicates. Some practical examples will clarify this.

A first example would be the lack of access for a relevant part of the population to banking and financial services. If a person without stable substantial revenue needs to take a loan or to finance an acquisition or an expense, the refusal of the banks will turn him toward individuals with considerable liquidities. These individuals are generally linked to criminal groups that take charge of the recovery of the debt if the debtor cannot honor the terms of the agreements which in these cases are very aggressive, with double-digit interest rates and a very strict payment schedule. The extortion or the shylock business is the segment of the chain value where creditors make their profit. It is known in the extortion world that unpaid interest is topped up on the principle that the debt thus increases exponentially and puts the debtor into a distressed situation. At this point the extortionists take over the assets of the debtor as collateral. Despite this worst case scenario extortionate lending represents an efficient source of financing especially during periods of economic distress, as was witnessed in the 1930s and in the recent postsubprime crisis.

In Italy, organized crime groups like the Sicilian *Cosa Nostra*, the Neapolitan *Camorra*, or the Calabrian *'Ndrangheta* generate profits equivalent to about 7% of national output with multi-billion euros in liquidity became the nation's number one bank as some recent studies have shown.[1] Extortionate lending had become an increasingly sophisticated and lucrative source of income. The classic street loan shark was restructured in organized loan-sharking that was well connected with professional circles and operated with the connivance of high-level professionals. It estimated that in Italy about 200,000 businesses were tied to extortionate lenders and tens of thousands of jobs had been lost as a result. Small businesses, which have struggled to get hold of credit during the economic slowdown, may have been increasingly tempted to turn to the mafia. Typical victims of extortionate lending were middle-aged shopkeepers and small businessmen. These are the categories which, more than any other, were exposed to the economic crisis and need alternative methods of finance to overcome this economic distress. This form of illegal shadow banking gained a new dimension with the development of peer-to-peer lending. Peer-to-peer lending aims to bring more liquidity to the credit market in a context where banks restrict the access to finance. Peer-to-peer lending platforms can be a perfect disguise for those classic usury lending activities. This is an example which uses innovation to bypass financial regulations. A second example is the tax system and the various criminal enterprises gravitating around tax fraud. The taxation policy of any country is submitted to regular changes linked to political or economic circumstances. Rigorous tax control of each individual in each company is theoretically impossible. Only a small portion of business are inspected by tax authorities. This leaves the gates wide open to all kinds of tax fraud, the sole intention of fraudsters being to pass under the radar or that their rogue schemes are low profile enough so they can garner significant proceeds. Tax crime is probably one of the most lucrative areas of organized crime and has gained significant momentum over the past decades. This phenomena is also the result of stiffer sentences against crimes involving murder or drug trafficking. In Europe, the value-added tax fraud became so complex and evolved that fraudsters have developed or raided financial markets (ex energy markets) and investment vehicles in order to increase the scale of this activity. A review of the main national syndicates is needed as well as a projection of the tendencies existing in terms of the involvement in financial markets.

[1]La Padania/Le mafie brindano alla crisi E si mangiano il 7% del Pil, http://www.sosimpresa.it/24_xiii-rapporto-sos-impresa.html.

2 ITALIAN GROUPS

The relationship of the Sicilian Mafia with the financial world started to become *visible* in the 1980s. A series of characters involved in a network of connections between the Vatican, Mafia, and Italian politicians included:

- Michele Sindona, known as the Mafia's banker;
- Roberto Calvi, God's banker and head of the defunct Banco Ambrosiano, a bank backed by the Bank of the Vatican (*Istituto per le Opere di Religione*, IOR);
- Licio Gelli, the leader of the masonic lodge P2, one of the few survivors of that time.

Sindona, Banco Ambrosiano as well as the IOR had allegedly been involved in a series of financial crimes, like laundering the proceedings of the Mafia, stock and securities fraud in connection with the New York Italian American criminal groups. Sindona had been the financial services provider for both the Sicilian Mafia and the New York Gambino family. He established the basis of the first transnational financial crime enterprise by connecting the Italian and American criminal organizations, resulting in the so-called Bontade-Inzerillo-Gambino connection. Starting with Cornwell's [64] book written immediately after Calvi's death in 1982, a multitude of articles, researches, and books cover these events, thereby making it probably the most covered financial crime episode in history.

Closer to the present day, another organization from Southern Italy the 'Ndrangheta was at the center of two frauds that shocked the financial markets in the European Union in the late 2000s: the Voice over IP (VoIP) and carbon allowances tax frauds.

- In March 2010, an international warrant was issued for Silvio Scaglia, a reputed Italian telecom tycoon, one of the richest men in the peninsula. The arrest was part of a massive operation called "Operazione phuncards-broker" and targeting a significant number of people involved in tax fraud with VoIP and digital services. The prosecutors claimed alleged links of a 2.7 billion dollar money-laundering and tax-evasion scheme to the 'Ndrangheta. The fraud developed between 2003 and 2006 and is considered by specialists as state of art in terms of value-added tax fraud [65].
- The origin of 'Ndrangheta funds laundered through the VoIP market was the proceedings from another tax scam on the energy markets. Between 2008 and 2010 within the European Union the market for carbon emissions allowances was hit by a systemic tax fraud which was implemented through carbon organized exchanges. This fraud resulted in illicit funds of more than 13 billion dollars and 'Ndrangheta had a share of these proceedings along with other crime syndicates.

3 GENDAI GOKUDO: MODERN GANGSTERS

It is often said that Japan is the cradle of new trends in technology, art, or lifestyle. It seems that this statement can be extrapolated to criminal activity. Before dealing with the technicalities, it is useful to underline that the Yakuza has his own criminal pattern and way of being, different in a lot of ways from other groups. Unlike criminal organizations in other parts of the world Yakuza is not strict in terms of secrecy. In certain sections of Japanese society, Gokudo are not perceived as illegal, belonging to a Yakuza clan that is tolerated. In fact most members have offices with the gang's nameplate outside and put the gang's name on personal business cards, calling them consultants or entrepreneurs. They own cars that have special number-plates and just like famous actors give interviews to journalists, and sometimes hold press conferences. Their relationship with the police is considered normal and authorities have meetings with Yakuza gangs on various matters. This conflation of criminal and civil life opened the door for Yakuza to some unique opportunities to enter and influence Japanese society in the highest financial, economic, and political spheres. Yakuza's help to civilians during the Kobe earthquake (1995) and Fukushima tragedy (2011) strengthened in the eyes of the public their special status in Japanese society. Traditionally, the Yakuza activities were prostitution and gambling. Although both activities are illegal, the police recognized that they were impossible to stamp out, and they accepted having Yakuza members keep the peace in this potentially violent and lawless area. As the Japanese economy grew more powerful in the years 1960-1980, the gangs began to look for ways to increase revenue.

A recent survey taken by the Japanese National Police Agency[2] conducted on 2885 companies revealed that 337 or 11.7% reported run-ins with Yakuza shakedowns. Of those

[2]When the Yakuza come calling one in five Japanese companies admit to paying them off, http://qz.com/29270/when-the-yakuza-come-calling-one-in-five-japanese-companies-admit-to-paying-them-off.

companies approached by the Gokudo, 62 companies or 18% paid for protection. Payments in cash were typically between 120 and 1200 dollars. The most common targets of Yakuza shakedowns were construction companies and real estate firms. In 43% of the cases, the men demanding money or compensation without cause were not Yakuza members themselves but individuals with Yakuza backing. The four most common means of extortion were: finding fault with the company and demanding compensation, asking for purchase of goods or services, aggressively requesting donations or "association fees," demands for construction work and related contracts. For the companies that refused to give in to Yakuza demands 32.6% saw their business operations disrupted, their reputation damaged or defamatory postings on the Internet. Ironically, around 1990 a Yamaguchi-gumi boss wrote a series of articles about safety problems at the Tokyo Electric Power Company (TEPCO) Fukushima Nuclear Power Plant and was paid off by TEPCO to stop writing about them.

3.1 The Japanese Boom

The big step forward for the "Gokudos" came in the mid-1980s, when the government decision to implement quantitative easing and allow easy credit generated one of the most rapid economic expansions ever seen in the modern world. Many "noveaux riches" appeared during the 1980s, the years of Japanese economic expansion, in a similar way as happened in Russia 10 years later. Stock and property prices rocketed, banks and credit institutions injected a huge amount of liquidity into the economy. It was during this period that the larger and more sophisticated Yakuza syndicates launched themselves into mainstream business—stock and property markets, hotel, and golf course developments. *Keizai Yakuza* (economic Yakuza) was the title given to this new venture of the Gokudos. This unprecedented drift from "sword and sandal" criminal tales to complex financial crimes found the Japanese law enforcement agencies unprepared for this new phenomenon. It was probably difficult at that time to define this phenomenon as crime. For instance at the start of the *baburu keizai* (Japanese economic boom) Susumu Ishii, the head of Inagawa-kai, Japan's second largest Yakuza group, set up the Hokusho Sangyo Co as his first shell company for dealing in property. Within a few years he was a multi-millionaire, with Picassos and Chagalls on the walls of his house, a private helicopter and a country club, and close links with at least two of Japan's big four securities companies. Many other Yakuza gangs followed Ishii's example, and the police realized the era of the friendly hood was over. It became in the years after a common habit for the Yakuza to open business offices for consultancy or mediation.

The National Police Agency, Japan's main governmental body for fighting organized crime, estimated that the income of all Yakuza groups in Japan in 1989 when the Japanese stock market reached its peak was 13 billion dollars. It is allegedly believed that more than 40% of the defaulted loans and mortgages that came in the aftermath of the *baburu keizai* were linked to Yakuza owned companies or Yakuza associates.

One of the oldest recordings of criminal activities in the sector of capital markets is without doubt the "Sokaiya." Sokaiya gained momentum during the Japanese economic expansion and was one of the leading products of the Yakuza. Sokaiya has as its purpose the manipulation of shareholders' meetings. Typically the Sokaiya gangs will prevent legitimate shareholders asking questions that could embarrass the company's directors, either by direct intimidation or by shouting down the questioner from the floor. They also ensure that the shareholders' votes go in the direction wanted by the company. In order to assist at the shareholder meeting the Gokudos acquired shares that entitled them to assist at that meeting and received preferred payment for their services. Despite being outlawed in 1982, the practice was used until the late 1990s. Major Japanese companies were involved in Sokaiya scandals (Ito-Yokado, Nomura, Niko, Daiwa, Sumitomo, etc.) Another scam developed by the Yakuza was the infiltration of boards of directors of huge companies or threatening stock traders or brokers in order to gain inside information or to be able to manipulate the stock.

One bespoken example is the company Janome Sewing Machine Co, Japan's second-largest sewing-machine maker, which was listed on the main section of the Tokyo Stock Exchange. The company fell victim to the antisocial forces in the late 1980s. In 1987, a group of speculators with Yakuza connections acquired 20% of the company's stock. One of their representatives was given a seat on the board, and then reportedly suggested the company buy back the shares. Gangsters were allegedly sent to the home of Janome's president in order to put pressure on him. One of the biggest scandals involving the Goduko gangs and the securities companies arose in the summer of 1991.[3] It concerned the railway and property developer Tokyu Corporation, and Susumu Ishii, the reputed leader of the new wave of "financial" Yakuza. From 1987 Ishii started buying heavily into the blue-chip Japanese companies NTT, Nippon Steel, and Mitsui Metals.

In March 1989 Tokyu Corporation's CEO, Noboru Goto, died, leaving the company vulnerable to speculators or even a takeover bid. Between April and October 1989, Ishii bought up 27 million Tokyu shares, many of which were paid for with loans from Nomura and Nikko Securities, two of Japan's big four securities companies. Ishii bought the shares at prices between 1700 and 2000 yen. Later in October, Nomura started strongly pushing Tokyu shares to its other investors, and within a month the share price had rocketed to more than 3000 yen (Figure 1). Thus Ishii had made a profit of almost 2 billion dollars through his Tokyu investment. At the same time, Nomura and Nikko bought golf club memberships from Ishii for 20 million pounds each—although it turned out that the club was a public course. It is supposed that Ishii was aiming to take over the Tokyo corporation, but the previous CEO suddenly fell ill, and died in September 1992. In the same year Japan's Ministry of Finance started an investigation to see whether Nomura and Nikko had conspired to manipulate Tokyu's share price. Both banks denied the charge at the time, and also claimed they did not know Ishii had ties with the Yakuza when they were dealing with him. But as a result of the scandal, the chairmen of the two securities companies were forced to resign and some executives went to jail. The scam is very similar in many ways to the pump and dump scheme implemented by New York families on Wall Street or by Russian criminals on the Canadian Stock Exchange. It is worth noting that Yakuza was a pioneer among criminal syndicates in terms of involvement in financial crimes.

3.2 After 25 Years of Recession

The death of Susumu Ishii and the end of the Tokyo Corporation episode marked the end of an era, corresponding to the longest period of prosperity in Japan's history. What followed was more than two decades of recession with low interest rates and lower growth rate. In this context, the pool of activities exerted by the Yakuza shrank even more and they were forced to move rapidly into white-collar crime. As a consequence of the increased presence of Gokudo violence groups in the Japanese financial economy, in December 2006 the Tokyo Stock Market and the NPA announced the establishment of a joint committee to eradicate the Yakuza from the stock market. Investigators now closely monitor trading accounts, trying to sift out names that they think might have underworld connections.

[3]Japan's Crime Incorporated: The years of the bubble economy lured Japan's Yakuza gangs to muscle into big business, http://www.independent.co.uk/news/business/japans-crime-incorporated-the-years-of-the-bubble-economy-lured-japans-yakuza-gangs-to-muscle-into-big-business-terry-mccarthy-in-tokyo-explores-their-corporate-web-1479105.html.

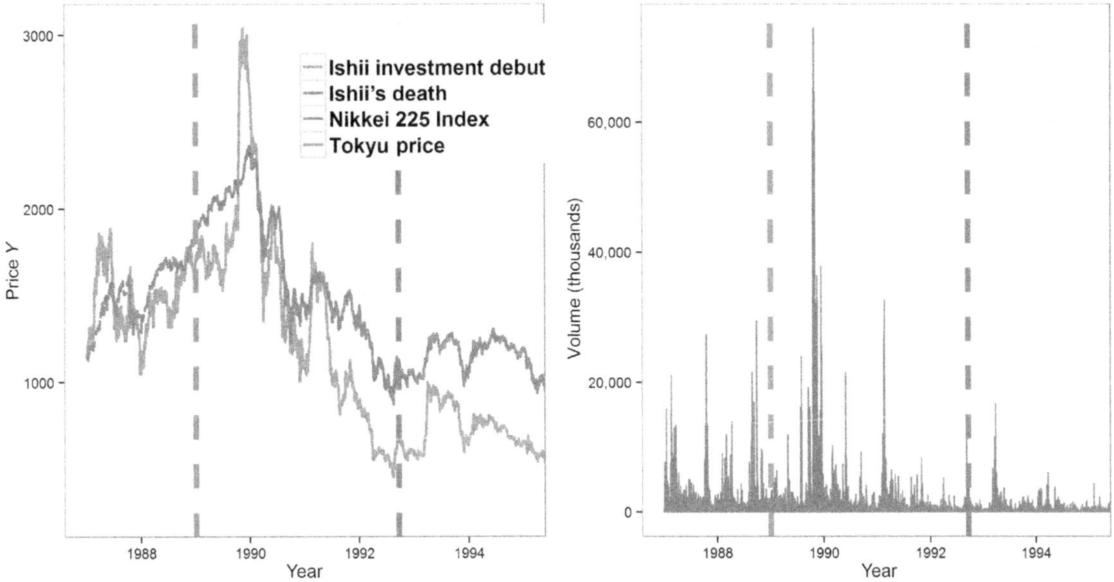

FIGURE 1 Tokyo Corporation stock. *Left*: The price of the stock peaked in 1990 after Ishii deployed his manipulation scam. The stock increased in value quicker than the Nikkei 225. *Right*: The daily volume peaked at the same time prices reached their maximum.

One of the most recent financial scandals involved one of Japan's biggest corporations, the optical equipment maker Olympus. In 2011, the scandal surfaced and a rich panelarray of characters appeared in the public domain with alleged ties to Yakuza. It is difficult to assess when the Olympus-Yakuza link started but certainly the nomination of a non-Japanese CEO, Michael Woodford from the UK, reshaped this relationship and plunged the company into an international scandal. A Japanese magazine uncovered in October 2011 that Olympus former chairman Tsuyoshi Kikukawa and other executives used a string of corporate acquisitions to cover up hidden losses dating from the 1990s. Suspect payments of more than 1 billion dollars were connected with the acquisitions. http://www.fraudconference.com/uploadedFiles/Fraud_Conference/Content/Course-Materials/presentations/23rd/cpp/5I-7I-Gerry-Zack.pdf.

Olympus's fraudulent scheme started sometime in 1985, thereby making it one of the longest schemes in white-collar crime at the time, when the company started a speculative investment strategy involving the purchase of higher risk securities. However, by the late 1990s, unrealized losses on those investments amounted to nearly 1.3 billion dollars. With the introduction of new fair value accounting rules that would require the recognition of these unrealized losses, Olympus needed to find a way to hide the substantial losses. Therefore, a loss separation scheme was conceived where the impaired assets were sold to off-balance-sheet vehicles ("receiver funds"[4]) that were established and controlled by Olympus. The sales of the depreciated assets were done at the assets' book values, not at the lower, impaired values, in order not to affect Olympus's balance sheet. The receiver funds

[4]Case studies: learning from the success of others case studies in financial statement fraud, http://www.fraudconference.com/uploadedFiles/Fraud_Conference/Content/Course-Materials/presentations/23rd/cpp/5I-7I-Gerry-Zack.pdf.

were able to pay Olympus for the acquired assets because the funds were financed by third-party financial institutions. These loans were secured with collateral pledged by Olympus. The receiver funds then acquired certain growth companies: three Japanese companies between 2003 and 2005 and one British company, Gyrus Group, in 2008, a case discussed below. Afterwards Olympus purchased these growth companies from the off-balance-sheet vehicle. These purchases were made at inflated prices and with the payment of exorbitant advisory fees, thereby allowing Olympus to foster good will. The payments for those acquisitions enabled the off-balance-sheet vehicle to repay the financial institutions, get the Olympus collateral released, and cover their operating expenses. Basically, the inflated purchase prices and advisory fees covered the hidden unrealized losses on the assets initially sold by Olympus to the off-balance-sheet vehicle. The bottom line of this scheme was that the unrealized losses of Olympus were converted into goodwill, enabling the deferral of any loss to future periods, when the goodwill could then be impaired. In some cases, Olympus recorded a write-down in value very soon after the acquisition, as some of the acquired companies had no revenue or business history, raising doubts about whether these companies were even legitimate businesses. This type of fraudulent scheme involving off-balance-sheet special purpose vehicles is called *Tobashi*, meaning "fly away" in Japanese.

OLYMPUS FALLING

Non-Japanese CEO

The Olympus scandal started when the company announced it had fired its British CEO Michael Woodford over management issues after just 2 weeks in the job. Woodford claimed he was fired after calling on authorities in Britain and Japan to investigate suspicious payments. Olympus's next CEO, Shuichi Takayama, admitted that Olympus's executives used a string of corporate acquisitions to cover up hidden losses dating from the 1990s. A Japanese magazine uncovered in October 2011 suspect payments of more than 1 billion dollar connected with the acquisitions. This highlighted the possible involvement in the scandal of a company suspected of having a relationship with the Yakuza.

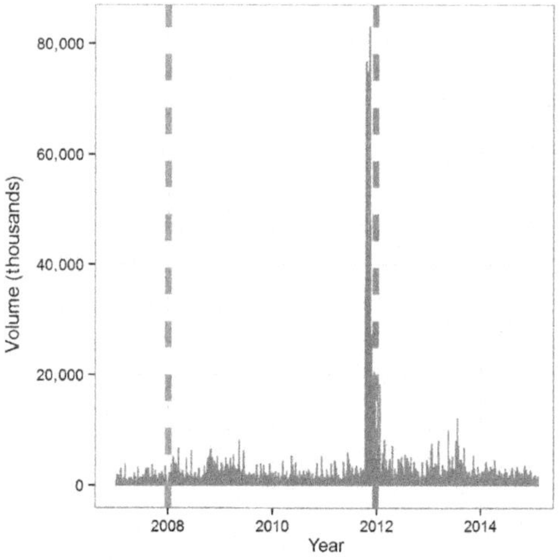

Olympus stock prices fell for the first time in 2008 when the acquisition of Gyrus took place. When the allegation of Yakuza ties surfaced the prices fell on a massive scale.

M&A fees

Olympus Corp. paid to obscure advisory firms and financial advisers (AXES and AXAM Investments) 687 million dollars in fees for the 2.2 billion dollars purchase of Gyrus, a British medical equipment manufacturer, in a record-breaking deal. The payment is the largest M&A fee ever made, surpassing the previous record of 217 million dollars involved in the 70 billion euro takeover in 2007 of ABN AMRO by RFS Holdings, a vehicle set up by Royal Bank of Scotland for acquiring the Dutch bank. The payment is equal to about a third of the acquisition price, much more than normal standards where advisers have fees of 1% or less of the transaction value for their M&A advisory services.

Another scandal irrupted in Japan in 2013 linking the Yakuza with the reputed bank Mizuho.[5] The bank was accused of extending more than 2 million dollars in loans via a partially bank-owned finance firm called Orient Corp to organized crime members. Orient, a company specializing in consumer credit, was accused of providing some 230 auto loans and other credits to clients who turned out to be "Yakuza" criminal members. The Japanese Bankers Association pointed out that these illegal transactions started before 2010.

No later than October 2014 the collapse of the Bitcoin exchange Mt Gox[6] based in Japan as a result of a criminal cyber-attack generated tens of millions of dollars of losses for many clients. There are many suspicions that this attack was orchestrated by Yakuza groups. The most phantasmagoric speculation goes further and claim that Bitcoin itself is a Yakuza creation for facilitating financial crime and its obscure founder Satoshi Nakamoto is actually a Gokudo alias.

4 AMERICAN LA COSA NOSTRA

There's a bubble there that's going to burst at some point and when it does it's not going to be good. I did a lot of things at times with people on Wall Street. A lot of guys are shady and they did shady things with me and I don't trust them.[7] ***Michael Franzese, former captain of the Colombo crime family, son of the New York underworld legend John "Sonny" Franzese, Sr.***

Franzese's views about the bubble could be accurate or not, but for sure the fact that he might have known in his prime people on Wall Street is without doubt a fact. Michael's involvement with the Colombo family in the 1980s was during a period of major turmoil for East Coast organized crime. The 1980s marked the start of the decline of the American La Cosa Nostra or at least of its traditional activities. The arrest of *the Dapper Don* John Gotti marked the end of this period, and the dawn of the street-type mobsters. With the Gambino family shaken down by the Federal Government, the Colombo family riven by an internal war, the Bonanno and the Lucchese reduced by consecutive indictments to glorified crews, the mob was confronted with a quest for survival. In those years changes in the structure of the blue-collar economy cut massive streams of revenue for the mob. The dissolution of its garbage cartels generated losses in revenue for the five families estimated to be 500

[5]Japan Mizuho bank mob loan orient Yakuza, http://www.ibtimes.co.uk/japan-mizuho-bank-mob-loan-orient-yakuza-514321. Japan's financial regulator to probe country's top banks, http://www.telegraph.co.uk/finance/financial-crime/10411178/Japans-financial-regulator-to-probe-countrys-top-banks.html.

[6]Bitcoin exchange Kraken joins the Mt Gox investigation the collapse still shrouded in darkness, http://www.japansubculture.com/bitcoin-exchange-kraken-joins-the-mt-gox-investigation-the-collapse-still-shrouded-in-darkness/.

[7]Mob boss calls a stock bubble, http://www.cnbc.com/id/101932292.

million dollars a year and the eviction in 1988 from the Fulton Fish Market historically handled by the Genovese family added another 50 million dollars of opportunity losses. Therefore, mob activity on Wall Street reportedly increased in the 1990s and American Mafia crime families switched to white-collar crime with a focus on small Wall Street brokerage houses.

4.1 Debut on Wall Street

The legacy of the mob on Wall Street can be traced to some time in the late 1970s.[8] One of the earliest known cases was when the US Attorney for New York and the Security Exchange Commission jointly announced indictments against Michael Hellerman, John Dioguardi, Vincent Aloi, and others for securities fraud. Aloi and Dioguardi were connected to the Gambino family. Hellerman, who later entered into the witness-protection program, disclosed later in a book [66] that he had been manipulating stocks for years and in association with the mob was behind some of Wall Street's biggest swindles, frauds that had ripped off millions of dollars from brokerage houses and banks.

In 1986, Marshall Zolp and Lorenzo Formato were investigated on allegations of manipulation of the stock of Laser Arms Corp, a purported maker of a self-chilling can, which was a bogus company which generated fictitious financial statements and nonexistent product. Zolp and Formato led the scam in association with organized crime. The Congressional hearings at which Formato testified led to passage of the Penny Stock Reform Act of 1990. In 1988, F.D. Roberts Securities, Inc., a New Jersey-based boiler room, and four associated persons were accused by the Security ExchangeCommission (SEC) of manipulating a microcap stock, Hughes Capital Corp. Dominick Fiorese, one of the indicted individuals, had reported ties to organized crime in the Gambino and Colombo families.

4.2 Operation Uptick

The pump and dump scam made the glory of the New York families in the late 1990s[9] and was depicted by David Chase in the series *The Sopranos*. One of the first serious cases from that period brought to justice was that involving the manipulation of the stock price of Health Tech, listed on NASDAQ as GYMM. In 1996, successful entrepreneur Gordon Hall began to conspire with members of the Bonanno and Genovese families in New York to "pump up" the price of common stock issued by Health Tech International, Incorporated. Hall was also the Chairman of Eagle Holdings, and also the CEO of Health Tech. He made an agreement with stock promoters Irwin Schneider, Claudio Iodice, and Eugene Lombardo, an associate of the Bonanno family in New York. In exchange for artificially inflating and supporting the stock price and volume of Health Tech common stock, Hall would pay Lombardo, Schneider, and Iodice with shares of the stock. He paid these shares of stock to Lombardo, Schneider, and Iodice under the guise of consulting agreements.

Whistleblowers from inside the company reported this activity to the Federal authorities and, after some preliminary investigations, agents and detectives working on a task force in New York City obtained court authorization to tape telephone calls of the group. For almost a year, working with the US Securities and Exchange Commission

[8]Testimony concerning the involvement of organized crime on Wall Street, http://www.sec.gov/news/testimony/ts142000.htm.

[9]In the late 1990s, the FBI launched Operation Uptick, which resulted in the arrest of more than 120 Wall Street stock manipulators linked to organized crime—one of the biggest Mafia busts in FBI history.

and officials from NASDAQ, agents and detectives conducted surveillance, intercepted conversations, analyzed complex business and trading records, and interviewed witnesses and experts to determine the extent of the conspiracy and develop the evidence necessary to indict and convict those involved. Lombardo, Schneider, and Iodice paid bribes to brokers under them who manipulated the price of the securities by artificially creating demand for them. These brokers made false claims to customers in order to induce them to buy Health Tech stock so the price would rise. The trading activity increased the price of the stock so conspirators could sell their shares at a profit, or "dump" them. When customers decided to sell the Health Tech stocks, brokers would refuse to take their calls or make unauthorized trades in the customers' accounts. In January 1997, sales of Health Tech shares increased almost four times over sales in December 1996. By the end of February, the stock price had risen to a high of 2.813 dollars per share, from its 0.87 dollars close on December 31 (Figure 2). This "pump and dump" scheme made millions of dollars for the conspirators.

The investigation showed that as the scheme continued, the Bonanno and Genovese families took control of two branches of Meyers, Pollack and Robbins, a major brokerage firm, and tried to expand the scheme to include other small-cap companies. Mobsters sought to control which brokers worked at the branch offices in order to avoid detection by law enforcement, and to control who would receive profits from the scheme. As disputes arose in these matters, LCN members resorted to their classic methodology to maintain control. They made threats of violence against individuals who were not backed by other LCN members and held "sit-downs" or meetings to resolve disputes with individuals who were backed by other families. In mid-January 1998, Jonathan Lyons, who managed one of the branch offices being used by the group, complained that the office was functioning solely for the conspirators to sell Health Tech and tried to keep Lombardo's brokers from working in the office.

Lombardo sent a Bonanno soldier and an associate to threaten Lyons. Lyons in turn sought protection through a friend from a Bonanno capo and another Bonanno soldier. Lombardo then contacted Frank Lino, a Bonanno family capo, who met with other Bonnano members to resolve the dispute. When the resolution did not satisfy Lombardo, he contacted Rosario Gangi, a Genovese family capo, to assist. Another meeting was held which included Gangi and Ernest Montevecchi, a Genovese LCN family soldier, and Lombardo prevailed. Gangi and Montevecchi were also instrumental in helping Lombardo control a second branch office of the firm. At one point, Lombardo, Schneider, and Iodice became dissatisfied with the method and timeliness of Hall's payments. Lombardo, Iodice, and another individual met with and threatened Hall and his senior vice president to ensure their continued cooperation and payment for the services of Lombardo and the others. Several telephone calls were intercepted in which Lombardo and others discussed their intent to hurt Hall. When interviewed by agents and detectives, victims of the scheme reported that they were told by brokers that they had hundreds of people working under them, they had invested heavily in the stock themselves, and they made promises as to the future performance of the stock. One customer had even recorded a sales call in which a broker falsely claimed to have 250 other brokers working under him and that he had purchased 1,000,000 Health Tech warrants himself.

As a result of the investigation, 33 people were indicted on charges of extortion, securities fraud, stock manipulation, and commercial bribery. The defendants included several members and associates of the Genovese and Bonanno families, as well as the principals of Health Tech and Meyers, Pollack and Robbins.

One of the breaches in regulation used by many of the fruadsters concerned the offshore

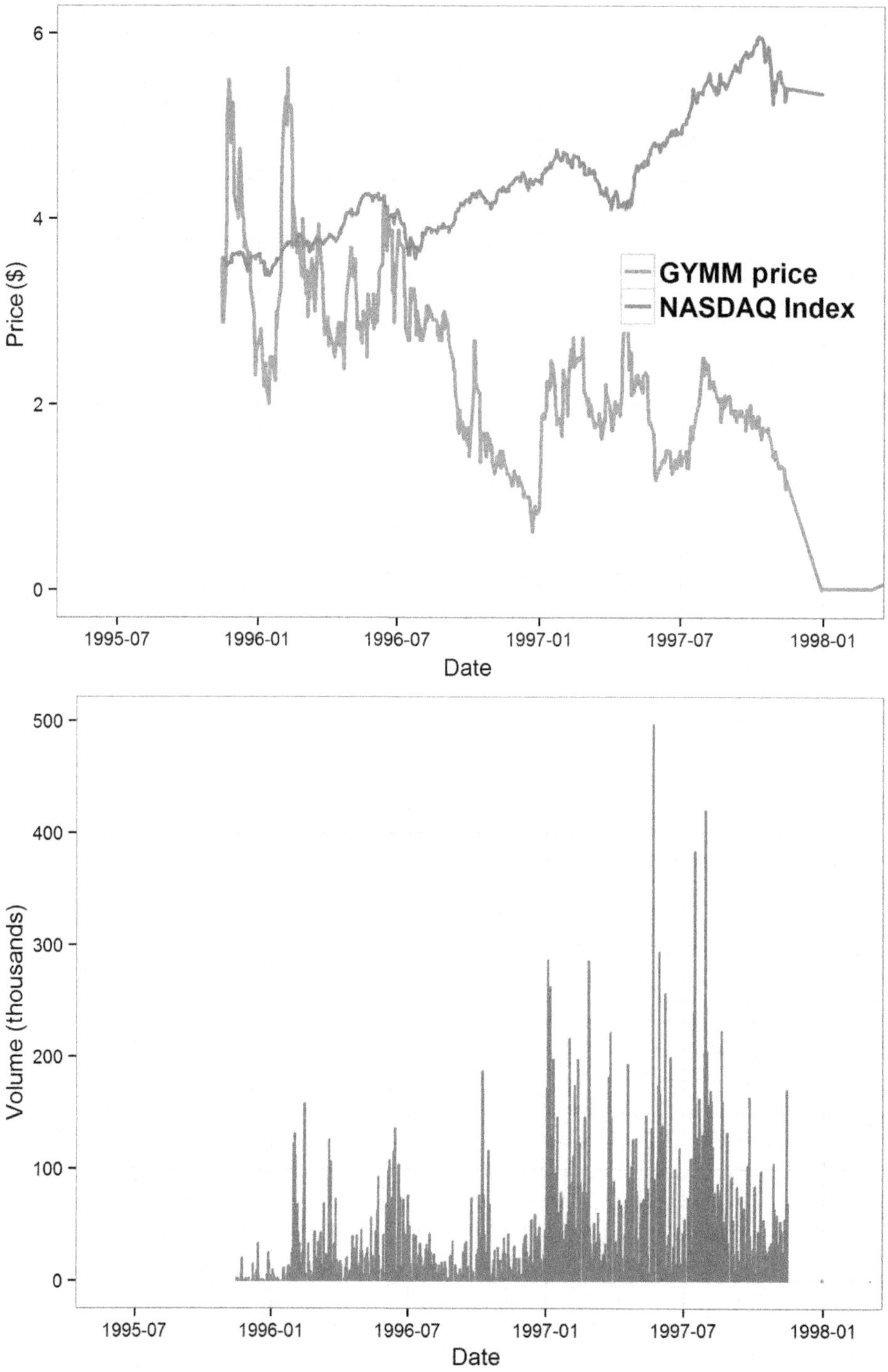

FIGURE 2 Health Tech stock prices and volumes: evolution during the period of organized crime involvement.

offerings. During the 1990s Regulation S provided a safe harbor from SEC registration for certain offshore offerings. Following the adoption of Regulation S, some issuers were using it as a means of indirectly distributing securities into the United States markets without registration. Organized crime used Regulation S offerings to obtain a cheap supply of stock for pump and dump.

Table 1 synthesizes the most relevant cases of mob involvement on Wall Street. The Genovese and Gambino families appear in most of the cases. Mob-linked short sellers were associated with the famous brokerage house Stratton Oakmont, owned by Jason Bentfort, who was the subject of the movie *The Wolf of Wall Street*, which appears in some of the cases which involved organized crime. The Russian groups that grew

TABLE 1 Timeline of Mob Involvement on Wall Street

Year	Companies	Crime synopsis	*Borgata*	Fraud size ($, millions)
1970		Manipulation of stocks prices	Gambino	≈5
1986	Laser Arms Corp	Penny stock price manipulation	Gambino	
1988	FD Robert Securities	Manipulation of microcap stocks	Colombo, Gambino	
1997	First Colonial Ventures	Manipulation of microcap stocks	Colombo	≈0.75
1997	Health Tech	Manipulation of microcap stocks	Colombo	≈5
1997	Stratton Oakmont, Hanover Sterling & Co.	Broker licensing test cheating	Genovese	
1998	Technigen Corp., TV Communications Network, Inc.	Manipulation of microcap stocks	Genovese	≈5
1998	Transun International Airways, Inc., Capital Planning Associates, Inc.	Manipulation of microcap stocks	Genovese	≈8
1998	Trump Financial Group, Sheffield Group	Forex derivative mis-selling	Gambino	
1999	Hanover Sterling, Norfolk Securities, Capital Planning	Pump and dump	Genovese, Colombo, Russian groups	≈100
1999	Sovereign Equity Management Corp.	Microcap pump and dump, Regulation S	Decavalcante	
2000	Stockinvestor.com	Microcap pump and dump, murder of Maier Lehmann and Albert Chalem	Decavalcante; Colombo	
2000	White Rock Partners	Pump and dump, Regulation S	Genovese, Gambino, Bonnano, Colombo	≈5
2000	Monitor Investment Group, Meyers, Pollock and Robbins, and First Liberty Investment Group	Pump and dump, Regulation S	Genovese, Gambino, Lucchese, Bonnano, Colombo	≈10
2008	Madoff advisory	Ponzi scheme	Genovese	≈50,000
2010	Realcast Live, BBC Gaming Inc.	Stock selling to elderly victims	Bonnano, Russian groups	≈12

quickly in the US during the 1990s are also present among the criminal groups. The mob had established a network of stock promoters, securities dealers, and boiler rooms to engage in "pump and dump" manipulations, controlling approximately two dozen broker-dealers, like the Hanover Sterling brokerage firm, which was under the control of the Genovese crime family.

4.3 Recent Years

In the year 2000, the Federal pressure on organized crime increased and as a result the reported cases of involvement in securities fraud decreased. This did not prevent the appearance in the top 10 list[10] of the most wanted white-collar criminals an associate of the Gambino family who operated in Florida. John Anthony Porcaro is wanted for his alleged involvement in a South Florida telemarketing scheme which defrauded more than 400 individuals throughout the United States out of more than 5 million dollars. Between February and December of 1998, the Trump Financial Group and the Sheffield Group were doing business as telemarketing firms which obtained money from investors for purported investment in foreign currency options in the foreign exchange markets. It is alleged that investors were promised as much as 700% returns based upon the rise and fall of Forex rates.

In 2010,[11] a notable figure of the Bonnano family Anthony Guarino was charged for criminal offenses. The top soldier was known by the Federal authorities for having ties with both Italian and Russian organized crime. In 2010, the Federal Court indicted a dozen mobbed-up suspects in a stock scam where elderly victims were duped into 12 million dollars of rogue investments. Guarino was identified in court papers as running the scam's daily operation. The scammers set up a boiler room operation, using the name Powercom Energy Services, in the Garment District. They sold stock between 2000 and 2009 in a pair of sham companies: Miami-based Realcast Live and BBC Gaming Inc. on Fifth Avenue. Indicted salesman Lance Barbarino, who pitched clients with a web of lies, admitted to a co-conspirator that his "mother will come out of the grave" before Realcast makes any money. Salesmen routinely collected 40% of the investment money as commission, with at least one major investor losing 50% off the top, the indictment charged. One investor lost his 50,000 dollar life savings, while another investor saw half of his 700,000 dollar stock buy disappear as commission.

But the most intriguing speculations around the involvement of the mob in financial crime are related to the Madoff case, discussed in detail in a separate chapter. This speculation claims that the Genovese family did not lose all its influence on Wall Street after the roaring 1990s and one of the feeding funds had ties with organized crime. Ironically Madoff is doing his sentence in the same facility as Carmine "the Snake" Persico, the historic leader of the Colombo family.

5 RUSSIAN-SPEAKING GROUPS

The widespread terms "Russian Mafia" or "Red Mafia" or "KGB Mafia" are as misleading as a term can be. *Russian Mafia* is not an accurate term due to the fact that within criminal groups from ex-Soviet countries ethnic Russians are not the majority. Moreover, the top positions of power are held by non-Russians. Thus ex-Soviet crime syndicates are a mix of various ethnicities, religious orientations, and education.

After the fall of the USSR during the Yeltsin era organized crime groups in the former

[10] America's most wanted white-collar criminals—2009-2011, http://www.businessinsider.com/americas-most-wanted-white-collar-criminals-2009-11?op=1#ixzz3Obu1sMMC.

[11] FBI: Mob fleeced seniors, http://nypost.com/2010/06/10/fbi-mob-fleeced-seniors/.

Soviet Union had grown from 785 during Gorbachev's reign to 5691. By 1996 this estimate had grown to 8000 groups, each with memberships of between 50 and 1000. The Government in Moscow estimated that the Russian mafia controls 40% of private business and 60% of state-owned companies.[12] In that period of the roaring 1990s from the ashes of the old Soviet Union in a picture dominated by violent killing a new group emerged, the oligarchs. The new class of Russian magnates took profit from dubious privatizations, many of them completed with the help of criminal brotherhoods (*bratva*). Privatization of public companies was the most disruptive episode that mixed violent and nonviolent crimes and will be addressed in a separate chapter.

5.1 Solntsevo Group

At that time every other guy claimed being from Solntzevo.

If the Yakuza's legacy toward sophisticated crime developed progressively with Japan's economic boom, in the case of Russian organized crime the drift appeared very quickly in less than 10 years. An American agency specializing in crime mentions in a report that the Moscow-based organization Solntsevo appears to be one of the most influential organizations. Originating as a gang of crooks from the neighborhood with the same name, the "Sunny Brotherhood" (*Solntzevo bratva*) quickly evolved into a reputed syndicate incorporating recently the collaboration of Semion Mogilevich, one of the Russian pioneers in worldwide crime. The Solntsevo criminal organization is widely perceived to be the most powerful Russian crime syndicate in terms of wealth, influence, and financial control. Its leadership, structure, and operations exemplify the new breed of Russian criminals that emerged with the breakup of the Soviet system. Rather than the traditional "thieves-in-law" who dominated the criminal underworld during the Soviet period and played more of a "godfather" role in overseeing loosely organized criminal networks, the leaders of Solntsevo and other post-Soviet Russian criminal groups are not only more flamboyant, aggressive, and politically savvy, but also well-versed in modern technology and business practices that allow them to operate efficiently across international borders. The power and wealth of the Solntsevo crime group derive largely from its financial and business network in Russia and highly placed political connections. According to press reports, Solntsevo benefits from Moscow city projects through its reported links to a construction, tourism, real estate, and utility conglomerate that obtained many of its properties from the city and holds others jointly with the municipal government. While dominating Moscow's criminal underworld—including the market for drugs, particularly cocaine—Solntsevo also has extensive worldwide operations. Solntsevo's international criminal activities are said to include trafficking narcotics and arms and money laundering.

Solntsevo started to drift toward financial crime in the late 2000s with the increasing pressure of the Russian federal security agency, FSB, on the criminal world. One of the first international scandals involving Russian criminals was the Bank of New York case, which surfaced in 1999. More than 10 billion dollars were laundered through a single account by the bank in the 1990s with proceedings from Russian criminals from the traffic of nuclear materials, drugs, precious gems, and stolen art as well as contract killings. The investigation led to another controversial character Semion Mogilevich and his ties with Solntsevo, then headed by Serghey Mihailkhov.

[12]The rise and rise of the Russian mafia, http://news.bbc.co.uk/1/hi/special_report/1998/03/98/russian_mafia/70095.stm.

5.2 Semion Mogilevich and Canadian Stock

One of the top 10 most wanted criminals on the planet is the Russian iconic legend Semion Mogilevich. Mogilevich had been a criminal carrier for some decades and in various countries and social organizations. A public portrait of Mr Mogilevich's criminal empire first appeared in May 1998 in *The Village Voice*, a New York newspaper. His legal issues started in the time of the former Soviet Union when he built part of his reputation. Mogilevich started as a small-time thief and counterfeiter in the 1970s, then made millions in the 1980s from Jews leaving the Soviet Union. He took their art, jewelry, and other valuables, promising to sell them and send the money, but kept most of the proceeds. Not long after the Berlin wall came down and the Soviet Union collapsed, making travel easier, Mogilevich set up operations in Budapest, where he ran a prostitution ring out of a topless bar called the Black and White Club. Though raised in a Communist society, Mogilevich quickly adapted the ways of fast business dealing. After the fall of the USSR he moved abroad to the United States where he forged a reputation in the underworld. The geographical and political changes were accompanied by a focus on a new type of crime, white-collar stock exchange manipulation.

5.2.1 Stock Manipulation

In the bull financial market of the 1990s, public companies offered criminals the chance to make even more money by artificially pumping up the stock price and milking investors. Mogilevich's move into the North American equity markets began with a company he set up in suburban Philadelphia called YBM Magnex. Its primary business was the manufacture of industrial magnets at a factory in Hungary and later at a factory the company bought in Kentucky. YBM attracted a blue-ribbon board, its books were audited by two prominent American accounting firms, it issued glossy annual reports and it had its own website. All of this turned out to be sophisticated cover for what was also a vast money-laundering operation.

The YBM case was the first public demonstration of the manipulation and infiltration of world financial markets by Russian organized crime according to crime surveillance officials. After revealing the crime in a negotiated agreement, YBM pleaded guilty to securities fraud in the Federal District Court in Philadelphia. After the affair went public Mogilevich was barred from entering the United States, but he was still free to travel in the western world with his Israeli citizenship, as are several other prominent Russians involved in crime. In the 3 years between the British action and the American authorities' penetration of YBM's corporate façade, the company had raised 114 million Canadian dollars on Canada's capital markets. Helped by glowing claims about sales and profits, YBM's stock soared, and Mogilevich and some of his associates sold their shares for millions of dollars in profits.

The shares were traded in Canada, attracting some American investors, while the company awaited approval for listing on the NASDAQ exchange in the United States. The company had sales but it also exaggerated them. It had customers, but it also maintained fictitious customer lists. It paid suppliers, but some were companies controlled by associates of Mogilevich. Some YBM officers and directors were complicit with Mogilevich, but others thought they were engaged in a legitimate business. In putting together YBM, he used offshore locales where secrecy prevails over disclosure, sophisticated financial transactions and wire transfers to move money quickly and beyond the prying eyes of regulators.

In the beginning Mogilevich set up a company based in the Channel Islands in 1991 called Arigon. Eventually, through a series of complex transactions and takeovers, Arigon acquired control of YBM Magnex. To finance YBM's first public offering, in Canada, Mogilevich sent 2.4 million dollars from Arigon's bank accounts in the Channel Islands. YBM was headed by one of Mogilevich's trusted associates, Jacob Bogatin. Bogatin, who had a doctorate in powder metallurgy from Volgograd State University, came to the United States in the 1980s and eventually became a citizen. From 1996 to 1998, he was president and chief executive of YBM. The company's glowing claims propelled YBM's stock from a few cents at the time of the first offering in 1994 to 5 Canadian dollars in early 1996, to more than 20 dollars 2 years later. Figure 3 shows the evolution of the YBM stock price benchmarked to the Toronto Stock Index. YBM prices increased exponentially in two years.

5.2.2 *Rogue Accounting*

In its 1996 annual report, for example, the company boasted of "record sales and earnings," with sales up 79% over the previous year. It also claimed that revenues from buying and selling crude oil increased from 13.6 million to 20.4 million Canadian dollars. YBM's books were audited for 1996 by Parente, Randolph, Orlando, Carey & Associates in Philadelphia. The firm reported that the financial statements "present fairly in all material respects" the company's financial position. In the summer of 1997, when YBM was preparing for another public offering, Ontario securities regulators asked Deloitte & Touche to conduct a "high-risk" audit. In the securities world, this means that the authorities were suspicious and wanted the accounting firm to apply extra scrutiny and diligence. Deloitte & Touche gave YBM a clean bill of health. One Canadian analyst who issued a "buy" recommendation noted that the company had emerged from the Deloitte audit with stronger perspectives. In November 1997, YBM completed a public offering of 3.2 million shares, at 16.50 Canadian dollars each, bringing in a total of nearly 53 million dollars.

Deloitte & Touche underlined that the company had carried out the audit "in accordance with applicable professional standards" and had vigorously defended itself against the suits. In June 1998, Deloitte resigned as YBM's auditors after it became concerned about "questionable transactions."

5.2.3 *Money Laundering*

An audit of YBM's books was undertaken in December 1998 by a Philadelphia accounting firm, Miller Coffey Tate, which the company hired when Canadian securities regulators raised questions, and YBM's annual reports, public statements and filings with regulatory agencies in Canada.

Miller Coffey Tate underlined money laundering and unusual transactions as suspicions in YBM activity. At the center of these transactions was a company called United Trade, which was incorporated in the Cayman Islands and was run by Igor Fisherman, who was also the chief operating officer of YBM. Fisherman, who has a master's degree in mathematics from Ufa State University in Russia, immigrated to the United States in the late 1980s and later became an American citizen. On one occasion, 3.2 million dollars were transferred from a bank in Lithuania to a United Trade account in Hungary. It was then quickly transferred to Chemical Bank in Buffalo for the benefit of six ostensibly different companies. At the same time, United Trade sent money to Chemical Bank for a Buffalo lawyer, Paul F. Fallon. In addition, the companies involved in the transactions, those in Lithuania, Hungary, and the United States, all had the same address—that of Mr Fallon's office in Buffalo. As for the oil sales, which YBM said had done so much for its profits, in reality the company never had any oil to sell.

After the YBM case Mogilevich disappeared and surfaced in the late 2000s, being arrested in Moscow in 2009. After a short incarceration he was released in the same year. Based in Moscow he has alleged ties with a major Russian crime

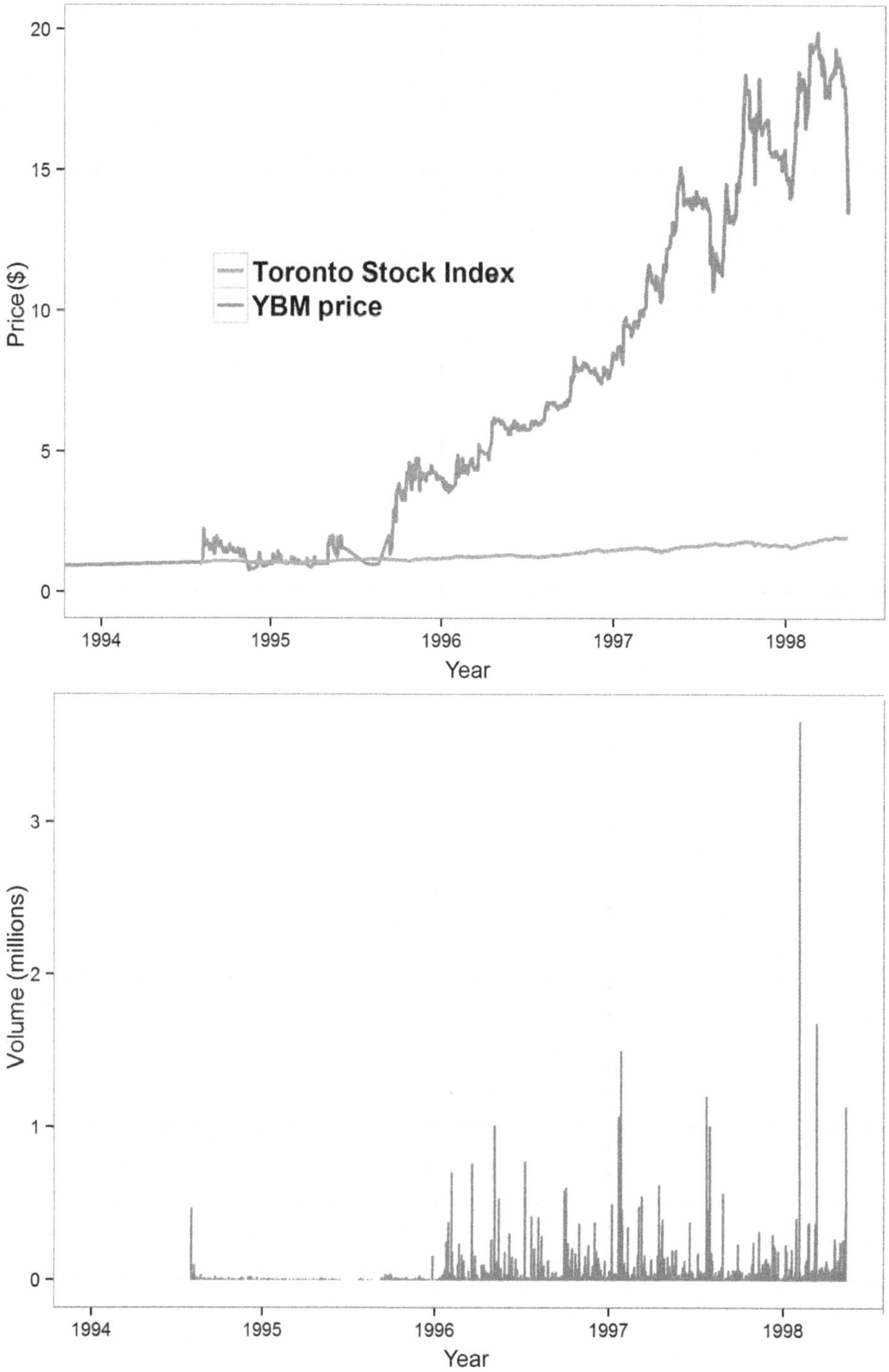

FIGURE 3 YBM stock. *Top*: Evolution of the YBM stock price benchmarked to the Toronto Stock Index. *Right*: Evolution of the traded volumes during the fraud period.

syndicate Solntsevo, involved in financial crime and money laundering across Europe.

These cases indicate that crime syndicates are able to infiltrate different technical and complex sectors of stock markets and have the means to address areas such as accounting, corporate financing, or regulation.

6 NEW WAVES OF ORGANIZED CRIME IN FINANCE

6.1 White-Collar Organized Crime

White-collar organized crime is not strictly speaking a crime syndicate in the sense that La Eme, 'Ndrangheta, or Yakuza are. In fact, this type of organized criminal behavior includes mainly people with no criminal record, well educated and coming from the upper classes of society. Nevertheless this category when mandated to act as agents for a financial institution in order to interact with the market or with clients do change their pattern of behavior and tend to carry out illegal actions. In addition in many cases they associate with other rogue agents from other firms in order to sustain their criminal acts over extended periods of time. Moreover, the pattern of this behavior is transmitted to other agents that are newly recruited into firms in the same division or department. This form of crime, including governance persistence over time and transmission to new recruits, ticks all the boxes necessary to be categorized as organized crime. The recent cases of Forex manipulation, LIBOR and Euribor fixing involve many traders or agents from some institutions that have been associated with these criminal enterprises. Those rigging rings existed for almost a decade and the new agents that were recruited in those banks colluded in this type of rogue behavior. This pattern of behavior is less studied in the literature and constitutes an exception to all perceptions about organized crime.

6.2 Latin American Drug Cartels

Less tied currently to financial markets, the drug cartels involved many reputed institutions in money-laundering scandals. The cases of Wachovia and HSBC investigated recently are overwhelming due to the enormous size of illegal transactions.

- In 2010, US authorities brought criminal proceedings[13] against Wachovia, which settled for 110 million dollars in forfeiture, for allowing transactions later proved to be connected to drug smuggling, and incurred a 50 million dollar fine for failing to monitor cash used to ship 22 tons of cocaine. More shockingly, and more importantly, the bank was sanctioned for failing to apply the proper anti-laundering strictures to the transfer of 378.4 billion dollars, an amount equivalent to one-third of Mexico's gross national product, into dollar accounts from currency exchange houses in Mexico with which the bank did business.
- In December 2012 HSBC, Europe's biggest bank,[14] was accused of failing to monitor more than 670 billion dollars, almost twice the amount Wachovia laundered, in wire transfers and more than 9.4 billion dollars in purchases of US currency from HSBC Mexico. The bank settled for a historic top penalty of 1.25 billion dollars forfeiture and 665 million dollars in civil penalties under the settlement.

Obviously these cases concern wire transfer and international Forex transactions, but with the pressure of controls on these types of

[13]How a big US bank laundered billions from Mexico's murderous drug gangs, http://www.theguardian.com/world/2011/apr/03/us-bank-mexico-drug-gangs.

[14]HSBC Judge approves $1.9b drug-money laundering accord, http://www.bloomberg.com/news/articles/2013-07-02/hsbc-judge-approves-1-9b-drug-money-laundering-accord.

operations, cartels might look in the future to launder through more complex methods involving securities or financial markets.

6.3 Chinese Triads

Less known to the Western world and less glorified by the mainstream film industry the Triads are, along with the Japanese Yakuza, the most powerful organization in Asia Pacific. The legends surrounding the origins of the Triads date to around the time of the fall of the Ming dynasty and the takeover of the Manchurian Qing. The first official records go back to the eighteenth century in Hong Kong, which is still today the basis of the origination. The term Triad depicting the dark societies is not a Chinese term (neither Mandarin nor Cantonese) and is in fact the English translation of "Sam Ho Wui" or literally the three united associations, the triangular banners based on the three characters representing heaven, earth, and man.

Broadhurst and Lee [67] showed that the substantial changes in the political economy of Hong Kong from a manufacturing to a financial services market and from colonial to neocolonial rule and the rapid economic development of mainland China have served to modernize, "gentrify" and transform the organization of the Triads. The Triads ways of functioning have become more corporatized and boundaries moved beyond traditional predatory street crime, extortion, and drug dealing predicated on brand violence to diverse "gray" business activities that also include trafficking (anything profitable), vice, copyright, Internet, and financial service crimes such as money laundering and financial fraud. Lo [68] explained further the mutation suffered by the Triads after the end of the British dominion in 1997. The leaders of the People's Republic of China applied a tactic to recruit Hong Kong Triad societies to the Communist camp. Consequently, Triad leaders were able to set foot in China and link up with officials and state enterprises. Lo [68] explains how the Triad leaders converted the social capital they developed in mainland China into economic capital through illegitimate means in the stock market. The many waves of immigration from Canton toward the United States and the European Union also brought the Asian criminal gangs. The boom of the Chinese economy in the years 2000s, bolstered Chinese capital investment overseas. The negative externality of the Chinese capital outflow is linked to transnational financial crime. A particular sector touched on is gambling. The involvement of Asian groups in match-fixing and rogue-betting schemes is already a main focus for investigators. The Dan Tan character arrested in 2014 is an iconic figure in this. Yet the involvement of the organized groups has not yet surfaced in this respect. In this respect, a new development came into the public domain linked to the investigation of the controversial Hongkongese tycoon Carson Yeung.[15] Yeung, who acquired the English football club Birmingham City, faced up to 14 years in jail for charges involving multi-million dollar money laundering. The investigators claimed around 93 million dollars passed through bank accounts connected to Yeung between 2001 and 2007. Yeung made a fortune in the late 1990s and early 2000s by obscure means. He claimed that a beauty parlor, gambling, and penny stock trading made up most of this fortune. He explained in front of the court that after the 1998 Asian stock market crash, he accumulated a stock portfolio of around 75 million dollars by 2007. The investigators also suggested a link between Yeung and Cheung Chi-Tai, an alleged Triad boss. Yeung's story is certainly not unique and many other entrepreneurs from Hong Kong with ties to the underworld managed to do business at global level. With a highly prized financial sector,

[15]Football: Birmingham's Yeung faces money-laundering verdict, http://financialcrimeasia.org/tag/triads/.

thriving initial public offering market, low taxes, and high activity of physical trades, Hong Kong is the perfect place to conduct financial crime and local groups would certainly lead this trend.

6.4 Transnational Organized Crime

On July 24, 2011, President Obama issued the Executive Order 13581 (Blocking Property of Transnational Criminal Organizations) aimed to target and disrupt significant transnational criminal organizations. A year later in 2012 the US Department of the Treasury took the first measures to tackle transnational syndicates and designated key members and associates of the Brothers' Circle crime syndicate as well as the largest group within the Japanese Yakuza, the Yamaguchi-Gumi, and two Yamaguchi-Gumi leaders. The US treasuries proceeded to freeze any assets the designated persons may have had within the jurisdiction of the United States and prohibited any transactions with them by US persons. The Brothers' Circle, a name unknown to the public prior to the treasury announcement, is the first case of a multinational crime network mainly focused on dealing in weapons, narcotics, and precious metals but also involving financial fraud. This organization has its roots in the former Soviet Union and operations in Europe, Asia, and the Middle East. The American authorities mentioned that Brothers' Circle "serves as a coordinating body for a number of criminal networks," directing members' criminal activity globally. The governance of this circle includes the central figure of Vladislav Leontyev, a Russian criminal originally from Nijni Novgorod. While the existence and the real scope of the Circle are still debated by experts, transnational organized crime is a reality and authorities started to became aware of this connection able to involve the biggest crime syndicates in the world. The fact that the alleged Circle was coordinated from Russia is not by chance. In fact the coordination would most likely have a financial connotation as Russian groups are reputed to be able to move funds across countries and markets via some ingenious approaches. Liberty Gold is an example in this respect that will be discussed in a later chapter.

6.5 Islamic Organized Crime

After the tragedy that took place early in 2015 in Paris at the headquarters of the satirical journal Charlie Hebdo the fear of fundamentalist terrorism became more acute than ever. The question of terrorism financing surfaced in debates. Yet the only thing that passed under the scrutiny of media and of public opinion is the ties with criminal gangs and the emergency of crime groups with Islamic backgrounds. The financing of the Charlie Hebdo operation had a terrorist background but the procurement and the logistics had a crime connection. In Europe, it is well known that extremist imams have close ties with the gang leaders from projects heavily involved in drug and weapon traffic. Most of the gang leaders from Muslim backgrounds the propagators of religious hatred, despite the fact that Islam is very categorical about those types of crimes. Violence preaching imams and violent practicing "caids" (gang leaders) tolerate each other in Europe's peripheral projects and in some cases do collaborate. The emergence of this type of crime would make it possible to join a large number of ethnicities and geographical backgrounds based on common faith. Chechnians, Tartars, Albanians, Pakistanis, and Maghrebians can easily join in illegal ventures. If the financing is added to this dimension all the elements for increasing the propensity toward white-collar crime are present.

This type of crime venture has proved to be effective on some occasions. One of the most relevant is the recent fraud on the carbon markets that took place in the European Union. The most disruptive syndicate that acted during that fraud was the ring which included Pakistani, Arab, and Turkish citizens centered around Dubai.

7 OUTLOOK

Tomita, Shiroyama, you both know nothing about futures trading, foreign exchange nor hedge funds.
Excerpt from Autoreiji, Beyond

In the light of recent cases three trends seem to characterize the involvement of organized crime in financial markets. First, the financial system will become a prevalent target of organized crime to the detriment of classic racketeering activities. Therefore, these groups will be a threat not only from the outside but also from the inside. Criminals tend to take over or register financial entities in low-regulation areas (i.e., brokerage houses, commodity trading houses, or hedge funds). Second, the financial crimes tend to be transnational with various syndicates forming joint ventures. In addition, these syndicates might collude or involve rogue operators from the banks. The allegation of mob ties to Jason Bradford and Bernie Madoff speak for themselves. Last but not least is the high leverage for innovation as a vector of spreading financial crime at a global level.

PART III

TYPOLOGIES OF CRIME ON FINANCIAL MARKETS

CHAPTER

3A

Insider Trading

OUTLINE

1 BACKGROUND

Efficient markets aim to capture through price the full information available for a particular asset, from both public and nonpublic sources. Therefore, no agent can generate excess returns on such a market. Most markets are rarely efficient and in the best case they follow the weak or the semi-strong forms of efficiency. This implies that prices adjust rapidly with the arrival of new public information. Therefore, an agent that executes trades by having particular information before it becomes public might be able to generate profits. These trades can have a *structural* relationship with the market if they concern a large share of the market liquidity and thus can affect the relevance of the price. They can also be *minor* if they represent only a small part of the market volume and they have little or no effect on the price.

Figure 1 shows the various relationships between information type and trades. If an agent has nonpublic information and deals in minor trades, it is often characterized as insider trading, with a small impact on prices. If the agent performs structural transactions in large volumes she can make the price oversensitive to the new information before it becomes public. If structural nonpublic information is made public it can also change the market equilibrium as the traders will try to adjust.

An agent can also alter the public information by generating fake rumors or hoaxes and this can change the market momentum, being considered as market manipulation. "Pump and dump" security frauds are a typical case where a person creates public information in order to distort market prices.

An agent can also, through structural trades, alter the price to give the impression to the market that there is virtual nondisclosed information. Spoofing, for example, is a practice where traders place limited orders outside the current bid and asking prices to give an artificial impression of an intention to buy or sell shares and to ultimately change the perception of other traders about the price. Short selling is another example of this type of inference.

http://dx.doi.org/10.1016/B978-0-12-801221-5.00005-1

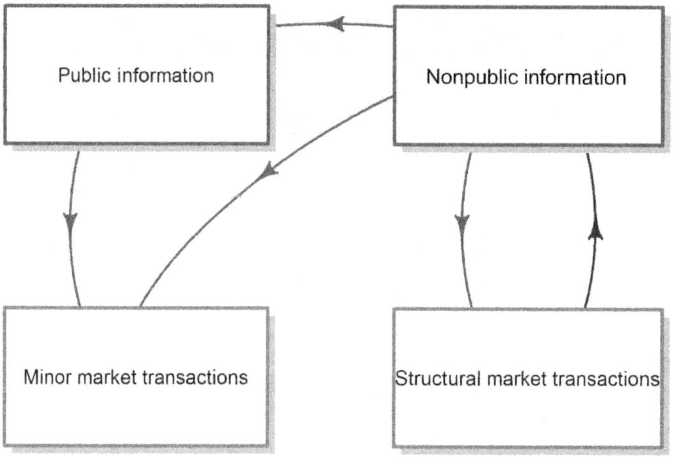

FIGURE 1 Information and market transactions: if an agent has nonpublic information and deals in minor trades it is often characterized as insider trading, with a small impact on prices. If the agent performs structural transactions in large volumes she can make the price oversensitive to the new information before it becomes public. If structural nonpublic information is made public it can also change the market equilibrium as the traders will try to adjust.

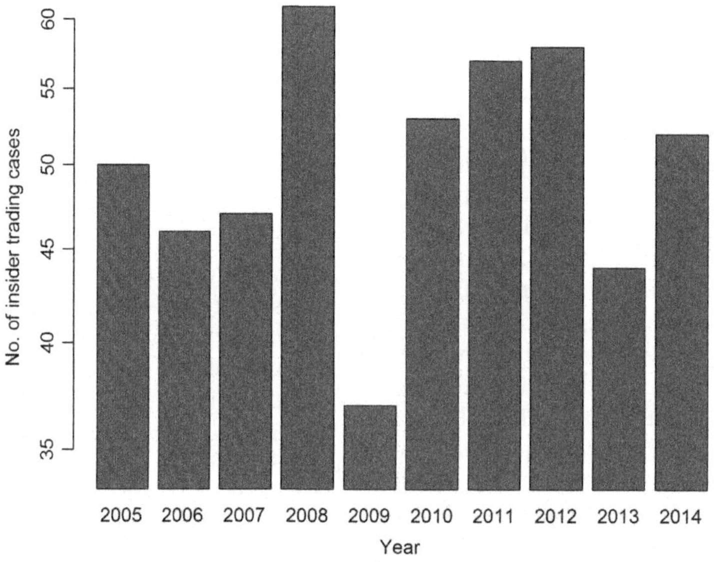

FIGURE 2 Number of insider trading cases reporting in the United States (SEC).

2 OVERVIEW OF INSIDER TRADING

Figure 2 shows the evolution of the number of insider trading cases in the United States as reported by the Security Exchange Commission (SEC). Insider trading is a term that most people associate with misconduct. But insider training also includes legal transactions when corporate executives, officers, directors, and employees, owning stocks or stock options in their own companies buy and sell those securities depending on the information that they might have working within that company. These types of trades should generally be reported to the domestic regulator. Nevertheless this is not an absolute rule; most likely in cases when employees from a company do trade, they have more information compared to other investors. Such a case occurred in 2006 among the Board members of the European aircraft constructor Airbus.[1] Senior managers had information about the delays in the delivery of the A380 super jumbo development, and they sold their shares before the market had that information.

AIRBUS CASE

Facts

The former Airbus CEO Noel Forgeard and current chief aircraft salesman John Leahy have been on trial since 2014 for selling Airbus stock in March 2006 even as they allegedly knew the A380 super jumbo development was behind schedule and the A350 long-range jet was to be redesigned. Soon after that episode Airbus shares fell sharply in June when the company disclosed delays on the A380 as shown in the graph below.

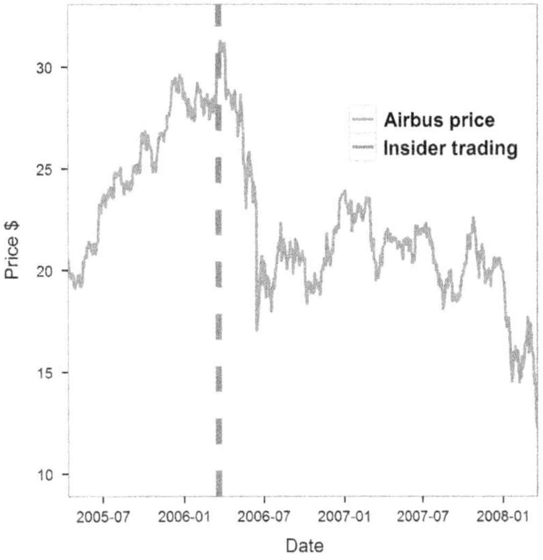

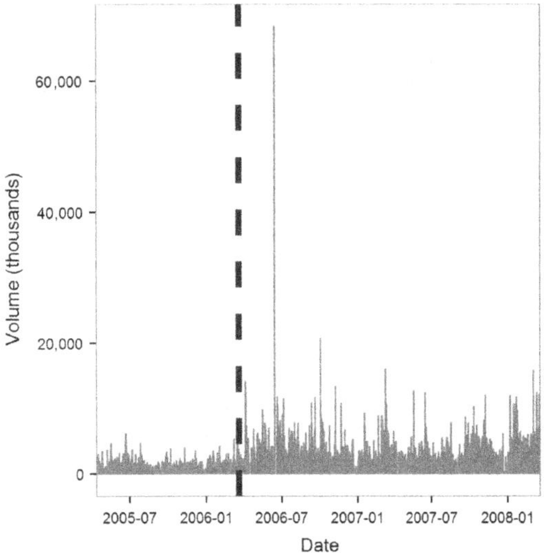

The insider trading had no particular effect in terms of volumes.

Aftermath

The French regulators investigated the insider trading charges for more than 3 years and dropped all charges against the 17 individuals accused at that time.

In the current trial, the French court considered that the executives and Airbus shareholders were

[1]Insider trading trial opens for current, former Airbus executives, http://www.wsj.com/articles/insider-trading-trial-opens-for-current-former-airbus-executives-1412350420.

privy to sensitive information about problems affecting the A380 and A350 programs, and should have refrained from selling their shares.

The court's criminal case is more focused on whether the executives had general knowledge that the A380 and A350 programs were headed for difficulties and how this affected the spread of this information to other investors. The seven individuals on trial face sentences of up to 2 years in prison and fines of up to 2.03 million dollars.

Illegal insider trading refers by the definition given by the SEC as the act of buying or selling a security, in breach of a fiduciary duty or other relationship of trust and confidence, while in possession of material, nonpublic information about that security. Insider trading breaches also include the action of spreading information or "tipping," to another person who uses that information for securities trading.

Despite the definition of insider trading being relatively straightforward, the typologies of real cases are much more numerous, and have several different causes. The term *material nonpublic information* is key in establishing a criminal case. The definition is purely qualitative and despite many guidelines in the jurisprudence there is still leeway in the comprehension of the term. Among other things the material feature of nonpublic information became observable only when action was taken on the basis of that information. For instance the change of color in the email signature of the CEO of a company can be considered immaterial. But if a trader that owns that nonpublic information does some trades that can be profit taking, the question about the materiality of that information may be the subject of debate. The materiality feature is often decided after action is taken. Another crucial point in insider trading cases is whether having that nonpublic information is the only factor that helped a trader to make a profit.

Insider trading cases can be distinguished depending on the flow the nonpublic information follows. First is when the nonpublic information is used by people with direct ties to the concerned company or asset. In this class can be included the cases when corporate officers, directors, and employees trade in the corporation's securities after having material nonpublic information about confidential corporate developments. Also these individuals can use this information through buffers including friends or family members who traded the securities after being tipped off with confidential material information. The second case is when the flow includes individuals with no direct ties to a corporation but who are bound by a contractual agreement to provide a specific service. This case includes attorneys, corporate finance advisers, strategy consultants, brokerage, and printing firms who obtain confidential material information when contracting for the corporation whose securities are traded. In this class should be mentioned also the employees of all regulatory bodies within a country or people working in governmental agencies with privileged access to nonpublic information.

Insider trading prosecutions are rare for some of the reasons outlined above. Regulators like the SEC in the United States try to keep the regulations in line with the outcomes of cases litigated in courts.

Insider trading is associated with high profile executives within corporations, but there are cases that can involve employees in support functions like printing or communication services. A relevant case is that of a print room employee from JPMorgan who passed on confidential information about mergers to an independent trader, who generated almost 1 million dollars in profits using the confidential information.[2]

[2]Ex-futures trader gets 4 years for using insider tips, http://www.bloomberg.com/news/articles/2013-03-11/selfemployed-trader-guilty-of-making-1-million-on-inside-tips.

Stealing Power Points

Richard Joseph, was an independent trader based in London, was found guilty in 2013 for making 1 million dollars on spread-betting between September 2007 and July 2008 with inside tips he received about forthcoming mergers. Joseph received the information from Ersin Mustafa, who worked in the print room at JPMorgan Chase & Co. Mustafa received around 400,000 dollars from Joseph for passing on this information along with others tips from his brother, Ali, who worked in the print room at UBS AG. Mustafa provided Joseph with M&A prospects he received in his printing room, that he sent electronically or printed.

Joseph's case was investigated in the FSA's Operation Saturn, which led to the arrests of eight men at the height of the financial crisis in 2008. Ersin Mustafa fled the UK in December 2009 and it is believed that he lives in Northern Cyprus on the Turkish side.

Trivia

Joseph pleaded not guilty to six charges of conspiracy to commit insider trading. He had worked in the finance industry in London in the late 1990s for a few firms and he made his reputation as a bond trader. He retired in 2008 in his late 30s and by that time he claimed to have 3.5 million pounds in the bank. His entourage claims that the regulators were hard on him, due to the fact that he was representing a minority in the City. He never worked for a big investment bank; he was self-taught, from a working class background, and black, thereby representing the upwardly mobile.

The detection of insider trading is far from being a simple task and the common signals like price and volumes rarely provide sufficient information or indicate abnormal activity. In many cases, the transactions following the use of material nonpublic information are not structural to the market and will not have much impact on the market equilibrium. If one adds to the equation spread betting and the trades involving derivatives having targeted securities as assets, the overall picture becomes more complicated. The surveillance of insider trading violations needs to be more sophisticated involving accounts with brokers and communications between various members of a corporation with access to privileged information.

One approach could be to build a social network of individuals within a corporation or among its contractors that have access to confidential information. The social network would have in each node the full picture of the person involved along with their immediate relations including family, colleagues, acquaintances, etc. Each node of the network should have knowledge of all the trades, communications or action related directly or indirectly to the confidential information. Once network has been set up, a link can be made between the different confidential information and the actions of people in the network.

An example of such an application of a social network is the case of Galleon Group and its flamboyant CEO, Raj Rajaratnam. In 2009,[3] Rajaratnam was arrested on charges of setting up a large insider trading scheme involving a hedge fund. Galleon Group's investor list had many technology executives including Anil Kumar, a McKinsey director, and Rajiv Goel, an Intel executive. Galleon has been accused in 2005 of illegal short selling and settled with the SEC for more than 2 million dollars.

The insider trading violation relied on a vast network of company insiders and consultants

[3] Arrest of hedge fund chief unsettles the industry, http://www.nytimes.com/2009/10/19/business/19insider.html?hp&_r=0.

to make more than 75 million dollars in profit from 2006 to 2009. The network involved a core of three individuals: Rajaratnam, Goel, and Kumar, all of them from Sri Lanka and educated at Wharton University. Each of the three indicted individuals had high profile positions in their companies and also were on the boards or had contacts with other big firms. For instance, Kumar was on the Goldman Sachs Board for a number of years. The network included executives from IBM and Intel.

In the aftermath Rajaratnam[4] was sentenced in 2011 to 11 years in prison and fined 92 million dollars, the largest penalty at that time for an insider trading case.

The case presented above underlines the role of service providing firms (finance advisors, consultants) in insider trading violations. Research published by Augustin et al. [69][5] investigated the presence of informed option trading around unexpected M&A public announcements. The analysis of the trading volume and implied volatility of the options underwritten on stocks over the 30 days preceding formal takeover announcements suggests that informed trading is more pervasive than one would expect.

A Logit model is proposed to describe the factors that drive the SEC-litigated insider trades in options ahead of M&A announcements characterized by a variable **Y**. **Y** takes the value 1 for a litigated case, which has a likelihood expressed as:

$$\mathbf{P}(\mathbf{Y}=1) = \frac{L}{1+e^{-kx}}$$

$$x = \beta_0 + \beta_1 S + \beta_2 C1 + \beta_3 C2 + \beta_4 C3 + \beta_3 T1 + \beta_4 P + \beta_5 C4 + \beta_6 T2 + \beta_7 F + \beta_8 \text{Region} + \epsilon_t),$$

where ϵ_t are the residuals, L and k are the parameters of the Logistic function, and β_i are the sensitivities of various factors. S takes the value 1 if the transaction is larger than the median M&A deal value, $C1$ indicates cash-financed takeovers, $C2$ identifies deals with a second bidder, $C3$ identifies completed deals that are not withdrawn or failed, and $T1$ indicates whether a bidder already had a toehold in the target company. **P** is 1 if the acquirer privatized the target postacquisition, $C4$ identifies transactions with a collar structure, $T2$ takes the value 1 for deals that have a termination fee that applies if the takeover negotiations fail, F indicates to the deal attitude, "Region" is 1 if the bidder is a US-based company. Augustin et al. [69] found that the driver for the SEC insider trading litigation is the size of a deal, and the completion of bids initiated by non-US bidders have a higher likelihood of litigation.

3 OUTLOOK

Wiretaps, lying and informants are the top reasons people get busted for insider trading today. [...]there were certain tricks of the trade you were expected to abide by if you were going to operate in the gray area:

- Never trade options on a sure thing, it is the first place they look.
- Always have a paper trail, an email pitching you the idea for every reason except the inside information.
- Buy more than you want and then sell some before the announcement. It shows misperception. If you knew about the announcement then why would you sell some right before?
- Never have inside information in print. Only use the phones (this one is changing).
- Find the derivative stocks that will benefit from the news, play those big.

[4]Judge fines Rajaratnam $92 million, http://www.hindustantimes.com/world-news/Americas/Judge-fines-Rajaratnam-92-million/Article1-766652.aspx.
[5]Study claims insider trading is more prevalent than previously thought, http://fortune.com/2014/06/17/insider-trading-study/.

- Be prepared for a phone call with the SEC. Play dumb, but have your story straight.
- Discuss the trading idea with other employees, but withhold the secret source.
- Reward your informant handsomely.

Turney Duff,[6] *a former trader at the hedge fund Galleon Group*

The interesting thing about insider trading is that as a financial crime it has many behavioral features in common with classic organized crime:

- Insider trading violations and classic organized crime tend to involve an inner circle of people, which facilitates the transmission of the information.
- Inside traders, like any other criminals, tend to avoid any traces or leaving any audit trails, thereby the investigations are based in many cases on informants.
- Inside traders, as any other criminals, have perfect alibis and proof showing that they were not involved in misconduct.

Therefore, tacking this type of crime needs ways and means different from other crimes like market manipulation. Firms do keep records of all conversations of their traders and firms' mobile and landline phones are taped, in case an investigation is required. With the increased numbers of insider trading investigations, many investment and trading firms have set up the practice of the *second phone*. The second phone is given by the firm but is not taped and is used for discussions which are *off the record* or are in the gray area. This makes the investigation work harder and this is the reason why in cases of insider trading authorities should use techniques specific to organized crime, like wiretapping or placing informants.

[6]The truth about insider trading, http://www.cnbc.com/id/101586358.

CHAPTER

3B

Ponzi Schemes

OUTLINE

1 BACKGROUND

The Madoff scandal brought to the attention of the public an old scam in the investment world based on a pyramidal-like structure. Generally speaking, in a pyramidal game or structure with multiple layers the marginal utility or gain of individuals from layer K is generated by the addition of a new layer $K + 1$. Without reducing the generality if each individual has the same utility then the number of individuals from the layer K should be higher than the number of individuals from layer $K + 1$ ($N_{K+1} > \kappa \cdot N_K$) where κ is a constant depending on the size of the marginal promised gain.

Figure 1 shows the mechanism of a pyramidal-like scam, the newest member fueling the gains of the previous members. Pyramidal processes are common in many walks of society from religions to multilayer marketing and from social security systems to financial investments. Nevertheless in the investment industry Ponzi schemes are deemed as illegal and generally lead to massive losses for investors.

According to the Security Exchange Commission a Ponzi scheme is an investment scam in which the gains paid to existing investors originate from funds contributed by new investors. Ponzi scheme organizers often deploy hard selling techniques to persuade investors to go for their high-return, low-risk opportunities. A successful Ponzi scheme needs an increasing number of investors and an increasing volume of investments. Both the number and the size are critical.

There are some semantic differences between pure pyramidal scams like multilevel distribution and financial Ponzi scams. In a pyramidal distribution scam, the newcomer makes one upfront payment and earns profits by finding others members to become distributors of a product. A Ponzi scheme generates high investment returns by simply handing over the money from the newcomers to the previous members.

http://dx.doi.org/10.1016/B978-0-12-801221-5.00006-3

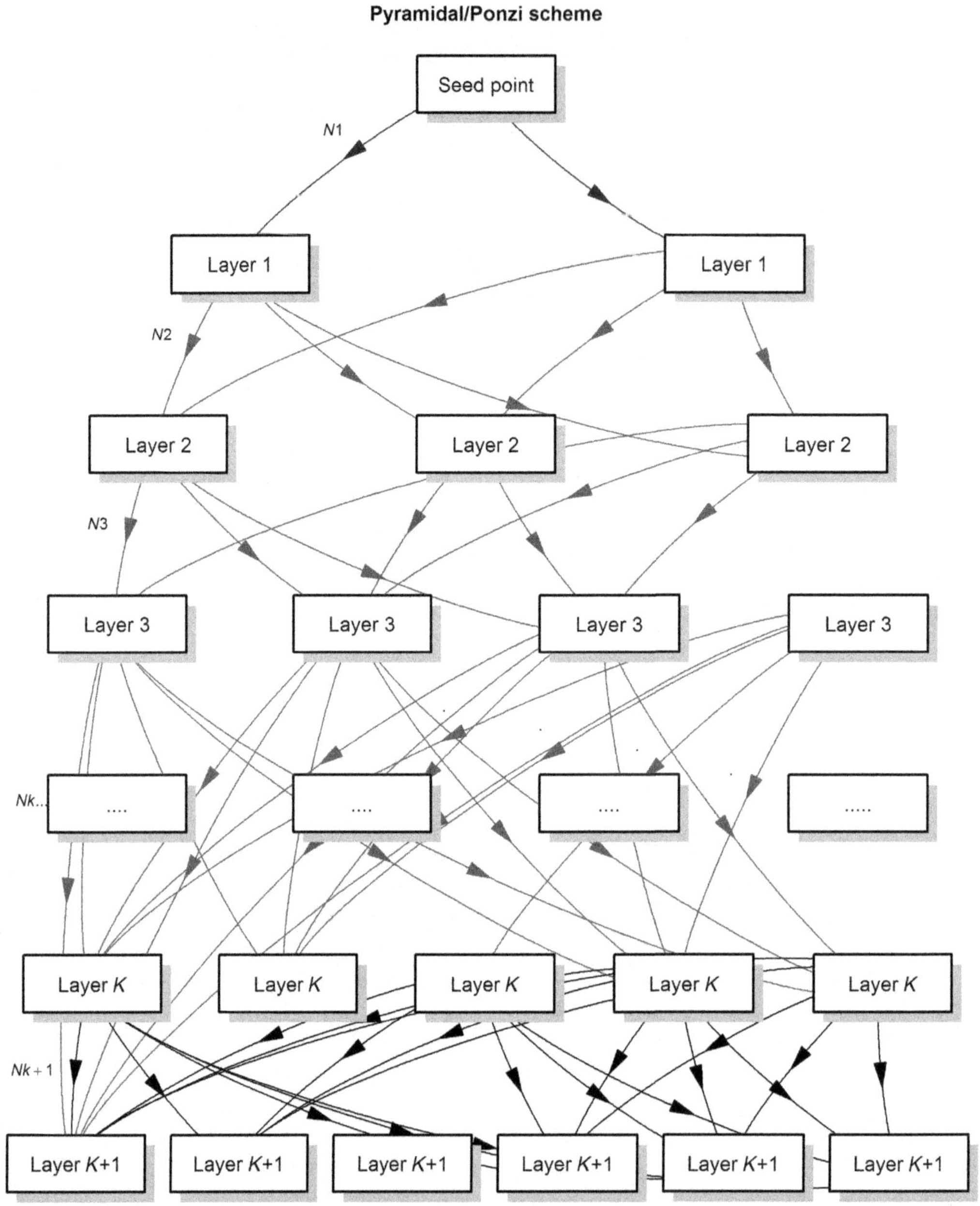

FIGURE 1 Ponzi/pyramidal scams. The scam structure is based on adding new members with an increasing contribution. To be sustainable the scam needs to add a high (infinite) number of members and a high volume of flows.

A common trait of both scams is that often the investment or the product does not exist or is profitable only to a small percentage. Another common point is that both are based on new layers of members that can provide the profits for the previous ones. In pyramidal scams, each member is responsible for building the next layer, while in Ponzi scams the process is centralized.

Also in the initial stage it is critical that the scam quickly finds new investors in order to pay the previous ones. Once completed the seeding stage the news about investors taking home high returns spreads. Having a growing number of investors is important as it then interests as many potential investors as possible through the spread of this news in the investment community. Having a growing volume of funds is crucial to be able to fulfill the promised return for the previous investors from the previous layer. As shown in the Figure 1, a Ponzi scheme needs an infinite number of layers in order to avoid collapse, but this is obviously impossible in reality. Therefore, any means of getting new investors or convincing new investors to reinvest their gains in the scam are used. More sophisticated pyramids use leverage in order to keep the pyramids alive or introduce constraints in the withdrawal of the funds. Social security systems in Europe for instance are, according to some recent research, involved in a Ponzi pyramid. With an inverse age pyramid and an economy in recession the only way to avoid collapse is by issuing new governmental debt, as is the case in European Union countries or Japan.

The first large-scale pyramidal scam is attributed to Charles Ponzi, who engineered in roaring 1920s, Boston an investment strategy aiming to provide 100% profit in over three months. The notable thing about that episode was that everything took place very quickly and the scam collapsed in the Summer of 1920 generating a loss that today would amount to 230 million dollars.

Among the regions where Ponzi scams emerge are the emerging economies or countries that have experienced political unrest. Ex-Soviet bloc countries are a good example in this sense. In Yeltsin's Russia in the 1990s a famous Ponzi scam occurred. Sergey Mavrodi founded the *MMM company* promising dividends of 1000%, through media and television. Mavrodi took at least 1.5 billion dollars within 5 years from at least 2 million people. When raided by the police Mavrodi convinced these investors that it was the government's fault and he was even elected to the Russian Duma, thereby obtaining immunity.

Russia's southern neighbor Romania experienced a Ponzi rush between 1992 and 1994 when the *Caritas* scam originated in Transylvania's capital Cluj. After going bust in 1994 the losses amounted to almost 1 billion dollars from at least 4 million people.

Ponzi scams in relation to financial markets do appear clustered since the Madoff event in 2008 as revealed by Ponzitracker.com, a database with all scams detected since 2008 mainly in the United States.[1]

In the same year, another scam generating a loss of 3.6 billion dollars was brought down by the federal US Government. The scam's central figure was Tom Peters, once the owner of the prestigious Polaroid brand. He generated a loss of 3.6 billion dollars in a Ponzi scheme. Table 1 shows some examples of large-scale Ponzi scams, illustrating that the biggest losses are from those schemes based in the United States. There is a growing trend of Ponzi scams in Asian countries with much more diversification in assets (commodities, crypto-currencies, etc.).

Innovation is a facilitating vector in Ponzi scams. The recent failure of the Hong Kong

[1]Ponzitracker.com, http://www.ponzitracker.com/ponzi-database/.

TABLE 1 Examples of Ponzi Scams

Year	Country	Initiator	Vehicle	Losses (million dollars)
1920	The USA	Ponzi	International reply coupons	265
2008	The USA	Thomas Petters	Hedge funds	3650
2008	The USA	Madoff	Hedge funds	18,000
2009	The USA	Allen Stanford	Financial services	7000
2009	The USA	Scott Rothstein	Investment funds	1500
2010	The USA	Nevin Shapiro	Investment funds	800
2011	The USA	James Fry	Investment funds	1500
2012	Indonesia	Jaya Komara	Meat trading	600
2013	India	Sudipta Sen	Real estate/film	335
2013	Singapore	Lee Song Teck	Gold	7
2014	The USA	Galemmo Glenn	Investment funds	34.5
2015	China	Hong Kong	Bitcoin	390

Note: *Since 2008 many scams have been discovered, mainly in the United States, accounting for billions of dollars in losses.*

Bitcoin exchange *MyCoin*,[2] which had over 3000 clients who invested an average of nearly 13,000 dollars, is a good example. MyCoin promised investors short-term returns exceeding 100% on an initial minimum 52,000 dollars investment, often hosting local events at luxury hotels. In December 2014, the company modified its withdrawal rules by preventing customers from fully cashing in their accounts unless they were able to recruit more investors. The company's website also quotes the price of one Bitcoin at 1.36 dollars, the market value in early 2015 being approximately 218.28 dollars per Bitcoin.

2 QUALITATIVE FEATURES

Ponzi schemes have some common features that can be assessed qualitatively, through the diligence process.

A Ponzi investment is generally presented to potential customers as high yield but with a guaranteed feature. High-yield returns are often associated with high risk. If an investment is promoted as bearing less or no risk it should raise questions.

As revealed by the Madoff case, Ponzi's returns are regular, positive, and less correlated with fundamentals regardless of overall market conditions. Investment returns, especially high yield, show fluctuations, and are irregular, due to the fact that they employ leveraged strategies. If an investment performance reports shows a smooth time series of returns then this can be an alarm signal.

The strategies which produce these guaranteed returns are generally not fully disclosed by the scammer, leaving a secretive aura. The companies promoting this scam are closely knit, meaning that there are few or no independent auditors, custodians, and asset keepers. The scammers control the process from start to finish.

When suspicions are aroused or after a certain time, investors might want to withdraw their investment and the returns. Most likely the broker or the sales of the fund start to be difficult to assess, requiring heavy paperwork and trying to encourage investors to "roll over" their positions.

Ponzi schemes usually involve investments that have not been registered with the regulators. The sellers of those strategies are advisors or brokers who are also unlicensed. Most Ponzi schemes operate through unregulated intermediary firms.

[2]Investors file police complaints alleging MyCoin Bitcoin fraud, http://www.ibtimes.co.uk/investors-file-police-complaints-alleging-mycoin-bitcoin-fraud-1487561.

3 QUANTITATIVE FEATURES

Artzrouni [70] provided a straightforward attempt to model a Ponzi scheme. The dynamics of a Ponzi scheme are described using a first-order linear differential equation. The model is based on a promised, unrealistic interest rate r_p, the actual, realized nominal interest rate r_n, the rate at which new deposits are accumulated r_i, and the withdrawal rate r_w. Assuming that all these rates are constant and that the withdrawal rate r_w applies at each time t to the promised accumulated capital including the promised rate, then the withdrawal amount at time t by those who invested an initial amount K at $t = 0$ can be written as: $r_w \cdot K \cdot e^{t(r_p - r_w)}$. In addition, we assume that those who invested $s(u)$ at time u will want to withdraw at time $t > u$ a quantity $r_w \cdot s(u) \cdot e^{(rp-rw)(t-u)}$.

The total withdrawal at time t from initial and new layers that were added between times 0 and t is the sum of the integral of the withdrawals from new layers added between 0 and t and the previously calculated withdrawals from the initial deposit K, giving a cumulated amount at time t of

$$W_t = r_w \left(K \cdot e^{t(r_p - r_w)} + \int_0^t s(u)\, e^{(r_p - r_w)(t-u)}\, du \right) \quad (1)$$

A simple assumption that can be made for the dynamics of the cash inflow $s(t)$ is an exponential function:

$$s(t) = s_0\, e^{r_i t} \quad (2)$$

where a positive r_i denotes an increased inflow and a negative r_i an exponentially decaying inflow. With this assumption the amount withdrawn at time t has the following analytical form:

$$W_t = r_w\, e^{r_p - r_w} \left(K + s_0 \frac{e^{t(r_w + r_i - r_p)} - 1}{r_w + r_i - r_p} \right) \quad (3)$$

If S_t is the amount in the Ponzi fund at time t then the temporal dynamic can be written as:

$$\frac{dS_t}{dt} = r_m \cdot S_t + s(t) - W_t \quad S_0 = K \quad (4)$$

As shown in Artzrouni [70] the dynamic of the total in a Ponzi scheme can be expressed in a closed analytical form:

$$S_t = a \cdot e^{(b + r_m) \cdot t} + c \cdot e^{(d + r_m) \cdot t} + f \cdot e^{r_m \cdot t} \quad (5)$$

where a, b, c, d, and f are constants that depend on r_m, r_i, r_w, and r_p.

The maximum amount of funds gathered by a Ponzi scam ($\max(S_t)$) and the time when this maximum is reached (t_{max}) are expressed as[3]:

$$\max(S_t) = a \left(\frac{-cd}{ab} \right)^{\frac{b}{b-d}} + c \left(\frac{-cd}{ab} \right)^{\frac{d}{b-d}} + f \quad (6)$$

$$t_{max} = \frac{\ln(\frac{-cd}{ab})}{b - d} \quad (7)$$

Figure 2 shows the dynamic of the fund for a Ponzi scheme, showing a profit which reaches a maximum before going on to collapse. These results are in agreement with the findings of Cunha et al. [71], who presented a computational approach to the mathematical model described above.

A more advanced model was proposed by Parodi [72], which developed a Ponzi Geometric Brownian Motion model for exponentially growing capital (S_t^{sto}) following the stochastic differential equation:

$$dS_t^{sto} = (r_m \cdot S_t^{sto} + s(t) - W_t) \cdot dt + S_t^{sto} \sigma\, dB_t \quad (8)$$

where B_t is the noise term.

The solution of this stochastic differential equation has the following form:

$$S_t^{sto} = \zeta_t S_0^{sto}\, e^{(r_m - 0.5\sigma^2)t + \sigma B_t} \quad (9)$$

where ζ_t is a function depending on:

$$\zeta_t = \zeta(t, r_m, r_p, r_i, r_w, \sigma) \quad (10)$$

[3] Two conditions are required: $\frac{cd}{ab} < 0$ and $\frac{1 + cd/ab}{b-d} < 0$.

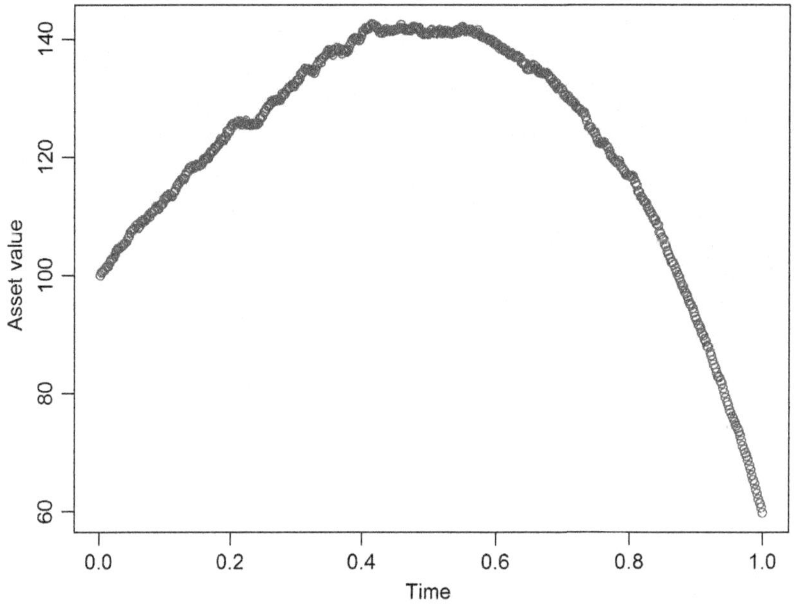

FIGURE 2 Evolution of total assets of a Ponzi scam assuming no volatility.

Under a stochastic dynamic the expected value of the assets is:

$$\mathbf{E}[S_t^{\text{sto}}] = a \cdot e^{(b+r_\text{m})\cdot t} + c \cdot e^{(d+r_\text{m})\cdot t} + f \cdot e^{r_\text{m}\cdot t} \quad (11)$$

where $a, b, c, d,$ and f are the constants introduced above and the expected value is expressed as $\mathbf{E}[S_t^{\text{sto}}] = S_t^{\text{sto}}(\sigma = 0) = S_t$.

Based on Equation 9 the evolution of the stochastic form S_t^{sto} can be simulated using through a Monte Carlo approach with a high number of trajectories (N_{sim}), therefore the probability of collapse (PC, the probability of the total funds going to zero) given a certain time horizon as well as the total time to collapse can be computed:

$$\text{PC} = \frac{(S_t^{\text{sto}} < 0)^*}{N_{\text{sim}}} \quad (12)$$

Figure 3 shows some trajectories of total funds of a Ponzi scheme with a volatility of 25%. The results are discussed in the following sections.

3.1 Volume Is Critical

An important feature of running a Ponzi fraud is to keep a steady flow of new investors. Naturally like in every investment industry these inflows should exist, but the rate at which this happens is also critical. Like any other pyramidal-like structure the inflow will decay exponentially as it gets more and more difficult to bring in new investors. If the decay rate r_i is too high then the PC increases and also the time to collapse decreases. The scam needs to keep the growth rate of the inflows positive in order to avoid collapse and suspicion. Figure 4 shows the relationship between the probability and time of collapse and the inflow rate r_i. The lower the inflow rate the higher the PC and the shorter the collapse time. For negative inflow rates (decreasing amount of new investments) collapse is almost certain.

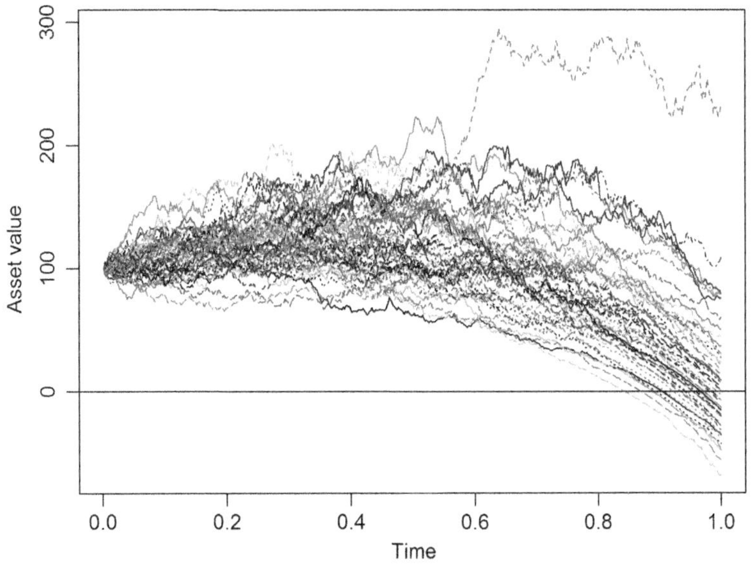

FIGURE 3 Volatility of Ponzi assets using Monte Carlo simulation.

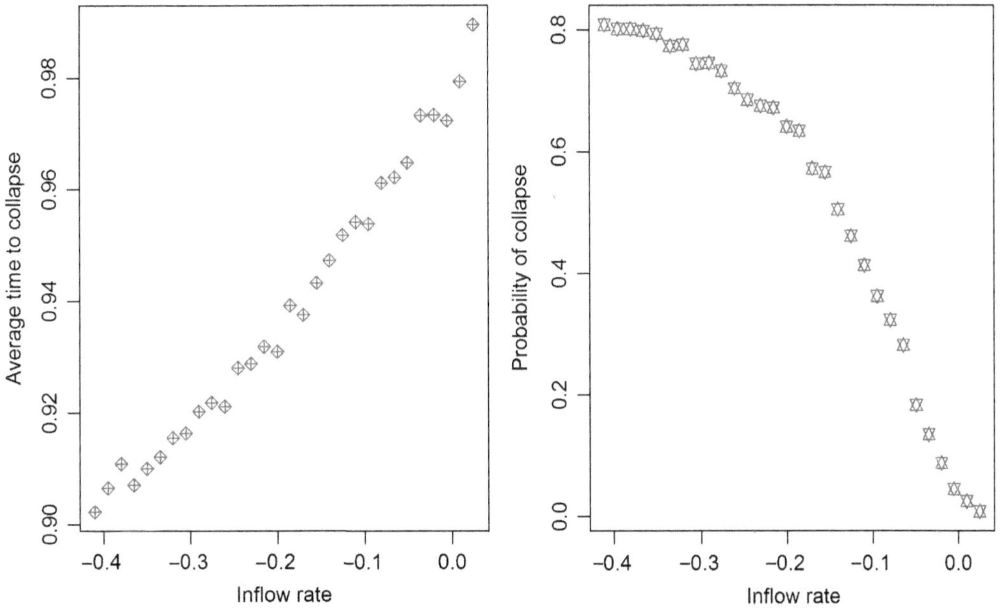

FIGURE 4 Ponzi scheme with various capital inflow rates. The lower the inflow rate the higher the probability of collapse and the shorter the time to collapse. For negative inflow rates (decreasing amount of new investments) collapse is almost certain.

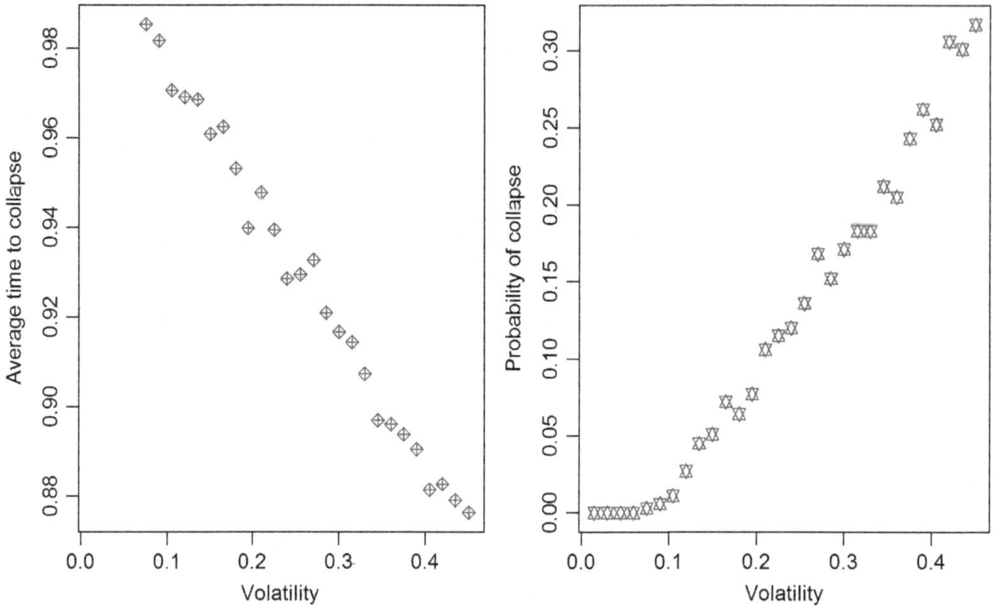

FIGURE 5 Ponzi scam and volatility. The higher the volatility the higher the probability of collapse, despite the fact that there is more legitimate investment in the funds.

3.2 A *Risk-Free* Scam

Ponzi scams have the option to invest parts or all of the proceedings in real investment assets to get returns that are risk free. This would, however, expose the portfolio to volatility. In the simulation presented in Figure 5 different return volatility combinations are assessed with the excess return to volatility ratio kept constant. Interestingly a Ponzi scam has no incentive to produce an excessive return as the higher the volatility, the higher the PC, and the shorter the time to collapse. Allegedly Ponzi had limited knowledge of finance and investment strategies, but this would not have helped him because as proven above the lower the market risk the longer the survival of the scam. The same conclusion was found in the case of Madoff's scam. He never deployed the strategy on NASDAQ as he claimed, the market liquidity not being able to absorb orders corresponding to the 50 billion dollars of assets he was managing.

3.3 Problems With Withdrawal

The big risk for a scam is if customers start suddenly to demand their funds back. The same Monte Carlo approach shows that the PC increases sharply with the increase of the withdrawal rate; if the withdrawal rate is higher than the promised rate the collapse probability tends toward 1. One conclusion of these simulations is that the scam should make withdrawal more difficult as time goes on. It also requires reinvestment of the returns of the initial investors. Many Ponzi scams have operated in this way strategies to delay the payments, including difficulties in reaching the investment company, paperwork issues, etc. Figure 6 shows the relationship between the probability and time of collapse and the withdrawal rate r_W. The higher the inflow rate the higher the PC and the shorter the collapse time. For high inflow rates (decreasing amount of new investments) collapse is almost certain.

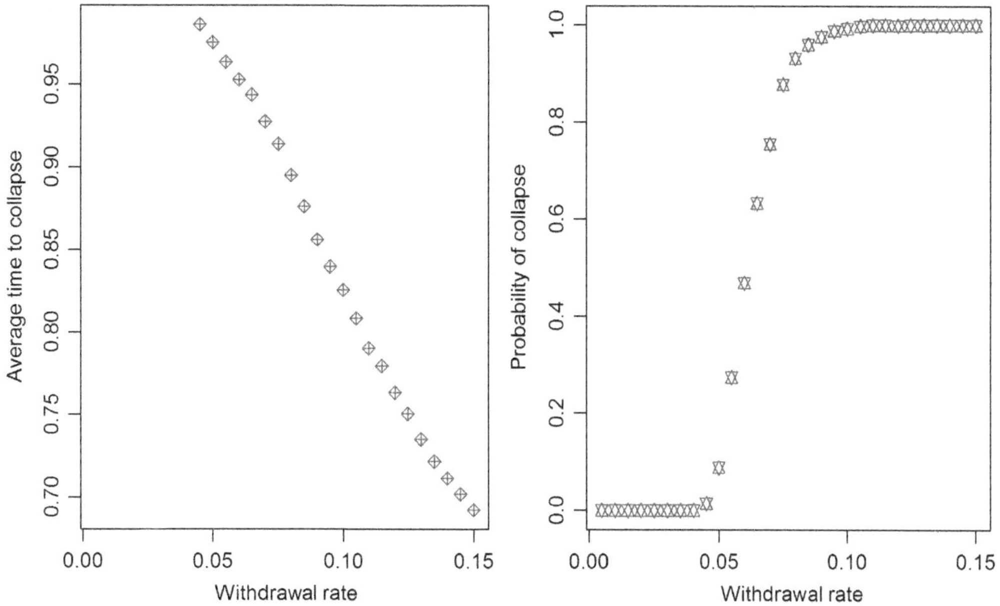

FIGURE 6 Relationship between the Ponzi scam and the withdrawal rate r_W. The higher the inflow rate the higher the probability of collapse and the shorter the time to collapse. For high inflow rates (decreasing amount of new investments) collapse is almost certain.

3.4 Statistical Testing of the Ponzi Scam

A way to test if an investment has a Ponzi pattern is to assess whether the evolution of its total funds follows the trajectory described in the previous section. Statistically for a given discrete time series of total assets from a fund $S^*_{t_i}$ where $t_i, i = (1, 2, \ldots, N)$ are the reporting dates of the fund's performance which are generally monthly:

$$\mathbf{E}(S^*_{t_i}) = a \cdot e^{(b+r_m)\cdot t_i} + c \cdot e^{(d+r_m)\cdot t_i} + f \cdot e^{r_m \cdot t_i} \quad (13)$$

Assuming that the expected value for the Ponzi funds can be represented as the functional form $\Im(\theta)$ with $\theta = (a, b, c, d, f)$ for a given series of funds the parameter θ can be estimated by minimizing the following function:

$$\mathbf{F}(\theta) = \sum_{i=1}^{N} \left| \frac{S^*_{t_i} - \Im(\theta)}{S^*_{t_i}} \right|^2 \quad (14)$$

If parameters θ are not significant for a given confidence interval than the respective fund is not suspicious. Assessing the relevance of the estimated parameter can be done analytically in a number of ways, but this can lead to many false positives. Employing a resampling method for the confidence interval of parameter θ has two advantages. First, it makes no parametric assumptions about the underlying distributions of the series and second it can assess the various subsamples based on different parts of the history of $S^*_{t_i}$. The asset levels are variable so the resampling cannot be done purely randomly and the time sequence should be respected. Therefore, a modified jackknife method is proposed:

1. Form the time series of asset values $S^*_{t_i}$ with a percentage h (h can be around 20%) of the observations "jackknifed", but keep the temporal order for the rest, thereby generating a new series $S^{*,1}_{t_i}$.

2. Values of parameters θ_i^* are estimated by minimizing the functional form from Equation 14.
3. Repeat the first steps for a large number of simulations Nt, generating a distribution of the parameter set θ_j^* with $j = (1, 2, \ldots, Nt)$.

TABLE 2 Results of Ponzi Pattern Test

Country	No. of funds testing positive	Total no. of funds	Ratio of funds testing positive (%)
Australia	2	48	4.17
Bermuda	1	51	1.96
Canada	1	116	0.86
Cayman Islands	4	61	6.56
France	18	181	9.94
Germany	4	360	1.11
Ireland	1	85	1.18
Liechtenstein	1	10	10.00
Luxembourg	2	156	1.28
The Netherlands	1	25	4.00
Singapore	1	45	2.22
South Africa	2	29	6.90
Switzerland	8	712	1.12
The UK	12	1010	1.19
The USA	71	2397	2.96
Vanuatu	1	1	100

Notes: *The number of funds for which the test did not reject the Ponzi pattern as well as the total number of funds are listed. Interestingly countries with less strict regulation like tax havens have a higher proportion of suspicious funds.*

Once the distribution of the parameter estimate θ^* is found, the confidence interval can be computed and it can be assessed if the parameter is relevant or not.

Table 2 shows the results of the test above for the performance of the Hedge Funds included in the Barclay Hedge Funds database, a total of 5823 funds. The number of funds for which the test did not reject the Ponzi pattern as well as the total number of funds are given. Interestingly countries with less strict regulation like the tax havens have higher proportion of suspicious funds.

4 OUTLOOK

Almost a century after Charles Ponzi tricked many honest investors from Boston, the scam that bears his name along with the many similar pyramidal schemes have for many years left many investors out of pocket. With the structural issues of economic growth in the Western countries and the slowdown of emerging economies the Ponzi schemes will probably find fertile ground, especially in those countries or markets with less or no regulation. Thus Asian countries with a growing middle class population but with less regulation in the investment field will be susceptible to new Ponzi schemes. In the same way crypto-currencies like Bitcoins and even less sophisticated digital currencies or other online-based markets can be exploited by the Ponzi schemers.

CHAPTER

3C

Pump and Dump—Market Manipulation

OUTLINE

1 BACKGROUND

Described by Joseph de la Vega[1] in the late seventeenth century as common practice in the Amsterdam Stock Exchange, market manipulation embraces many forms and employs many methods, that have evolved over the time. From classic stocks and commodities futures to sophisticated derivatives almost all financial instruments can be subjected to manipulation. From a legal perspective market manipulation is defined as an intentional act aiming to deceive investors by controlling or artificially altering the market for a security. Manipulation techniques are diverse and include: spreading misleading information, taking control over the available asset for trading, or creating an artificial image upon the demand for a security by speculative trading.

Table 1 shows a glossary of manipulation techniques often encountered in securities markets. Cornering the market is one of the better known to the public, occurring in stock and commodities markets. Pump and dump techniques are one of the most disruptive techniques as they imply the spreading of misleading information concerning a stock. Enron was probably the best known example of stock pumping, but generally this technique does not target big caps and focuses more on microcaps, or shares traded over-the-counter.

From Table 2 it can be seen that manipulation has many typologies. A more systematic classification is given in the seminal work of Allen and Gale [73], which proposed three main categories, completed by a fourth category that gained momentum with the increase in high-frequency trading:

[1] "Among the plays which men perform in taking different parts in this magnificent world theater, the greatest comedy is played at the Exchange. There, the speculators excel in tricks, they do business and find excuses wherein hiding places, concealment of facts, quarrels, provocations, mockery, idle talk, violent desires, collusion, artful deception, betrayals, cheatings, and even tragic end are to be found." **Joseph de la Vega, Confusion of Confusions [20].**

http://dx.doi.org/10.1016/B978-0-12-801221-5.00007-5

TABLE 1 Brief Glossary of Terms Used to Describe Various Market Manipulation Activities

Technique	Description
Painting the tape (screen)	A group of traders creates trading activity and spread rumors to drive up the price of a stock or a benchmark
Front running	If a trader places a large order (buy) and the other traders are aware, they will try to buy the market ahead in order to profit from the large trader
Quote matching	A trader who knows the price at which another large trader will place a future trade will place the very exact same order ahead of it, in order create an advantageous position
Wash trading	A trader is selling through a broker and repurchasing with another broker the same security to generate activity and increase the price
Bear raiding	A trader or a group of traders is involved in heavy selling or short selling in order to push down the price of a stock
Cornering	A trader purchases a big share of a particular stock or commodity to gain control of the supply to increase the price. Cornering can be done through both spot and futures markets
Short squeezing	A trader squeezes a group of short sellers out of their short positions, by taking a big position in the spot market
Spoofing	A trader who is long in a security makes a series of buy orders for that security and immediately cancels them, thereby increasing the impression of activity and demand and bringing more traders that will increase the price
Marking the close	A trader places a large number of orders before the close of the market, in order to drive up the value of a portfolio or a fund
Fomenting	A trader creates a false impression about a company through rumors or trades with brokerages in order to drive its stock one way or another
Pegging	A practice of an investor buying large amounts of an underlying commodity or security close to the expiry date of a derivative held by the investor
Pump and dump	A trader long on a microcap stock spreads a lot of false news about the firm in order to pump the price up. Once the price reaches the target the trader dumps the stock
Short and distort	A trader short on a stock spreads a lot of false news about the firm in order to decrease the price
Boiler room	A group of salespersons contact a potential client and persuade them with hard sales techniques to pursue an investment

TABLE 2 Examples of Market Manipulation

Year	Commodity	Synopsis
1863	Harlem Railroad	A famous financier cornered the market of Harlem Railroad stock
1901	American Steel	The company's directors bear raided the stock, by closing production capacities
1994	Venezuelan bonds	A hedge fund tried to manipulate the price of the bonds for activating a barrier option
2006-2012	Gold and Silver	A group of banks manipulated the prices of Gold and Silver
2006-2008	LIBOR/EURIBOR	A group of banks manipulated the average of the individual LIBOR and EURIBOR contributions
2008-2012	FX	A group of banks used techniques like wash trading and painting the tape to manipulate the benchmarks of many currencies
2014	NASDAQ-listed stocks	Athena capital was the first case of market manipulation involving high-frequency trading

- *Action-based manipulation*, which is based on actions that change the actual or perceived value of the assets. The American Steel example is such a case. Action-based manipulation can also occur in commodities markets when a party can reduce or increase the production of that commodity in order to change the price levels.
- *Information-based manipulation*, which is based on spreading misrepresentations and false information to the investor community. The avenues used for spreading false news have evolved over time according to technology. Initially newspapers and boiler rooms were the main tools for pumping stocks. Also, those with privileged relationships with brokers could spread rumors to clients for big fees from the stock pumper. Emails and the Internet represented the first technological jump in pumping techniques, allowing the dissemination of false news to a larger number of people. Spam filters tried to address this issue, but the arrival of social media and social networks made it possible for false claims to be disseminated on Facebook and Twitter. Bots, automatic programs that create and distribute content online, are another sophisticated development in pump and dump schemes.
- *Trade-based manipulation*, which is based on simple long and short trades of a speculator, without taking any publicly observable actions to alter the value of the firm or releasing false information to change the price. Corners and short squeezes are examples of trade-based manipulation, being based on simply longing the market.
- *Order-based manipulation*, which is a type of manipulation based on canceled or nonexecuted orders. A trader or a group of traders place many orders (limit orders) to artificially create the image of a direction in the market or to simply congest the market.

Another feature in differentiating the manipulation is the time horizon over which the market price is maintained at "abnormal" levels. These types of manipulation can be allocated to the following classes:

- *Long-run manipulation* (3 months to years): Manipulating prices over a long period of time requires a complex mechanism, which should pass under the radar of analysts and investors. Enron is a good example of this, the company managing to capture the imagination of market with rogue information for some years. The LIBOR manipulation is another example, the level of LIBOR being kept artificially low for many months during the financial crisis in 2008.
- *Medium-run manipulation* (2 weeks to 3 months): Information-based manipulation such as that concerning biotech firms. False information about a product is discriminated to current and potential investors.
- *Short-run manipulation* (1 day to 2 weeks): Manipulation involving derivatives. When a counterparty hedges its derivatives portfolio, the hedging trades might have a massive impact on the underlying price.
- *Daily manipulation* (<1 day): Daily manipulation includes many avenues like "banging the close," the use of dark pools and the typical high-frequency trading schemes that will be discussed in a separate chapter.

2 TRADE-BASED MANIPULATION ECONOMICS

During the prohibition years in New York the numbers game was very popular. In this game, a lot of people played a number and the winner was chosen from a random number generator. The random numbers at that time were the betting odds on dog races. An accountant, Otto

Berman,[2] working for reputed mobster Dutch Schultz, was able to work out in his head the amount of money one should bet in order to move the betting odds in line with the number played in the numbers game. Otto Berman was able to solve this mentally to optimize the problem and to provide a risk-free strategy.

Similarly to that anecdotal episode, the economics of trade-based manipulation as introduced by Allen and Gale [73] and further developed by Aggarwal and Wu [74] are modeled with three type of investors:

1. Informed party investors who have information about the future moves of the price up or down with respective stock prices S_u and S_d. These types of investors which is the most important can be *truthful investors* if they buy when the stock goes up or *manipulators* if they long the market when they know it will go down.
2. Information seekers who try to develop strategy based on past prices and on the trades observed on the market.
3. Uniformed investors, who do not have any type of information or trade. They constitute the biggest category in terms of numbers.

Figure 1 shows the possible evolution of such a configuration. Following Aggarwal and Wu [74] we assume that an informed trader can be a manipulator with probability γ, a truthful investor with probability δ or can remain indifferent and take no action with probability $1-\gamma-\delta$. The informed trader takes a position at $t=1$ and sells at $t=2$. If he is truthful the price may end up as S_u or S_d. If he is a manipulator the price will end up at S_d. For this framework a key point is the assumption made by Allen and Gale [73] that considers that uniformed traders are uncertain whether the informed trader is truthful or whether he intends to manipulate the price. This pooling hypothesis facilitates profits in a manipulation economy.

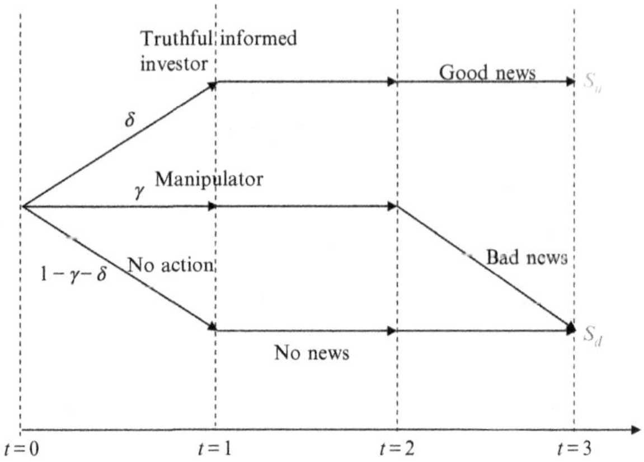

FIGURE 1 Manipulation flow. The informed trader can be a manipulator with probability γ, a truthful investor with probability δ or can remain indifferent and take no action with probability $1-\gamma-\delta$. The informed trader takes a position at $t = 1$ and sells at $t = 2$. If he is truthful the price may end up at S_u or S_d. If he is a manipulator the price will end up at S_d.

To determine the equilibrium state of the manipulation economy S, the market price of the stock is linearly related to Q, the quantity demanded:

$$S(Q) = c + s \cdot Q \tag{1}$$

where $Q < \frac{S_u - c}{s}$ is the total amount of stock outstanding corresponding to a price S_u.

To find the optimal manipulation economy Aggarwal and Wu [74] conjectured that the manipulator and the truthful informed party pool their strategies, by buying the same quantity of shares at time 1 and selling these shares at time 2. Assuming N information seekers each demanding q_2^{Di} at time 2 the final price and the profit for each party are determined by the maximization of the profit for each information seeker and for the informed party. Uninformed investors are considered to ignore optimality. The optimization should satisfy each party as follows:

[2] The famous quote from *The Godfather Movie*: "*Nothing personal it is just business*," is attributed to Otto Berman.

1. An informed trader buys $q1$ shares at time $t = 1$ and sells them at time $t = 2$. The price of acquisition depends on demand, being the only buyer at the time: $c + s \cdot q_1$. The selling price is determined by the demand at time $t = 2$, generated by the information seekers who follow the trend and decide to enter in the economy given the trade of the informed trader.
2. Each of the N information seekers buys at time $t = 2$ a quantity q_2^{Di} at a price $(c + s \sum_i q_2^{Di})$ that will be set at S_u or at S_d depending on whether the informed trader is legitimate or rogue. The probability of the two states at time $t = 1$ is $\pi = \delta/(\delta + \gamma)$ for S_u and $1 - \pi$ for S_d.

The global optimization is written as:

$$\underbrace{\max}_{q_2^{Di}} \left\{ (1-\pi) \left[S_u q_2^{Di} - \left(c + s \sum_i q_2^{Di} \right) q_2^{Di} \right] + \pi \left[S_u q_2^{Di} - \left(c + s \sum_i q_2^{Di} \right) q_2^{Di} \right] \right\} \tag{2}$$

$$\underbrace{\max}_{q_1} \left\{ (c + s \cdot q_2^D) q_1 - (c + s \cdot q_1) q_1 \right\} \tag{3}$$

where $q_2^D = \sum_i q_2^{Di}$.

The optimal profit for each information seeker and for the manipulator are

$$\text{Profit}_i = \frac{((S_u - c) - \pi(S_u - S_d))^2}{(N+1)^2 s} \tag{4}$$

$$\text{Profit}_M = \frac{N^2((S_u - c) - \pi(S_u - S_d))^2}{(N+1)^2 4s} \tag{5}$$

For this result it can be seen that the profit of the manipulator relative to the profit of the investment seekers increases with N, the number of investors from the investment seekers category.

This framework occurs in many areas of manipulation. A good example would be the Abacus case involving Goldman Sachs, a Wall Street firm, Paulson & Co a hedge fund, and IKB, a German bank. Here Paulson was the informed trader (truthful) that anticipated the fall of the credit market, Goldman Sachs the alleged manipulator and IKB the information seeker. Paulson and Goldman entered into a pooled strategy creating Abacus, the product intended to benefit from a rise in the credit market. Before the crisis they sold the product to IKB, which took the losses and also shorted the credit market.

3 DARK POOLS

As discussed in the previous sections, traders of large orders face the risk of manipulative schemes like front-running and quote-matching, when the other traders in the market are informed about the large order [75]. Some alternative trading systems providing large traders with liquidity that would avoid this problem have been seen in the past decade. In fact exchanges and over-the-counter are not the only avenues a trade can take for execution. Figure 2 shows the various alternatives, including dark pools and the electronic communication network (ECN). Dark pools are alternative trading systems where trades are anonymous and executed in small blocks. They are used mainly by large traders who do not want to affect the market price with their large orders and consequently obtain adverse prices for their trades. An ECN collects, displays, and executes anonymously orders from major brokerages and individual traders without a middleman.

Dark pools started to gain market share in the United States after 2005 when the new Regulation National Market System encouraged newer and faster electronic trading centers to compete with the traditional exchanges and broker dealers. The same trend was followed in Europe.

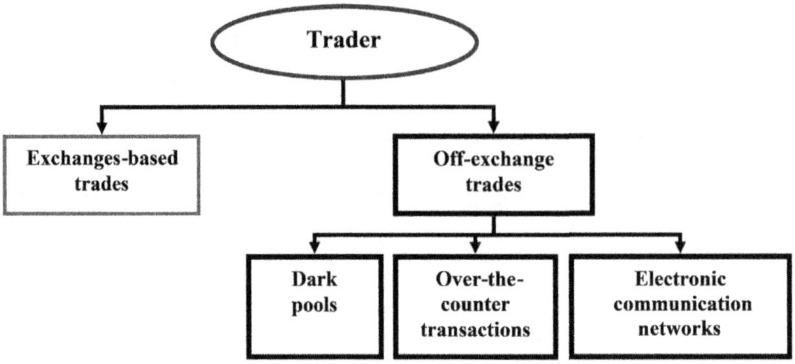

FIGURE 2 Avenues for a trader: off-exchange-based trades, dark pools and ECNs are cost-effective alternatives. Dark pools are alternative trading systems where trades are anonymous and executed in small blocks. They are used mainly by large traders who do not want to affect the market price with their large orders and consequently obtain adverse prices for their trades. An ECN, displays, and executes anonymously orders from major brokerages and individual traders without a middleman.

The lack of transparency[3] of dark pools and the fact that they are used extensively by high-frequency transfer was underlined by the popular work of Michael Lewis [76]. Without doubt the fact that large traders are protected from front running is not entirely positive in the price discovery process. A basic example would be if a trader wants to sell a big volume of a stock due to the fact that he knows that the company has losses. If he executed the trade through an exchange or with a broker the information that the company might face distress will be spread to other traders and thus they will come with lower bids. On the other hand if the stock is sold through a dark pool, completely anonymously and executed in small blocks, the information will not be available to the market and thus the seller will have a much better price than on an exchange. But the drawback is that the price will not reflect the full information about the stock. Traders could use this to control the flow of information between dark pools and exchanges: hence new manipulation schemes can be developed.

[3]Dark markets may be more harmful than high-frequency trading, http://www.reuters.com/article/2014/04/07/us-markets-darkpools-analysis-idUSBREA3605M20140407.

4 DERIVATIVES AND MANIPULATION

Derivatives markets have become prominent in the past two decades, and investment banks saw the options market as a new business opportunity. When a derivatives is marketed the underwriter takes hedging positions.

VENEZUELAN BONDS[a]

In November 1994 LM International, a US hedge fund, purchased $500 million of "knock-in" put options from Merrill Lynch and other dealers, for Steinhardt Management (hedge fund led by Michael Steinhardt), having as assets Venezuelan bonds. The barrier of up-and-in puts was established at $0.51 with a strike of $0.45. For this type of option ($K = \$0.45, H = \$0.51$) the payoff can be written as:

$$\text{Payoff} = (K - S_{\text{T}})^{+}\mathbf{1}_{\{\max_{0\le t\le T} S_t > H\}} \quad (6)$$

where S_t is the price of the Venezuelan bond and T is the maturity of the option. Ideally for the hedge funds the Venezuelan bond should rise as high as 51 cents in order to activate the option and than to fall below the strike level of 45 cents as shown in the figure below.

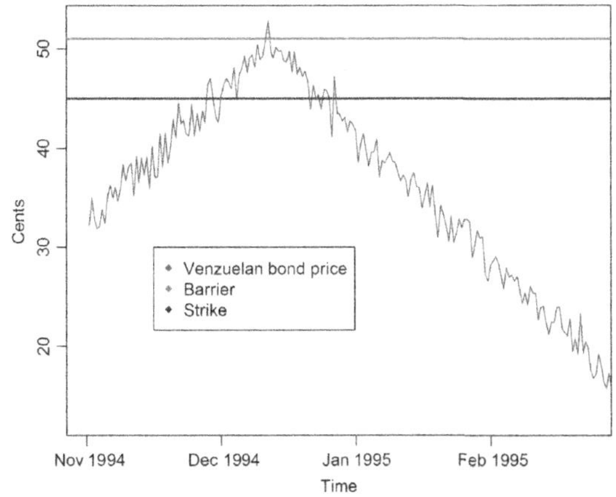

Thus after buying the barrier put options the hedge funds tried to boost the prices through longing call options and the underlying bonds. The sellers of call options needed to buy the assets to insure the risk neutral hedge. The total value of bonds accumulated by the hedge funds was between \$0.8 and \$1 billion, representing 13% of the outstanding total. In early December, the bonds increased from about \$0.45 to almost \$0.51. During those days the market flashed a "bid" price of \$0.51 but the respective brokerage house indicated that was an error.

Aftermath

In January the bonds felt to \$0.3875, thereby making the put option valuable if it was knocked in. The hedge funds and the underwriters (Merrill Lynch) entered into a dispute whether the barrier was activated. The Security Exchange Commission also began an investigation into alleged price manipulation.

[a] Funds, Merrill Battle over Venezuelan bonds, *Wall Street Journal*, February 15, 1995.

Gallmeyer and Seppi [77] proposed a straightforward framework to model the actions of agents who wish to manipulate the value of their derivative holdings by placing market orders in the underlying market, which alter the price temporarily. The model can be extended when the manipulators place an order on another derivative, which will oblige its sellers to place market orders in the underlying market. Gallmeyer and Seppi [77] imposed a price dynamic $S(t)$ which depends on the $\Delta\theta_t$ variations of the aggregate assets for all active traders as follows:

$$S(t, r_t, \Delta\theta_t) = S_{\mathrm{F}}(t, r_t) \cdot (1 + g(\Delta\theta_t)) \qquad (7)$$

where the fundamental price $S_{\mathrm{F}}(t, r_t)$ is expressed as:

$$S_{\mathrm{F}}(t, r_t) = S_{\mathrm{F}} \prod_{s=1}^{t} (1 + r_s) \quad r_s \in \{u, d\} \qquad (8)$$

where S_{F} is the price of the asset at $t = 0$ and r_{s} is the price variation obeying a binomial tree model in which the price can go up or down with the returns $\{u, d\}$. The risk neutrality condition implies that the risk-free rate is the weighted sum of up and down returns $r_{\mathrm{f}} = p_{\mathrm{u}}u + (1 - p_{\mathrm{u}})d$, p_{u} being the probability of the price going up. The function $g()$ describes the relationship between share prices and the net changes in the stock holdings:

$$g() = \begin{cases} g_0 & \Delta\theta_t \geq g_0 \\ \gamma\Delta\theta_t & g_0\gamma \leq \Delta\theta_t < -g_0 \\ -g_0 & \Delta\theta_t < -g_0 \end{cases} \qquad (9)$$

To illustrate this type of manipulation we assume that a purchaser of a barrier call[4] *down and in* option (strike K_{e} and barrier H) enters into a manipulation and to alter the price he also buys a vanilla put from various market makers and

[4] In regard to the barrier option the reputed financier George Soros affirmed: *Knock out options relate to ordinary options the way crack relates to cocaine* [78].

brokers with strike K_v and also shorts the market of the asset. The problem for the manipulator is to find the right quantities of puts in order to be sure that she can end up with a positive profit. Specifically for the barrier option the strike K_e is 80, the knock-in barrier H is 70 and the strike of the vanilla put K_v is 100, the option being at the money $S_0 = 100$. What the manipulator wants to achieve here is to push the price so low in order to activate the barrier and to make her barrier option valuable. Initially the barrier option is very out of the money and is therefore very cheap. On the other hand, the put option is at the money, thereby maximizing the volume of spot which will be shorted by its seller for hedging purposes. If the quantity of put is big enough the hedging action will push the price down according to Equation 8. In addition, the manipulators also shorten the asset in order to add momentum to the bearish trend. The final value of the manipulator's transactions at the expiration of the option T is:

$$\begin{aligned} V(T) =&\beta \max(K_v - S(T, \Delta\theta_T), 0) \\ &+ \max(S(T, \Delta\theta(T)) - K_e, 0)\mathbf{1}_{\{S_t<H\}} \\ &- P_v(0) - P_e(0) + \Delta\theta_0^m(S_{t^*} - S(0)) \end{aligned}$$

where β is the volume of puts bought by the manipulator, $\Delta\theta_0^m$ is the amount of the asset which is shorted by the manipulator, and $t^* = \min_{0\leq t\leq T} S_t < H \quad \underbrace{\min}_{\{0<t\leq T;\, S_t<H\}} \quad t$ is the time when the price hits the barrier. $P_v(0)$ is the price paid for the put and $P_e(0)$ is the price paid for the barrier option.

The economics behind this scheme is to find the amount of puts to be bought and the amount of short positions that would maximize the portfolio at maturity:

$$\underbrace{\max}_{\Delta\theta,\beta} E(V(T)|\Delta\theta, \beta) \qquad (10)$$

A second-degree effect appears when the price hits the barrier, and the delta of the barrier call jumps in value. Thus the seller of the barrier option will start to buy shares, thereby pulling the price up, while the put seller will cut their hedging position. Therefore, the barrier option will enter positive payoff territory.

The optimization of Equation 10 can be done by simulating the price and the volumes through a Monte Carlo approach. Figure 3 shows the value of the manipulation profit depending on the amount of puts held. It can be observed that at the break-even point there is a jump from a loss to a profit. For that volume of puts the price can be pushed to the barrier level.

Furthermore for a better understanding of the mechanism the results of the simulations are shown for a failed manipulation (Figure 4) and for a successful manipulation (Figure 5). For a failed manipulation the value of the barrier call remains low over time, and the put finishes in the money as the price ends in a bearish region. It is assumed that the manipulation makes the price of the asset nonstationary. The P&L of the manipulator oscillates around zero for the horizon of the option.

In the case of a successful manipulation the price of the barrier option increases constantly over time. The delta of the barrier option jumps when the spot price reaches the barrier. Therefore, the seller of the knock-in option will start to hedge the option, buying the spot and supporting the price signal. The price of the vanilla put drops and the option ends up out of the money.

Figure 5 also shows some large swings in gamma level. If the underwriter of the barrier call wants to be gamma neutral and he hedges the gamma risk by buying and selling the vanilla option, this action might also influence the market of plain derivatives and implicitly the level of the implied volatility. Therefore, a further step in developing the above model is to incorporate the effect of option traded volume at the level of the implied volatility. In the following equation, the dynamic of the volatility level can be expressed as

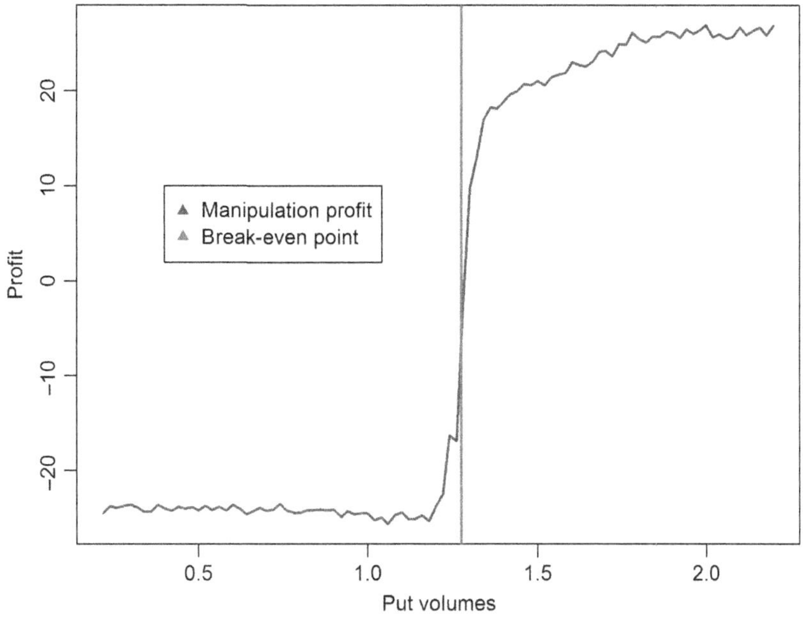

FIGURE 3 The value of the manipulation profit is dependent on the amount of puts held.

$$\sigma(t, \Delta\theta_t^o) = \sigma_{\mathrm{F}}(t) \cdot (1 + g_\sigma^o(\Delta\theta_t^o)) \quad (11)$$

where $\Delta\theta_t^o$ is the variation in the volumes of vanilla options and $g^o()$ captures the relationship between the volatility level and the variation of option volumes. The fundamental volatility $\sigma_{\mathrm{F}}(t)$ can follow a classic stochastic process expressed as:

$$\mathrm{d}\sigma_{\mathrm{F}}(t) = a(t, \sigma_{\mathrm{F}}(t))\,\mathrm{d}t + b(t, \sigma_{\mathrm{F}}(t))\,\mathrm{d}B_t \quad (12)$$

where $a(t, \sigma_{\mathrm{F}}(t))$ and $b(t, \sigma_{\mathrm{F}}(t))$ are characteristic functions of the dynamic.

Horst and Naujokat [79] expanded this framework for cases of illiquid markets, whereas option traders may have an incentive to increase their portfolio value by using their influence on the dynamics of the asset. It should be recalled that Jerome Kerviel, the rogue trader of Societe Generale, was a market maker of turbo options and was using his huge positions in big European stock indexes in order to alter the likelihood of those options ending up in the money.

Kraft and Kühn [80] showed that a large trader might have an incentive to issue options if they are valued by markets based on traditional Black-Scholes prices. He can *underhedge* if he has a negative price impact, thereby manipulating the option's payoff. For a positive price impact he has an incentive to overhedge the option position generating extra profit from the stock position exceeding a perfect hedge.

5 OUTLOOK

No matter what I bet, life is decided. But what kills you is usually not one point, but the ace of spades.
Vladimir's Central, Michael Krug, Russian poet and composer

Altering the price discovery process in financial markets through manipulation reduces efficiency. Manipulative tactics have evolved over time and employ the latest innovation like

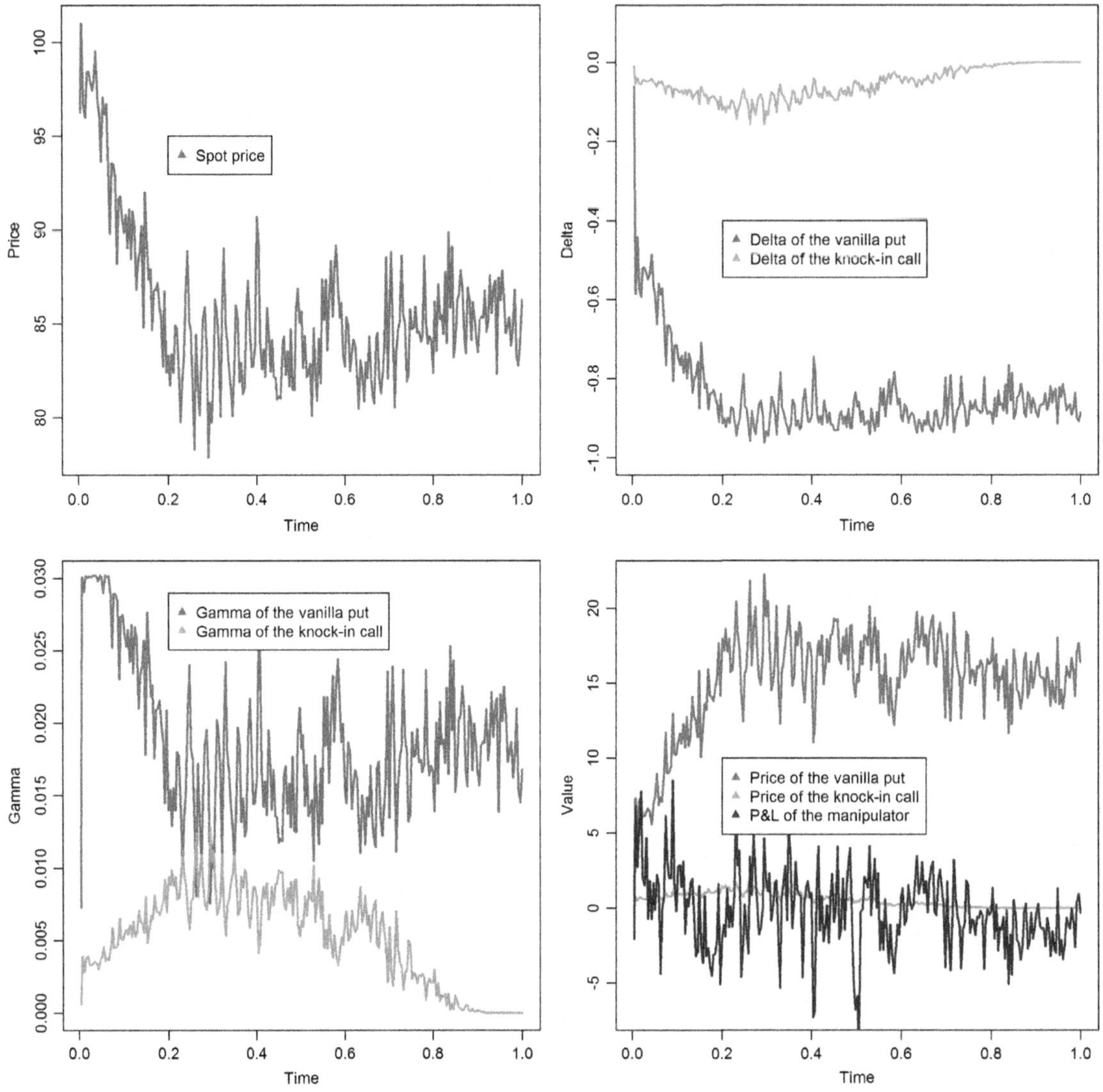

FIGURE 4 Failed manipulation: the value of the barrier call remains low over time, and the put finishes in the money as the price ends in a bearish region. It is assumed that the manipulation makes the price of the asset nonstationary. The P&L of the manipulator oscillates around zero for the horizon of the option.

the Internet and social media, thereby necessitating a renewal in the theories concerning manipulation.

Large traders could also have disadvantages in traditional exchanges, which were demonstrated by the FX manipulation cases. Informed traders can take profit from a foreseeable big order in the market with techniques like front running. The extensive use of dark liquidity pools can open avenues for other types of manipulation which are so far less understood and studied.

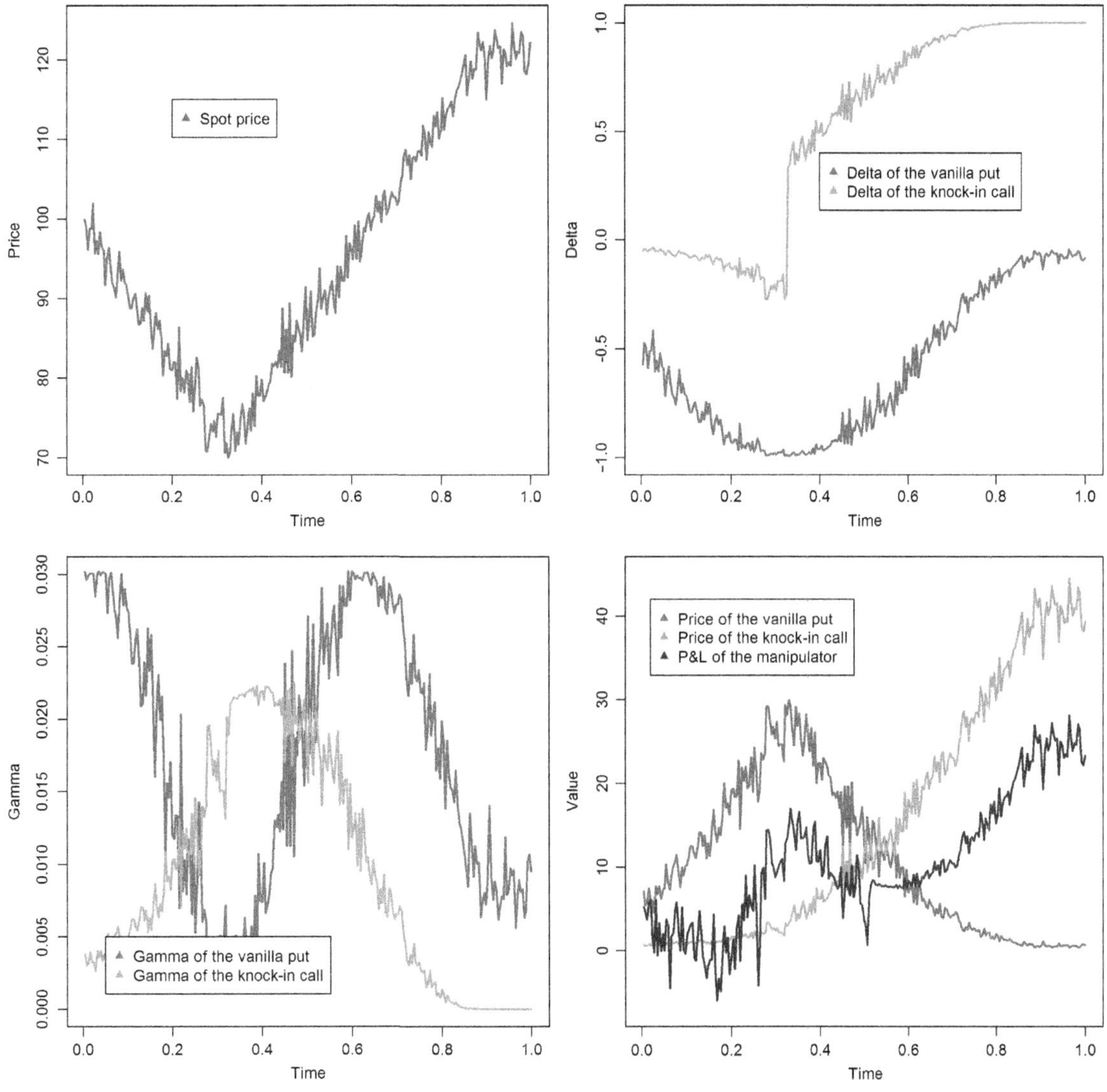

FIGURE 5 Successful manipulation: the price of the barrier option increases constantly over time. The delta of the barrier option jumps when the spot price reaches the barrier. Therefore, the seller of the knock-in option will start to hedge the option, buying the spot and supporting the price signal. The price of the vanilla put drops and the option ends up out of the money.

There is less focus on the very stringent issue of derivatives in relation to market manipulation. Markets can be efficient but the corresponding derivatives market might not be. Trades in the derivatives market which are usually over the counter are delta hedged on the spot market. Therefore, a big position in a derivative can cause a large change in the asset price. Furthermore, if the seller of the derivative, in particular an exotic derivative, hedges the gamma risk or the correlation or the cross-asset risk this could also have an impact on the sampled values of market parameters like volatilities and correlations.

CHAPTER

3D

Rogue Trading

OUTLINE

1 BACKGROUND

A rogue trader is an employee of a financial institution which makes independent decisions on buying and selling financial instruments, despite not having the authorization to execute them for the accounts of clients or for proprietary trading. Rogue traders take large speculative positions very often through directional trades trying at the same time to hide the real accounts of their transactions.

Rogue traders can be classified based on their approach of exposing the bank to those large positions and their intention to commit a criminal act (Table 1). In most of the publicized cases like that of Nick Leeson the real rogue positions were hidden through sham accounting or through fictitious positions. The forging or manipulation of accounts is the key element that allows the accumulation of this kind of position over a long period. Other cases of rogue trading do not involve false accounts but within the limits allowed by the bank the trader can create huge exposure over time especially when the market conditions change over time. One example is that of the London whale Bruno Iskil.

An intermediate case is when a trader does not commit any accounting manipulation or fraud but tries to trick the controls, by giving the impression that his positions are within the normal limits. For example a trader who has a large position in the futures markets and at the end of the day would write a series of sell tickets equal to the quasi totality of the position. When the risk managers review the trading book, they would find only a small percentage of the real position on the books. The trader would repeat these tactics each day, canceling the sell transactions and retaking them in order to mask the real underlying position. These kinds of actions to hide the rogue trades are not easy to detect, if the risk manager is not aware of the scam.

The crucial question is whether the rogue traders can be considered as criminals or not. Traders like Leeson, Adobolis, and Kerviel have

http://dx.doi.org/10.1016/B978-0-12-801221-5.00008-7

TABLE 1 Types of Rogue Trading

Features	Trade dissimulation	No dissimulation
No criminal intent	*Kerviel, Leeson*	*Iskil*
Criminal intent	Adobolis Hamanaka	Hunter

been sent to prison on criminal charges. Nevertheless their actions were not intended to generate profits for their banks nor to undermine their activities. Furthermore the main figures of rogue trading did not personally benefit from their unauthorized actions. There are also cases when there is criminal intent in rogue trading, where the trader carries out a criminal enterprise that would bring benefits to the trader.

Yasuo Hamanaka, aka Mr Five Percent, Sumitomo star copper trader, is an example of a rogue trader who used unusually large positions in both copper spot and futures trades to manipulate the market, which is a criminal offense. He managed to keep the copper market high for many years, and despite the official story that his trades were unknown to his management, allegedly Sumitomo were aware of his actions. When the market turned its cap the corporation made a massive loss and dismissed the trader who controlled 5% of the copper market. A case of rogue trading with criminal intent which did not have any dissimulation in the trading books was that of Brian Hunter, a star gas trader who ruined the hedge fund Amaranth generating losses of more than 6 billion dollars while trying to manipulate the North American gas market.

2 HISTORIC OVERVIEW

According to Toshihide Iguchi,[1] the rogue trader from the 1995 class, *less than 5% of unauthorized financial trading cases may have been reported.* They correspond to those big losses which are above a certain threshold and cannot be hidden from the public. Losses of a few billion are difficult to hide, while smaller losses of millions of dollars are easier to conceal.

Table 2 shows a compiled dataset of trading losses that have occurred over the past 20 years, underlining the rogue trading cases. Interestingly Leeson's loss that pushed Barings into bankruptcy is currently in 12th place on the list. The top trade is surprisingly not classified as rogue trade and comes from Morgan Stanley's credit desk in the turmoil of the financial crisis. Jerome Kerviel generated the biggest loss among the rogue traders. It can be observed that most of the losses, both trading and rogue, occurred during the financial crisis of 2008.

The real questions that arise in this context are:

- What is the real size of all rogue trading cases including those accounting only for a few million?
- What is the real frequency of rogue trading including those rogue trades that generated profits?

Among the series of small rogue trading losses is the case of Rochdale Securities,[2] a 60-person brokerage house in Connecticut that in 2012 experienced a loss of more than 5 million dollars, 1000 times smaller than the Kerviel case, but bigger than the firm's capital could absorb, thereby forcing into a bankruptcy situation. The rogue trader was Rochdale's employee David Miller, who bought 1.625 million shares of Apple stock in the hours before Apple announced its third-quarter earnings in 2012. If the company's stock price rose, he planned to take the profits, and if it dropped, he hoped to claim it was an

[1]Ex-Daiwa rogue trader says most unauthorized trades hidden, http://www.bloomberg.com/news/articles/2014-04-30/ex-daiwa-rogue-trader-says-bulk-of-unauthorized-trades-hidden.

[2]Morgan Stanley pays $4 million fine in rogue trader case, http://dealbook.nytimes.com/2014/12/10/morgan-stanley-pays-4-million-fine-in-rogue-trader-case/?_r=0.

TABLE 2 Trading Losses Ranked by Size Indicating (in Bold Face) the Cases of Rogue Trading

Rank	Rogue trading	Loss ($, billions)	Country	Bank	Asset	Year	Trader's name
1	No	8.67	United States	Morgan Stanley	Credit Default Swaps	2008	Howie Hubler
2	Yes	6.95	France	Société Générale	European Index Futures	2008	**Jerome Kerviel**
3	Yes	6.69	United States	Amaranth Advisors	Gas Futures	2006	**Brian Hunter**
4	No	5.85	United States	Long Term Capital Management	Interest Rate and Equity Derivatives	1998	John Meriwether
5	Yes	5.80	United Kingdom	JPMorgan Chase	Credit Default Swaps	2012	**Bruno Iksil**
6	Yes	3.46	Japan	Sumitomo Corporation	Copper Futures	1996	**Yasuo Hamanaka**
7	No	2.43	Brazil	Aracruz	FX Options	2008	Zagury/Sotero
8	No	2.38	United States	Orange County	Leveraged bond investments	1994	Robert Citron
9	No	2.28	Germany	Metallgesellschaft	Oil Futures	1993	Heinz Schimmelbusch
10	Yes	1.83	United Kingdom	UBS	Equities ETF and Delta 1	2011	**Kweku Adoboli**
11	No	1.82	China	CITIC Pacific	Foreign Exchange Trading	2008	Frances Yung
12	Yes	1.78	Singapore	Barings Bank	Nikkei Futures	1995	**Nick Leeson**
13	No	1.74	United States	Deutsche Bank	Derivatives	2008	Boaz Weinstein
14	No	1.56	Austria	BAWAG	Foreign Exchange Trading	2000	Flottl/Elsne
15	Yes	1.50	Japan	Daiwa Bank	Bonds	1995	**Toshihide Iguchi**
16	No	1.46	United Kingdom	Soros Fund	SP 500 Futures	1987	George Soros
17	Yes	1.06	France	Groupe Caisse d'Epargne	Derivatives	2008	**Boris Picano-Nacci**
18	No	1.05	Brazil	Sadia	FX and Credit Options	2008	Ferreira/Ballejo

error in trading. Apple's shares fell and a big loss was generated, closing Rochdale's activity and landing Miller in prison for 30 months. In the aftermath of the affair the prime broker, Morgan Stanley, was fined 4 million dollars for failing to respect the trading limit of Rochdale, which accounted for 200 million dollars on a daily basis. But the Wall Street giant increased in that day the trading limit to 750 million dollars which allowed the rogue trader to take a long position on Apple shares.

This example shows that rogue trades can be very heterogeneous in morphology and the severity and frequency of these losses can be complicated to assess.

3 JEROME KERVIEL CASE

One of the best documented cases in the rogue trading world is the Societe Generale episode. Following the outbreak of the scandal in January 2008 the internal auditor conducted a special audit called project GREEN[3] which was made public and provided much useful information about the way the fraud was perpetrated over time. At the time his rogue position was uncovered Jérôme Kerviel was a trader with the Delta One[4] desk on the Turbo warrants[5] market within the equity derivatives division.

The report's first conclusion was that this position was built over some years including the following phases:

1. The initial phase had episodes in 2005 and 2006 with some fraudulent transactions (up to 15 million euros on positions between June 2005 and February 2006, up to 135 million euros from February 2006 onwards, mainly on the equity markets).
2. In the second phase from late January 2007 Kerviel constituted a short position on index futures reaching 28 billion euros on June 30, 2007 and generating a total profit of 1.5 billion euros.
3. The final phase between January 2 and January 18, 2008 consisted in a long position on index futures, 49 billion euros, discovered on January 20 then unwound between January 21 and January 23, leading to gross losses of 6.4 billion euros and a net loss of 4.9 billion euros).

Interestingly Kerviel was positive in the books just a few weeks before being discovered and went from a positive to a negative position in a very short time.

Working previously in the Back/Middle Office team he was fully aware of the control system and he employed a series of techniques to conceal his fraudulent directional positions including:

- booking "fictitious trades," canceling positions and latent earnings generated by fraudulent positions;
- booking pairs of fictitious transactions of equal quantities of the same stock for different "off-market" prices in order to conceal the realized earnings without creating a directional position; and
- booking "provision flows," consisting of the modification of the Front Office mark to market valuation. This option was available on the desk in order to adjust for the model bias, but should have been accessible only to the assistant trader and not the trader himself.

[3]MISSION GREEN, https://www.societegenerale.com/sites/default/files/20%20F%C3%A9vrier%202008%20Rapport%20d%27%C3%A9tape%20du%20Comit%C3%A9%20sp%C3%A9cial%20du%20Conseil%20d%27administration%20de%20la%20Soci%C3%A9t%C3%A9%20G%C3%A9n%C3%A9rale.pdf.

[4]Delta One desks have a mandate to track an asset as closely as possible by taking positions on other instruments ($\Delta = 1$); it is often associated with exchange traded funds (ETFs) and swaps. Delta One desks trade in various clusters like FX, equities, interest rates, and commodities.

[5]The bank had an activity of market making on the barrier option, selling a call option with a known out barrier ("calls down and out"). Kerviel was in charge of the delta hedging of this product.

Some warning signs were there before the day when the fraud was discovered, but Kerviel's controllers and managers ignored them.

The first warning signs were generated by the extent of the initial margin and by the margin calls. Having huge positions in the futures exchanges they indeed required message liquidity inflows to cover the initial margin. One of the exchanges EUREX sent a letter to SocGen in 2007 about Kerviel's positions but was ignored for unknown reasons. Figure 1 shows the evolution of cash flows sent by SocGen to Fimat brokerage comparing the proportion used for Kerviel's trades with the total amount for all SocGen positions. After January 2008 the amounts allocated for covering Kerviel's margin call represent an important part of all fees paid to Fimat.

A second warning sign was the origin of Kerviel's P&L as well as the evolution of his Mark to Market, which raised issues to the risk manager but for some reason was never audited in detail. Each month his emails to the Back/Middle Office contained all kind of explanations for his fictitious positions. For example on December 31, 2007, the risk manager sent an email to Kerviel on the subject "Valuation JK + EUR 1,464,129,513," representing an amount close to the real earnings as recalculated in the aftermath. The positive positions

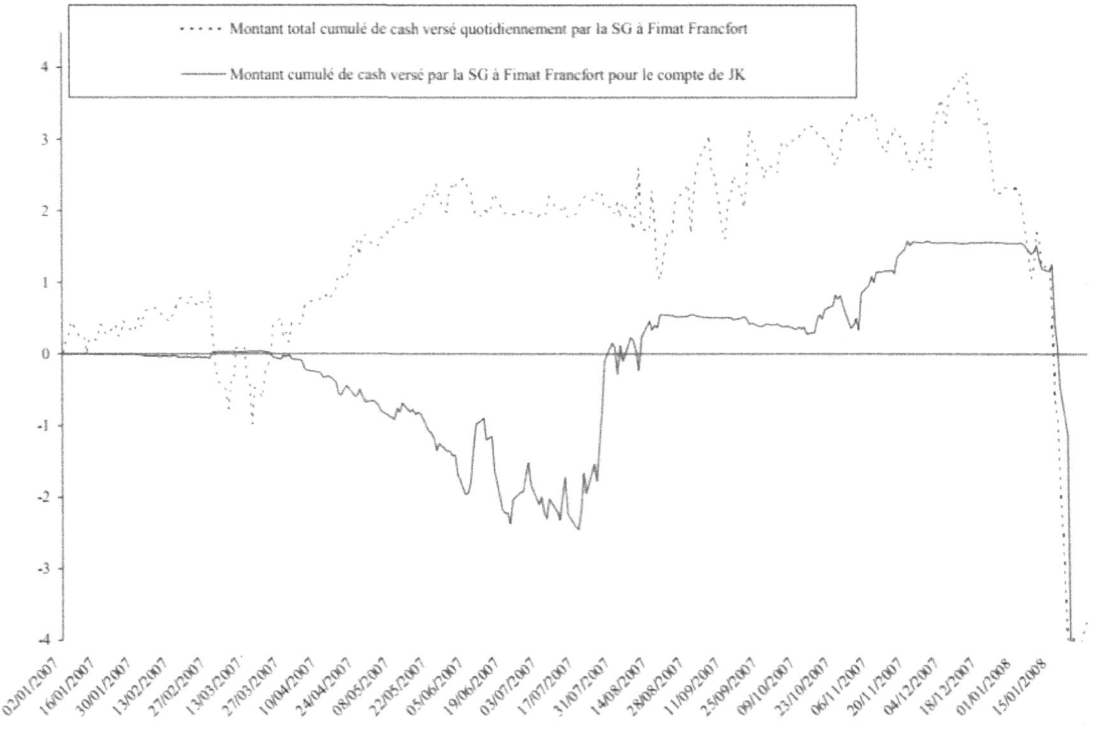

FIGURE 1 Evolution cash flows sent by SocGen to Fimat brokerage comparing the proportion used for Kerviel's trades (plain line) with the total amount for all SocGen positions (dashed line). After January 2008 the amounts allocated for covering Kerviel's margin call represent an important part of all fees paid to Fimat. *Source: Societe Generale GREEN report.*

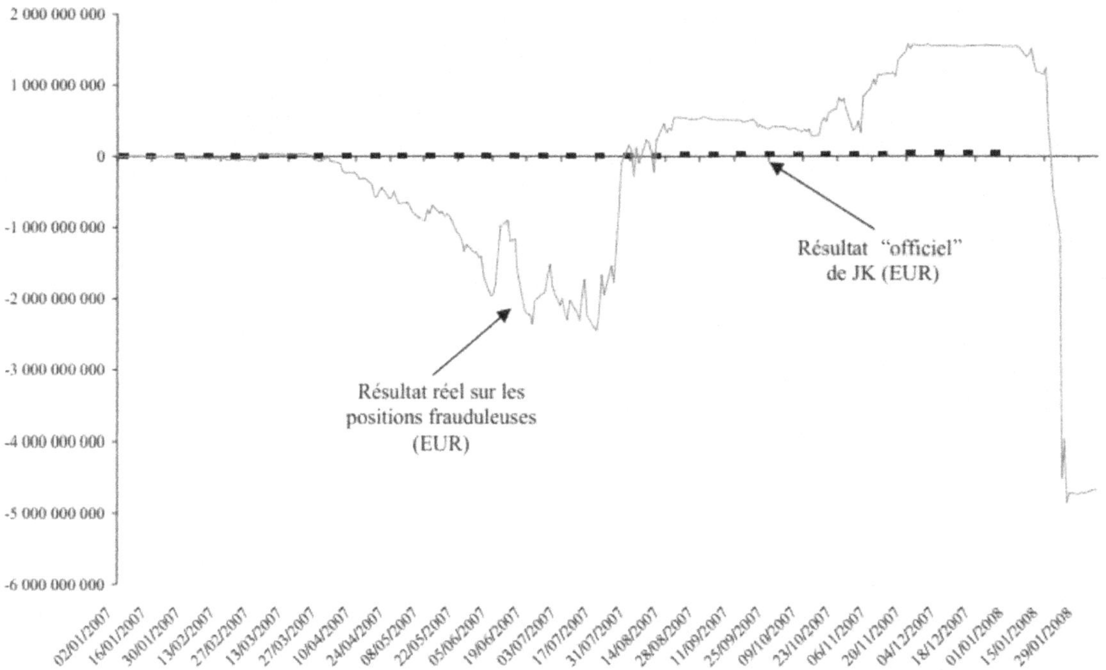

FIGURE 2 Evolution of actual earnings on the unauthorized positions taken by Kerviel (solid line) compared with his declared P&L (black bars). His official earnings were much lower than the real positions. *Source: Societe Generale GREEN report.*

in December 2007 are shown in Figure 2, which shows the evolution of actual earnings on the unauthorized positions taken by Kerviel. Indeed his fraud generated almost 1.5 billion euros at the end of 2007 before going into negative territory in January 2008. Figure 3 shows the evolution of the fictitious trades taken by Kerviel. They were designed in such way to compensate the unauthorized trades and hence to hide the real position. Kerviel was long on the equity market, which started to be bearish anticipating the Lehman disaster which followed 8 months later. Most likely if the market was not so bearish in those early days of 2008, implying a huge amount of margin call for his long position, the fraud would have remained undiscovered, and if there had not been a crisis, Kerviel would have taken home another bonus.

3.1 A 7 Billion Dollars Loss, But Not Kerviel's Loss

The SocGen audit report indicates on January 24 that Kerviel lost almost 4.9 billion euros, representing 0.25% of France's gross domestic product. The reality is slightly different as Kerviel was forbidden to enter the banks in the week prior to the report. The realized losses were generated during that week by the bank's decision to suddenly cut his unauthorized positions on the main European equity indexes. Kerviel allegedly held massive positions on the main European equity future index controlling for instance 20% of the German DAX index futures. When SocGen suddenly decided to unwind those positions this caused the price to plummet and the execution price of the unwinding was lower because of this. Many analysts felt that SocGen's behavior

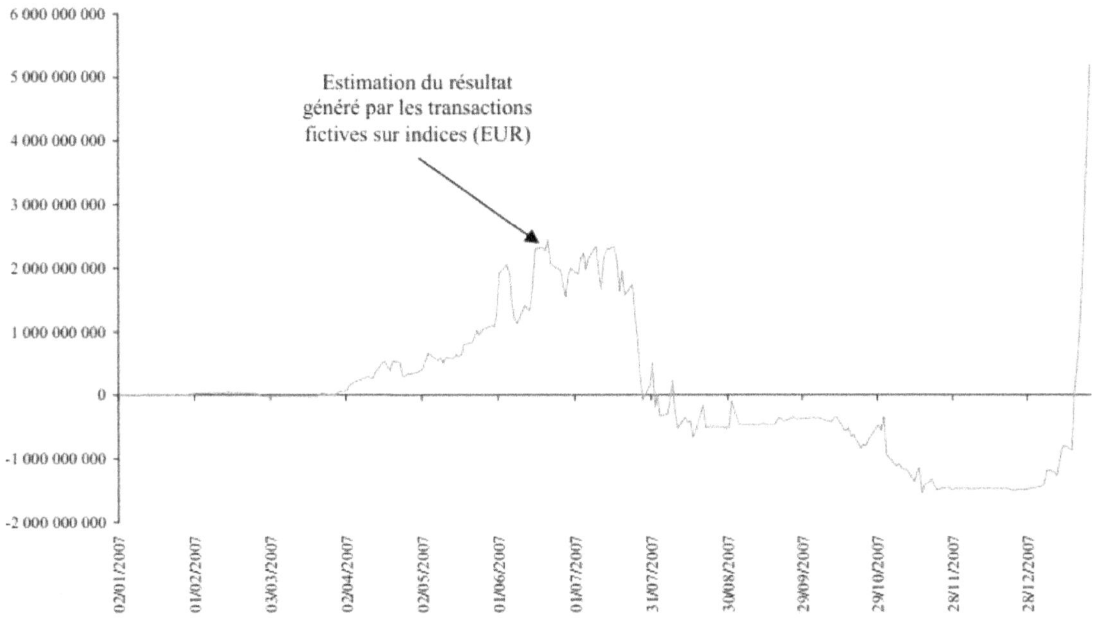

FIGURE 3 Evolution of earnings for the fictitious trades undertaken by Kerviel. They were designed in such a way to compensate the unauthorized trades and hence to hide the real position. *Source: Societe Generale GREEN report.*

was unreasonable and the 4.9 billion loss could have been mitigated if the sell had been executed over a few days via fewer traders. Figure 4 shows the market's response after SocGen unwound Kerviel's unauthorized positions. He was long on the futures of the main indexes including EUROSTOXX50, FTSE (UK), CAC40 (France), and DAX (Germany), which plummeted on the day SocGen shortened the unauthorized positions. On a nominal exposure of 49 million euros a small variation of 1% would account for almost 0.5 billion euros. Kerviel's attorneys underlined that his position when he was fired had a negative mark-to-market which was smaller than the 4.9 billion communicated on January 24 by the bank, also accusing SocGen of market manipulation.

4 TACKLING ROGUE TRADING

Whenever an abnormal event occurs within an organization generating massive losses, the information concerning that event is generally recorded by people, systems, or processes from that environment. Furthermore in most of the best-known cases of rogue trading, the institutions concerned had a certain degree of awareness but did not manage to see the full picture and to realize the gravity of the situation in order to assess the risk. Nevertheless those institutions were not able to predict or stop the rogue trading in real time due to a structural inadequacy in their systems, governance and procedures. The relevant information existed but like in the Kerviel case was clustered in various locations across the business units and systems, without a unitary view which would eventually allow the irregularities to be identified. The governance of risk management and control functions is tailored to deal with day-to-day operations and to assess the risk of the trades with a profit and loss profile around the core of the distributions. A risk control function close to the desk trader does not have the scope and resources to address

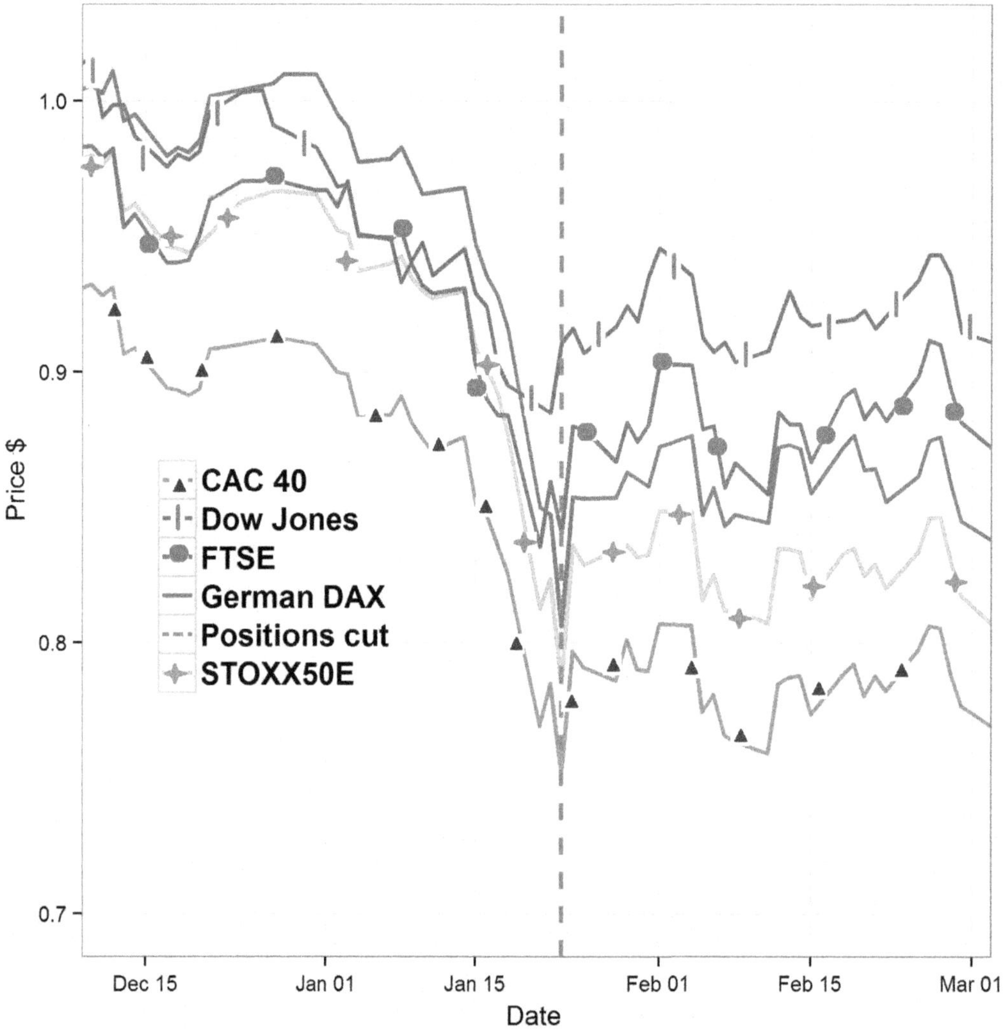

FIGURE 4 Market response after SocGen unwound Kerviel's unauthorized positions. All major European stocks indexes had a technical minimum due to the massive volumes sold. The fact that the index price plummeted due to the volumes unleashed suddenly on the market amplified Kerviel's loss. *Source: Societe Generale GREEN report.*

the structural issues of a rogue trader which can accumulate over a certain period of time. The rogue trading would need a dedicated function with the appropriate tools to control those specific scenarios across an organization.

The control and surveillance procedures did not include the aspects that could generate a rogue trade event. In fact the various functions on a desk floor have at center "the trader." This concept allowed many traders to extend their area of influence and control upon the Back Office and Middle Office functions. In some industries like military or aerospace, the roles and responsibilities are strictly separated in order to not allow one person to gather intelligence on all the industrial flow. This scheme aims to avoid industrial espionage cases. In investment banking, this scheme is not implemented and in many cases those institutions depend on a small group of people who have an influence on clients, strategies, and risk. Therefore, an optimal solution for addressing rogue trading within organizations would address all three aspects, with the following principles:

- *Develop systems and analytical tools for organizational and business units.* Kerviel's irregularities were signaled in the counterparty risk department due to the increasing amounts of initial margin required to keep his huge positions running. Therefore, a surveillance system integrating data from the various risk functions, data about the behavior (i.e., the number of canceled trades, access times from home) of the trader and the trading performance would be in a much better position to address this issue. Once the system is in place an analytical framework needs to be developed in order to compile all the available information. Clustering analysis can be a good start in order to define profile clusters and to assess if a certain trader is behaving differently from the peer group. Vendor solutions proposed by Actimize, BAE systems, SAS, and IBM have already become popular with banks.
- *Implement appropriate procedures in terms of surveillance.* Following the recent rogue trading events banks introduced some specific policies concerning the two-week holiday, which would imply that another trader takes over the positions and can raise alarms if irregularities are detected. Also, canceled orders order and daily reconciliations needed better assessment as they are leading indicators in those cases. Probably the most important change concerned the remuneration of traders. The cash proportions of trader's bonuses have been capped in many countries, the remaining part being deferred over a period of time (2 years).
- *Develop dedicated governance.* A dedicated function complete with independent governance for day-to-day operations is necessary for the effective use of an interdepartmental system of analytical tools and for following dedicated procedures. This transverse function should have a complementary role to that of risk managers.

5 OUTLOOK

It is with great stress that I write this mail. First of all the ETF (Exchange Traded Funds) trades that you see on the ledger are not trades that I have done with a counterparty as I previously described. I used the bookings as a way to suppress the PnL losses that I have accrued through off-book trades that I made.
Excerpt from Kweku Adobolis's email to his line manager before he was found to have been rogue trading.

The Kweku Adobolis case seems to replicate the Kerviel episode. Both were young promising traders, both on Delta One desks, exposed to equity and ETF markets and able to manage huge directional trades. Probably many other small-scale rogue trading events are similar to Kerviel's positions from 2005 to 2006, floating around financial institutions' trading desks without being discovered or being known to the public. The main questions from this rogue trading from 2008 should focus on two aspects. First, from a behavioral perspective there is a need to understand why some young bankers when introduced to this hypercompetitive milieu deviate from their usual pattern. Why do those individuals with a high-level education and an upper class social background spread lies, use forgery, misrepresent their work and engage in huge risk-taking operations, in most cases without gaining any real personal benefit? The answer probably has more ramifications going beyond the banking industry itself and is rooted somewhere in the social trends of modern society.

Second, from a technical point of view there is a need to change the paradigm of assessing the risk on trading floors and more generally in banks. Systems, analytical tools, and processes should be implemented holistically in order to enable the controller to navigate across all departments in the bank.

CHAPTER

3E

Initial Public Offerings

OUTLINE

1 BACKGROUND

Capital markets are one of the most attractive sources of liquidity for private companies intending to go public. Listing a company and having public ownership in the capital structure is not only a technical change, but also involves a drift in the firm's culture. Figure 1 shows the evolution of the number of initial public offerings (IPOs) and of the capital raised worldwide. The past two crises that followed the Internet bubble in 2000 and the credit crunch had a huge effect on the number and the capital raised through public offerings.

Figure 2 shows the geographical breakdown of the IPOs in terms of the number of companies and the capital raised. North America leads the way in terms of total capital raised, but Asia with its Hong Kong, Shanghai, and Tokyo exchanges has shown strong growth in terms of the number of listed companies.

The specificity of IPO-related frauds is reflected by the view of public offerings in the eyes of investors. "Hot" IPOs are somehow seen as an above average investment support. Wang et al. [81] and Povel et al. [82] argued that a firm's incentive to commit fraud when going public varies with investor beliefs about industry business conditions and the propensity for fraud increases with the level of investor beliefs about industry prospects but decreases in the presence of extremely high beliefs.

Povel et al. [82] proposed a two-regime model explaining the probability of fraud committed by managers in order to get funds from investors. The probability of fraud depends on the *ex ante* expectation of having above average profitability. In this model very and high expectations of profit raise fewer suspicions of IPO fraud but a reasonably high expected return also leads to closer monitoring from potential investors.

Among the IPO frauds the most frequent are the listing of bogus businesses, pre-IPO frauds involving underwriters and the misrepresentation of the firm before and during the IPO process.

http://dx.doi.org/10.1016/B978-0-12-801221-5.00009-9

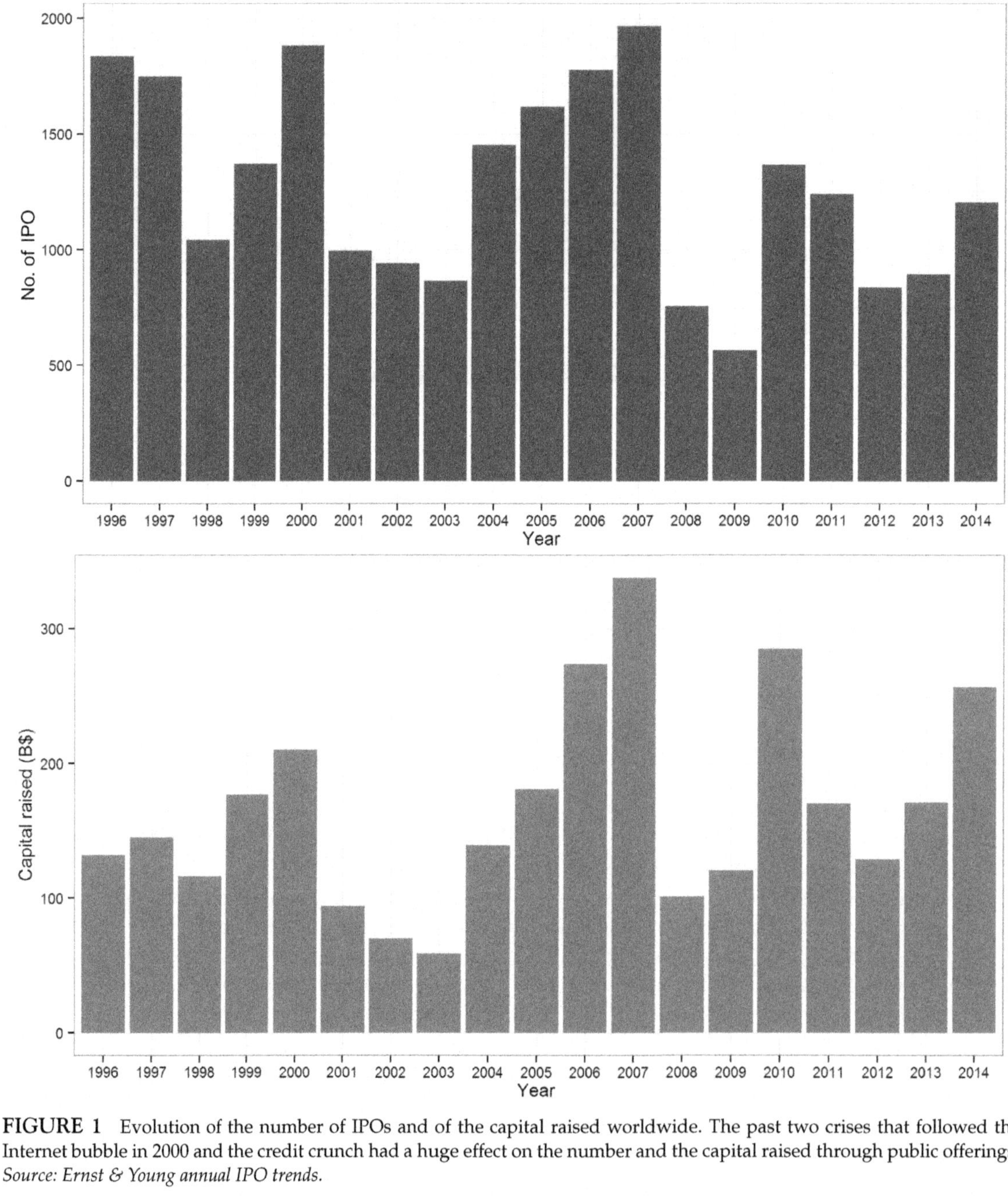

FIGURE 1 Evolution of the number of IPOs and of the capital raised worldwide. The past two crises that followed the Internet bubble in 2000 and the credit crunch had a huge effect on the number and the capital raised through public offerings. *Source: Ernst & Young annual IPO trends.*

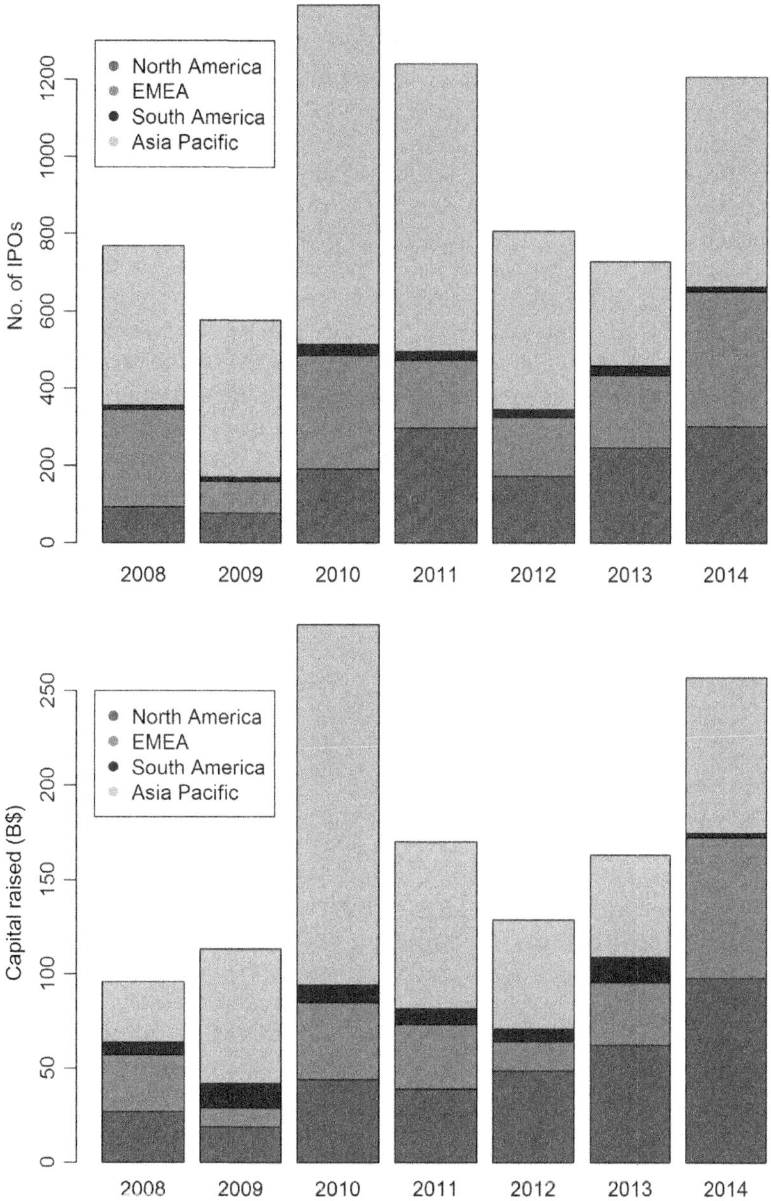

FIGURE 2 Geographical breakdown of IPOs in terms of number of companies and capital raised.
Source: Ernst & Young annual IPO trends.

2 FAKE IPOs

Listing companies with irrelevant or bogus businesses and selling them as hot prospects is the most basic fraud in the IPO arena. Jordan Belfort, the broker portrayed in Scorsese's *Wolf of Wall Street*, and his firm Stratton Oakmont[1] were involved in such affairs, attempting to list businesses like judo schools, bagel makers, newfangled water purifiers, or a recovering alcoholic selling shoes. An important element of the scheme was that the Stratton IPO stock was not really sold to the public—it was sold to Stratton. Securities laws forbid underwriters like Stratton from buying more than a small percentage of the IPO stock they issue. To avoid this roadblock, Stratton sold all of its IPO stock to its associates, which sold them back at a higher price, thereby creating a momentum in stock price and attracting naive investors.

3 PRE-IPO SCAMS

Buying shares of a company before the company actually goes public, known as pre-IPO investing, can expose unwary investors to many risks. This type of proposal is frequent in start-up companies in the technology sector. Pre-IPO offerings targeted at the general public are often fraudulent and illegal because many of the brokers proposing such schemes are not registered with any regulatory body and are in fact bogus. Hence, the buyer will lose all their money. In addition when those brokers are regulated they might sell unregistered securities which may be extremely difficult to sell, as they have to be held for a given period of time. The biggest risk though is when the company never goes public.

The Facebook IPO in 2012 attracted much interest from investors but also from scammers. By 2013 the Security Exchange Commission's (SEC's) Enforcement Division laid fraud charges against a Florida financier Craig Berkman, a former candidate for Governor of Oregon, for a Ponzi-like scheme that promised investors cheap access to pre-IPO shares of Facebook and other companies, like LinkedIn, Groupon, and Zynga.[2] Berkman raised $13.2 million from 120 investors the main portion of the money being for his personal use.

In the pre-IPO scam, a crucial role is also played by the underwriters. Aggarwal et al. [83] explained the extremely high level of IPO underpricing during the Internet bubble years of the late 1990s based on the allocation practices of underwriters and their manipulative behavior. Lowry and Shu [84] explained that firms employ underpricing as a form of insurance against future litigation costs, firms with greater litigation risk tending to underprice their IPOs by a greater amount.

Two illegal practices related to IPOs and involving underwriters are spinning and laddering [85].

Spinning is the allocation by underwriters of the shares of hot IPOs to company executives in order to influence their decisions in the hiring of investment bankers and/or the pricing of their own company's IPO.

Laddering investors agree to purchase shares in the aftermarket of an IPO in exchange for being granted access by the underwriter to invest in the IPO at the offer price. The underwriter engages in the sale of IPO shares to clients with the implicit agreement that more shares will be purchased post-IPO, leading to the creation of a minibubble and resulting in big gains for both parties. Once the price increases to a certain level,

[1] How the "Wolf of Wall Street" really did it, http://www.wsj.com/articles/SB10001424052702303453004579290450707920302.

[2] SEC: Florida financier used Facebook's pre-IPO frenzy to swindle clients, http://www.forbes.com/sites/steveschaefer/2013/03/19/florida-financier-charged-with-using-facebooks-pre-ipo-frenzy-to-swindle-clients/.

"insiders" then sell their shares and take their profits.

4 EMERGING EXCHANGES

The growing number of IPOs on the Asian exchanges, mainly in Hong Kong and Shanghai, aroused much suspicion about the soundness of the IPO process in those regions. China, one of the biggest markets for IPOs, was confronted with serious issues on this topic. In 2011, the China Securities Regulatory Commission (CSRC) fined Minsheng Securities, a brokerage company, $326,000 for failed due diligence in Shanxi Tianneng Technology's attempt to launch an IPO in 2011. It also gave a warning to Nanjing Securities for a similar violation when it advised Guangdong Xindadi Biotechnology in 2012. Both IPOs were halted after frauds were uncovered.[3] Following fraud allegations the Chinese regulator banned the IPOs in 2005 for almost one year. The same thing happened in 2012 when the CSRC banned the IPOs until the end of 2013, creating a waiting list for listing of no less than 800 firms. Given the Chinese ban many of the questionable Chinese companies gained access to US capital markets through the back door, by acquiring listed companies.

5 IPOs AND RISK OF LITIGATION

IPOs of bogus start-ups claiming a unique patent for curing some rare disease or having a unique energy generating technology have been quite common. The Internet bubble was followed by a series of IPO litigations in relation to technology firms listed on NASDAQ.

One of the consequences of misrepresentation of the firm due to the intention of the management to overstate the situation of the firm to raise more funds in the IPO process is reflected in the post-IPO class actions. If the price of the IPO does not reach the desired target the investors tend to blame it on managers who misrepresented the situation. The fraud on the market theory provides the legal framework for class action. With the new technology bubble companies like Facebook or Groupon became subject to IPO litigations.

A database of IPO-related class actions is provided by the Stanford Securities class action clearing house,[4] accounting for almost 414 cases since 1997. Other databases concerning IPOs provided by Kenney and Patton [86] and IPOScoop.com[5] allow us to construct a sample of listed firms that became the subject of IPO litigation. The database provided by Kenney and Patton [86] gives valuable information like the offering price and, the discount on the volume of shares offered. The other database IPOScoop.com, which is an independent online rating service for IPOs, provides details about the opening day performance of the stock. The dataset of 2551 IPOs is completed by the time series of the prices on the first 100 trading days of the stock. Figure 3 shows the distribution of the various features of IPO shares through a benchmark between the litigated and the nonlitigated firms.

Interestingly the ratio of shares offered to the public to the total outstanding volume seems to be a distinguishing feature as the litigated firms have a lower ratio than the nonlitigated firms. Opening day returns (both opening and closing prices) appear to be different for the two categories. Surprisingly the maximum return over the first 100 days seems to have the same distribution for both populations. The absolute difference between the volatility of return over the first 100 days and the median of the sample is also

[3]China punishes two brokerages in IPO fraud crackdown, http://www.reuters.com/article/2013/06/01/us-china-brokerages-idUSBRE95002X20130601.

[4]Securities class action clearing house, http://securities.stanford.edu/.

[5]https://www.iposcoop.com/.

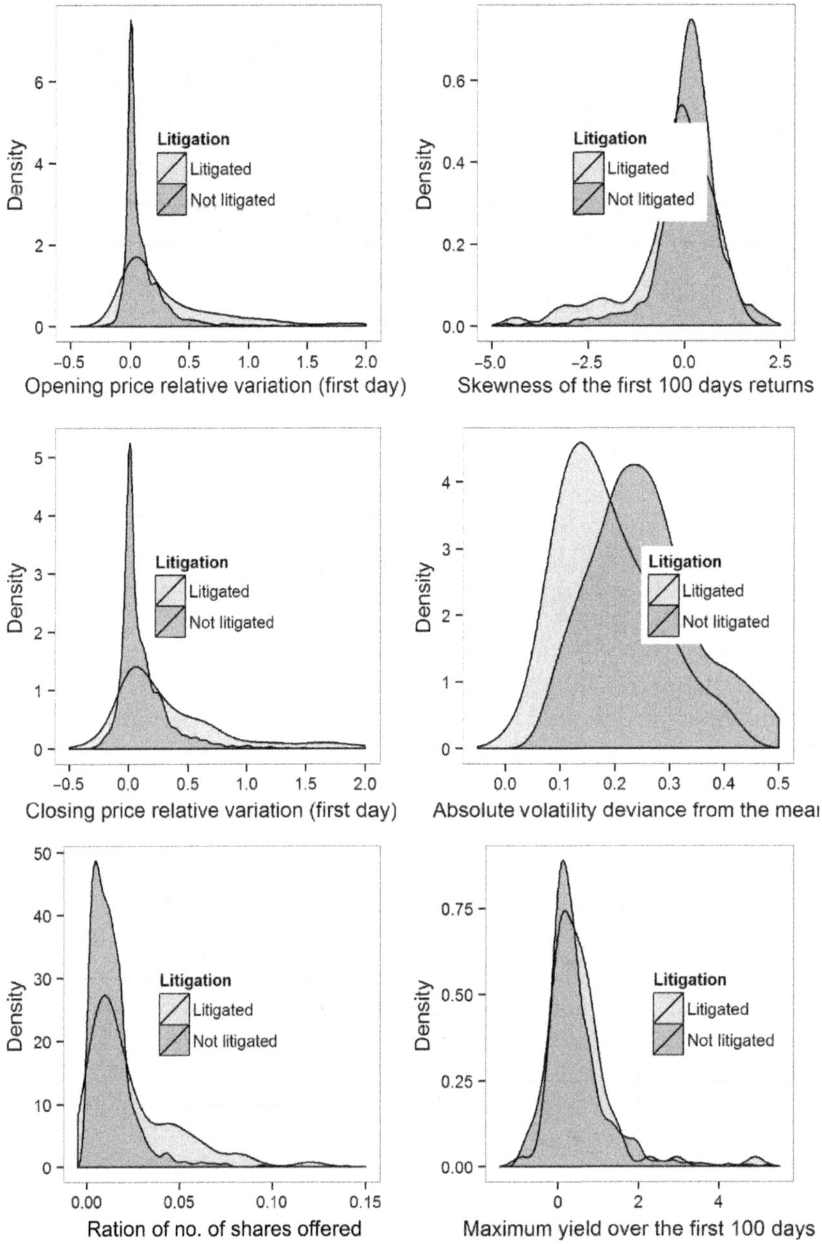

FIGURE 3 Distribution of the various features of IPO shares through a benchmark between the litigated and the nonlitigated firms.

a factor that has some discriminatory features. This volatility metric is based on the idea that volatility is mean reversion and capture is how much it deviates from the long-term trend.

If the risk of litigation is assumed to be a proxy for the risk or fraud on IPOs a straightforward model can be developed as follows:

$$Z_i = \text{Const.} + \beta_1 \cdot \text{DR}_i + \beta_2 \cdot \text{VR}_i + \beta_3 + \text{AV}_i + \beta_3 \cdot \text{SK}_i + \epsilon_i \qquad (1)$$

where Z_i is the dependent variable and takes the value 1 if the firm i was involved in litigation regarding its IPO process and 0 otherwise. DR_i is the opening return on the first day compared to the offer price, VR_i is the proportion of shares offered to the public relative to the total available shares, AV_i is the absolute difference between the volatility of the returns during the first 100 days and the median volatility of the sample, SK_i is the skewness of the returns during the first 100 days, and ϵ_i are the residuals.

The results of the regression are shown in Table 1, with R_2 being around 15%.

TABLE 1 Regression Results for the Factorial Model in Equation 1

Parameter	Estimate	Std. error	*t*-Statistic	*p*-Value
Const.	0.10065	0.05284	1.905	0.05805
DR	0.19376	0.05931	3.267	0.00125
VR	−0.30584	0.16280	−1.879	0.06155
AV	2.39826	1.08625	2.208	0.02823
SK	−0.04671	0.01628	−2.869	0.00450

The results show that a big jump in the opening price might be linked to a higher probability of litigation. If high opening returns are related to underpricing this may be an argument sustaining the points behind the results of Aggarwal et al. [83].

6 OUTLOOK

Efficiency in markets is not a given state and is in fact a process. The information flow during the cooling period around an IPO as well as the role played by the underwriters in relation to investors are major points of concern in the transparency of IPOs. The behavior in the opening days of the newly listed stock provides information that can indicate whether the process was fair or not.

CHAPTER

3F

Mis-Selling

OUTLINE

1 BACKGROUND

Mis-selling is defined as an unethical practice where an institution or an individual misrepresents or misleads an investor about the characteristics of the provided product or service. Special attention has been paid mis-selling in the structured products field, when an institution tries to convince a client about the desirability of the product and the fact that the product suits the client's profile even though a sound analysis would suggest serious doubts and risks.

In the aftermath of the financial crisis, the mis-selling was often associated with structured products which had embedded exotic derivatives with sophisticated payoffs. The development of markets for structured products (Collateralized Debt Obligation, Target Accrual Redemption Note [TARN], structured credits, etc.) reflects the appetite of banks' clients for sensible products that provide them with tailored solutions to address their specific hedging need or risk profile. At the time of purchase of a structured product, the probability of loss is often underestimated by either the low probability of an adverse market movement or an incorrect assessment of the product's risk profile.

The complexity and sophistication of derivatives is probably analogous to the difficulty of valuation by nonfinancial institutions, a small regional bank or municipality risk profiles and performance proposed solutions. Buyers entered into financial transactions which gradually changed from the original objective of risk management and plain protection against unwanted risks to a quest for financial gain (not necessarily backed by the exposures of their assets or their liabilities) with the objective improved *vis-à-vis* competitive competitors.

http://dx.doi.org/10.1016/B978-0-12-801221-5.00010-5

In the early 1980s, the development of panel derivatives including caps, floors, swaps, etc. has allowed companies to manage their interest rate risk profile. In the case of swaps, it was easy to understand that if a company having a fixed rate debt was covered by a swap, any decrease in the level of interest rates would be in the company's favor and any rise in rates beyond the fixed rate swap would be unfavorable. These positions were not intended to be "marked to market" *per se* and their outcome was materialized in the evolution of the cost of corporate financing. Caps and floors played a role similar to an insurance product guaranteeing a company its financing costs will not exceed a threshold established at the start of the contract.

But structured products have an even higher degree of complexity and are usually constructed by combining a set of derivatives whose resulting risk profile is a nonlinear function. Theoretically, the price of any derivative is precisely equal to the present value of future expected gain with which is associated. For structured products embedding derivatives with long maturities (10-40 years) with a very illiquid underlying market the valuation is complex and can vary depending on the assumptions taken into account, classic models such as Black-Scholes having limited applicability.

Generally speaking, the notion of "fair value," in the sense proposed by the International Financial Reporting Standards, becomes obsolete, given the low liquidity of these instruments and the framework in which they were developed. Hence, fair value resulting from complex probabilistic models gives way to the "business value" or value of acceptance representing the price the customer finds acceptable to buy the product. It is important to remember that the unwinding costs of this type of product are high, and that their purpose in most cases is to be held to maturity and not to be "negotiated" on the market, because any early unwinding can generate additional costs.

Some recent court decisions like the condemnation of Deutsche Bank by the Federal Court in Karlsruhe[1] for mis-selling suggest that the information asymmetry and expertise between the financial institution and the client plays a crucial role in the outbreak of moral hazard in the sense outlined by Adam Smith: "Maximization of individual interest without consideration of the consequences adverse decision on the collective interest."

2 DERIVATIVES INVOLVED IN FINANCIAL MALPRACTICE

Mis-selling refers mainly to providing clients with products that are not really suitable for their profile. Another side of mis-selling is the sale of products to a client by misusing it in order to achieve targets through unorthodox or illegal methods. In this category, a serious focus is attached to derivatives used for financial malpractice.

The seminal work on financial malpractice by Schilit [87] showed that derivatives can be used to disguise the balance sheet or for smoothing the income. Enron misuse of derivatives to obfuscate their financial statements is the best studied case in the field. The example presented below completes the picture of the situations in which derivatives are used in this way.

2.1 Smoothing the Income

The implementation of rule SFAS No. 133 of the US accounting GAAP since 2000 which implied the valuation of derivatives in mark to market which introduced more volatility in the balance sheet and in earnings [87]. Many

[1] On March 22nd the Federal Court of Justice in Karlsruhe ordered Deutsche Bank to pay 541,074 euros ($768,942) damages, plus interest, for failing to advise a middle size client on the true risk of a complex swap transaction. *Rhyme and reason*, http://www.economist.com/node/18442065.

companies then used derivatives as a way to smooth their earnings in order to give the impression to investors and markets that the firm stable and sustainable prospects. An example is Freddie Mac, which used interest rate derivatives to smooth underreported net income by nearly $4.5 billion between 2000 and 2002.

2.2 Hedging vs Speculation

The basic use of derivatives for corporations is to hedge their exposure to market randomness. For instance, a French cognac exported to the United States is indirectly exposed to the EUR/USD exchange rate as its costs are in euros and the revenue in dollars. Therefore, the French producer could hedge its exposure using a forward contract or derivatives in order to insure its operational margin. Similarly a Kentucky-based wheat producer exporting in Japan and being paid at the average annual price should cover its exposure to the yen with forwards or with an Asian option. If the hedging potions does not fit entirely with the exposure the hedging position becomes speculative and needs to be accounted as such. Over- and underhedging are current practices in firms with market exposure and have specific features from an accounting perspective.

Schilit [87] gives the example of General Electric, which in 2002 *overhedged*, or entered into more swaps than required to hedge their interest rate exposure due to the issuance of commercial paper. Under the accounting rule SFAS 133 the company was required to include the outcome of overhedges in their accounts, which would have resulted in a fine of 200 million dollars. Instead the company created a new accounting approach in order to avoid this punishment, but some years later the Security Exchange Commission penalized them for accounting fraud.

Schilit [87] also states that: "Investors should be cautious when a company reports large gains from hedging activities, as these ineffective (sometimes called economic) *hedges* may really be unreliable speculative trading activities that could just as easily produce large losses in future periods. In addition, investors should look out for ineffective hedges that produce gains well in excess of the loss in the underlying asset or liability."

In fact, the reality is much more complex and each firm that uses derivatives for hedging is automatically involved in speculation. For example, a wholesale wheat distributor who wants to cover against a rise in the purchasing price of wheat will subscribe to an option at the money on the wheat price. Nevertheless the banks selling the option will cover the position in a delta neutral strategy and will buy 0.5 of the nominal positions, contributing to the directional momentum of the market. In addition, many firms with exposure to the market have a risk arising from their house hedging (trading) desks. The in-house trader will have a tactical maneuvering limit to take controlled risk in order to anticipate the market's moves. Hence the firm will not be perfectly hedged and will always have an overround on the delta relative to the exposure.

2.3 Public Finance Malpractice

The legacy of the problems in Greece and the Eurozone crisis have shown that a simple derivative can be used as a Trojan horse in the public accounts of a country that can lead to a butterfly effect in the European Union (EU). The Trojan horse was a portfolio of currency swaps that the Greek Government acquired duplicitously from Goldman Sachs in the early 2000s to cover its real debt situation. By the time the EU had officially confirmed this information markets plunged into the red and its economies entered into a long recession. Figure 1 shows the evolution of the debt to GDP ratio for Greece.

Greece had public debts denominated in dollars and yen, before entering the euro area. Goldman Sachs proposed a currency swap to convert the debt into euros. Thus a currency swap took place between Greece and Goldman, Greece being indebted in dollars. Entering into a currency swap entails paying interest and a

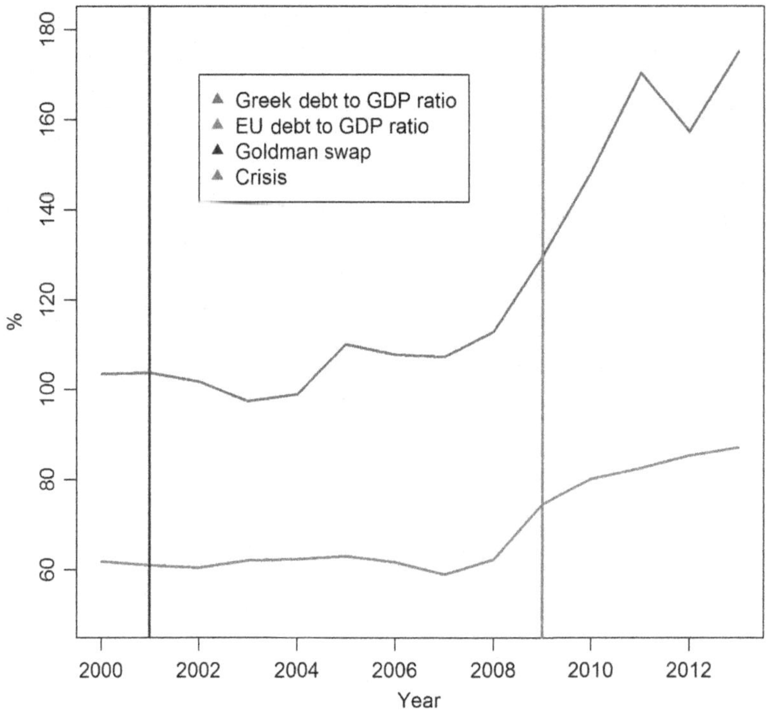

FIGURE 1 Evolution of the debt to GDP ratio for Greece and the European Union.

nominal fee in euros to Goldman Sachs which paid the dollar interest to Greece. Thus Greece's debt was now denominated in euros. In a currency swap, the nominal exchange takes place at the end of the swap. In practice, Goldman Sachs went further, as it had proposed an dollar/euro exchange rate, which allowed Greece to reduce its debt by means of malpractice. At the time of the swap, the exchange rate was 1 euro for 1 dollar. Goldman Sachs proposed 1 euro for 0.9 US dollars (the rate of the previous year). A swap has generally a null mark to market at initiation but in this case the Greek swap has a positive mark to market. The amount involved was about $10 billion. Goldman has paid a cash payment of $1 billion corresponding to the premium of the swap. Nevertheless at the maturity of the swap, which was 10-15 years, Greece had to repay $12 billion (including interest). Thus the currency swap with premium served to disguise debt as the 1 billion premium did not appear in the public finances of the Greek state.

3 TOXIC CREDIT PRODUCTS

The Eurozone crisis and the economic distress that hit the US following the credit crunch in 2008 revealed to the public a series of cases of town and municipalities that took loans from banks in the form of structured products with exotic derivatives embedded.

For example at least 5500 French towns including Saint Tropez have taken out toxic loans from various banks including the failed French-Belgian bank Dexia, the failed British bank Royal Bank of Scotland and Societe Generale. With no means to unwind that debt, and no way to pay it back, these towns turned to the government for bailouts. The total amount seems to be approaching 60 billion dollars in France alone.[2] Many of the towns were already in a distressed situation and could not afford classic bullet bonds which would be too expensive. Thus investment banks proposed leveraged loans with derivatives embedded in an attempt to reduce these debts. The following boxes exemplify some of the types of embedded derivatives in the toxic loans.

STRUCTURED CREDIT

Bank is paying:

Fixed rate: 4.1%

Maturities: every 3 months

Client is paying:

Fixed rate: 2.1%

Payments: every 3 months for the first 3 years of the deal

Structured rate: max(12.5% − 10 × (Reference rate 1 − Reference rate 2), 2.1%)

Reference rate 1: GBP Constant Maturity Swap (CMS) 10 years

Reference rate 2: GBP CMS 1 years

Payments: every 3 months after the first 3 years until the maturity of the deal in 20 years

Observations:

For the first three years the client receives 2% from the bank. After three years the coupon depends on the difference between the short-term rates and the long-term rates. The yield rate curve being upward, the short rates are lower than the long rates. Therefore, the structural rate remains at a low level.

When the financial crisis took hold in 2008 and the central banks cut interest rates, the difference

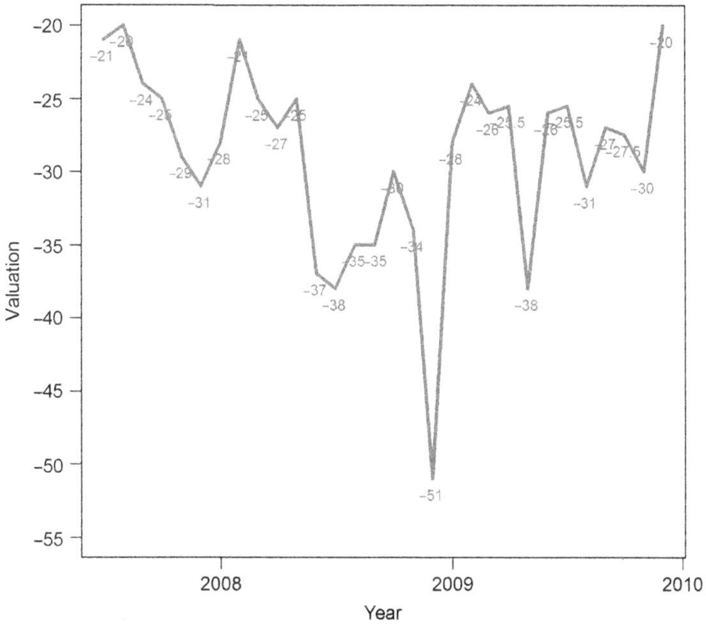

between long and short rates decreased and the city faced the possibility of paying more coupons. As shown in the figure above, the mark to market/model falls during the crisis.

[2] French towns discover toxic assets, ask for bailout, http://www.globalpost.com/dispatch/news/regions/europe/france/120221/french-towns-toxic-assets-dexia-euro-debt-crisis.

STRUCTURED CREDIT WITH EMBEDDED SWAP

Bank is paying:

Fixed rate: 3.6%

Payments: every 3 months over the maturity of the deal (10 years)

Client is paying:

Structured rate: max(3.60% + 67.6% × (EUR/USD rate − EUR/CHF rate), 3.60%)

Payments: every 3 months after the first 3 years until the maturity of the deal in 10 years

Observations:

This structured swap is based on the difference between two exchange rates. The main issue is that a municipality raising taxes in euros is exposed to currency risk of yen or Swiss franc. During the mis-selling litigation for these types of structured loans it was claimed to be a major point of misrepresentation for the client.

STRUCTURED CREDIT WITH EMBEDDED SWAP

Bank is paying:

Structured rate: 4.1% − 10 × max(−0.15% − (CMS EUR 30Y − CMS EUR 1Y), 0)

Payments: every 3 months over the maturity of the deal (20 years)

Client is paying:

Structured rate: 0.00% for the first year 7.60% − (10 × CMS GBP 10Y − CMS EUR 1Y)

Payments: every 3 months after the first year for 20 years

Observations:

The swap is leveraged in two directions: first, there is the difference between the short- and long-term rates in euro and the spread between British pound and euro yield curves. Like in the other case the client does not pay any interest in the first year. The product was built on the idea that in early 2000 the long-term GBP were rates in

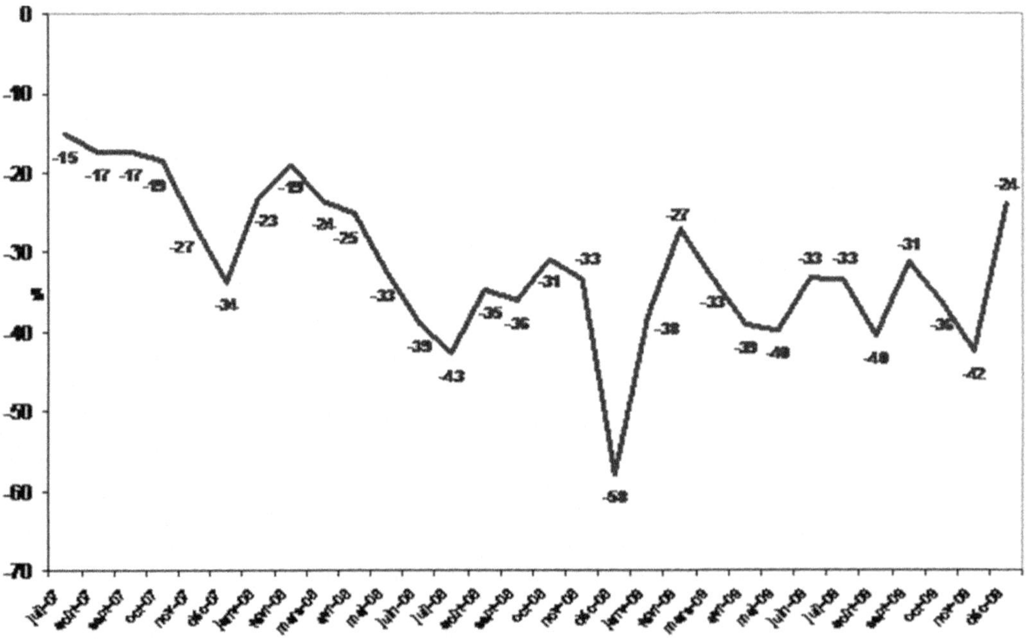

relatively lower than the EUR rate due to the structural difference between the two yield curves. This relationship is true for the later payment dates but for the earlier dates this relationship is not valid. Therefore, this product has the potential for forward spread at low level and with time the spread increases in value, thereby generating a profit (ease in interest payment) for the client.

During the crisis when the rates were cut the yield curve changed and the client ended up paying high structured interest.

STRUCTURED CREDIT WITH EMBEDDED SWAP

Bank is paying:

Structured rate: Euribor $1Y + 15 * (V - 0,91\%)$,

V is the premium of straddle swaption for a 5-year swap starting in 1 year.

Client is paying: Euribor 1Y.

In this case, the swap aims to create an advantage to the client based on arbitrating the volatility forward curve. The valuation of the straddle depends on the volatility of the underlying swap and in the case of a structured loan depends on the forward volatility curve. This volatility curve is in backwardation for as long as the maturities volatility is smaller than the spot volatility. On such a product as above this effect implies that the client buys the forward straddle cheap attached to the load and with time the value of straddle increases as the forward start swaption will become at one time a spot swaption.

When the crisis hit the market the volatility curve changed shape and the mark to model/market of the product became negative for the client.

$$\frac{dF_k(t)}{F_k(t)} = \sigma_k(t)\, dW_t^{k+1} \tag{1}$$

This is the fundamental equation of the Libor Market Model introduced by Brace et al. [88] and is based on the instantaneous volatility $\sigma_k(t)$.

This form, expressed as a forward neutral risk measure, needs to be adjusted in a unique measure such as:

$$\frac{dF_k(t)}{F_k(t)} = -\sum_{i=k+1}^{N-1} \frac{\delta_i F_i(t)}{1+\delta_i F_i(t)} \sigma_i \cdot \sigma_k + \sigma_k(t)\, dW_t^{k+1} \tag{2}$$

$$\sigma_j(t) = k_j(a + b(t_j - t)) \cdot e^{-c(t_j - t)} + d \tag{3}$$

A parametric form for correlation was introduced by Rebonato [89] having the following expression for two maturities i and j:

$$\rho i, j = \rho_\infty + (1 - \infty) \exp(-\beta |i - j|) \quad \beta > 0 \tag{4}$$

The toxic loans with their embedded derivatives are generally analyzed using Monte Carlo methods.

4 STRUCTURED INVESTMENT PRODUCTS

Another category of structured products which involved the courts was when underwriting institutions used structured investment notes with sophisticated payoffs. Here the investors litigated because allegedly they were not fully aware about the product's dynamics.

After experiencing losses of $32 million an investor filed a lawsuit against ICICI Bank for mis-selling. The bank sold financial products such as snowball interest rate swaps, TARN options, and box options.[3] One popular structured product proposed to investors over the past two decade is the power reverse dual-currency note (PRDC).

Similar to the current situation in the EU and United States during the mid-1990s, Japan saw

[3]Five entities file lawsuit against ICICI Bank UK alleging mis-selling, http://smartinvestor.business-standard.com/pf/Investments-285025-Investmentsdet-5_entities_file_lawsuit_against_ICICI_Bank_UK_alleging_mis_selling.htm.

its interest rate declining in yields. For instance, the long-term rates fell from a high of 6% to almost 1%, while the short-term rate tended to zero. Therefore, the Japanese investors looked for structured products that provided higher yields than the yen interest rate. Investment banks looked elsewhere, in foreign markets where the interest rate markets had a significant differential. This is how the PRDC appeared and it can be perceived as a product betting that the domestic currency is not going to strengthen as much as predicted by the forward FX rate curve [90].

The coupon of the PRDC at time t denoted as C_t is:

$$C_t = \min\left(\max\left(r^f \cdot \frac{S_t}{f_0} - r^d, b_f\right), b_c\right) \quad (5)$$

where r^f is the interest rate of the foreign currency, r^d is the interest rate of the domestic currency, S_t is the spot exchange rate at time t, and f_0 is the forward exchange rate at initiation for maturity t.

There are some exotic versions of the PRDC including Bermudan Cancelable PRDC Swaps, Knockout PRDC Swaps, and the TARN [90].

In a Bermudan cancelable PRDC swap, the issuer of the product has the right to cancel the PRDC swap at any established date t_i after the exchange of fund flows scheduled on that date.

A knockout PRDC includes an up-and-out FX-linked barrier and the PRDC swap is knocked-out on the swap date t, if the spot FX rate S_t exceeds a specified level.

A TARN is a version of the PRDC that terminates when the accumulated PRDC coupon amount, including the coupon amount scheduled on that date, reaches a predetermined target cap. TARN coupons are expressed as:

$$C_{t_i} = \max(\beta(S_{t_i} - K), 0) \quad i \in \left\{1, 2, \ldots, \hat{N}\right\}$$
$$A_{t_i} = A_{t_{i-1}} + C_{t_i}$$
$$\hat{N} = \min(i : A_{t_i} > U) \quad i \in \{1, 2, \ldots, N\}$$

where β is a constant, K is the strike, and t_N is the maximum maturity of the swap.

A straightforward modeling based on a Hull-White formalism [90, 91] for a domestic risk neutral measure in the domestic rate is detailed as follows:

$$\frac{dS_t}{S_t} = (r_t^d - r_t^f) \cdot dt + \sigma_s \cdot dW_t^s \quad (6)$$
$$dr_t^d = (\theta_t^d - a^d \cdot r_t^d) \cdot dt + \sigma_d \cdot dW_t^d \quad (7)$$
$$dr_t^f = (\theta_t^f - a^f \cdot r_t^f - \rho_{fs}\sigma_f\sigma_s) \cdot dt + \sigma_f \cdot dW_t^f \quad (8)$$

where σ_s, σ_d, and σ_f are the volatilities of the spot exchange rate, domestic foreign interest rate, and foreign interest rate. $\left\langle dW_t^s dW_t^d \right\rangle = \rho_{ds} dt$, $\left\langle dW_t^s dW_t^f \right\rangle = \rho_{fs}\, dt$, and $\left\langle dW_t^f dW_t^d \right\rangle = \rho_{fs}\, dt$.

The valuation of such products is made using Monte Carlo methods, thereby making the assessment of such products inaccessible to common investors. Many of the litigation issues around this products arose from the symmetry in information between the investors and the underwriters. For long-term PRDC the market of products for calibration of the model parameter is very thin liquidity and the market makers are the very same banks that underwrite the products. Therefore, the price of those derivatives is driven directly by the volumes of PRDC sold, thereby raising other questions about the relevance of the valuations of these products.

5 STRUCTURED PRODUCTS TO RETAIL COSTUMERS

With the scandals around the mis-selling of structured products to municipalities and towns, banks tried to push these products to the retail market including small and medium enterprises (SME). In 2014, the British Financial Conduct Authority announced that nine banks including Barclays, the Royal Bank of Scotland,

Lloyds Banking Group, and HSBC[4] were paying out 2.4 billion USD in redress to SMEs that were mis-sold interest rate swap agreements, which included 450 million dollars in consequential loss payments, after sending out 17,000 redress determinations to customers. The banks involved also agreed to review their sales of IRHPs1 made to unsophisticated customers since 2001.

6 MIS-SELLING AND VALUATION ISSUES

Many of the structured products mentioned above are classified from an accounting viewpoint as Level III, implying that the parameters used for their valuations are not observable and bearing all the issues specific to this class of financial instruments. The valuation of the structured products includes some aspects that make them less transparent and more likely to be candidates for mis-selling litigation.

- Incomplete markets: The exotic derivatives embedded in structured products are traded or hedged with options which are traded on incomplete markets. In those markets (i.e., long horizon CMS), the valuation methods differ thereby implying more than one price. If three assessors evaluated the price of an exotic derivative using the same parameters they most likely find different answers. Therefore, the mark-to-model being used as input in the accounting of fair value can already generate discrepancies between the buyer and the seller.
- Model risk: The more exotic the underlying derivatives, the more dependent the valuation is on the model assumption. For example, the valuation of a barrier option can vary significantly depending on whether the asset increases in value or not. In the interest rate products, the parameterization of correlation among the various forward rates on the yield curve is an important part of the model and the various assumptions can have an impact on the valuation. In addition, some of the unobservable parameters, including correlation and volatilities for some maturities where the corresponding derivatives (i.e., swaptions) are not liquid, are established based on trader's or structurer's views. The parameters based on subjective opinion are a serious source of issues in the valuation process at the initiation and during the life of the product. For example when a client enters into an exotic swap proposed by a bank and intended to be of null value at initiation, she might find that depending on the model and parameter the swap could have a negative mark to model/market. In this case from the initiation a client who does not have the means to value the products independently might enter into an asymmetric relationship from the beginning. Similarly during the lifetime of the swap the mark to model/market establishes the payment of each party and are another source of asymmetry.
- Market manipulation: It is useful to recall that many of the structured products mentioned above used either LIBOR, EURBOR rates, or FX rates as inputs in the payoff. All those markets have been subject to manipulations from the major banks organized in cartel-type structures. The investigations revealed that many of the manipulations occurred when the banks sold the derivatives their clients.

Figure 2 shows the valuation of the same products by three different agents: the structurer, the risk manager, and an independent assessor.

[4] Mis-selling derivatives: British banks complete SME case reviews, http://www.ibtimes.co.uk/mis-selling-derivatives-british-banks-complete-sme-case-reviews-1469944.

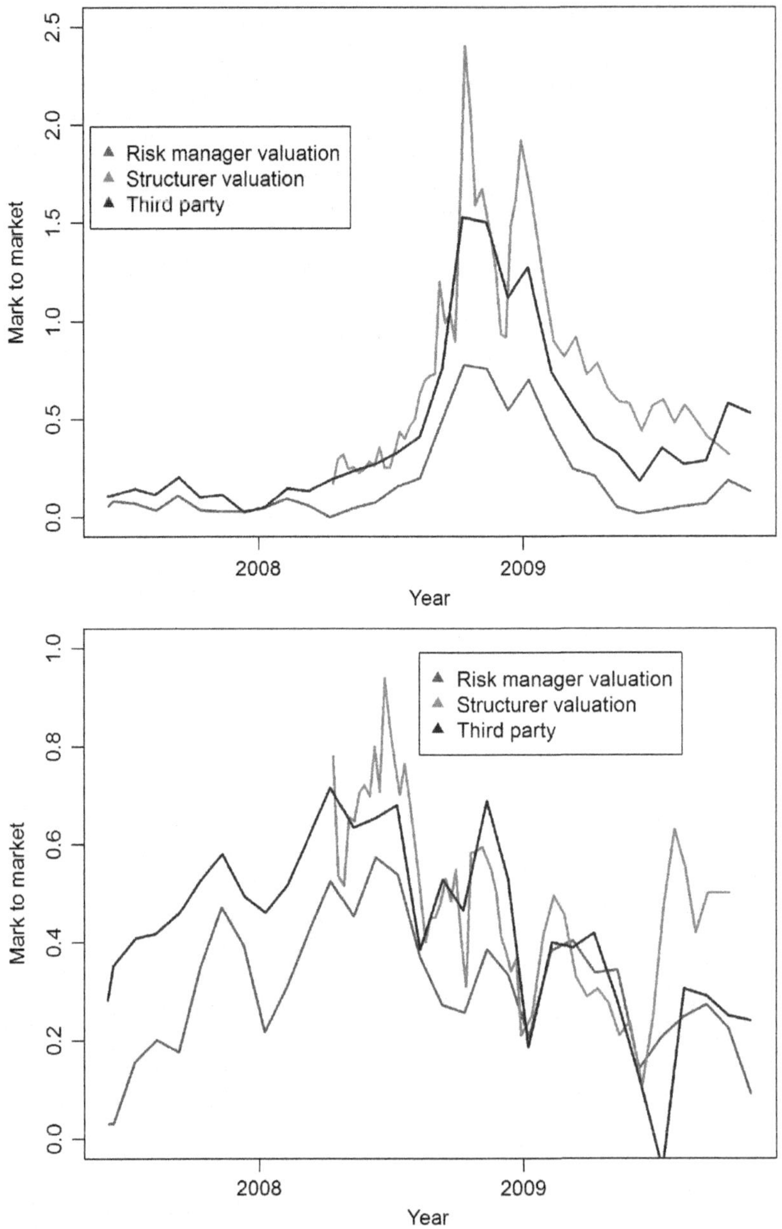

FIGURE 2 Valuation of an exotic derivative embedded in a structured product. The top graph corresponds to a derivative indexed on the difference between the long-term rates and the short-term rates. The bottom graph is the valuation of a derivative indexed on the difference between long-term rates in two different currencies.

This is a perfect example of how the same product can have different valuations from different parties with the same input values, underlining the issues of valuation in incomplete markets and the role played by model risk.

7 OUTLOOK

Although "demonized" after the recent financial crisis, structured products can play a significant role in economic development when they are well controlled. This control imposes a set of rules which must be clear to all parties (banks, investors, auditors, etc.). This is particularly important for the clients, which should engage in this type of transaction only if they are able to understand, assess and manage the product and its risks. It is necessary to recall that many entities including municipalities and SMEs have taken positions on structured products bearing complex P&L profiles without being able to dynamically control and value them.

To avoid this type of situation, some commonsense rules should be put in place. Thus, the structured product must be built given the risk exposure/profile of the customer. As an example it seems unlikely that a municipality from Detroit collecting taxes in dollars should have on its balance sheet structured debt indexed to the FX rate JPY/EUR. If this logic is clear, explicit, and well understood, this will mitigate any hazardous valuations that can sometimes lead to wrong decisions during periods of market turbulence. This of course requires that the client would be able to value alone or with an independent agent the subscribed product and understand the potential impact of market changes on its dynamics. Finally, the customer should have full control over the accounting impact of such a product on its balance sheet and income statement.

Beyond the many consequences of using complex, structured products the foundations of the current debate revolve around the concept already mentioned of moral hazard and the powers given to regulators to monitor and validate the activities of investment banks. Today, despite the efforts of the G20, the roles and responsibilities of regulators worldwide are very heterogeneous with very few genuine policies. Strengthening and harmonizing accounting rules and regulations at the international level would offer a more serene environment for businesses, municipalities, banks and also that support them in a crisis and taxpayers who are indirectly paying the bills.

CHAPTER

3G

Money Laundering in Financial Markets

OUTLINE

1 BACKGROUND

Typically money laundering is the process of transforming illegal funds of criminal origin into legal funds flowing in the legal economy. The process has three stages: placement, layering, and integration.

- *Placement* is the initial stage of introduction of illicit cash into the financial system. There are cases when brokerage houses accept cash for alimenting accounts, but generally the use of cash in securities transactions is relatively unusual and is actively discouraged by securities firms and their regulators [92]. Nevertheless with the new crime involving less cash and more electronic money forms, the placement has begun to change in nature and to represent the insertion of any illicit type of fund or liquid assets in the economy.
- The second stage, the *Layering*, represents the transfer from one account to another or the change in nature of the initial inserted funds in order to hide the criminal source of the funds and to cut the links with the offenders. The financial markets are mainly concerned with this stage as they can move the *value* of the crime proceedings across assets, across countries, and across counterparties, involving realized or unrealized fund transfers. The ability to move the value without effectively moving the money from one account to another is a particularity and

http://dx.doi.org/10.1016/B978-0-12-801221-5.00011-7

also an advantage of financial markets compared to other layering methods.
- The last phase, the *Insertion*, consists of investing the illegal gains in the legal economy and making it generate legal profits. Once this has been achieved, the likelihood of commingling the illegal funds with legal investments is very high, thereby making the investigation process more complex. Financial markets are a good investment vehicle for the last stage, with a large choice from structured products to bonds and from crowdfunding to private equity.

From the late 1990s there were signals that markets are being used to launder money [92]. The British police had identified schemes to launder money through the London Stock Exchange. Warning signals raised on the United States Over-the-Counter Bulletin Board (OTCBB) have made it a prime target of money launderers.

2 THE INDUSTRY OF MONEY LAUNDERING

One of the strong tendencies in global crime is the separation between the process of crime and criminal proceedings. Criminals understand that in the current environment it is very likely they will face justice sooner or later. Therefore, dealing with the legal system becomes just another variable of the crime business. The main outcome for a criminal or a group of criminals of court proceedings is the foreseeable impact on their assets. The court's decision can be adjusted but the freezing of assets cannot.[1] Losing their assets and the incumbent power is one the means of cracking down a crime across the world. Thus the ultimate defense for criminals is to break the connection between the crime and the money flows that lead to court proceedings in the legal economy. Based on this fact money laundering became a standalone industry, disconnected from the underlying crime. By decoupling these two dimensions the investigative work became more difficult and court sentences were less likely to address the full picture. It is unlikely that an investigation would wipe out a money-laundering platform and all its underlying crime. The consequence of this diversification implies that funds from a securities fraud are not necessary cleaned though the financial markets, and crimes on the streets are not necessarily cleaned by pizza restaurants or kebab takeaways. In fact the more disconnected are the crime and the laundering, the harder it is for investigators to complete the puzzle. Thus basic protection tax proceedings can end up in an Over-the-Counter (OTC) derivative shell company in Jersey, credit card scams can end in Bitcoins and manipulation of the real estate market in Spain. But for a launderer the dilemma is quickly solved as the supports can be decoupled and funds can be channeled into different investments as many times as necessary to sidetrack the investigators.

The financial flows generated by financial crime and cleared in the money-laundering process tend to be directed toward a certain number of countries amenable to banking secrecy for their clients. Table 1 shows a classification of the top countries in terms of bank secrecy. Despite its traditional image Switzerland appears in 24th position, the list being dominated by Caribbean countries and Pacific islands.

3 MECHANISM OF MONEY LAUNDERING ON MARKETS

The financial markets, deprived of liquidity after the recent financial crisis, went through a phase of being very fragile and they were exposed to money-laundering risk, due to the ability of launderers to inject quick liquidities [93, 94].

[1] *I processi si aggiustano, le confische no*, Michele Scarcella, ex boss of Sacra Corona Unita, Ugento, Puglia, Italy.

TABLE 1 Countries with a High Level of Banking Secrecy

Rank 2013	Country	Secrecy score
1	Samoa	87.6
2	Vanuatu	86.67
3	Seychelles	85.23
4	St Lucia	84.4
5	Brunei Darussalam	84.13
6	Liberia	83.23
7	Marshall Islands	81.63
8	Barbados	81
9	Belize	80.4
10	San Marino	80.13
11	Mauritius	80
12	Antigua and Barbuda	80
13	Bahamas	79.93
14	Bermuda	79.87
15	St Kitts and Nevis	79.57
16	Malaysia (Labuan)	79.53
17	Maldives	79.47
18	Liechtenstein	79.27
19	United Arab Emirates (Dubai)	79
20	Nauru	78.93
21	Lebanon	78.87
22	Gibraltar	78.6
23	Dominica	78.53
24	Switzerland	78.4

Note: Financial Secrecy Index, http://www.financialsecrecyindex.com/.
Source: Financial Secrecy Index.

Levi [95] was one of few researchers to identify that the phenomenon of laundering money on financial markets covers a large range of typologies from simple unregistered securities to exotic derivatives. The main difference from the other types of laundering is that the forensic accounting is less efficient in detecting these schemes, mainly when they involve complex products. Therefore, understanding of the big picture and the mechanisms of the flows are crucial in the investigations process.

Bearer securities are a basic example of how a security can be used for laundering money. Bearer securities are shares or bonds whose owner's name is unregistered in the registry of the issuer, and which are payable to its holder or presenter. This type of security is available in some European countries and the owner does not appear in any files as registered securities owners do.

A more complex scheme presented by Pemberton [92] as the Misappropriation Model allows criminals to repatriate dirty money from offshore and use it onshore while avoiding paying income tax on the money.

Crime groups with large sums in offshore accounts start by taking control of a publicly traded shell company. It can be a technology company or penny stock shell with no real business. After they have taken over and hold majority control, the criminals appoint either themselves or in most of the cases associates as directors and officers of the company. They create a " buzz" around the company with some new product or innovation or big business ongoing. This justifies the fact that later the company's shares are sold to anonymous offshore companies in return for the original illegal funds. This type of scheme is often associated with market manipulation frauds. The shares are offered to the public through special financial products like the issuance of restricted Regulation "S" or Regulation "D" shares available in the United States.

3.1 Focus on Derivatives

The role of derivatives is less studied and less well known in the money-laundering process. A basic laundering mechanism is the execution through a brokerage house of a long and short position on the same asset (buying and selling the same future contract or buying a call option and a put option or buying and selling a vanilla swap). The broker will pay the client for the position ending up in the money with clean money and will cancel in his records the out of the money transaction to avoid any audit trail. Technically only the transaction fee and the broker's margin are costs for the client dealing with illegal funds, but in this way they manage to obtain proof of origin for the funds.

BANK OF CREDIT AND COMMERCE INTERNATIONAL—THE FIRST MONEY LAUNDERING

Background

Founded in 1972 by the Pakistani banker Agha Hasan Abedi, and having Bank of America as the main shareholder, BCCI became at one time the biggest private bank in the world. Incorporated in Luxembourg BCCI operated from London and Karachi. From the 1980s the bank became a main platform for global money laundering and was under scrutiny from many regulators and law enforcers.

Derivatives and money laundering

A well-known example is that of the Bank of Credit and Commerce International[a] and its derivatives arm Capcom led by Syed Ziauddin Ali Akbar, who explained the above scheme to undercover Agent Robert Mazur from US customs in 1988. Agent Mazur testified how Akbar used pairs of long short trades that was called "mirror image" trading to launder huge sums of money. Mirror image trading involved two accounts controlled by the same person and the bank was buying contracts for one account while selling an equal number from another account. Since both accounts are controlled by the same individual any profit or loss is effectively netted. One main advantage of this strategy is that being a zero-sum game it can pass under the radar of auditors among many millions of dollars worth of legitimate transactions, thereby making it untraceable.[b]

Trivia

Until its fall in 1991, the BCCI served many dictators and criminal groups including the ex-Iraqi president Saddam Hussein and the Medelin Cartels. The CIA also held accounts with the bank to fund the Afghan resistance against the Soviet army, the forerunner of modern Talibans.

[a] The origin and early years of BCCI, http://fas.org/irp/congress/1992_rpt/bcci/03hist.htm.

[b] Money laundering with derivatives, http://www.wolfgang-hafner.ch/media/Geldw%C3%A4sche/ARIF%20Money-laundering.pdf.

The mirror trading scheme was also favored by a regulation concerning bunched orders of derivatives, which are orders entered by an account manager that are executed as a block and allocated after execution to customers so the trades may be cleared and for post trade allocation. The Commodity Futures Trading Commission (CFTC) regulation 1.35(a1) allowed a derivatives broker to not identify his client's trade allocations during a trading session. The broker could do this in the post trade without specific rules. This specific regulation allowed all types of misconduct in the derivative world including money laundering.

The regulation in the United States changed in 2012 when the CFTC imposed new rules on time limits for bunched orders, requiring that bunched orders be allocated as soon as practicable after execution, but also providing absolute deadlines by which allocation must occur. For trades that are cleared, allocation must occur sufficiently before the end of the day the order is executed to identify the ultimate customer for each trade. Account managers are forbidden from giving any account or group of accounts consistently favorable or unfavorable treatment relative to other accounts, in order to reduce the risk of mirror trades.

If the cleared derivatives market requires strict monitoring of its participants, the OTC derivatives market offers more maneuver for launderers.

3.1.1 OTC Derivatives

OTC derivatives are bilateral agreements between two counterparties, that are not traded or executed on an exchange. In some cases, OTC deals can be registered via an exchange without the margin mechanism. Compared to the listed derivatives which are standardized, the OTC products are tailored depending on the needs of the two counterparties. The warning signals in these type of transactions are in the following situations:

- The features of the OTC derivative are very different from the cleared versions. A swap with a premium at initiation is generally not a sign of confidence. The Goldman's Sachs swap offer to the Greek treasury is one example of a derivative used as for malpractice. But in reality this type of instrument can hide other fund exchanges in a laundering scheme.
- There is no economic basis for explaining that derivative. As an example a small retail enterprise based in Wales with all costs and revenues indexed in GBP, enter in an OTC Forex forward on YEN/CAD. In these cases, the OTC derivative can justify a one-time payment or flow. Not being marked to market regularly the settlement can occur whenever a fund needs to be transferred.
- The valuation of the derivative is sophisticated and uses models which are based on traders' opinions (Level 3 assets). An example can be a Swiss trading company entering in an OTC accumulator option[2] on chrome prices with a Russian metal exporter. As the chrome market is illiquid with not many derivatives listed, the pricing of such a product is almost impossible. This ambiguity can be used to justify a fund transfer between the two firms, part of a laundering scam.

Figure 1 shows a simple example of money laundering using OTC derivatives. A criminal group owning a company seeded with illegal funds makes an investment with a specialized firm. This firm does not need to be a financial company, and could easily be a trading house or an importer exporter. The investment firms purchase in OTC exotic derivative products from offshore firms. Sporadic settlements based on "mark to model" ("mark to mob") justify a fund transfer to the offshore firm. The offshore firm has the same OTC derivative back to back with another counterparty controlled by the crime group, but with a clean record. The same "mark to mob" valuation justifies the transfer of funds to the counterparty resulting in clean funds. The very same scheme is used currently by firms to reduce their tax bills in countries with high taxation rates.

3.2 Private Equity and Venture Capital

Private equity and venture capital firms are the less scrutinized area of the financial industry by regulators. The Patriot Act in the United States and other recent regulations across various jurisdictions (i.e., Financial Action Task Force recommendations) increased the surveillance effort mainly concerning the origin of the funds and the focus on Know Your Client policies. Over the past decade the private equity industry has become more global and involved more transnational fund flows than before.

With the recent crisis the role of private equity firms featured more prominently in the economic picture due to the massive regulatory pressure on banks that were urged to reduce the credit flow to economies and also the financing of cross-national deals (Figure 2). Thus private equity industry increased its total assets under management since the recent crisis to more than 25%.

[2]An accumulator option is a regular forward contract where the notional value of the forward is determined over the life of the option up to the expiry date rather than by a predefined value.

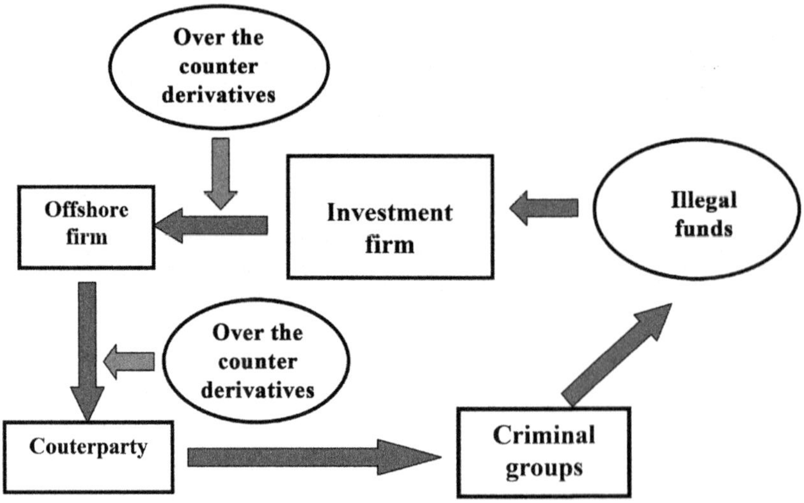

FIGURE 1 Money-laundering OTC derivatives: *Placement*: A criminal group owning a company seeded with illegal funds makes an investment with a specialized firm. This firm does not need to be a financial company, and could easily be a trading house or an importer exporter. The investment firms purchase OTC exotic derivative products from offshore firms. *Layering*: Sporadic settlements based on "mark to model" ("mark to mob") justify a fund transfer to the offshore firm. The offshore firm has the same OTC derivative back to back with another counterparty controlled by the crime group, but with a clean record. *Insertion*: The same "mark to mob" valuation justifies the transfer of funds to the counterparty resulting in clean funds.

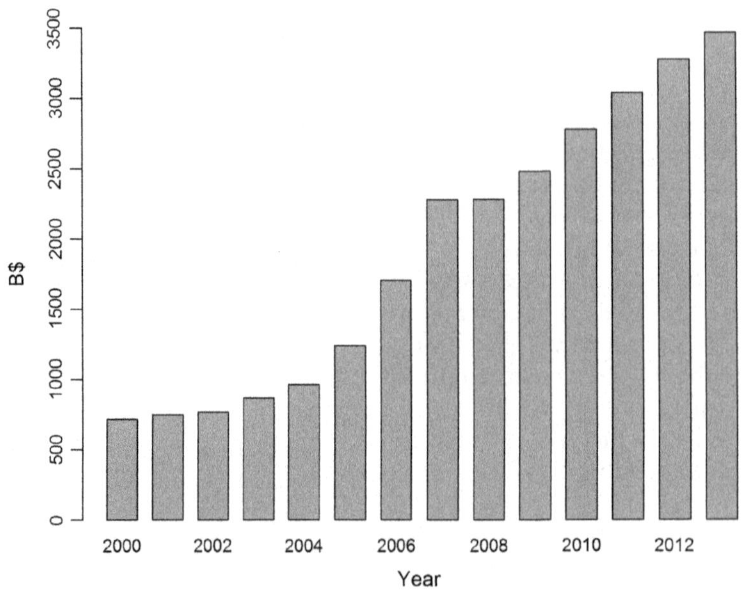

FIGURE 2 Private equity industry. Evolution of the total assets under management. *Source*: *The 2014 Preqin Global Private Equity Report*.

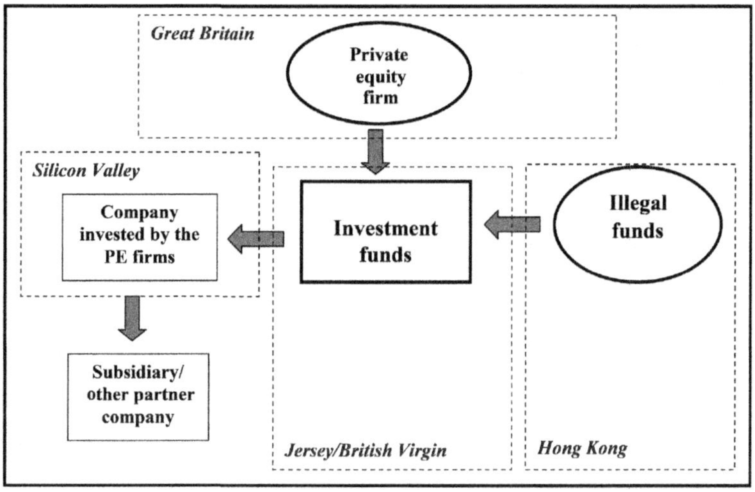

FIGURE 3 Money-laundering schemes in the private equity sector. In this example, illegal funds originating from Hong King are invested in a private equity company with an office in London, but with its funds incorporated in an offshore island. The private equity firm takes shares in a technology start-up based in the United States, having a subsidiary or subcontracting relationship with a company based in China. This last piece of the puzzle is generally linked to the individuals who placed the money in the private equity fund. Therefore, the funds' transfer cycle is closed and represents an avenue for money laundering.

In the example shown in Figure 3 illegal funds originating from Hong Kong are invested in a private equity company with an office in London, but with its funds incorporated in an offshore island. This phase represents the placement stage. In the layering stage, the private equity firm takes shares in a technology start-up based in the United States, having a subsidiary or subcontracting relationship with a company based in China. This last piece of the puzzle represents the integration stage and is generally linked to the individuals who placed the money in the private equity fund. Therefore, the funds' transfer cycle is closed and represents an avenue for money laundering.

Another variable that makes the picture more complex is the partnership between private equity firms and the development banks or supranational investment agencies like the World Bank. Such an example is Emerging Capital Partners, a private equity fund backed by Britain's Department for International Development, which in 2012 was under criminal investigation by the European Union and Nigerian anti-corruption authorities for its alleged involvement in fraud and the laundering of millions of dollars looted by James Ibori, the ex-Governor of Nigeria's oil-rich Delta State.[3] This scandal was amplified by the fact that the private equity fund was in partnership with the International Finance Corporation, the World Bank's private sector arm, as the first participant in the World Bank's Private Equity Africa Climate Change Investment Support Program.[4] Furthermore the World Bank initiated a 100 billion dollar for tackling climate change

[3]UK development fund implicated in money-laundering investigation, http://www.globaljustice.org.uk/news/2012/apr/16/uk-development-fund-implicated-money-laundering-investigation.

[4]IFC's private equity investments cause controversy, http://www.brettonwoodsproject.org/2012/02/art-569564/.

with investment in Third World countries. This could give an indication about the risk to which the private equity sector is exposed in the new globalized picture.

4 NEW FINANCING TOOLS AND MONEY LAUNDERING

4.1 Crowdfunding

Crowdfunding aims to decouple the financing of entrepreneurs from the harsh world of Private Equity, Venture Capital, and LBO firms. Thus crowdfunding gathers small amounts of funds from a large number of participants to finance a new business venture. Crowdfunding uses all kinds of networks including the main social networks to attract investors.

By its nature crowdfunding is susceptible to money-laundering abuses or can be a tool itself for laundering money. The crowdfunded securities are generally low-priced for reasons of accessibility and are placed in offerings exempted from registration and not subject to specific regulatory scrutiny. Two scenarios of laundering exist:

- A firm controlled by criminals is crowdfunded with proceedings coming from crime or illegal activities.
- A crowdfunding platform is in criminal hands and various funds are directed toward the appropriate business that can represent the final phase of the laundering process.

4.2 Structured Products

Structured products are financial instruments generally dealt OTC aimed to fit specific investors' profiles. In most cases, structured products have exotic derivatives embedded which are exposed to the same problem as OTC derivatives. Here things are much easier as the underwriter of the product can propose a valuation of the product again based on mark to model that can justify a big fund transfer to an investor. Many structured product investments are domiciled in tax havens in order to optimize the investor's gains. This adds another degree of complexity to the scheme.

4.3 Digital and Crypto-Currencies

With the many advantages brought by the emergence of digital and crypto-currencies also comes many threats. Forming basically a non-centralized and distributed system, parallel to the current banking system, the digital/crypto-currencies are a first choice for many money launderers today. The case of Liberty Reserve, one of the biggest platforms for washing illegal funds, and the current scrutiny of Bitcoins are warning signals about the role of innovation in the money-laundering industry.

5 MAJOR CASES INVOLVING REPUTED INSTITUTIONS

Money-laundering cases, like many other financial crimes, require the involvement of big financial institutions for various reasons. First, to transfer large amounts of money in an effective way the involvement of major banks facilitates the task. Second, in terms of reputations, a transfer coming from a reputed company like JPMorgan would be regarded as less suspicious by an investigator compared to a transfer from a bank incorporated in Vanuatu. Last but not the least is that even those criminals that want to avoid reputed banks should be aware that small banks often have links with the bigger firms and when an international transfer is made the major bank takes part in the operations.

Few major banks or institutions have been caught in the web of money laundering over the past few decades. There is more or less material evidence of the fact that they use financial markets as tools for laundering money, but the aim of the following examples is to support the following conjecture:

Proposition 1. *Whenever a large-scale crime (financial or not) occurs, in order to clear and clean the proceeds of that crime a major financial institution with an international presence needs to be involved.*

Argument. A first issue is that of correspondent banks. In theory, a major bank could have a myriad of correspondent banks across the globe, with various profiles of risk. When a client uses the services of a small bank for transferring money abroad it benefits from the fact that the small bank has as correspondent a major bank with global coverage. Banks of this type are shell banks with no physical presence in any country for conducting business with their clients, offshore banks with licenses limited to transacting business with persons outside the licensing jurisdiction, or banks licensed and regulated by jurisdictions with weak anti-money-laundering controls that invite banking abuses and criminal misconduct.

A 2001 US Senate report explains that the prevailing principle among US banks has been that any bank holding a valid license issued by a foreign jurisdiction qualifies for a correspondent account because US banks should be able to rely on the foreign banking license as proof of the foreign bank's good standing. US banks have too often failed to conduct careful due diligence reviews of their foreign bank clients, including obtaining information on the foreign bank's management, finances, reputation, regulatory environment, and anti-money-laundering efforts.

A second issue is that of the complexity of operations that can be handled by a small bank or an offshore shell bank. More sophisticated schemes including the use of exotic derivatives, structured products, share in private equity, or access to exchanges are offered only by multi-business institutions. These tools make the laundering process easier to disguise and in fact one would take less risk in passing 10 million dollars through a bank with thousands of billions of assets compared to passing them through an offshore bank with 100 million in assets.

5.1 Bank of the Vatican

Since the death in 1978 of John Paul I, the 33-day Pope, the number of stories, movies, and books around the *Bank of the Vatican* continue to increase. The initial leitmotif of the tormented 1980s in Italy involving the Sicilian Mafia, the American La Cosa Nostra, the Italian politicians, and the lodge P2 fueled many Hollywood film scripts. The IOR was involved in the collapse of the famous Banco Ambrosiano after the disappearance of $1.3 billion in loans made to companies in Latin America.

The second leitmotif reemerged in early 2010 when Pope Benedict VI, with the participation of law enforcement, produced a big turnaround in the Vatican's finances. Bank of the Vatican is most likely a euphemism; the two most representative institutions of the Vatican are the *Institute for Religious Works* and *Administration of the Patrimony of the Apostolic See.*

The Institute for Works of Religion (Istituto per le Opere di Religione, IOR) was constituted on June 27, 1942 by Pope Pius XII in Vatican City. The newly established IOR absorbed the former Administration of the Works of Religion (Amministrazione delle Opere di Religione, AOR), which had originated in the Commission for Pious Causes (Commissione ad pias causas) established by Pope Leo XIII on February 11, 1887. The AOR was initially a type of central administration for the Pope's remaining assets after the loss of the Papal States.

The changes in the Vatican started in 2010 when IOR's chairman, Ettore Gotti Tedeschi, and its director general, Paolo Cipriani, were investigated[5] for money laundering. Money transfers from IOR's account with other correspondent Italian banks amounting to more than 30 million dollars triggered the attention of the

[5]Money-laundering inquiry touches Vatican Bank, http://www.nytimes.com/2010/09/22/world/europe/22vatican.html?_r=0.

investigators. Major financial institutes, including JPMorgan, ceased doing business with the IOR because of a lack of transparency. Following these events Benedict VI replaced Ettore Gotti Tedeschi in 2013 with Ernst von Freyberg, a German banker, with the aim to reestablish order in the Vatican finances.[6] But in 2014 the picture became more complex when Monsignor Nunzio Scarano, a former Vatican prelate, was arrested for money laundering while trying to smuggle across the border some 20 million euros in 500 euro notes.[7] A close look at the 2012 IOR annual report[8] nevertheless provides a very different reality check. The bank serves 18,900 clients compared to 21,000 clients in 2011. The total assets represent 4.9 billion euros and net assets 0.769 billion euros. The net result of the bank is almost 87 million euros. This equates the IOR with an average level subsidiary of a medium-sized commercial bank in Germany, far from those scenarios that imagined billions were being laundered. The question that comes naturally is why such a small institution with assets lower than the total funds laundered by the Bank of New York (BNY) in 1990 is constantly depicted as a center of financial crime?

The annual report of the IOR as well as the reforms started by Pope Benedict VI and continued by Pope Francis seem to have brought more clarity to the financial activities of the Vatican. But the main problems were unfortunately not tackled in a satisfactory way either by media or by investigators. The recurrent target of all approaches since the 1980s was the Vatican, the Italian Cardinals, and the "Bank of the Vatican." But the big picture was completely forgotten. In fact the Catholic church has an extended patrimony spread over almost all continents that has been built up in the course of its bimillennial existence. The value of this patrimony, including both liquid and illiquid assets, is much higher than the few billions on IOR's balance sheet. The way that this huge institution of the Catholic Church and also of humanity is governed and managed is far from being understood.

5.2 Bank of New York

In 1999, the US Justice Department started an investigation against BNY for participating in a Russian tax-evasion scheme amounting to a total of 7 billion USD. The initial allegations were that Russian citizens transferred funds into the US avoiding local taxation and BNY facilitated the transfer. Slowly with the participation of the European investigators the case revealed itself to be a massive money-laundering scheme for Russian organized crime that came to prominence during the troubled Yeltsin era.[9] Beyond the BNY scandal many sources indicate the presence of Semion Yudkovich Mogilevich,[10] the very same person who was at the center of a pump and dump and money-laundering scam on the Canadian Stock Exchange in the late 1990s.

The scandal revealed a weakness of the banking systems around the correspondent account. A correspondent bank can conduct business transactions, provide services, accept deposits, and gather documents on behalf of

[6]The money-laundering Vatican Bank comes clean, http://www.thedailybeast.com/articles/2014/05/19/the-money-laundering-vatican-bank-comes-clean.html.

[7]Arrested Vatican prelate in new money-laundering charge, http://www.reuters.com/article/2014/01/21/us-vatican-bank-monsignor-idUSBREA0K0DE20140121.

[8]Rapporto Annuale 2012, http://www.ior.va/Portals/0/Content/Media/Documents/AnnualReports/425x00sc399T!/IOR_RapportoAnnuale_2012.pdf.

[9]US investigators missed Russian Mob in NY Bank scandal, http://www.thekomisarscoop.com/2002/08/us-investigators-missed-russian-mob-in-ny-bank-scandal/.

[10]Elite's underworld links exposed, http://www.theguardian.com/world/1999/sep/05/paulfarrelly.theobserver.

TABLE 2 Recap of the Main Public Investigations Concerning HSBC

Year	Misconduct/crime	Aftermath
2015	Gold and silver manipulation[a]	Under investigation
2014	Platinum and palladium price manipulation[b]	Ongoing class action
2012	Mis-selling financial products[c]	Fined $2.3 billion
2012	LIBOR manipulation[d]	No fines followed the investigations
2013	EURIBOR manipulation[e]	No fines followed the investigations
2012	Money laundering[f]	Penalties of $1.9 billion
2015	Tax evasion[g]	Under scrutiny
2014	FX manipulation[h]	Fines of $618 millions

[a] *Banks face US manipulation probe over metals pricing, http://www.bloomberg.com/news/articles/2015-02-24/banks-said-to-face-u-s-manipulation-probe-over-metals-pricing.*
[b] *HSBC, Goldman Rigged Metals Prices for Years, Suit says, http://www.bloomberg.com/news/articles/2014-11-25/hsbc-goldman-rigged-metals-prices-for-years-suit-says.*
[c] *HSBC pays $4.2 billion for fines and mis-selling in 2012, http://www.bbc.co.uk/news/business-21653131.*
[d] *Libor scandal: EU slaps six banking giants with $2.3-billion fine, biggest penalty yet for rigging lending benchmarks, http://business.financialpost.com/2013/12/04/libor-scandal-eu-slaps-six-banking-giants-with-2-3-billion-fine-biggest-penalty-yet-for-rigging-lending-benchmarks/.*
[e] *Three banks accused of rigging Euribor, http://www.telegraph.co.uk/finance/newsbysector/banksandfinance/10843666/Three-banks-accused-of-rigging-Euribor.html.*
[f] *HSBC to pay $1.9 billion in US money-laundering penalties, http://www.bbc.co.uk/news/business-20673466.*
[g] *HSBC aided tax avoidance, http://www.moneyexpert.com/news/hsbc-aided-tax-avoidance/800583223.*
[h] *Six banks fined 2.6bn by regulators over Forex failings, http://www.bbc.co.uk/news/business-30016007.*

other financial institutions. Criminals used those smaller correspondents bank to transfer funds into the United States. The scheme involved many companies mainly based in France and Italy which were dedicated to laundering funds for the Russian criminal organizations.

5.3 HSBC

The case of HSBC is one of the most interesting, the prominent British bank over the past five years going through a series of scandals involving all areas of its activity. Table 2 shows a recap of the main public investigations, the money-laundering scandal in relation to the South American drug cartels being one of the most problematic for the bank and mainly for its North American business. HSBC settled the case in the US court for a near 2 billion dollar fee.[11]

Among the accusations it was pointed out that the bank failed to monitor more than $670 billion in wire transfers and more than $9.4 billion in purchases of USD from HSBC Mexico representing vehicles for money laundering. This allegedly allowed the Sinaloa drug cartel in Mexico and the Norte del Valle cartel in Colombia to move more than $881 million through HSBC's US unit from 2006 to 2010.

The allegation does not concern activity on the financial markets, focusing only the currency

[11] HSBC Judge approves $1.9bn drug-money laundering accord, http://www.bloomberg.com/news/articles/2013-07-02/hsbc-judge-approves-1-9b-drug-money-laundering-accord.

exchange activity in branches. Nevertheless HSBC is one of the main players on the FX markets and the huge sums involved in the allegations are not likely to have influenced the market activity of the bank. Furthermore being a major FX player probably allowed it to have some advantage in hedging the plain spot transactions.

Beyond being a cautionary tale this episode shows that banks that became too big, too diversified, and too global are difficult to manage as a unitary entity and local dysfunctions might occur.

5.4 Julius Baer

Swiss private banks are perceived by the public as a gray area due to suspicions of money laundering and tax evasion. Regarding tax evasion there has been much research and many investigations pointing out the various mechanisms and assessing the loss for various governments. As regard money laundering in relation to financial markets, there are fewer public cases.

One case that was reported in the media in 2014 concerned Julius Baer, the reputed private bank that was investigated for receiving funds in a Swiss account that were linked to value-added tax (fraud in the EU Emissions Trading System) and failure to perform adequate client checks.[12]

The fraud on the carbon markets discussed in a separate chapter is a unique case involving tax evasion, money laundering, and cyber-crime using a financial instrument. This type of crime carried out criminal groups in almost all cases requires the participation of a large institution in order to redirect the huge financial flows. Institutions like Deutsche Bank or Julius Baer which took part directly or indirectly in the fraud made the transfer of large amounts of money easier.

[12]Swiss bank Julius Baer says cooperating in EU carbon market tax fraud probe, http://www.reuters.com/article/2014/09/30/julius-baer-carbontrading-fraud-idUSL6N0RV55Z20140930.

6 OUTLOOK

All right, $16,000 laundered at 75 cents on the dollar, minus my fee, which is 17%, comes out to $9960. Congratulations, you've just left your family a second-hand Subaru. ***Saul Goodman, Breaking Bad***

Money laundering in relation to financial markets, despite many warning signals, a field which has not been sufficiently covered by investigators, regulators, and researchers. Money laundering is currently assessed through a framework adapted for the classic paradigm of blue-collar crime cash proceedings that need to be placed into the legal economy. Modern crime imposed radical changes on the laundering process. Thus money laundering became a standalone industry which services different types of crimes ranging from traditional to modern white-collar crime. The placement phase does not deal only with cash but also with deposits from offshore banks, electronic accounts (PayPal), securities, or digital currencies. In this new environment, the financial markets can be an efficient tool due to their speed of transactions and complexity, which makes it easier to hide compared to classic real estate laundering schemes, and their global coverage. OTC derivatives as well as structured products have the enormous advantage that their valuation is based in many cases on subjective assessment which can favor the integration stage of the laundering process. Crypto-currencies require a special focus in the context of money laundering. Currently Bitcoins and other similar currencies do not have the critical mass to clear huge amounts of funds. But if one day they are able to do so, the assumption regarding the reliance on big financial institutions for laundering large-scale crime proceedings should be reassessed.

PART IV

MODERN FINANCIAL CRIME

CHAPTER

4A

Hedge Funds

OUTLINE

1 BACKGROUND

In the current environment involving more regulatory burdens for both investors and managers it is difficult to give a precise definition of hedge funds and to point out the differences that separate them from traditional funds or even funds of funds. Nevertheless in the common view of the Wall Street, hedge funds are associated with above average returns in the double-digit area, generated through the use of sophisticated investment strategies involving leverage, long/short and derivative positions in both domestic and international markets. Most hedge funds are organized in the form of private investment partnerships and until very recently they were much less regulated. On the top of that, for tax reasons many hedge funds are incorporated in tax havens like Cyprus, Bermuda, etc. The foundation of the hedge funds industry was often associated with the image of Alfred Jones, but the first organizations

http://dx.doi.org/10.1016/B978-0-12-801221-5.00012-9

seemingly having hedge fund activities can be traced to the years prior to the Great Depression. The rationale behind a hedge fund is to provide a tool dedicated to high wealth individuals that would understand and foresee the advantages and risks associated with placing funds into such an investment. The strategies in hedge funds vary from very common ones like long/short on futures market to those on very illiquid markets like weather derivatives. This rationale became biased over time as many less wealthier individuals targeted the hedge funds to obtain higher returns. Thus many pensions funds, accumulation and sovereign funds started to invest in hedge funds mainly to diversify their portfolio.

As shown in Figure 1 a hedge fund and generally a fund is surrounded by many another actors who contribute directly or indirectly to the investment process.

From the perspective of access to the markets the most important role is that of the prime broker. Given the complexity of their strategies hedge fund managers execute trades with a number of brokers though a certain number of markets. The role of the prime broker is to provide a global service which involves the aggregation of orders, trades, and settlement with all brokers. This confers the advantage of having a centralized view on the trades and on their market value. Through this consolidated view the prime broker is able to provide financial services on behalf of collateral held and securities borrowed. On top of that many other services can be provided by the prime broker like risk management, advisory, technology services, custodianship, etc. Nevertheless the central clearing and the borrowing services can make the relationship between the prime broker and hedge funds very privileged. In conditions of distress, the prime broker can allow extra credit lines to the hedge funds or can cut the financing.

Another element in the picture is the custodian and depository institutions that have the role of safe-keeping the assets of the hedge funds and providing valuation services to the hedge fund. This service can be independently provided by a separate firm or by the prime broker or even internalized by the hedge funds. The net asset value (NAV) of the fund and its evolution over time is one of the key inputs for assessing the performance of a hedge fund. Compared to other traditional investment vehicles, hedge funds do not often disclose their books.

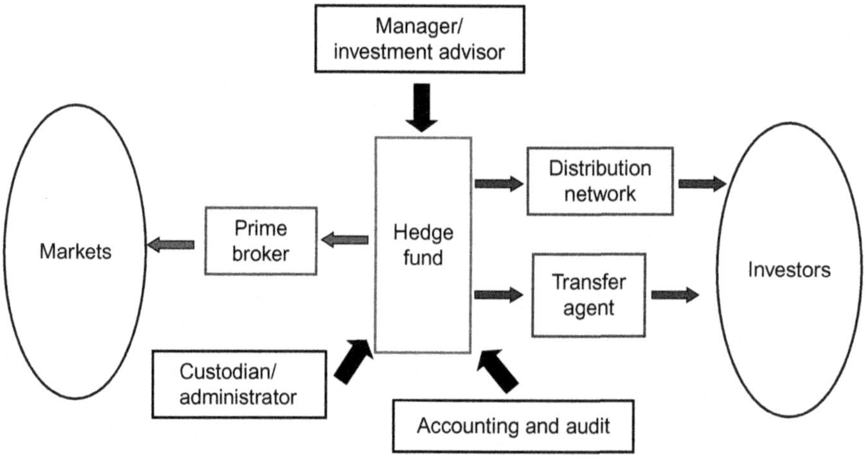

FIGURE 1 Hedge funds industry: service providers in the hedge fund industry.

The external auditor brings an independent view on the performance of the hedge funds and on its accounts. Two points should be addressed in this context. First is the ability of current accounting rules to capture the performance of hedge funds when the strategies are sophisticated and complex products are harbored in the books of the funds. The issues around the valuation of Level III assets in bank balance sheets are discussed in a separate chapter. This is also applicable to some hedge funds. Second is the asymmetry of information and ability to understand a market between the fund managers and the auditor. Complex strategies might imply the booking of immediate profit under an assumption that is difficult to verify. With the exception of those strategies focusing on liquid assets, many funds use markets which are niche and are difficult to understand for someone who is not an expert.

Even if these features are understood by the accountant how accurate can a static balance sheet reflect the situation of a company that has a value indexed on many stochastic parameters?

Going back to the global picture of the hedge sector, Figure 2 shows the evolution of the total assets under management in the hedge fund industry and a breakdown of the various types of hedge funds. Over the past 20 years hedge funds increased their managed assets over ten types. The recent financial crisis represented a massive drawback as the total assets under management

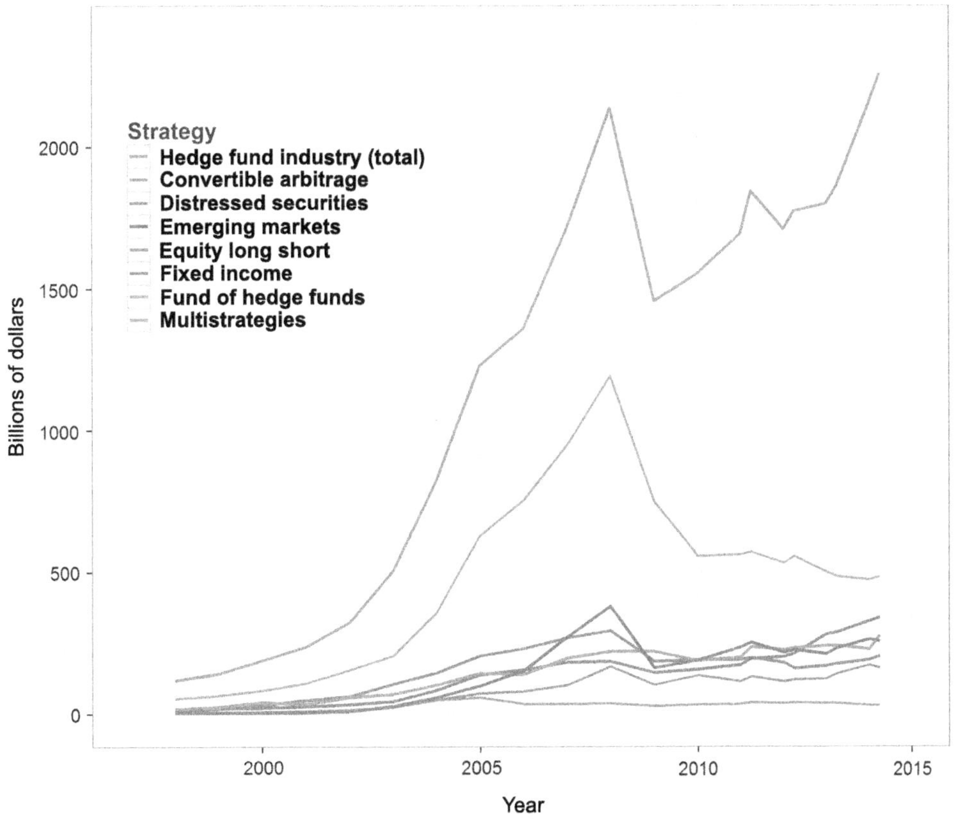

FIGURE 2 Evolution of the total assets under management in the hedge fund industry.

shrunk significantly. Post Lehman, the fund of funds was the most affected with a negative trend in terms of assets under management. Fixed income assets as well as multi-strategy funds had managed to keep a steady amount of new inflows.

In terms of returns hedge funds traditionally gave superior returns compared with other vehicles, as shown in Figure 3. Nevertheless since the financial crisis these assumptions changed and the performance of started to contract. For instance the Barclay hedge funds index had an inferior performance relative to the S&P 500 total returns index. Moreover even the Hedge funds Long/Short Index or Global Macro Index, which were historically less affected by the crisis in terms of returns, showed an inferior performance to equity indexes.

Beyond the change in terms of performance, the hedge fund industry suffered a more profound change in terms of activity and role within capital markets.

Prior to the 2008 crisis, the hedge fund industry provided vehicles for alternative investment, able to generate return/risk profiles appropriate for certain types of investors or with a diversification strategy for a conservative portfolio.

The numerous defaults and their consequences on the market underlined that hedge funds acted as concentrators of systemic risk as

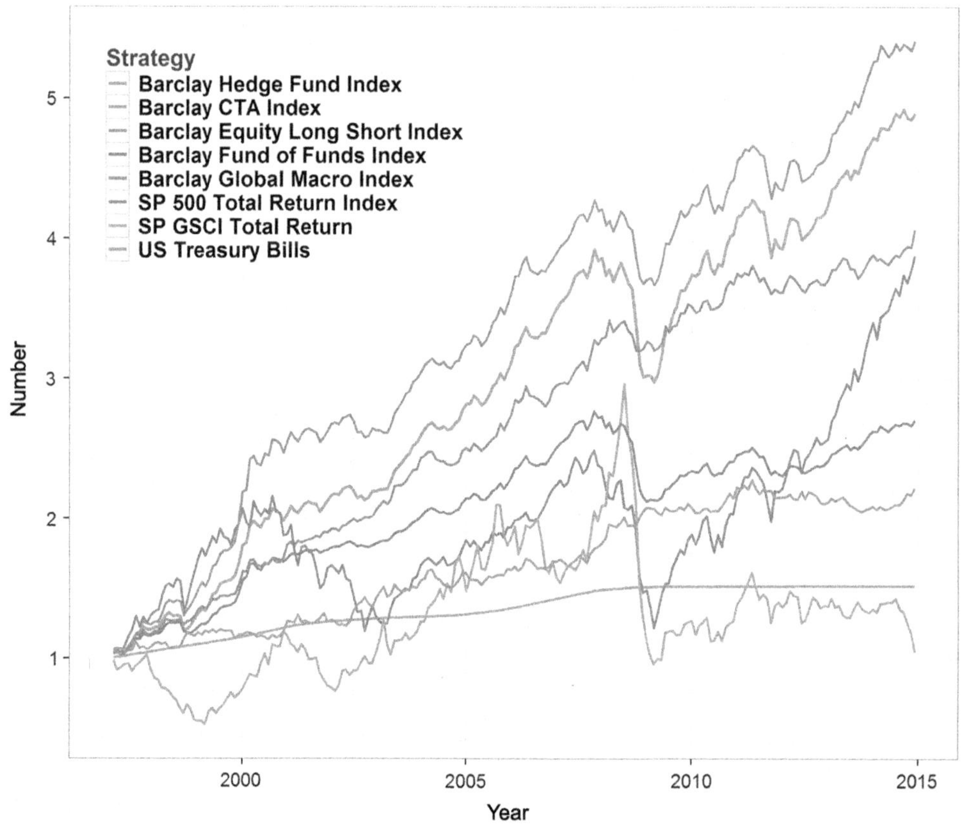

FIGURE 3 Hedge fund benchmark performance indexes: before the crisis hedge funds over-performed the classic market indexes. After the crisis the returns showed less growth compared to the S&P 500 total return index.

a consequence of the massive inflow of funds in the industry and the use of leverage.

Even before the Lehman event, hedge funds were perceived in some cases as having a strong impact (negative) on the real economy. The use of leverage and of strategies including short selling enables hedge funds to put strong pressure on listed companies, currencies, commodities, or even governments (if we take into account the role of hedge funds in the Argentinian default). Disposing of significant liquidity hedge funds can easily raid a market or an asset, thereby inducing bullish or bearish momentum, depending on their strategies. Regulation tries to tackle this behavior but its heterogeneity made things more complicated and had only partial effects.

In the post crisis era, the role and position of hedge funds started to evolve, mainly as a consequence of the new regulatory waves. Thus hedge funds picked up many functions from banks due to their less prudential requirements. Indeed banks on both the commercial and the investment sides saw their capital burden increasing exponentially after 2009, thereby limiting the panel of operations and activities that would be profitable.

For instance, the structured notes activity which represented the peak of complexity and profitability for investment banks almost disappeared, but surfaced in the hedge fund industry. With the new regulations and charges on counterparty risk (XVA, CVA-VAR) and market risk (Stressed VAR) banks shrunk their proprietary trading and market-making activities, which increased in size in hedge funds.

But the main behavioral drift occurred in traditional banking activity. With Basel III, banks were in the impossible position of having to finance the economy due to the capital burden of lending activities. Thus hedge funds started to develop commercial lending offers to small and medium corporations. With less prudential requirements, hedge funds were able to offer better conditions to industries.

One of the main innovations in terms of commercial credit is peer-to-peer lending, often proposed within dedicated hedge funds. Peer-to-peer lending proposes a unique tool which mediates and manages the interaction between the supplier and the demander of credit. The hedge fund selects a portfolio of possible facilities and makes this proposal to an investor. Securitization transactions are possible on the top of those lending lines. The difference from traditional banks is that in the case of a hedge fund the fund holder is not protected by a deposit scheme. He is not perceived as a deposit holder but as an investor, thereby bearing the consequent risk.

Banks kept an exposure to these activities by financing or investing in hedge funds, without bearing all the regulatory burden associated with the presence of those businesses on their balance sheet.

2 ORIGINS OF FRAUD IN THE HEDGE FUND INDUSTRY

The year 1998 is not only remembered by the public for France winning the association football World Cup or the twilight of the Yeltsin era in Russia, but also for the collapse of Long-Term Capital Management (LTCM), a reputed Wall Street hedge fund that employed at that time two Noble Prize winners (Scholes and Merton). Ironically they shared the Nobel Memorial Prize in economic sciences one year prior to the default of the fund.

The failure of LTCM and its consequences on the financial markets pointed to the fact that hedge funds play a structural role in the market's equilibrium. Many hedge funds opt for strategies on illiquid markets or products. For instance, there are managers specializing in out-of-the-money derivatives or in correlation basket derivatives. Many of these products are classified by the accounting rules as Level III instruments, their valuation depending on the opinion of management concerning the valuation parameters. Thus in some markets or sectors of the market hedge funds play a very big role as they can act as liquidity providers or even market makers. A good example would be the correlation products. These products are exposed to the correlation of two or more commodities, as their payoff depends on the evolution of certain assets. Generally even on markets like foreign exchange or interest rate correlation products are not liquid and are very difficult to replicate or hedge. At the highest level of sophistication, investment banks were heavily involved in structured products on fixed income and credit markets. They relied massively on the hedge fund market to obtain prices for those products or for various hedges. A very delicate situation occurred in the midst of the crisis when market volatility did not allow banks or hedge funds to have prices for those types of products. Dealing with inefficient and illiquid markets makes hedge funds perfect candidates for development of financial offenses. Controls and supervision of hedge funds' strategies become more difficult and almost impossible when the strategy is sophisticated. The collapse of the American hedge funds Amaranth in 2006 due to bad timing of a weather forecast pointed out the crucial role played by the prime brokers in the relationship with the hedge funds. Before analyzing some big failures in the industry and cases of fraud it is important to position the funds in the global context of the investment process.

A hedge fund traditionally remunerates itself as well as its managers through two streams of income:

- A portion of assets under management, generally 2% of AUM.
- A percentage of the net profit generated by the fund, about 15–20%.

This reward structure implies two tendencies intended to maximize the revenue, which are at the genesis of most of the fraud cases. First, a hedge fund has an incentive to increase the maximum amount of assets under its management. This is also for the structural reason of achieving the optimal scale and to have appropriate access to the market. Prime brokers generally have a preference toward funds of large size and are backed by reputed financial institutions. Second and most important is the need to generate high returns in order to increase the reward of the managers. These two points have crucial implications for the risk of fraud within the hedge fund industry. The main issue is related to the reliability of hedge funds' performance reports and how they can be altered, manipulated or scammed in order to attract more investors or to artificially inflate managers' rewards. In the absence of above average returns, hedge funds might turn toward other forms of illegal activity like money laundering or market manipulation.

Hedge funds involved in fraud or misconduct can be divided into three typologies:

1. *White funds*, established as legal hedge funds that starts as a legitimate activity with serious managers employing reasonable and transparent strategies. At a turning point they tend toward misconduct in order to dissimulate losses and to fraud or forge performance to keep the activity going. The role of moral hazard, presented in a separate chapter as a vector for crime propagation, is fundamental in these cases.
2. *Dark funds*, registered entities having from the start the aim to conduct or to facilitate criminal activities. Their purpose is to provide criminal groups with an investment vehicle to ensure an interface with the legal economy or to enter into fraudulent transactions. Being less regulated, hedge funds are the most cost-effective vehicles for crime in order to interact with the financial world.
3. *Gray funds*, established as legitimate activities that can be involved voluntarily or involuntarily in financial crime or misconduct. The illegal activities are

collateral and the hedge fund keeps its focus on its legitimate businesses. This typology is the most complicated to assess from both economic and legal points of view.

3 HEDGE FUND RISK ASSESSMENT

Hedge funds operate under a heterogeneous and less strict regulatory framework compared to other financial institutions. In the US hedge funds benefit from the "safe harbor" exemptions relative to the 1933 Securities Act, the 1940 Investment Company Act, and the 1940 Investment Advisers Act. The main outcome is that hedge funds are submitted to less disclosure and record-keeping requirements. The massive growth of the hedge fund industry in terms of assets under management and the lack of transparency with which hedge funds operate resulted in an increased number of frauds. Thus the Security Exchange Commission (SEC) adopted in 2006 Rule 203(b)(3)-2 for hedge funds in order to increase the prudential framework and to add clarity.

Few indicators can raise an alert flag for fraudulent activity within a hedge fund. Hedge funds with unusually strong performance claims over a long period of time, with a shorter period of negative returns, can be a strong indicator of misconduct. The term hedge fund[1] is in many ways inappropriate as the manager does not hedge, but speculates, thereby implying risk-taking strategies that can lead to periods high losses. Most hedge funds experience losses in some periods of their activities, as a normal consequence of their leveraged strategies.

Short selling is another red flag for most hedge funds. A typical fraud occurs when a fund takes a short position in a stock and orchestrates efforts to disseminate unfounded or materially false negative information about the stock, eroding the price, and allowing the fund to profit on the short position. The negative information is not always disseminated through classic support. It is enough that a manager or a group of managers start to trade intensively in a stock and to put in many bearish orders to give the impression that the stock is losing value. The stock manipulation is not operated through real support but by creating premises leading to a bearish momentum. Therefore, the short-selling-related crimes are complex cases for investigators.

Hedge funds investing in illiquid assets are difficult to audit and control due to the fact that the valuation of their strategies depends on parameters which are not observable. Thus managers have a free embedded option to overvalue investments in order to increase the performance and their reward. Moreover, the manager can use related parties as fund valuator in order to be able to influence the NAV.

If the hedge funds are not audited by reputable or independent accounting firms it can be a leading signal of a foreseeable fraud. For instance, many fraudulent funds are audited by accountants with a link to the managers. A good indicator is the ratio of audit fees to the total management fees.

If the relationship of hedge fund managers with that market access provider (broker, broker dealers, or prime brokers) is too close it can be an indication of a lack of independence and increased likelihood of involvement in collusive schemes. Investor complaints or involvement in previous litigation cases can be warning signs that the fund might be involved in misconduct.

4 SHAVING ASSETS

The case of private Asian investors who put money into a Hong Kong-based hedge fund with

[1] In French hedge fund is translated as *fond speculatif* (speculative fund), emphasizing clearly the risk-taking strategies of this type of funds.

alleged investment in stocks of a vodka refinery in Uzbekistan, who never got their money back, is probably symbolic of the most basic hedge fund scam. This type of fraud consists of extracting funds from the firm or spending them on various services and then informing the clients that the investment was not productive or filing for bankruptcy or simply vanishing.

The shaving assets scam is very often reported as a Ponzi scheme or a misrepresentation of performance. Indeed, Ponzi structures or rogue performances are employed by the managers in order to gain time and to gather as many funds as they can from the investors. Nevertheless the initial and ultimate goal is to pocket the money from the firm.

A version of this fraud developed as a scenario of operational risk is the fund theft by a senior manager of the funds. In this case, the fund along with the investors are victims of fraud. The classic example is that of a hedge fund CFO who stole funds from his firm to finance his gambling activities.[2]

5 MISREPRESENTATION OF RETURNS

Some hedge fund advisers misrepresent hedge funds' performance and *cherry-pick* investments for their clients. Some advisers also changed their methods for determining the value of securities in their funds. In a recent survey of the investment industry, SEC's Office of Compliance, Inspections, and Examinations revealed that more than 200 hedge fund advisers included misrepresentation in their material. Misrepresentations include the following three typologies which are depicted in the examples below:

- A hedge fund manager/adviser can alter the performance of the funds including the Sharpe ratio and the alpha. As shown in the following sections traditional risk metrics can be easily manipulated in order to present the results in a better light. In an SEC investigation[3] the New York-based hedge fund firm Think Strategy Capital Management LLC (520 million dollars in assets) and its sole managing director Chetan Kapur were charged with fraud in connection with two separate hedge funds they managed. Kapur misrepresented the funds' performance in order to bolster their track record, size, and credentials.
- When a hedge fund has illiquid assets, the manager can misrepresent the valuation of those assets. He can collude with third parties like brokers or valuation firms.
  In 2011, an SEC investigation[4] dismantled a scheme involving Michael Balboa, a former portfolio manager with Millennium Global Emerging Credit Fund, and two European-based brokers. They inflated the fund's reported monthly returns and NAV by manipulating its supposedly independent valuation process. From at least January to October 2008, Balboa surreptitiously provided its brokers with fictitious prices for two of the fund's illiquid securities holdings for them to pass on to the funds outside valuation agent and its auditor. The scheme caused the fund to drastically overvalue these securities holdings by as much as 163 million dollars in August 2008, which in turn allowed the fund to report inflated and falsely positive monthly returns. By overstating the fund's

[2]Ex-hedge fund exec who admitted theft for gambling habit denied leniency, http://www.nj.com/business/index.ssf/2012/06/judge_denies_leniency_to_ex-he.html.

[3]Think Strategy Capital Management, http://www.sec.gov/litigation/complaints/2011/comp22151.pdf.

[4]Millennium global emerging credit fund, http://www.sec.gov/litigation/complaints/2011/comp-pr2011-252.pdf.

returns and overall NAV, Balboa was able to attract at least 10 million dollars in new investments, defer about 230 million dollars in eligible redemptions, and generate millions of dollars in inflated management and performance fees.

- A manager can present to her clients a strategy with a given performance but implement *de facto* a different strategy which bears more and/or different risks. The final investment could be a company or a cluster in which the manager has a direct interest.

The indictment case against G. Rooney in 2011[5] was for fraudulently misusing the assets of the Solaris Opportunity Fund LP, for which it was the investment adviser. Rooney made a radical change in the fund's investment strategy, contrary to the fund's marketing materials, by becoming wholly invested in Positron Corp., a financially troubled microcap company. Rooney, who had been Chairman of Positron since 2004 and received salary and stock options from Positron since September 2005, misused the Solaris Fund's money by investing more than 3.6 million dollars in Positron through both private transactions and market purchases.

6 MONEY LAUNDERING

Being less regulated, operating on alternative markets and sometimes being incorporated in tax havens make hedge funds perfect candidates to enter in money laundering or terrorism financing schemes. The exposure of the hedge funds industry to the tax haven countries diminished significantly over the past two decades as shown in Figure 4. Currently less than 5% of the total hedge fund assets are run by managers incorporated in tax havens, compared to more than 15% 20 years ago.

The regulatory pressure around tax havens most likely affected this tendency. If the hedge funds had a certain degree of scrutiny, the origin of funds injected by investors is a blind spot of the scheme. Hedge funds operated for a long time without any rules regarding their anti-money-laundering policy.

After the 9/11 terrorist attacks, the American Congress passed the Patriot Act [96], which targeted as a priority the financial aspect of terrorism and had a wide remit. The International Money Laundering Abatement and Anti-Terrorist Financing Act arising from the Patriot Act, imposed a host of anti-money-laundering obligations on financial institutions. Title III altered existing law primarily by amending the Money Laundering Control Act of 1986, which set criminal penalties for money laundering, and the Bank Secrecy Act of 1970 (BSA) was a reporting statute aimed at banks. Section 326 of the Patriot Act required financial institutions to collect specified information from entities seeking to open an account. Financial institutions were also required to comply with section 352 by implementing anti-money-laundering programs by 2002. Hedge funds were exempted from section 326 requirements pending further study, and exempted from section 352 requirements until 2002. The aim at that time was to enforce the anti-money laundering dedicated to hedge funds. Nevertheless after a few years and some proposals in 2009 FinCEN indicated it was prioritizing issues and that hedge fund anti-money-laundering rules were simply not at the top of the list. Thus currently the hedge fund industry in the US lacks a clear framework for addressing money-laundering issues.

The money-laundering framework involving funds of hedge funds is summarized in Figure 5. In the placement phase, illegal money can be

[5]Solaris Management LLC, http://www.sec.gov/litigation/complaints/2011/comp22167.pdf.

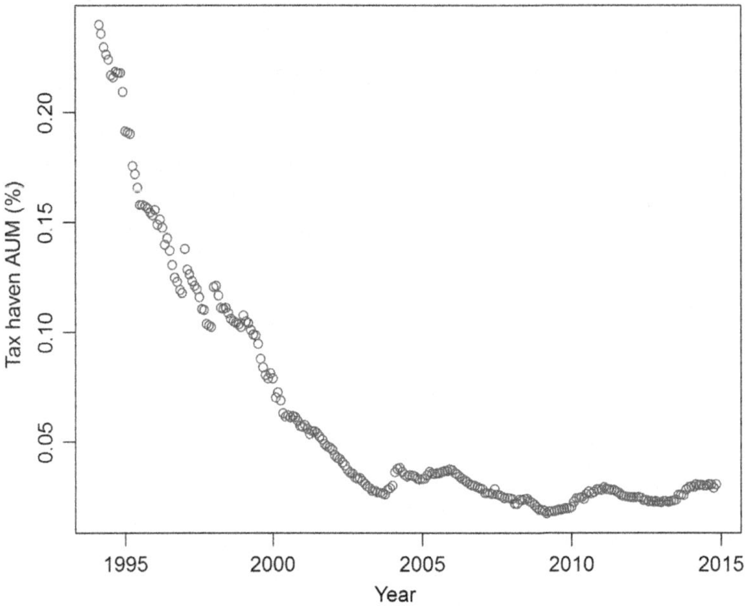

FIGURE 4 Hedge funds in tax havens: less than 5% of the total hedge fund assets are run by managers operating in tax havens, compared to more than 15% 20 years ago.

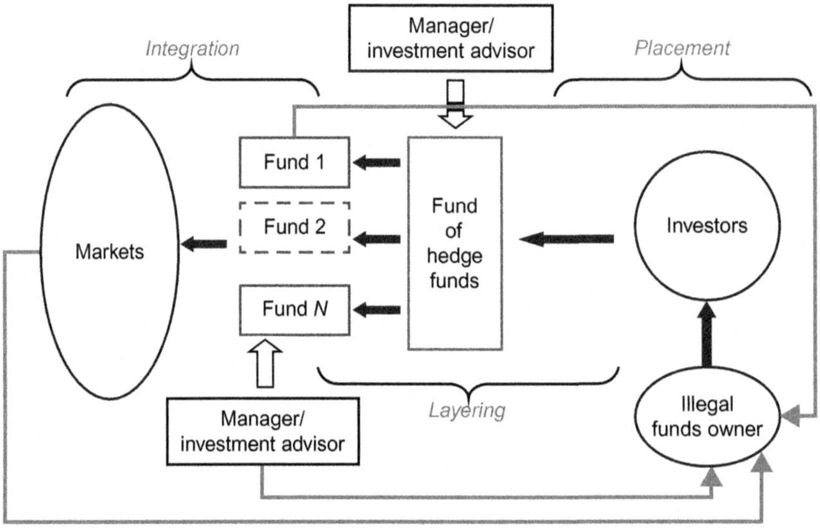

FIGURE 5 Fund of hedge funds money laundering: Red arrows (black in print versions) indicate the inflow of illegal funds. Green arrows (gray in print versions) reflect the dynamic of *cleaned* money. Illegal funds can be placed in the system directly or through third-party investors. The fund of hedge funds can introduce liquidity into their funds, with the proceeds of the investments. Investment can represent independent assets or supports controlled by the owner of the illegal organization (like a stock in a microcap). Funds return cleaned either from the manager in the form of consulting fees, or from performance return from the funds or from the final investment controlled by the perpetrators.

introduced into the system directly or through third-party investors. In the layering phase, the fund of hedge funds can introduce liquidity into their funds, with the proceeds of the investments. During the placement phase the investment can be independent assets controlled by the owner of the illegal organization (like a stock in a microcap). Funds return cleaned either from the manager in the form of consulting fees, from the manager, as gains from the fund itself or as profit from the final assets controlled by the perpetrators.

A recent small-scale example occurred in 2009 when the Federal Bureau of Investigation[6] targeted two financial professionals in Florida and Nebraska in an international probe against the German hedge-fund firm K1 Group. K1 Group, a firm that invested in other hedge funds, was in the middle of an international inquiry after saddling lenders including Barclays Plc, JPMorgan Chase, BNP Paribas, and Societe Generale SA with about 400 million dollars in losses. K1's founder, Helmut Kiener, was investigated for fraud and breach of trust. As a result of this case US prosecutors brought indictments against Stefan Seuss and Thomas Meyer, linked to K1, for money laundering. The two professionals agreed in 2007 to help a person to move about 500,000 dollars offshore. That person was in fact an undercover federal agent. Seuss ran a Miami consultancy called Seuss and Partners, helping clients set up offshore companies and foreign bank accounts to shield investments.

This example indicates that rogue hedge funds in an international context with transnational ramifications enable them to enter into money-laundering schemes using brokers, advisers, and independent promoters.

7 MARKET MANIPULATION

Hedge fund managers and investment managers generally might tend to look for easy rides in the markets. When a manager disposes of a few hundred million dollars he can invest in markets where this amount will be infinitesimal compared to the market's open interest or in markets where this amount can make a difference. Thus all types of market frauds relative to stock manipulation can easily be implemented by a small number of hedge funds. Large caps are not spared from being targets of hedge fund manipulation. The fact that large caps have many analysts and investors buying and selling actively means the stock can even be an advantage of the manipulator.

A manipulating strategy can start with a naked short sell of a stock with a significant amount of funds and the operation can affect the price of the stock. If the target is a small cap, even a small short volume can put a bearish pressure on the stock. When prices are sufficiently low the hedge fund will buy the stock at a lower price. Afterwards when the market corrects they will be able to make a profit from selling the stock at a higher price.

For medium and large caps the mechanism starts similarly but involves a behavioral aspect that differs from other investments. Many active managers have trigger signals and stop-loss orders on their positions. The trigger of the stop loss is activated if a large negative variation is observed during a period of time (daily trading). If the short seller manages to plunge the stock below the trigger and to activate the stop-loss orders, many investors will automatically cut their positions, selling their shares and thereby putting additional pressure and negative drift on that stock. Later the hedge fund buys the stock at a lower value and makes a profit when the

[6] K1 hedge fund said to be linked to FBI money laundering sting, http://www.bloomberg.com/apps/news?pid=newsarchive&sid=a.i0Az7wASBw.

market corrects this effect. The pump and dump scenario is also possible on small caps and hedge funds can also use this type of manipulation to generate profits.

JIM CRAMER'S FOMENTING

Background

In 2009 in a very controversial edition of the CNBC show *Mad Money* the guest Jim Cramer exposed some rogue techniques that he employed previously for manipulating stock markets through his hedge fund.[a]

Manipulating stocks

Cramer explained how he was able to move the futures market in short positions: *A lot of times when I was short at my hedge fund, and I was positioned short, meaning I needed it down, I would create a level of activity beforehand that could drive the futures.*

Cramer explained the market manipulation through short selling in order to give the impression a stock is down, which he calls fomenting: *You can't foment. That's a violation...But you do it anyway because the SEC does not understand it.* He adds, *When you have six days and your company may be in doubt because you are down, I think it is really important to foment.*

Most important Cramer explained how to bypass the possibility a third party could acknowledge a misconduct. *What's important when you are in that hedge fund mode is to not be doing anything that is remotely truthful, because the truth is so against your view it is important to create a new truth to develop a fiction,* Cramer advises. *You can't take any chances.*

Controversies

In 2006, the SEC investigated Jim Cramer and his research firm TheStreet.com for allegations of collusion between short sellers and a stock research firm. Cramer started to work in the hedge fund industry with Michael Steinhardt, a previous colleague of Ivan Boesky and son of Sol Steinhardt, reputed associate of the Genovese organized crime family.

[a]Jim Cramer shorting stock, http://www.huffingtonpost.com/2009/03/11/jim-cramer-shorting-stock_n_173824.html.

7.1 Manipulation on the Stock Market

In order to address the issue of short selling the SEC introduced Rule 105 of Regulation that prohibits the short sale of an equity security during a restricted period, generally five business days before a public offering, and the purchase of that same security through the offering.

One of the largest crackdowns[7] in the hedge fund industry occurred in 2013 when the SEC has taken legal action against 23 firms and hedge fund managers for short-selling violations. The funds agreed to pay 14.4 million dollars to settle the market manipulation charges. The SEC charged major firms including: Blackthorn Investment Group, Claritas Investments Ltd., Credentia Group, D.E. Shaw & Co., Deerfield Management Company, and Hudson Bay Capital Management. The firms charged in these cases allegedly breached Rule 108 and bought offered shares from an underwriter, broker, or dealer participating in a follow-on public offering after having sold short the same security during the restricted period.

[7]Hedge funds pay 14 million dollars to settle SEC market manipulation charges, http://www.hedgeco.net/news/09/2013/hedge-funds-pay-14-million-to-settle-sec-market-manipulation-charges.html.

PENNY STOCK MANIPULATION

Background

Jurgen Homm, a German hedge fund manager[a] who was on the run for more than five years, was arrested in Italy on federal fraud charges that accused him of orchestrating a market manipulation scheme designed to artificially improve the performance of his funds, a fraud that led to at least 200 million in losses to investors around the world.

Modus operandi

Homm was the Founder and Chief Investment Officer of Absolute Capital Management Holdings Limited, a Cayman Islands-based investment adviser who managed nine hedge funds from 2004 until September 2007. The criminal complaint filed in the US District Court in Los Angeles alleged that Homm directed the hedge funds to buy billions of shares of thinly traded, United States-based penny stocks. Homm caused many of the purchases of penny stocks to be made through Hunter World Markets Inc., a broker-dealer in Los Angeles that Homm co-owned. Homm also allegedly obtained shares of the penny stock companies through various businesses he controlled.

After the hedge funds invested hundreds of millions of dollars in the illiquid penny stocks, Homm caused the hedge funds to trade the stocks among themselves in "cross-trades" made through the Los Angeles-based broker-dealer. As part of the stock manipulation scheme, Homm and others allegedly sold their own shares of the penny stocks to the hedge funds managed by Homm. The cross-trades served to increase the trading prices of the previously illiquid stocks and, in turn, to boost the NAVs and apparent performance of the hedge funds. This apparent performance improvement at the hedge funds generated additional fees for Homm and Absolute Capital, as well as boosting Absolute Capital's stock price on the London Stock Exchange, Alternative Investment Market.

Aftermath

The allegedly fraudulent conduct caused at least 200 million in losses to investors in the hedge funds. The scheme allegedly netted Homm and his co-schemers more than 53 million via trades made through Hunter World Markets alone.

[a] Fugitive hedge fund manager arrested in Italy, http://www.fbi.gov/losangeles/press-releases/2013/fugitive-hedge-fund-manager-arrested-in-italy-in-u.s.-case-alleging-market-manipulation-scam-that-led-to-at-least-200-million-in-losses.

7.2 Manipulating the Market to Embellish the Performance

Manipulation can occur not only for structural profit-taking reasons, but also to inflate the performance of a portfolio by increasing the NAV of the fund. The NAV is computed at agreed reporting dates and is computed using the settlement or closing prices of the market. Thus one could try to put order in the market in such a way that the closing prices would appear inflated, thereby embellishing the global picture of the fund.

In a popular piece of research, Ben-David et al. [97] assessed whether hedge funds manipulate the stock market and presented evidence of significant price manipulation at the stock level by hedge funds on critical reporting dates. The study measured stocks in the top quartile of hedge fund holdings and showed abnormal returns of 30 basis points in the last day of the month and a reversal of 25 basis points the following day. A significant part of the return is earned during the last minutes of the last day of the month, at an increasing rate toward the closing bell. This evidence is consistent with hedge funds' incentive to inflate their monthly performance by buying stocks that they hold in their portfolios. Higher manipulations occur with funds that have higher incentives to improve their ranking relative to their peers and a lower cost of doing so.

Cici et al. [98] show that hedge fund advisers intentionally mismark their stock positions. Manipulation is documented even after eliminating issues inherent in the pricing of illiquid securities. Hedge fund advisers mark their positions up (down) following poor (good) performance of their equity holdings. Mismarking is more pronounced for advisers who are audited less frequently, are domiciled in offshore locations, self-report to a commercial database and report more frequently to investors. Furthermore, equity mismarking is related to some of the reported return patterns documented in previous studies, such as a discontinuity in the distribution of returns around zero and smoothed returns.

7.3 Manipulation in the Commodities Market

Commodities and especially niche markets can be easy targets for hedge funds due to a mix of both high volatility and thin liquidity. In these conditions, hedge funds with only some tens of millions of dollars with an appropriate leverage can take over a market.

In December 2014, the Federal Energy Regulatory Commission[8] proposed approximately 30 million in fines for a Pennsylvania-based hedge fund and a trader working on its behalf over electricity market manipulation allegations. Powhatan Energy Fund LLC and Houlian Chen allegedly violated the anti-manipulation rule through so-called up-to-congestion trading in markets administered by a regional transmission organization, PJM.

The *Up-To-Congestion* product was proposed by a regional transmission organization and is a purely financial product that allows for hedging of congestion and losses throughout the system. The product has no energy component associated with it, and no physical delivery of energy. The regional transmission organization clears the product in the Day-Ahead market as a Virtual Transaction without expectation of physical delivery.

Being on a very niche market this product, dedicated mainly to electricity producers and consumers, had some pitfalls as a financial product. Chen realized he could be paid simply for placing trades and intentionally placed millions of megawatt-hours of offsetting trades between the same two trading points in the same volumes and the same hours in order to cancel out the financial consequences of any spread between the two trading points while collecting the payments, through a mechanism specific to that market known as marginal loss surplus allocation. Electricity cannot be stocked and therefore in each trade that affects the supply/demand equilibrium the gap should be filled instantly in order to avoid jumps in prices. This would imply reallocation of surpluses to market participants. The mechanism, not being dedicated to financial investors, had some pitfalls exploited by the hedge fund.

In the commodities, world hedge funds started to target recently physical investment, mainly in stock of agricultural commodities. The convenience yield representing the advantage of having the ownership of the physical asset compared to the futures position is specific to commodities markets. Besides investing in the physical commodity hedge funds started to target storage capacities, agricultural land, and other related infrastructures. The massive flows of liquidity can contribute to increase in prices and volatility of some commodities.

[8] FERC seeks $30M in hedge fund, trader manipulation fines, http://www.law360.com/articles/605976/ferc-seeks-30m-in-hedge-fund-trader-manipulation-fines.

In 2010, the hedge fund Armajaro made a 992 million dollar investment[9] in the cocoa physical markets, corresponding to almost the entire European chocolate consumption. The investment was originated by Anthony Ward, co-founder of Armajaro in 1998 and ex-chairman of the European Cocoa Association. The physical delivery was very unusual for a hedge fund, which usually deals with the futures markets. The idea behind this investment was that if a trader gets control of the whole supply of cocoa, then she could easily corner the market and generate profits. Although the investment did not raise suspicions with regulators, some lobby groups tackled the transactions, due to the negative impact of speculation on the real agricultural economy. Following this event the World Development Movement, an anti-poverty group, started to put serious pressure on the United Kingdom and European Union to follow the example being set by the United States and introduce limits on the amount of money speculators can put into markets. This investment had no illegal connection, but it underlines the power that a hedge fund can have on a niche market. Therefore, in these type of environments the likelihood of market manipulation on both physical and futures is high due to the asymmetric liquidity access of hedge funds and other nonfinancial traders.

7.4 Hedge Fund Cartels

LIBOR and Forex manipulations showed that banks worked in cartels in order to rig the benchmarks. The same thing could happen with hedge funds. In an industry having almost 1 trillion dollars if some hedge funds collude in deploying manipulation strategies it could be a very successful enterprise especially on mid-cap markets, but also on bigger markets if big hedge funds are involved. At the dawn of the Eurozone crisis there were rumors of hedge funds trying to deploy speculative attacks against distressed sovereign debts.

8 HEDGE FUND PERFORMANCE METRICS AND THEIR ISSUES

The assessment of hedge fund performance uses a series of metrics aimed to provide an accurate prediction of the risk-adjusted returns for a fund or a strategy. Most performance measures are computed based on historic data, but backtested on their ability to forecast the future. The issue with the classic performance metrics is that they can be smoothed or manipulated in order to provide a more optimistic impression about the activity of the funds. The following sections will address how each metric can be manipulated.

8.1 Sharpe Ratio

The Sharpe ratio was introduced by Sharpe [99] and summarizes two measures (mean and variance) in one. The Sharpe ratio was build on Markowitz's mean-variance paradigm, which assumes that the mean and standard deviation of the distribution of one-period returns are sufficient statistics for evaluating the prospects of an investment portfolio. Practical implementations use *ex post* results while theoretical discussions focus on *ex ante* values. Implicitly or explicitly, it is assumed that historic results have at least some predictive ability. We consider δ as the excess return of the returns R_X over the risk-free rate r_f; $\delta = R_X - r_f$ σ_δ is the standard deviation of δ. The Sharpe ratio is defined mathematically as:

$$S_X = \frac{E(R_X - r_f)}{\sigma_\delta} \tag{1}$$

[9]Cocoa investor buys 650 million pounds of beans, http://www.bbc.co.uk/news/business-10682433.

As shown by Goetzmann et al. [100], the Sharpe ratio is invariant to scaling when it is maximized, so it can fix the expected excess return at any positive value $\bar{\delta}$ expressed as

$$\bar{\delta} = \sum_{i=1}^{m} \pi_i \delta_i \tag{2}$$

where π_i are the probabilities of occurrence of state i and δ_i the excess returns under the physical measure.

Hence, the Sharpe ratio can be reshaped as:

$$S_X = \frac{\sum_{i=1}^{m} \pi_i \delta_i}{\sqrt{\sum_{i=1}^{m} \pi_i \delta_i^2 - \bar{\delta}^2}} \tag{3}$$

Under the risk neutral measure characterized by the state probability $\hat{\pi}_i$ in respect of $0 = \sum_{i=1}^{m} \hat{\pi}_i \delta_i$, for $E(\hat{R_X}) = r_f$ the maximum possible Sharpe ratio is expressed as:

$$S_X^* = \sqrt{\frac{\hat{\pi}_i^2}{\pi_i} - 1} \tag{4}$$

From a dynamic perspective at any given moment the Sharpe ratio can be manipulated, adjusting the difference between the realized returns and the future anticipated returns.

We assume that a manager has an historical average excess return of $\bar{\delta}_h$ with a standard deviation of σ_h and that the portfolio's average excess return and standard deviation in the future are $\bar{\delta}_v$ and σ_f. The Sharpe ratio over the entire period can be written as:

$$S = \frac{\pi_h \bar{\delta}_h + (1-\pi_h)\bar{\delta}_f}{\sqrt{\pi_h(\bar{\delta}_h^2+\sigma_h^2)+(1-\pi_h)(\bar{\delta}_f^2+\sigma_f^2)-(\pi_h\bar{\delta}_h+(1-\pi_h)\bar{\delta}_f)^2}}$$

$$S = \frac{\pi_h \bar{\delta}_h + (1-\pi_h)\bar{\delta}_f}{\sqrt{\pi_h \bar{\delta}_h^2(1+S_h^{-2})+(1-\pi_h)\bar{\delta}_f^2(1+S_f^{-2})-(\pi_h\bar{\delta}_h+(1-\pi_h)\bar{\delta}_f)^2}}$$

where π_h is the weight of the past historical state.

To maximize the Sharpe ratio from the previous expression the target mean excess return in the future should take the form:

$$\bar{\delta}_f^* = \begin{cases} \frac{\bar{\delta}_h \cdot (1+S_h^{-2})}{1+S_f^{-2}} & \text{if } \bar{\delta}_h > 0 \\ \infty & \text{if } \bar{\delta}_h \le 0 \end{cases} \tag{5}$$

which in simple terms means that if the manager had a better performing Sharpe ratio in the past then the target future excess return should be lowered compared to the past excess. If the manager had a poor past Sharpe ratio compared to the expected future ratio then the expected excess return should be above the historical excess.

Therefore by smoothing the targeted returns a maximum for the Sharpe ratio is achieved using the following expression:

$$S^* = \begin{cases} \sqrt{\frac{S_h^2 S_f^{*2} + \pi_h S_h^2 + (1-\pi_h) S_f^{*2}}{1+(1-\pi_h)S_h^2+\pi_h S_f^{*2}}} & \text{if } S_h > 0 \\ S_f^* \sqrt{\frac{1-\pi_h}{1+\pi_h S_f^*}} & \text{if } S_h \le 0 \end{cases} \tag{6}$$

Figure 6 shows a dynamic manipulation of the Sharpe ratio for a series of hedge fund returns, following the procedure introduced by Goetzmann et al. [100] and described above.

Some other metrics related to Sharpe's ratio like Jensen's alpha, Sortino's ratio or Treynor-Mazuy timing measures can also be dynamically manipulated.

9 FRAUD INDICATORS

The first study about the accuracy of hedge fund returns was performed after the Enron event by Liang [101]. The study shows that audited funds have a much lower return discrepancy than nonaudited funds. Also it points out that there is a significantly positive correlation between the auditing dummy variable and

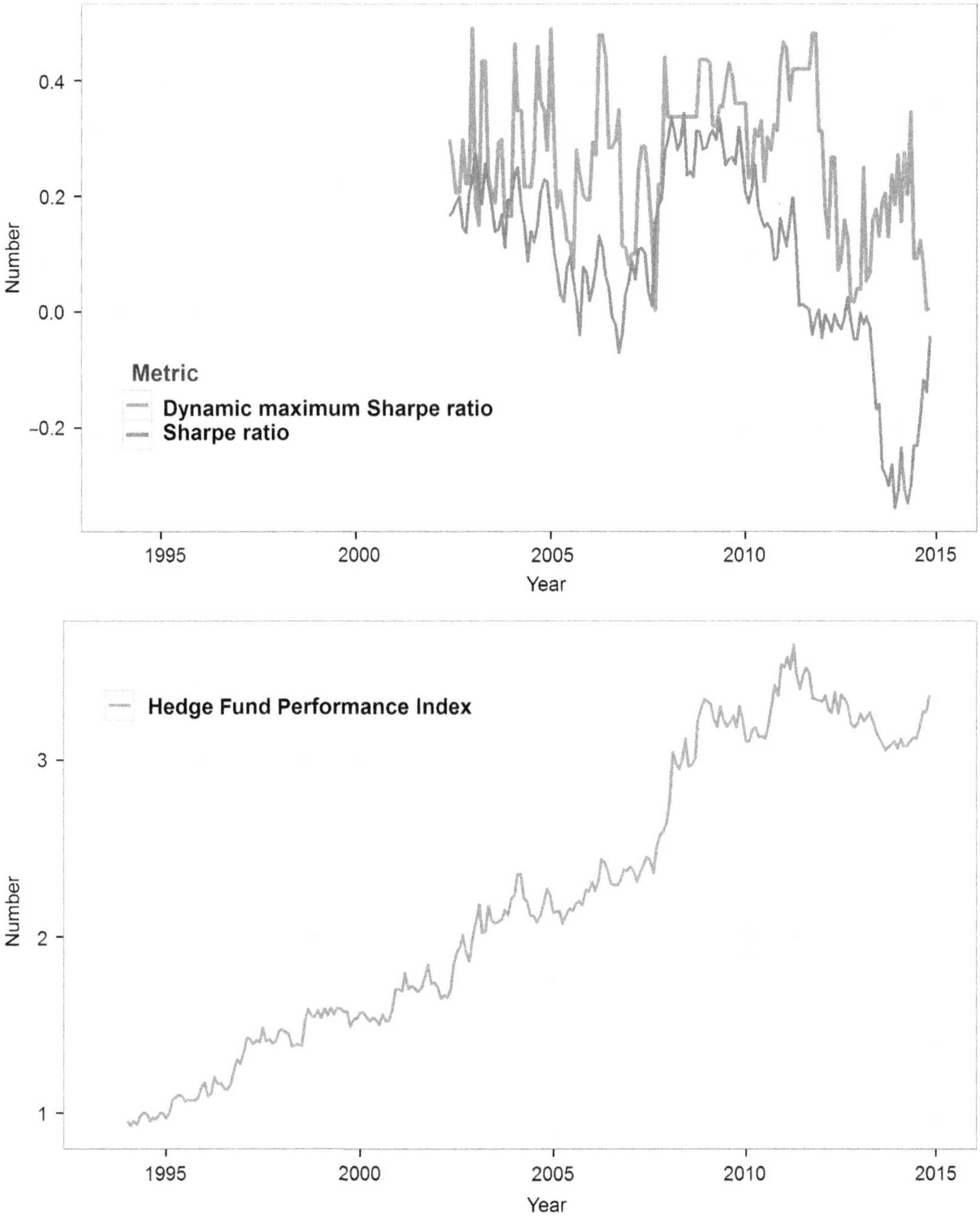

FIGURE 6 Dynamic manipulation of the Sharpe ratio for a series of hedge fund return.

fund size. Large funds tend to be audited while small funds tend not to be, because large funds can afford to have an auditor and there is a greater need to audit their large money pools or complicated portfolio positions. Funds listed on exchanges, funds of funds (compared with hedge funds), funds with both US and non-US investors, funds open to the public, funds invested in a single sector (compared with multiple sectors), and unleveraged funds have better data quality than the other funds.

9.1 Bias Ratio

The bias ratio, introduced by Abdulali [102], is the most popular metric used for assessing whether returns are manipulated or not [103, 104]. During the Madoff events the bias ratio had allegedly indicated abnormal values as presented by software providers of the hedge fund industry.[10]

For a given set of returns R_i with mean μ_R and standard deviation σ_R, in its discrete form the bias ratio can be expressed as:

$$\mathrm{BR} = \frac{\sum_{i=1}^{M} R_i \cdot \mathbf{1}(0 \leq R_i \leq \sigma_R)}{\mathrm{Const.} + \sum_{i=1}^{M} R_i \cdot \mathbf{1}(-\sigma_R \leq R_i \leq 0)} \tag{7}$$

In its continuous form the return distribution is expressed as:

$$\mathrm{BR} = \frac{\int_{-\infty}^{\infty} R \cdot \mathbf{1}(0 \leq R_i \leq \sigma_R)\, \mathrm{d}R}{\mathrm{Const.} + \int_{-\infty}^{\infty} R \cdot \mathbf{1}(-\sigma_R \leq R_i \leq 0)\, \mathrm{d}R} \tag{8}$$

The bias ratio is similar to a test for randomness, as it is a mathematical technique that identifies abnormalities in the distribution of returns [105]. The bias ratio metric is nothing more than the ratio of the frequency of positive returns to the frequency of negative returns to within one standard deviation of the observed return distribution, thereby assessing the asymmetry of the return distribution.

The bias ratio has the following properties:

1. $0 \leq \mathrm{BR} \leq \infty$
2. If $R_i < 0,\ \forall i > 0$ then $\mathrm{BR} = 0$
3. If $R_i > \sigma_R,\ \forall i > 0\ R_i > 0$ then $\mathrm{BR} = 0$
4. If $\mathbf{E}(R_i) = 0$ and $\mathbf{E}(R_i^3) = 0$ then $\mathrm{BR} \rightarrow 1$.

As depicted in the last property from the above list, the bias ratio for a highly liquid fund in an efficient market should be close to 1. Highly illiquid securities have high serial correlation and hence the bias ratio of such a fund will be greater than 1. A high bias ratio for funds intended to be invested in classic strategies should be an alarm signal.

9.2 Return Distribution Discontinuity

When the performance indicators are manipulated by managers usually the frequency of performance improvement is higher than the frequency of negative variations, thereby generating discontinuities in the distribution of the performance variation around the critical points (i.e., management target performance).

Discontinuity in performance metrics was discussed for the earnings reported by Burgstahler and Dichev [106]. A straightforward statistical test to find discontinuities in returns was presented by Takeuchi [107].

Let $R_i, i = 1, 2, \ldots, M$ be a set of independent random variables with distribution function $\mathbf{F}$. Assuming equally spaced points $-\infty = \zeta_0 < \zeta_1 < \zeta_2 < \cdots < \zeta_k = \infty$, where $\zeta_k - \zeta_{k-1} = z$, the empirical frequency for each bin is given by:

$$Z_j = \sum_{i=1}^{M} \mathbf{1}(R_i \in (\zeta_{j-1}, \zeta_j)) \quad \text{for } (j = 1, 2, \ldots, k) \tag{9}$$

Z_j follows a multinomial distribution and therefore it can be developed as:

$$p_j = \mathbf{P}(R_i \in (\zeta_{j-1}, \zeta_j)) = \mathbf{F}(\zeta_{j-1}) - \mathbf{F}(\zeta_j) \tag{10}$$

[10] Hedge funds risk and replication, https://www.riskdata.com/resources/hedge_funds_risk_and_replication.html

where the expectation of Z_j is $E(Z_j) = Mp_j$ and the variance can be written as $\text{var}(Z_j) = Mp_j(1 - p_j)$.

The statistical discontinuity test is:

- *H0*: In the bin j, the distribution is smooth, $(p_{j-1} + p_{j+1})/2 - p_j = 0$.
- *Ha*: Alternatively the distribution cannot be characterized as smooth in bin j.

The statistics of the test can be expressed as:

$$\tau_{\text{BD}} = \frac{(p^*_{j-1} + p^*_{j+1})/2 - p^*_j}{\sqrt{\text{var}((p^*_{j-1} + p^*_{j+1})/2 - p^*_j)}} \quad (11)$$

The empirical probability of an observation being in bin j is $p^*_j = Z_j/M$, with the variance of the test being:

$$\text{var}((p^*_{j-1} + p^*_{j+1})/2 - p^*_j) = \frac{1}{M}(p^*_j(1 - p^*_j) + p^*_j((p^*_{j-1} + p^*_{j+1})) + 0.25(p^*_{j-1} + p^*_{j+1})(1 - (p^*_{j-1} + p^*_{j+1}))) \quad (12)$$

Under the null hypothesis the test follows the normal standard distribution:

$$\tau_{\text{BD}} \propto \mathbf{N}(0, 1) \quad (13)$$

Based on this formulation it can be assessed on the basis of the value of τ_{BD} whether the smoothness hypothesis can be rejected at a given confidence interval level.

9.3 Number of Zero Returns

As a corollary of the previous test a discontinuity frequently accounts for zero returns. Following Bollen and Pool [108], under the assumption that true returns are distributed normally $N(\mu, \sigma)$, the probability p^0 that a given return is reported as 0.0000 for a fund that is rounded to the nearest basis point is given by:

$$p^0 = \int_{-\eta}^{\eta} \frac{1}{\sqrt{2\pi}\sigma} \mathrm{e}^{-0.5(\frac{x-\mu}{\sigma})^2}\, \mathrm{d}x \quad (14)$$

where η is the rounding convention. Hence the probability of observing as many as k zeros in a series n observations long is obtained through the Bernoulli distribution:

$$p^0_{k,n} = \binom{n}{k}(1 - p^0)^{n-k}(p^0)^k \quad (15)$$

Critical values for observing k zeros are then established by the cumulative distribution function based on the probabilities expressed above. An alarm trigger is set when the probability of generating the observed k zero returns or more is below a certain threshold.

For the case of negative returns the probability is expressed as for a rounding convention η:

$$p^- = \int_{-\infty}^{-\eta} \frac{1}{\sqrt{2\pi}\sigma} \mathrm{e}^{-0.5(\frac{x-\mu}{\sigma})^2}\, \mathrm{d}x \quad (16)$$

and hence the probability of observing k negative returns in a series n observations long is equal to:

$$p^-_{k,n} = \binom{n}{k}(1 - p^-)^{n-k}(p^-)^k \quad (17)$$

An observation threshold as in the previous case can be put in place for $p^-_{k,n}$.

9.4 Manipulation-Proof Performance Measure

To address the issue of performance ratio manipulation, Goetzmann et al. [100] introduced a manipulation-proof performance measure (MPPM) having three properties:

- The score's value should not depend upon the portfolio's dollar value.
- An uninformed investor cannot expect to enhance his estimated score by deviating from the benchmark portfolio. At the same time informed investors should be able to produce higher scoring portfolios and can always do so by taking advantage of arbitrage opportunities.

- The measure should be consistent with standard financial market equilibrium conditions.

At the same time the metric should respect some basic conditions for every performance metric:

- The score must increase with the return.
- The score should be concave to avoid increasing the score with added leverage or more risk.
- The score should be time separable to prevent dynamic manipulation of the estimated statistic.
- The score should have a power utility form.

We assume a score function $\Theta(r_i, S_i)$ depending on the return r_i at a state S_i. The measure Θ is manipulation free if $\Theta(r_i^1, S^0) > \Theta(r_i^2, S^0)$ implying that $\Theta(r_i^1, S_i) > \Theta(r_i^2, S_i)$ for any states S_i. In other words, the relative performance based on measure Θ cannot be changed based on changing the underlying state.

Therefore, the manipulation-free measure can take the form:

$$\Theta(r) = \Upsilon\left(\frac{1}{M}\sum_{i=1}^{M}(\theta(r_i, S_i))\right) \tag{18}$$

where Υ is a function taking the power form.

The proposed MPPM has the following form:

$$\Theta(r) = \frac{1}{(1-\rho)\cdot\Delta t} \ln\left(\frac{1}{M}\sum_{i=1}^{M}\left(\frac{1+r_{rf}+\delta_i}{1+r_{rf}}\right)^{1-\rho}\right) \tag{19}$$

where δ_i is the excess return at time i and ρ is the risk aversion of the investors. This form annualizes the one-period geometric excess on the basis of the time Δt related to the frequency of observing the returns r_i.

9.5 Doubt Ratio

Browna et al. [109] proposed a new measure, the doubt ratio (DR), to detect suspicious funds based on the MPPM. As mentioned before, the MPPM is a decreasing function of the relative risk aversion, given the observed returns and the risk-free rate. For example, if a fund has a positive expected excess return and no volatility of returns, the fund's implied risk aversion is infinity and each observed return is the same, $r_1 = r_2 = \cdots = r_N$, and the MPPM will also not fluctuate, $\Theta(1) = \Theta(2) = \Theta(3) = \cdots = \Theta(N)$.

The proposed expression for the doubt ratio is:

$$DR = \frac{\Theta(2)}{\Theta(2)-\Theta(3)} + 2 \cong \frac{2\bar{\delta}}{(s_\delta^*)^2} + 1 \tag{20}$$

where $\bar{\delta}$ is average excess return, $s_\delta^* = s_\delta \cdot \sqrt{(T-1)/T}$ and s_δ is sample standard deviation of excess return. Thus for a series of returns with no negative returns the doubt ratio goes to infinity.

9.6 Conditional Serial Correlation

Getmansky et al. [110] underlined that the returns to hedge funds and other alternative investments are often highly serially correlated, which is most likely explained by illiquidity exposure and smoothed returns. Therefore, the propensity for managers to misreport by smoothing is increasing in the illiquid market, since the market trades are scarce and valuation is done through mark to model, which generates serial correlation.

Bollen and Pool [108] proposed a straightforward approach to test for conditional serial correlation, the distinction between a fund's observed return R_t^O at the reporting date, and R_t, the actual return of the fund's portfolio is again important. We make the assumption that the degree of smoothing, and hence serial correlation, is a function of the actual lagged return:

$$R_t^O = b_0 + b^+ \cdot R_{t-1}^O \mathbf{1}_{R_{t-1}^O \geq \mu} + b^- \cdot R_{t-1}^O \mathbf{1}_{R_{t-1}^O < \mu} + \epsilon \quad (21)$$

where ϵ are the residuals and μ is the average of the previous returns.[11]

Therefore, b^- aims to capture the serial correlation for below average returns. A positive b^+ coefficient indicates that serial correlation is high for above average returns, which is consistent with a performance embezzlement. The test consists of assessing whether b^+ is positive within a certain confidence level, which would raise an alarm signal.

9.7 Digits Test

When the performance reporting is smoothed by managers' intervention, the digits of the communicated figures will follow some particular patterns. These types of patterns can be tested with methods like Benford's law already used in financial crime assessment.

9.7.1 Uniformity Test

Straumann [111] developed a statistical testing methodology that can detect patterns in hedge fund returns exhibiting peculiar and most likely "man-made" patterns, which are worth examining. As described by Straumann [111], the uniformity test compares the percentage of observations ending in each digit 0 through 9 to its expected value of 10% under the null of a uniform distribution. The classic goodness-of-fit test U is asymptotically distributed:

$$U = \sum_{d=0}^{9} \frac{(D_d - M \cdot 0.1)^2}{M \cdot 0.1} \quad (22)$$

where D_d is the total number of observations ending in digit d and M is the total number of observations. The U statistic is asymptotically distributed as a χ^2 distribution with 9 degree of freedom:

$$U \propto \chi_9^2 \quad (23)$$

if the test statistic exceeds the $1 - \alpha$ percentile of the χ_9^2 distribution, α being the confidence level.

If this test is applied to the set of monthly returns included in the Barclay hedge fund databases the number of suspicious performances is around 13.4% for the pure hedge funds, 9.2% for the funds of funds, and 15.7% for the CTAs, as listed in Table 1.

TABLE 1 Digit Test Applied to the Set of Monthly Returns Included in the Barclay Hedge Fund Databases

Type of fund	Suspicions	Total	Percentage
Hedge funds	496	3697	13.4
Funds of funds	94	1018	9.2
CTA	158	1003	15.7

9.7.2 Benford's Law

An empirical alternative to assess rogue performance reporting is through Benford's law, which deals with the probability of occurrence of a digit as a decimal in a set of numerical data Benford [112]. It should be recalled that the Benford law states that the distribution is given by:

$$P(d) = \log(d+1) - \log(d) = \log(1 + 1/d) \quad (24)$$

Figure 7 shows the first digit distribution for the Global Barclay Hedge Funds performance index. The observed distribution for this case follows the theoretical law. Various approaches for testing the agreement with Benford's law are discussed in a separate chapter. Figure 8 shows the first digit distribution for the returns of the Fairfield fund, which was Madoff's main feeding

[11] Bollen's approach proposes in fact to test if the fitted actual returns R_t are above or below the average.

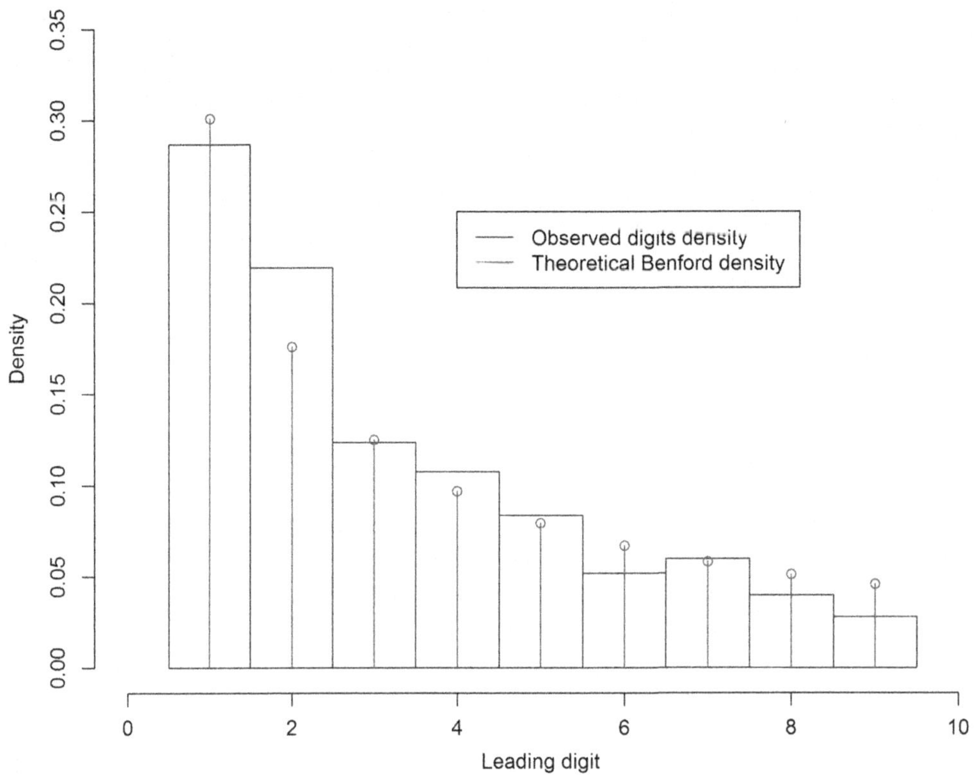

FIGURE 7 First digit distribution for the Global Barclay Hedge Funds performance index.

TABLE 2 Benford Test Applied to the Set of Monthly Returns Included in the Barclay Hedge Funds Databases

Type	Suspicions	Total	Percentage
Hedge funds	593	3697	16.0
Funds of funds	349	1018	34.2
CTA	148	1003	14.7

fund. Table 2 shows the results of applying the χ^2 test for the Benford law fitting to the monthly performance of funds from the Barclay database. Funds of funds seem to exhibit the most suspicious pattern, more than 34% not following Benford's digit law.

10 OUTLOOK

In December 2014, HSBC[12] closed all accounts and ended the relationship with the Jersey-based hedge fund Global Advisers, which was the world's first regulated investment support for Bitcoins. The decision of the bank was allegedly justified by the threat of Bitcoins being used as a money-laundering tool and also by the still open wound left by the penalty given to the bans by the North American authorities in relation to cleansing funds from South American cartels. The news seemed to have all the ingredients of

[12]HSBC severs links with firm behind Bitcoin fund, http://www.bbc.co.uk/news/world-europe-jersey-30261976.

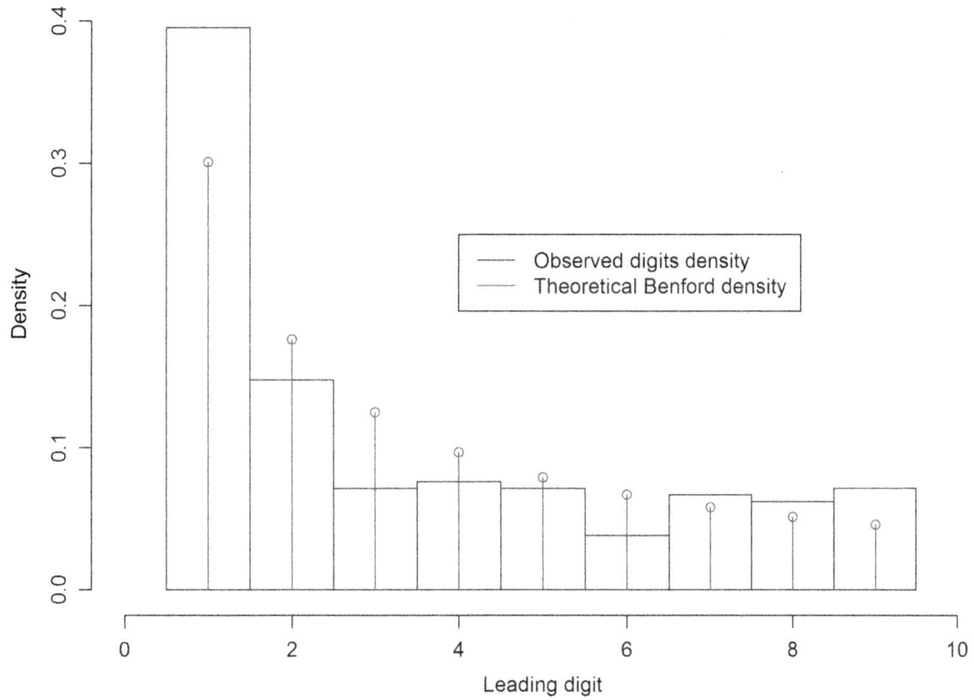

FIGURE 8 First digit distribution for the returns of the Fairfield fund, which was Madoff's main feeding fund.

a big story: tax haven, crypto-currency, hedge funds, money laundering, and HSBC.

Nevertheless, the idea behind it is that the hedge fund industry advances very rapidly toward new areas not yet covered by prudential authorities or intersection of sectors with no fully fledged regulatory status. Another example would be the peer-to-peer lending market that grows rapidly as the financing from the banking sector seems tainted, especially in countries with high levels of sovereign debts.

In the current environment, the hedge fund industry will continue to grow, and financial crime will surely follow in terms of sophistication and size. Having less mandatory fillings, the hedge fund industry remains secretive in many respects, a fact also justified by its competitive nature. But in this context it became a difficult if almost impossible task to predict if something abnormal occurred within a hedge fund. The case of Harry Markopulos revealing some years before the collapse the big Madoff scam is unique in this respect.

Therefore, the hedge fund diligences should be based more on instinct and *fuzzy* reasoning than on basic due-diligence questions like: "How many members of the risk committee are directors in the firm?" But to be able to exert such diligence the potential investor should have the right *a priori* information. Wealthy individuals or even family offices would not be able to have the type of insight with regard to assessing whether a hedge fund is rogue or manipulative. Looking closely at the fraud indicators described above can provide an efficient means of understanding whether the performance of a fund is authentic or *man made*. The bias ratio alarmed Madoff's investors for some years without any relevant consequences. Only individuals with experience and contact in the milieu would be able to have a fair opinion about the real risk a hedge fund poses to its investors.

CHAPTER

4B

Emerging Markets and Financial Crime

OUTLINE

1 BACKGROUND

The structural changes that occurred in the geopolitical equilibrium during the 1990s as well as the rapid development of the economies of South America, Far East Asia, and Africa marked a turning point in the development of financial markets. Thus new financial hubs like Dubai, Hong Kong, Shanghai, and Moscow gained importance at a global level and started to play an important role in international financial transactions.

With these developments came also some dangers concerning the way financial tools were (mis)understood in those regions. The first source of threats originates from the fact that in many of the emerging countries the economy previously controlled by the government passed into the hands of private individuals. In the Eastern European bloc, this passage was far from transparent and as a result a generation of tycoons, magnates and oligarchs have risen to power. The transfer of property from public to private hands involved in most cases local criminal organizations which took over the local industries directly or through protection taxes.

The second source of troubles was the lack of experience of those countries with free markets and especially with financial markets. Therefore, market manipulation and insider trading are business as usual in many of the emerging stock markets. The securities frauds were linked in many cases to the privatization process as many privatized companies became listed, therefore constituting an additional opportunity for those involved in corruption and crime to profit from the financial market mechanisms.

The third source of threats in the emerging economies is represented by *the war on commodities and supply capacities* (shipping and freight). Many of the emerging economies like the ex-USSR, South American, and African countries have enormous resources of all kinds. Two examples are oil production and aluminum production.

http://dx.doi.org/10.1016/B978-0-12-801221-5.00013-0

TABLE 1 Geographical Distribution of the Oil Reserves in 2013

Country	Thousand million barrels	Percentage
Saudi Arabia	265.9	15.8
Canada	174.3	10.3
United States	44.2	2.6
Venezuela	298.3	17.7
Iran	157	9.3
Iraq	150	8.9
Kuwait	101.5	6
United Arab Emirates	97.8	5.8
Russian Federation	93	5.5
Libya	48.5	2.9
Nigeria	37.1	2.2
Kazakhstan	30	1.8
Qatar	25.1	1.5
Total emerging	*1038.4*	*61.5*
Others	165.2	9.8
Total	1687.9	100

Source: BP.

TABLE 2 Geographical Breakdown of Worldwide Aluminum Production

Country	Percentage	Quantity (million tons)
United States	4	1.644
Others	19	7.809
Australia	5	2.055
Canada	7	2.877
Norway	3	1.233
China	39	16.029
India	4	1.644
Middle East	6	2.466
Brazil	4	1.644
Russia	9	3.699
Total emerging	*62*	*25.482*
Total production	100	41.1

For example, many of the world's oil reserves are concentrated in emerging countries,[1] with more than 60% of the global reserves, while North America and Saudi Arabia have just under 30% of the total (Table 1).

In regard to the global metal resources and production the emerging countries account for almost 62% of worldwide aluminum production[2] (Table 2).

As a comparison 40 years ago the United States produced more than 30% of the global aluminum.

The commodities war has involved some battles, one being on financial markets and another taking place at geopolitical level with the various spheres of influence. Furthermore the war has two dimensions:

- A first dimension is the ground physical economic battle which has at stake the ownership of resources (mines, oil, and gas fields) and infrastructures (transportations and transformation of raw materials). In some African countries, this phase of the war is brutal, sometimes involving real wars against various factions for the ownership and exploration of various resources. Governments and private entrepreneurs are involved in financing of the exploration projects in direct contact with the local governments. In low gross domestic product (GDP) per capita, countries corruption

[1]There are various definitions of the emerging economies but here for simplification we consider nondeveloped emerging countries.

[2]The global aluminum industry, http://www.world-aluminium.org/media/filer_public/2013/02/25/an_outlook_of_the_global_aluminium_industry_1972_-_present_day.pdf.

scandals and other white-collar crime are usual. In this context, some countries like China, a big consumer of raw commodities, established strategies mainly in African countries for insuring the supply chain of material from the local mining phase to transportation and delivery.

- A second dimension of the battle is linked to the financial markets and is closely linked to the previous one. The feasibility of exploration projects depends to a high extent on the market price of the explored resource. A small market price could lead to stopping and abandoning the project. One example was the case of the iron mining exploration in Sierra Leone, which ended up in a difficult situation due to the sharp decline of iron prices in the context of bearish commodities markets. Thus on niche markets specific manipulation can play a strategic role in boosting or obstructing a physical exploration project.

The bottom line for emerging markets is that the three sources of threats are linked as many companies involved in commodities exploration or energy supply are privatized and afterwards are listed on markets.

2 PRIVATIZATION IN THE EASTERN BLOC

In this context, the term privatization refers to the transfer of ownership of a business or property from a government or a governmental agency to a privately owned entity or private individuals. A massive wave of privatization occurred in the countries of the Communist bloc during the 1990s and more gradually in China over the past two decades. The main arguments that led to the privatization of government-owned companies was to increase their efficiency as a result of private ownership. The increased efficiency would come from private owners focusing on profit maximization as compared to the government, which tends to be concerned about the social redistribution of the potential profit.

A research paper published in 1992, one year after the fall of the Soviet Union, by Cohen and Schwartz [113] had a very realistic and even forward-looking content predicting the outcome of the privatization process in the ex-Eastern bloc countries. The authors identified some trends about the privatization process and predicted correctly that criminal groups would commingle in this process. The work underlined that in Eastern European countries privatizing ownership will not change the governmental firms into efficient and innovative entities, as private ownership makes sense in the context of already established capitalist firms. The linkage between firms as well as the political aspects that interconnected the firms and their traditional markets makes Eastern Europe "an unsuitable candidate for rapid privatization." During the asset auctions in the privatization process the networks of officials and plant managers, with their criminal allies, had enough capital and liquidities to bid. Cohen and Schwartz [113] also pointed out that corruption will certainly be an issue and inexperienced East European market regulators will not be able to implement efficient policies to control the markets. Most importantly, the study predicted that market rigging, stock manipulation, inside information to kickbacks, and money laundering with organized crime will be inevitable.

All these prophecies came true as the privatization process took place and generated probably a new form of economic paradigm: "gray capitalism." The structures, the behaviors, and the governance of business in this new economic environment had specific rules, different in many ways from the traditional Western enterprises.

Thus it is crucial to present the typical governance of a company in the Eastern European context. After the fall of the Berlin Wall a lot of opportunities arose, with very lax legal framework. The business in the new capitalist countries was less clear and regulated compared to the Western economies and usual transactions implied naturally doubtful transactions, extortion activities, corruption, etc. With the arrival of foreign capital the business structure could not be presented as such to potential investors. After the fast pace of privatization since the 1990s, in the early 2000s business ventures from the ex-Communist bloc reorganized their activities in order to separate the operations from the ownership structure. Previously an "entrepreneur" had personal control on companies' assets, workers, suppliers, customers, and banking services (Figure 1). To make it acceptable for modern business practice such a company was restructured around management entities owned by the entrepreneur or group of entrepreneurs. This entity owned all the assets, tangible and intangible, managed the relationships with the accounting and legal services and insured the relationship with the banks. All operations involving production, stock and trading were executed through dedicated subsidies, the profits being consolidated to the managing entity. The operational entities leased the assets from the managing entity and paid fees for all the common services. Thus the managing entity had a clean record and the operating

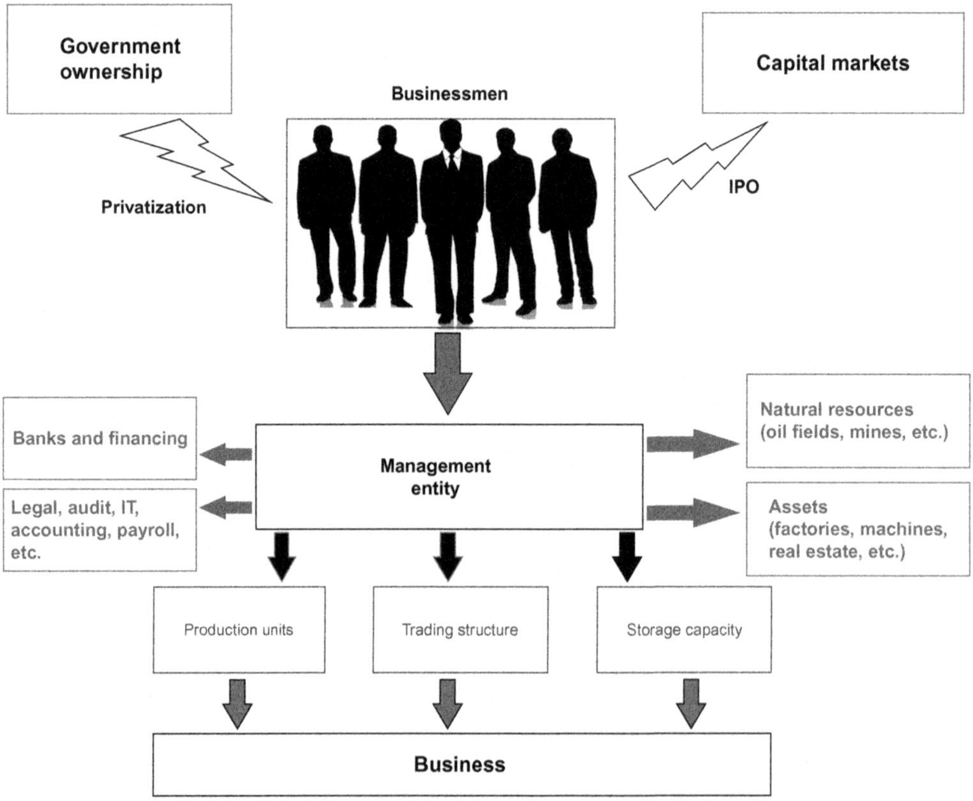

FIGURE 1 Governance structure of a privatized company. The operations were separated from the ownership structure. Some of the companies went from difficult privatization to stock exchange listing.

entities continued business as they usually did in the 1990s [1]. In the late 2000s, the managing entities started to be consolidated in holding companies placed in tax havens, Cyprus and Dubai being a common destination. Some of the companies that survived had greater ambitions and became listed on major stock exchanges.

Moscow is one of the cities with the biggest concentration of millionaires and in the colorful picture of ex-Soviet tycoons a particular niche is occupied by those oligarchs that survived the change from the roaring 1990s Yeltsin era to new modern Putin hegemony, among which Oleg Deripaska is the best-known figure in financial circles. The best example of the 1990s privatization in ex-USSR is the Russian aluminum producer RUSAL, which went through all the steps from an opaque privatization, harsh restructuring to finally seeing the light of the modern capital markets. Behind RUSAL was the iconic figure of Oleg Deripaska, one of the top five Russian oligarchs, close to the Russian Government. In the early years of the Yeltsin era Deripaska was an eminent student at the Moscow State University in theoretical physics (a renowned fizmat faculty where many oligarchs studied). Probably if the former president Andropov was alive today there was more chance of hearing about Deripaska's theorem than about Basic Elements, which is his current investment holding. After university Deripaska started as a metal trader in the early 1990s, when a ton of aluminum was valued at 400 dollars and sold it for 1200 dollars generating returns of 1000% a year. Deripaska took over the various aluminum plants during the roaring 1990s in the so-called "aluminum wars."[3] The aluminum wars from the 1990s took place for the control of the production capacities mainly based in Siberia at sites in Siberia (Krasnoyarsk, Irkutsk, Bratsk) and close to cheap hydropower plants which confered an advantage in terms of production price. In this war, Deripaska was backed by a reputed Russian-Israeli businessman and criminal authority called Michale Cherney. Also Deripaska recognized that he paid protection tax to local crime groups.

After the consolidation of the group RUSAL went public in January 2010, being listed in Hong Kong and Paris and raising more than 2.24 billion dollars by selling 1.61 billion shares, or 11% of its market capitalization (Figure 2). The initial public offering (IPO) in 2010 was clouded by controversy surrounding its massive debt amounting to 15 billion dollars and a lawsuit against its owner. At least four investment banks issued "buy" calls on RUSAL's stocks in their Thursday notes to investors as the coverage blackout expired. RUSAL's stock was rated "outperform" by Credit Suisse. Bank of America, Merrill Lynch, Liberum Capital, and Hong Kong-based Bank of China International gave "buy" recommendations based on the fact that *RUSAL's low-cost hydroelectric power at its Siberian-based plants help make RUSAL one of the lowest-cost global aluminum producers.*

The IPO attracted criticism that Hong Kong regulators were undermining the Chinese territory's credibility as a financial hub by allowing a company struggling with nearly $15 billion of debt to list shares. Reacting to these concerns, the Hong Kong Stock Exchange restricted prospective buyers to investors willing to purchase at least HK$1 million ($129,000) in shares and warned potential investors of the significant risk involved in the issue. By floating a 10.6% stake, RUSAL raised $2.2 billion in this IPO and cut its debt from $14.9 billion to $12.9 billion. Credit Suisse said in its research note that it expects RUSAL to benefit from the aluminum price recovery. The bank noted that it expects aluminum prices to rise to $1 a pound this year

[3]The aluminum wars are accurately depicted in the iconic Russian TV series *Brigada*. Arthur, the owner of a Siberian aluminum plant, is forced to pay a protection tax to the new generations of gangsters.

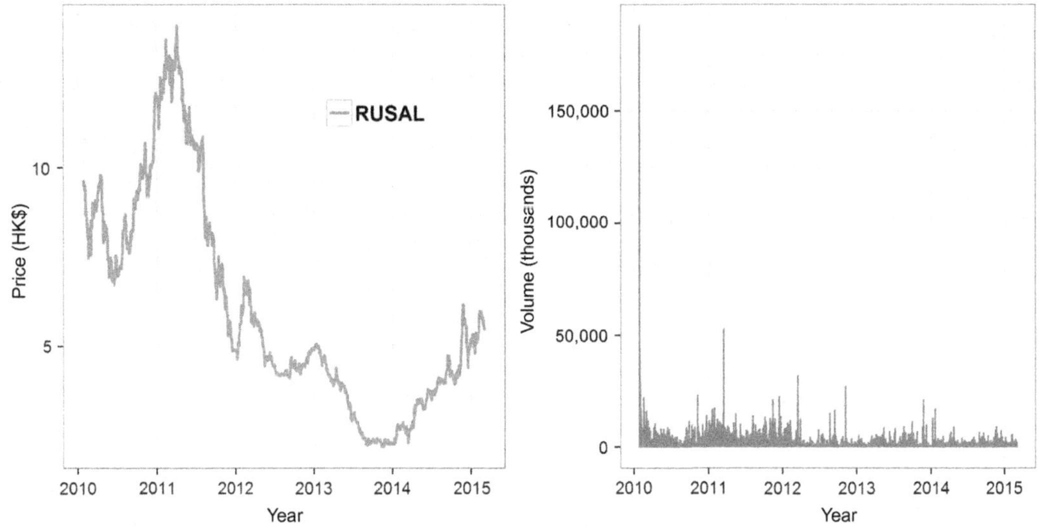

FIGURE 2 RUSAL prices and volumes. In January 2010, RUSAL listed in Hong Kong and Paris, raising more than 2.24 billion dollars by selling 1.61 billion shares, or 11% of its market capitalization.

from 86 US cents a pound in the second half of 2009.

OLEG DERIPASKA: PORTRAIT D'UN NOUVEAU RUSSE

First steps

During his studies he realized that money can be made by trading metal and commodities and opened a first brokerage firm with an investment of only 100 dollars.

Rebound after 2008 crisis

During the 2008 financial crisis Deripaska's wealth shrunk suddenly and he was close to losing everything as his main investment RUSAL suffered a 6 billion dollar loss in less than a year. Furthermore Deripaska, close to Vladimir Putin, was among the first recipients of bailouts from the state-owned development bank for an amount of 4.5 billion dollars, almost double the upper limit of a bailout fixed by the bank.

Trivia

Deripaska has close relationships with reputed British politicians including Lord Mandelson, the former Labor Cabinet Minister, and George Osborne, Chancellor of the Exchequer, and Nathanel Rothschild, socialite and businessman, a member of the powerful Rothschild dynasty.

3 FINANCIAL MARKET INTEGRITY

Among the emerging countries that experienced the biggest boom in the development of the stock market, China has without doubt the leading position. With its two financial hubs, Hong Kong and Shanghai, and GDP growth above 7% for almost two decades, China has all the prerequisites of a fast-growing stock market. In this scenario, the market integrity is not always guaranteed and the Chinese market has faced many cases of market manipulation and insider trading during the 2000s.

A recent probe launched by the China Securities Regulatory Commission focused its investigation on a practice that involves groups of investors pumping up prices of certain targeted stocks including small-cap companies, such as a maker of automobile tires in eastern China's Shandong Province and a government-controlled hydroelectric power company.[4]

A new type of market manipulation is that involving transnational firms with operations in mainland China and stocks listed in the United States. The company AutoChina International Limited is one of the many examples in this sense.

In 2012, the Securities and Exchange Commission charged AutoChina International Limited, a China-based firm and 11 investors, with conducting a market manipulation scheme to create the false appearance of a liquid and active market with its stock. One of the company's directors and others fraudulently traded AutoChina's stock in order to increase its daily trading volume on the US-based stock exchange. From October 2010, the defendants and others deposited more than 60 million dollars into US-based brokerage accounts and engaged in hundreds of fraudulent trades with the help of a Hong Kong-based broker-dealer. The fraudulent trades included matched orders, where one account sold shares to another account at the same time and for the same price, and wash trades, which resulted in no change of beneficial ownership of the shares. AutoChina and the other defendants engaged in the scheme after lenders offered AutoChina unfavorable terms for a stock-backed loan due to low trading volume in its stock. From November 2010 to January 2011, the average daily trading volume increased to more than 139,000 shares, the fraudsters accounts' trading accounting for as much as 70% of the trading turnover (Figure 3).[5]

Another case of transnational securities fraud goes further and uses high-frequency techniques to manipulate markets. Early in 2015 Aleksandr Milrud, a Canadian citizen, was arrested for wire and securities fraud conspiracy. His technique consisted of daily recruited stock traders in China and Korea placing high-speed buy or sell orders and then quickly canceling them, a method called spoofing. The activity would artificially raise or lower the stock prices and allow traders to exploit the price moves and book profits. The investigation found that the scheme yielded as much as 600,000 dollars in a day and generated between 1 and 50 million dollars per month.[6]

These two cases indicate that the emerging capital markets along with the access of investors from the emerging countries to capital markets bring to light new types of scams at a global level. The old boiler rooms in New Jersey have been replaced by transnational networks using advanced high-frequency trading techniques.

4 COMMODITIES AND ENERGY MARKETS

The economic boom in the emerging countries accompanied by the privatization process created a unique opportunity to transfer the ownership or the exploration rights of natural energy resources into the hands of private capital. This transfer involved not only huge amounts of money but also occurred during a period when the prices of commodities and fossil fuels went

[4]China investigates possible stock-price manipulation, http://www.wsj.com/articles/china-investigates-possible-stock-price-manipulation-1419231997.

[5]Security Exchange Commission charges China-based company and others with stock manipulation, http://www.sec.gov/News/PressRelease/Detail/PressRelease/1365171488190#.VPZkAvnz2lc.

[6]A brief history of Chinese day traders manipulating US stocks, http://tabbforum.com/opinions/a-brief-history-of-chinese-day-traders-manipulating-u-dot-s-stocks.

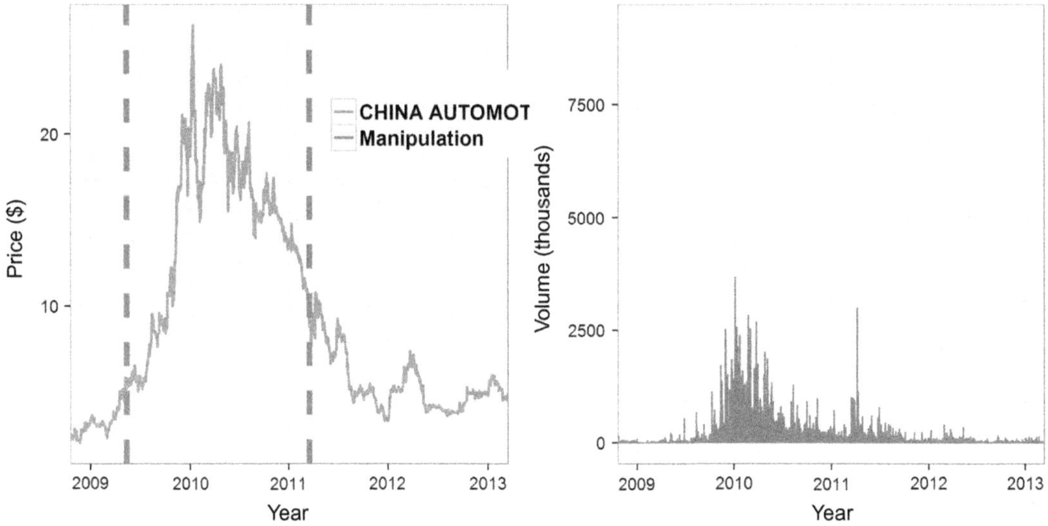

FIGURE 3 AutoChina's stock prices and volumes. From November 2010 to January 2011, the average daily trading volume increased to more than 139,000 shares.

through bullish times. A particular situation was that of the energy sector in Eastern Europe.

The first example is the case of one of the oldest oil companies in the world, a Romanian national company called Rompetrol. One name associated with Rompetrol is that of Dinu Patriciu, a charismatic entrepreneur who managed to take over the company through a series of financial operations involving a long and difficult process. His legacy in the oil business started in 2000 when he acquired a state-owned refinery for almost 50 million US dollars. Through a series of transactions on the stock market he managed to acquire the entire Rompetrol company around 2004. The investigators started to track him and his associates from 2006 until 2014. Patriciu was acquitted before his death in 2012 but his accomplices were given jail sentences. They were found guilty for embezzlement, money laundering, and setting up an organized crime group.[7]

The most serious accusation was nevertheless that concerning market manipulation. Employing affiliate brokers Patriciu made transactions in which he sold a large number of Rompetrol shares on April 7, 2004, when the company was listed on the Bucharest Stock Exchange. More than 2 billion Rompetrol shares were traded on that day, some of them for prices as low as 0.0025 USD per share, while the closing price for the shares was more than triple, at 0.01 USD per share. Figure 4 shows the evolution of the Rompetrol stock, which plunged in July 2005 after the news emerged about the investigation concerning the privatization process.

Among Patriciu's affiliates who were investigated for money laundering and market manipulation was Phil Stephenson, a Texas-bred lawyer and former US Treasury official during George Bush's presidency.[8]

---

[7]Romanian senator, former minister get jail sentences in Rompetrol refinery stock manipulation, http://www.romania-insider.com/romanian-senator-former-minister-get-jail-sentences-in-rompetrol-refinery-stock-manipulation/133031/.

[8]An oil Fortune bound in red tape, http://www.washingtonpost.com/wp-dyn/content/article/2005/08/15/AR2005081501483.html.

FIGURE 4 Evolution of the Rompetrol stock which plunged in July 2005 after the news emerged about the investigations concerning the privatization process. *Source: Financial Times.*

In the aftermath of the privatization the Romanian Government received 50 million dollars, but Patriciu made 2.7 billion dollars, making him one of the richest persons from the Eastern bloc (excluding the ex-USSR countries).

DINU PATRICIU PORTRAIT D'UN NOUVEAU RICHE

Background

During the years prior to the fall of Communism, like many other oligarchs and magnates from Eastern Europe, Patriciu had a bright academic career, being a reputed architect.

Rompetrol episode

In the years after the fall of the Iron Curtain, Patriciu started to become interested in the oil business, one of the most profitable sectors of the country. He coveted Rompetrol, the national oil company with a huge network of influence in the African and Arab countries. He engaged in a battle to take over the company, the main motivation being the "Libyan bill," which was a few billion dollars old debt that the now defunct Gaddafi regime had toward Rompetrol.

Later years

After cashing out the Rompetrol venture to a gas consortium KazMunayGaz from Kazakhstan Patriciu started to have many issues with the law relating to his Rompetrol takeover. In parallel his investments had suffered a massive contraction in terms of turnover during the years of the crisis.

Trivia

On the controversial list of HSBC costumers with hidden accounts in Switzerland, Patriciu appeared with a total amount of 800 million dollars.

Another example from the Eastern bloc is the energy sector in Bulgaria, which suffered a brutal and obscure privatization process in the late 1990s. Energy tycoons emerged during those years and among them there were figures with alleged links to organized crime. When Atomenergoremont, the company insuring the maintenance of Kozlodoy nuclear plant, was privatized in 2003, the main investors were organized in a veritable energy "inner circle" made up of a handful of controversial businessmen: Konstantin Dimitrov "Samokovetza," Vasili Bozhkov, Hristo Kovachki, and Bogumil Manchev. Some of these names raised in the recent past suspicions linked to their implication in various criminal activities (e-vestink, 2008). For instance, Konstantin Dimitrov, known as "Samokovetza," was wanted for heroin trafficking and racketeering from 2003 until he was killed in 2004 in Amsterdam. He was involved in various sectors, from tourism to energy. Another interested investor Vasil Bozhkov, known as "the Skull," was the owner of Nove Holding, with operations in the fields of insurance, infrastructure, and gambling. He had been charged with various illegal operations like illegal excavations and art trafficking.

The most complex case is without doubt that of the African countries with huge commodities resources: oil, metals, diamonds, and soft commodities, the battleground of many investors. Crime, inter-ethnic war, and corruption are just some aspects of this new rearrangement of the worldwide resources map.

5 OUTLOOK

Emerging countries and their markets have a very interesting mix of features including fast-growing economies, booming capital markets, and technology-driven innovations, all intensified by access to extensive energy and commodities resources. These features make the emerging economies fertile ground not only for investors but also for the emergence of financial crime. Organized crime had been to some extent part of the initial economic boom of some of the emerging economies. The new geopolitical equilibrium added new variables to the equation, which can also constitute new opportunities for the development of white-collar crime.

A 2025 Global Trends report signed by the American Intelligence Office[9] underlines that crime could be the most serious threat in Europe as Eurasian transnational organizations flush from involvement in energy and mineral concerns become more powerful and broaden their scope. One or more governments in Eastern or Central Europe could fall prey to their dominance. The danger of crime becoming a multinational enterprise, that could empower well-established personalities and even governments, is not new.

[9]Global Trends 2025: a transformed world, http://www.dni.gov/files/documents/Newsroom/Reports%20and%20Pubs/2025_Global_Trends_Final_Report.pdf.

CHAPTER

4C

From Terrorism Financing to Terror's Economy

OUTLINE

1 BACKGROUND

Certain events have reshaped the meaning of the word *risk* in the investment world, but none more so than the events of 9/11. Two buildings where many big financial firms from Wall Street operated collapsed in only a few hours. Beyond the issues around operational risk and business continuity challenges, the investment community understood quickly that terror is not only linked to extremism and violence, but involves also a robust network of financing. Since 9/11 two crises have hit the global economy and markets saw the price of fossil fuels going through the roof, until late 2014. Most likely fossil fuels should be seen today as the implied price of geostrategic equilibrium rather than a consumption commodity. Oil plays the role of a global currency with fluctuations dictated mainly by the unrest in the main zones of production.

Terror has had many forms throughout history, from the royal partisans that tried to assassinate Napoleon to the IRA in the United Kingdom, from the Red Brigade in Italy to Hamas in the Middle East. A common trait of all these organization is the complex system of financing based on crowd funding from individuals involved with the cause but mostly from bigger stakeholders who have direct interests in the unrest generated by those groups. Also these groups often bypass their political mandate and enter into traditional criminal activities.

What really changed with 9/11 is the fact that terrorism developed a nonmilitary feature, which actually made civilians weapons of destruction in thrall to an ideology. But in order to train, organize and command civilians for terrorist purposes numerous resources are needed and obviously mainly financial resources. With

http://dx.doi.org/10.1016/B978-0-12-801221-5.00014-2

oil prices rising in two decades from 10 to 100 dollars Middle East countries found themselves in possession of colossal liquidities. The roaring 2000 in the Middle East made possible the development of many national and private investment vehicles. With the war on terror many started to raise questions about the destinations of the petrodollars as the recipient countries of those funds were also those harboring individuals or organizations involved in financing the terror. At the peak of oil prices in 2008 the net value of Gulf overseas assets, public and private, was around 1600 billion dollars but this fell by 19% within a few months due to the financial crisis. The sovereign wealth funds concentrated almost 724 billion at the end of 2007, representing 45% of overseas investments.

This made possible a political investment expansion of Gulf countries overseas at strategic levels. For example, in a single transaction in October 2008, investors from Abu Dhabi and Qatar spent 12 billion dollars to purchase 16% ownership in Barclays Bank, a crisis-stricken British financial institution. At the end of 2013 the total current account of the top five Gulf countries (Table 1) totaled 302 billion dollars, representing almost 2% of US gross domestic product.

Without entering into a detailed discussion of the changes of the dynamics in direct foreign investment, one thing appears clear. The petrodollars have changed this picture over the past 15 years mostly due to the increase of oil prices. These changes have occurred alongside the rise of the terrorist threat from fundamentalist organizations and groups. Therefore, it is crucial to assess the possible links and flows that might link these two phenomena.

TABLE 1 Current Account of the Main Gulf Countries

Current account global ranking	Country	Current account ($, billions)
3	Saudi Arabia	132.2
5	Kuwait	69.13
13	United Arab Emirates	52.6
14	Qatar	47.5
27	Oman	0.7
	Total	302.2

2 MECHANISMS

Often in the literature and among experts terror financing is wrongly associated with money laundering. Field and Guiora [114] assert correctly that terror financing presents a wholly different concept from money laundering and, as such, money laundering aims to clean and conceal illegal funds while terror financing generally deals mainly with legal clean funds and rarely involves illicit money. Money laundering is a crime from the moment a person that knows that the funds are illicit handles them. Terrorism financing is a crime long after the fund transfers have taken place and only when the *end user* is involved in a terrorist act. A policy or system within an organization that targets illegal transfers will most likely find money laundering, but fail to detect terrorist financing. In money laundering, the criminal act begins when the illicit funds are earned, while in terrorist financing it occurs when the illicit funds are spent. Therefore, money laundering and terrorist financing follow opposite paths which can be harbored by the same network.

Traditionally nonprofit organizations and charities had already been identified as vectors for disseminating this type of financing.[1] Islamic charities are funded on the concept of Zakat, which represents the amount a Muslim believer gives out of his or her wealth to the neediest of Muslims. Zakat is one of the "five pillars" of

[1] Report: Blocking Faith, Freezing Charity, https://www.aclu.org/human-rights/report-blocking-faith-freezing-charity.

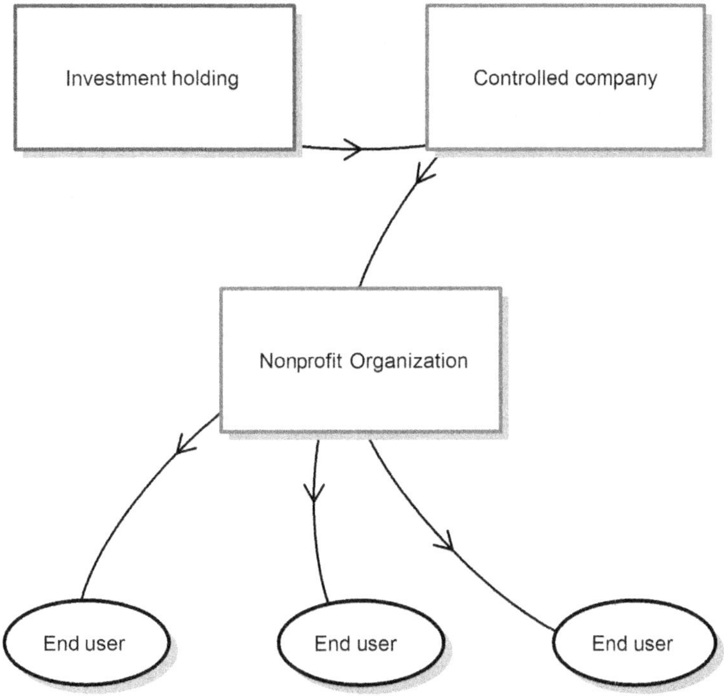

FIGURE 1 Basic terrorist financing scheme including an investment holding as a stakeholder in a corporation that contributes to charities or other nonprofit functions that could distribute funds to the "end users."

Islam and a religious obligation for all observant Muslims. Certainly the big operations like those seen in the Middle East with the rise of so-called Caliphate (ISIL/ISIS/Daech) cannot be financed only with the Zakat contributions. A more structural and coordinated financing source is needed. Also the multi-national dimension of this phenomenon with operations in many countries including recruiting training and logistics raises the question not only of the financing source but also of the payment network and tools.

Figure 1 shows a basic financing scheme where an investment holding is a stakeholder in a corporation that contributes to charities or other nonprofit functions that could distribute funds to the "end users" directly or by paying for services like travel and training supplies. The holding can be incorporated in a Middle East country while the corporation and the charities can be in Western or Asian countries. The payment across countries mainly in the West-East direction can also be made through the *hawala*[2] system in order to bypass international payment systems. The development of digital currencies and crypto-currencies like Bitcoin extend the range of possibilities for this type of transfer.

3 TERRORISM FINANCING AND FINANCIAL MARKETS

Terrorism financing is generally less linked to financial markets and it concerns mainly retail

[2]Hawala means bill of exchange in Arabic and is an informal system for transferring money without sending the money physically. The system is used across borders and involves a network of agents that transfers the funds exclusively based on trust.

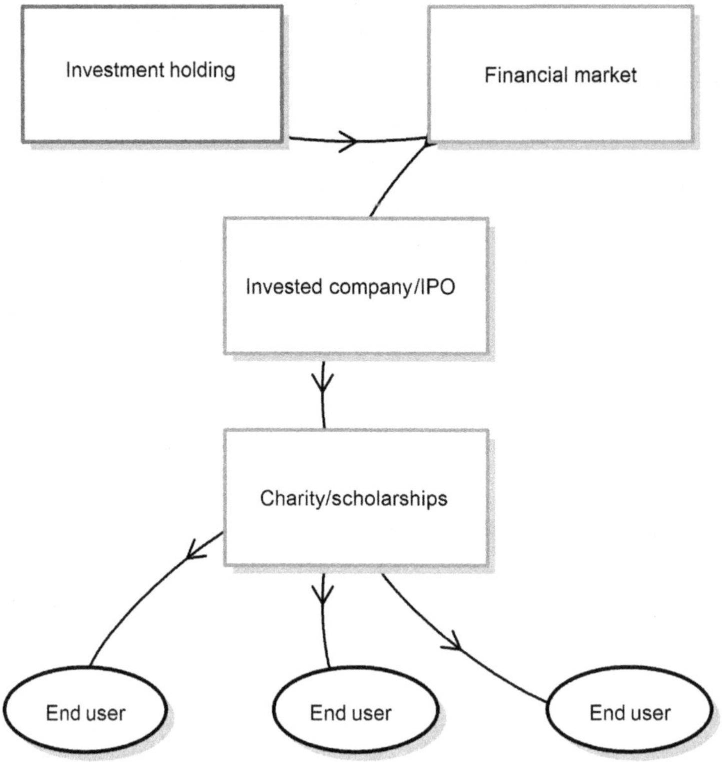

FIGURE 2 Scheme of terror financing through capital markets where an investment company takes control of a company-based overseas.

and commercial banks. But recent developments in the war against terror revealed interesting facts about an evolving element of terror financing on financial markets. Nevertheless big operations like the Taliban in Pakistan and ISIL[3] require massive amounts of liquidity which cannot be transferred through classic vehicles like charities without arousing suspicion. Financial markets can be an alternative for moving large amounts of money and to secrete in those investments operations linked of the terror economy. Figure 2 shows a scheme of financing using capital markets where an investment company incorporated in the Middle East takes control through the capital (stock) market of a company based in Europe, the Russian Federation or in Asia. A straightforward alternative can be via an initial public offering process. Once the company starts to operate under new shareholders involved in the terror economy it can finance various nonprofit foundations via subsidiaries.

Not only capital markets can be used for financing terror. As various reports show the *Daech* generates profits through oil trades by selling physically to neighboring countries. Other more sophisticated schemes include transactions

[3]Allegedly the organization is self-financed and has surplus assets of 2 billion dollars following the taking of Mosul, an important commercial point in the region. Also the organization generated a few millions a day from selling oil abroad. http://www.rand.org/content/dam/rand/pubs/testimonies/CT400/CT419/RAND_CT419.pdf.

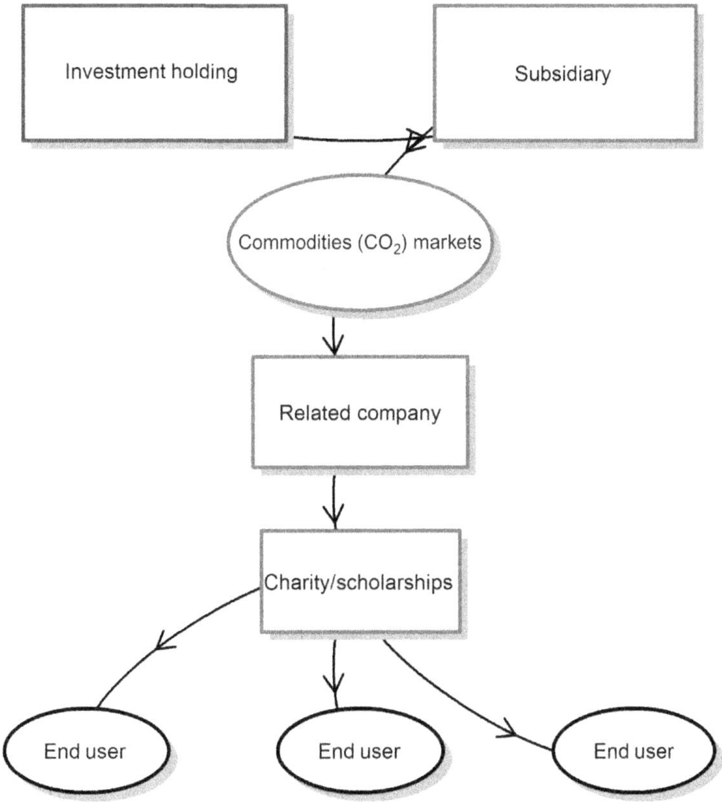

FIGURE 3 Sophisticated terrorist financing schemes include transactions on the energy markets aiming to transfer funds via transactions related to commodities.

on the energy markets involving the transfer of funds on behalf of transactions related to commodities or other assets from the energy complex. The aim of the transaction on these markets is not so much to make profits, but to have a legitimate explanation for transferring funds (Figure 3).

3.1 Emission Markets and Terrorism Financing

A relevant example is the case of financing of Taliban activities with the participation of companies incorporated in the European Union and Dubai operating on the carbon emission markets and mostly related to the value added tax fraud that occurred on this market between 2008 and 2010. Frunza [1] pointed out that the previous tax fraud cases in early 2000 were operating from the UK through the so-called Dubai connection. They were trading electronic goods and trades between the UK and UAE was revealed. The Dubai connection was revived toward the end of the 2000s on the emissions and generally speaking the energy markets, giving serious indications of further ties with terrorism financing that would lead toward Pakistan.

In 2014, a scandal emerged after a joint British and US operation against the Taliban in the border region between Afghanistan and Pakistan found documents in a cave not far from the town where Osama bin Laden was killed by US special forces in 2011.[4] The documents found in that cave were nothing more than trading books of companies incorporated in Italy and involved in the CO_2 emission markets. In relation to this case a British-Pakistani man was suspected by the investigators of involvement in an alleged 1 billion fraud in Italy. At the center of the investigation was a trading company called SF Energy Trading incorporated in Milan, Italy and owned by the alleged British-Pakistani fugitive and whose books were found by the American SEALs in Pakistan. After avoiding the payment of taxes the network of shell companies passed the illegal funds to bank accounts in Cyprus and Hong Kong before moving them to Dubai and the Emirates. The funds were then allegedly used to fund the terror economy in the Middle East. Therefore, the goal of the fraudster was not just to swindle VAT from the state, but also to use the CO_2 emissions market to transfer capital to extremists for terrorist activities.

[4]Danish CO_2 quotas part of colossal Italian fraud case, http://cphpost.dk/news/danish-co2-quotas-part-of-colossal-italian-fraud-case.11071.html.

4 OUTLOOK

The term terror financing should be enriched in the light of new developments in the concept of the terror economy. The economy of terror goes beyond financing and includes the products from all assets, capital and resources engaged by a terrorist organization to make profits channeled toward terrorist acts. This economy also includes a sociological dimension as not all elements involved in this economy are related directly to terror. Some of them are part of a lobby or participate on a high conceptual level or not at this level at all, looking only after financial profit.

The global dimension of the terror economy adds a new variable. For instance, Islamic State recruits come from almost 80 countries, the top suppliers being Saudi Arabia, Tunisia, the UK, and the Russian Federation. The multinational dimension of the terror economy should be understood in its specific context with its various layers from the top organization involved directly in supplying the terror to the smaller organization and companies paying some nonprofit organizations. Despite the appearance of independence between the various layers, this economy can be understood as a unitarian corpus and the financial markets facilitate the interaction of its various strata and geographical locations. The strategies related to the "war on terror" should also concern the aspects involving the terror economy with all its sociological, political, and financial consequences.

CHAPTER

4D

Cybercrime

OUTLINE

1 BACKGROUND

In 2010, the cyber-attack[1] carried out on the Natranz plant which is part of Iran's nuclear program marked a crossroads concerning the systemic risk arising from cyber-security issues.

The attack employed a computer worm named Stuxnet, which was designed to infiltrate the programmable logic controllers (PLCs) widely used in technological and industrial processes. The Stuxnet attack was allegedly carried out by a joint US-Israel task force after previous preparation. The attack took place in two phases spread over some years.

The initial attack, less known to the public, was designed to secretly gather information on the infrastructure of the Iranian plant to understand how the computers control via PLCs the centrifuges used to enrich uranium.

In the second phase, the virus infiltrated the machine controls with two main tasks. First, it targeted the gas centrifuges tasked with separating uranium-235 isotopes from uranium-238 isotopes at the Natranz plant. As a result, centrifuges were spinning out of control or were slowed down, stalled and in some cases self-destructed. Second, the worm overrode the communication with the plant monitoring systems in order to give the impression that the operations were working normally. It recorded what the normal operations at the nuclear plant were, then played those recordings back to plant operators, so that it appeared that everything was operating normally while in reality they were not.

[1]The Stuxnet attack on Iran's nuclear plant was "Far More Dangerous" than previously thought, http://www.businessinsider.com/stuxnet-was-far-more-dangerous-than-previous-thought-2013-11?IR=T.

http://dx.doi.org/10.1016/B978-0-12-801221-5.00015-4

In the attack's aftermath some parts of the Natranz operations closed, while others survived. Security experts agreed that most likely further phases of the attack will happen, the 2010 episode being part of a series.

Cybercrime is defined as a harmful activity conducted via the means of technology including hardware, software, and communication networks (e.g., Internet wireless telecommunications, GSM, etc.). The targets of cybercriminals are the confidentiality, integrity, and accessibility of computer systems, technology infrastructures and electronic communication hardware. The various typologies of cybercrime include:

- traditional crimes (i.e., fraud, forgery) conducted in cyberspace and executed over the various electronic communication channels;
- spreading of harmful information via electronic media, including websites, social media, emails, and phone messaging;
- Internet-based crimes including hacking, information theft, and denial of service; and
- reverse cybercrime representing the rogue use of technology in order to commit a crime in the real world—examples include the bots used to take control of a machine or a system.[2]

Despite being unrelated to financial institutions the Natranz episode provides some cutting-edge information about the cybersecurity threats. Cyber-threats whether they are cyber-attacks or cybercrime are the creation of an autonomous industry, similar to the antivirus software industry. There are consortia which develop and test software for cyber-threats. These cost-intensive activities are conducted by various groups of individuals (cybercriminals) from various backgrounds with various purposes. They can be classified as follows:

- *Criminal groups*, which conduct cybercriminal activities in order to generate illicit profit. Ex-Communist bloc countries have a high concentration of cyber-fraudsters.
- *Terrorist groups* are very active in the *online* environment and want to disrupt activities of big institutions or organizations in order to make their presence felt or to cause panic.
- *National military and intelligence agencies*, which can use cyber-attacks to shut down an enemy target, to spy or steal political or economic secrets from firms and nations.
- *Saboteurs*, which are individuals acting alone or on behalf of organization that steal, alter, or manipulate information.
- *"Hactivists,"* who are motivated by a political ideal or ideology, like ecologist groups, for example.

Cyber-threats and mainly cybercrime tend to target large institutions rather than private individuals. Traditionally cybercrime dealt mainly with credit card scams, account theft, etc. Over the past decade, cybercrime has targeted institutions of systemic importance like nuclear plants, payment systems, or exchanges, and have gained more momentum.

The real issue with cybercrime as illustrated by the Natranz case is the likelihood of committing the perfect crime. In addition to the crime itself, be it theft or spread of bogus information, cyber-fraudsters can cover their tracks, creating an alternative virtual reality where everything is normal. Not only would the alarms be delayed after the occurrence of the crime but the audit trails and investigations would be deleted or supplied with bogus information generated by cybercriminals.

Cybercrime in the financial sector is mainly associated with credit card scams and bank account withdrawals. Nevertheless there is a technical limit to how much money a cyber-fraudsters can make through classic cyber-rackets like credit card scams and account

[2]Among the speculation surrounding the disappearance of the Malaysian air flight MAS 370, one concerned the electronic hijack of the plane.

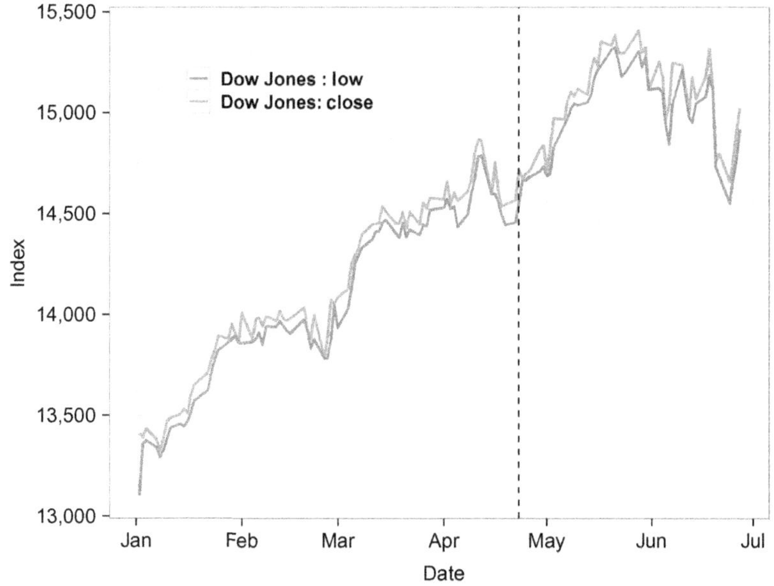

FIGURE 1 SEA cyber-attack and the effect on the Dow Jones Index.

withdrawals. But the amount of funds that can be pocketed by heisting a financial market is in theory unlimited. There is currently much less evidence or public material information concerning the attacks or intrusions of cybercriminals on market infrastructures. The usual cyber-scams on markets involve the spreading of the hoax through the web in order to alter the price of a stock, a typology detailed in a separate chapter.

The real threat is related to the fact that the entire market infrastructures rely mainly on Internet technology, thereby making it structurally vulnerable to hacking or disruptive cyber-attacks.

2 IMPACT OF CYBERCRIME ON MARKETS

The impact of systemic attacks can be very damaging, especially if the target has structural relevance, for example linked to national security. When news that "Two Explosions in the White House and Barack Obama is injured" diffused on April 24, 2013 around 1:07 PM exploded on the social media, the financial markets plunged into the red. Shortly afterwards the Syrian Electronic Army (a pro-Assad regime hacking group) claimed responsibility on Twitter "Ops! @ap get owned by Syrian Electronic Army! #SEA #Syria #ByeByeObama twitter.com/*Official$_S$EA6*/...." The account spreading the rogue news was soon suspended.

Figure 1 shows the impact of the alleged Syrian Electronic Army attack on the Dow Jones Index that dived almost 150 points within a day. The market recovered immediately when traders realized that the news had been a hoax.

Geopolitical conflicts involving cyber-attacks would gain a lot of momentum in the following years. Therefore, "Cold Wars" will most likely become "Cyber Wars." A relevant example in that sense is the cyber-attack that occurred in August 2014.[3] The FBI investigated a

[3]FBI examining whether Russia is tied to JPMorgan hacking, http://www.bloomberg.com/news/2014-08-27/fbi-said-to-be-probing-whether-russia-tied-to-jpmorgan-hacking.html.

cyber-attack originating from Russia against JPMorgan Chase & Co, resulting in the loss of gigabytes of sensitive data. The sophistication of the attack and technical indicators extracted from the banks' computers led the investigators to suspect a government-backed attack.

3 CYBERCRIME AND SECURITIES FRAUD

With the strong development of social media and web information platforms, cybercrime often targets the stock market. A McAfee[4] study about cybercrime estimates the annual cost to the global economy to be around 400 billion dollars. The report indicates that cybercrime becomes a very serious risk for financial institutions. Securities and brokerage firms and their customers are common targets of cybercriminals. The FBI[5] published a report about the typologies of cybercrimes in the financial markets. The typical crimes against these firms include spreading of false information, market manipulation schemes, and unauthorized stock trading. They can be summarized as follows:

- *Takeover of brokerage accounts and unauthorized transactions*. If the illegal takeover of bank deposit accounts or credit cards is common, this can also occur on online brokerage accounts targeting cash, shares, bonds, or the various trades. For example in December 2009, a Florida-based victim reported that 399,000 dollars disappeared from his online brokerage account. The cyber-takeover was conducted during the time the victim was also targeted by a Telephone Denial of Service (TDoS) attack, which cut off the communication with his broker. The trend in which cybercriminals initiated unauthorized financial transactions from bank or brokerage accounts has been pronounced over the past years. These transactions are combined with a TDoS attack, in which the victim's legitimate phone line is flooded with spam-like telephone calls to prevent the banks or brokerage firms from contacting the victim to verify that the transactions were legitimate.
- *Theft of nonpublic information*. Companies store most of their confidential nonpublic information in electronic repositories. By breaking into a company's networks or into the networks of its lawyers or accountants (which can sometimes be an easier target), cybercriminals can acquire inside information on acquisition and merger plans, quarterly revenue reports, or other data that could affect a company's stock prices.
- *Publication of false information*. Attacks against a bank, a stock or a market can be launched by spreading false information or hoaxes. Twitter and social media in general as well as the use of bot machines to automatically generate and follow news amplify the consequences of this type of crime.
- *Market manipulation*. Market manipulation can be based on cyber-scams. At one end of the spectrum manipulation can start via the spreading of rogue information about the asset. Criminals taking advantage of this information for trading can be hard to detect, as it might look like a normal trade, especially if it was carried out in another stock market. Using chatrooms and social media for "pump and dump," is a well-established technique, with criminals providing false information about a company's prospects and then cashing in

[4]Estimating the global cost of cybercrime, http://www.mcafee.com/fr/resources/reports/rp-economic-impact-cybercrime2.pdf.

[5]The cyber threat to the financial sector, http://www.fbi.gov/news/testimony/cyber-security-threats-to-the-financial-sector.

when the market reacts. At the other end of the scale, cyber-fraudsters can hack brokerage accounts and make unauthorized trades that can change the flow of the market.

- *Altering the book of trades and the strategy.* Accessing the trading book of a bank or a fund and being able to change that book can have all kinds of disruptive effects. With the emergence of HFT, the issue of their vulnerability became crucial due to their potential negative effect. BAE Systems reported in 2014 that hackers disrupted for eight weeks high-speed[6] trading at a large hedge fund and rerouted data that could have been used to make money in rogue stock-market transactions. Investigations found that the attack may have been linked to organized crime. The hackers inserted malicious software that delayed by several hundred microseconds the ability to trade. High frequency trading (HFT) relies on trades being executed in time windows that are much shorter than the reaction time of security systems. This structural gap makes HFT a relatively easy target and it is even easier not to be caught.
- *Disrupting the exchanges.* Cybercriminals target not only those who trade in securities but also the exchanges in which the securities are sold. TDoS and Distributed Denial of Service (DDoS) attacks show a desire by cybercriminals to focus their efforts on high-profile financial sector targets. FBI reports indicated that, in 2009, two US stock exchanges were victims of a sustained DDoS attack. The remote attack temporarily disrupted public websites but had no impact on financial market operations. A parent company of one of the exchanges stated that it had not experienced any degradation in service on its public website or core trading and data systems, which operated on a private network.
  In February 2011, criminal actors placed an online advertisement infected with malicious software onto the public website of a foreign stock exchange. The malicious advertisement appeared on the victims' computers as a pop-up, alerting the user to nonexistent computer infections in an attempt to trick the users into paying for and downloading rogue "antivirus" software.
  Also in February, the parent company of NASDAQ confirmed that they had been the victim of a security breach by unauthorized intruders into their Director's Desk web application, a system that was not directly linked to their trading platforms, but was instead used as an online portal for senior executives and directors to share confidential information.
- *Theft of electronic-stored assets.* Securities which are kept in depositories in an electronic format can be the object of theft if the depositories or custodians are hacked.
- *Theft of intellectual property.* Wall Street banks as well as hedge funds invest large amounts in their technology and methodologies that help them to generate profits. Those method-embedded systems are very valuable assets providing them with a comparative advantage, thereby making them a target for hackers and cyber-scammers. An investigation carried out by the FBI in 2010 dealt with two cases involving the theft or attempted theft of source code for high-frequency trading programs. The theft of these programs would have allowed a competitor to predict a company's actions in HFT trades, or give a competitor the opportunity to profit.

[6]Hackers sought monetary gain in hedge fund, http://www.bloomberg.com/news/2014-06-19/hackers-sought-monetary-gain-in-hedge-fund-attack-bae-says.html.

3.1 Cyber-Scams on Brokerage Accounts

An Security Exchange Commission (SEC) investigation from 2010[7] exposed a cyber-fraud involving forging of brokerage accounts, unauthorized trades, and market manipulation. Broco Investments had a legitimate account with the stock brokerage house Genesis. Broco and its executive director Valer Maltsev were part of a group of people that conducted in concert illegal cyber-frauds between 2009 and 2010. The fraud consisted of the repeated hijack of the online brokerage accounts of unwitting investors using stolen logins and passwords. Subsequently the fraudsters placed unauthorized trades through the compromised accounts.

Broco engaged in an elaborate scheme in which they manipulated, via account intrusions, the markets for shares of at least 38 issuers. The fraud involved the following steps:

- First Broco purchased thinly traded securities at the prevailing market prices using their own online brokerage account at Genesis.
- Shortly thereafter, individuals acting in concert with them, using stolen logins and passwords, intruded into the online brokerage accounts of other individuals held with various brokerage firms. Individuals acting in concert with them then used these intruded accounts to place a series of unauthorized buy orders (for shares of the same issuers purchased only moments earlier by Broco through the Genesis account), typically at prices well above the prevailing market prices for those thinly traded securities.
- In a short time window Broco sold its positions on the artificially inflated share prices of the targeted securities by selling the shares previously acquired in their account.

[7]SEC vs Broco Investments, Inc. and Valery Maltsev, http://www.sec.gov/litigation/complaints/2010/comp21452.pdf.

AMERISERVE FINANCIAL, INC. (ASRV)

Background

Among the stock manipulated through unauthorized trades by Broco, one of the most relevant examples is that of AmeriServe Financial Inc., which is a NASDAQ traded, Pennsylvania-based bank. The manipulation occurred on December 21, 2009 when the traded volume spiked at almost 277,500 shares from 11,300 shares per day as it did previously in the month. The stock traded in the $1.6-1.7 range and the manipulation took place in this thin range, thereby not affecting the price signal in a significant manner.

Manipulating stock

The manipulation took place in three phases within an interval of a few minutes. First, Broco bought a number of ASRV shares. Second, at Broco's request the three accounts from Scottrade brokerage were illegally accessed and unauthorized buy trades were placed to drive the price up. Third, Broco sold its shares at higher prices and then cut the unauthorized positions at a loss.

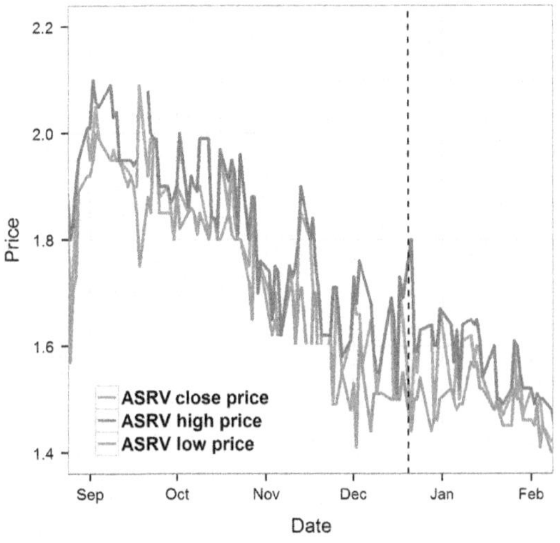

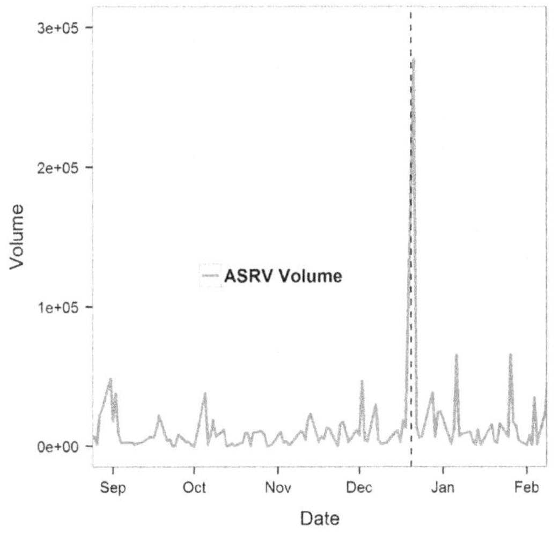

Aftermath

In that fraudulent operation Broco sold its shares for $141,500 in realizing a net profit of $17,760 and Scottrade's clients observed losses accounting for $20,355 following the unauthorized trades on their accounts.

Trivia

Valery Maltsev is a Russian citizen residing in or around Saint Petersburg, Russia. Maltsev was Broco's president and only officer, and has sole trading authorization for Broco's securities account.

In the aftermath the investigators estimated that the Broco account realized illegal profits of at least 255,000 dollars from its trading in the following 38 securities, at or around the time of unauthorized trading in compromised accounts. Broco attempted to withdraw 110,000 dollars from its brokerage account via wire transfer. In March 2010, Broco attempted to withdraw an additional 200,000 dollars from the account via wire transfer. Both withdrawals requested that the funds be wired Broco's bank account in Cyprus but the brokerage firm Genesis refused to process these requests. Online broker-dealers whose customers' accounts were compromised and used to make unauthorized trades suffered losses in excess of 600,000 dollars.

The Broco case caused limited damage but it shows how cybercriminals can execute attacks by employing different techniques in an organized and synchronized way. The main threat of cybercrime comes from its capacity to deploy means in a very short period of time and to conduct frauds using different techniques like hacking, market manipulation, DoS, etc. In addition, these types of attacks can be conducted from remote locations.

3.2 Cybercrime in Carbon Markets

The theft of assets in the commodities world is naturally a "blue-collar" type of crime. There are exceptions to this rule, one of them being the carbon emissions allowances. These allowances give the right to industrial companies within the European Union to emit CO_2. These rights are stored in electronic registries, which were once upon a time managed by each European Union country. In the emission rights market, being purely a regulatory-driven market, many pitfalls occured over time due to the fact that it was not initially conceived as a fully fledged financial market. Therefore, the national registries acting as electronic repositories of the European allowance (EUAs) had very low security standards and were not tested at all against cyber-attacks. This market suffered a number of abuses, including cyber-hacking of the registry accesses and electronic theft of the allowances. The security level of those systems being at that time low, accounts were relatively easily to hack. Once hacked the cybercriminal can transfer those rights to other accounts and then sell them on the market. An average European industrial company had in its account a few million allowances, worth around 14 dollars each [1].

The cyber-attacks started on November 30, 2010 when the Romanian subsidiary of Swiss cement producer Holcim reported that the Romanian National Registry for CO_2 allowances had been illegally accessed on 16 November of the same year. Unknown persons have accessed the accounts and stolen 1.6 million emissions permits. The "hackers" managed to obtain the login and the passwords of Holcim's Romanian registry accounts through a "Trojan horse" method. The security breach allegedly lay with the account holder and not with the registry itself.

Holcim was only the beginning of the saga of stolen EUAs. Only 6 weeks after the original incident on January 19, 2011 Austria's emissions registry recognized a massive theft of 488,141 EUA certificates on January 10. The theft did not involve the account of a company but was from a government holding account, thereby being the first reported theft of government-owned carbon permits. In the case of the *Austrian job* the criminals opened the cyber-offensive with a DoS attack, which implied that the hackers prevented the registry's system from functioning and stole the permits while the system was unavailable to its proper users. The stolen emission certificates were transferred to other accounts located in Liechtenstein and Sweden.

All the attacks occurred in a clustered manner and continued: on January 21, 2011 the Czech carbon permits registry announced that 1.3 million carbon permits were stolen from six different accounts between noon on January 18 and the morning of January 19. The allowances were transferred first to accounts in Poland, Italy, and Estonia. Interestingly the Czech police received a bomb threat around noon on January 18, which forced the registry to evacuate its personnel and operate the system from a backup site for several hours, which allegedly could have been the time of the cyber-attack. On January 27, CEZ energy group, the Czech Republic's biggest utility, confirmed that 700,000 CO_2 permits were missing from its account. The company detected two unauthorized transactions at the same time as the heist of the Czech national registry.

The series of attacks moved to Southern Europe and on January 31, 2011 an announcement was made that 300,000 EUAs had been stolen from a Greek cement firm. The emissions permits were stolen by cybercriminals on January 18 from the Greek emissions registry account of cement maker Halyps, which is part of Italy's Italcementi Group, the company said on Monday. The hackers penetrated the server system of the University of Patras, using it as a Trojan horse with a Greek IP and then hit cement company Halyps.

On February 8, 2011 an Italian official from the country's ministry of the environment confirmed the theft of 267,991 EUAs taken from an Italian CO_2 registry account on November 24, 2010. The theft was made public two months after the original incident. However, on December 2, 2010, the Italian registry found around 100,000 of the stolen allowances, probably from Romania, in an Italian account. The Italian investigators had tracked allowances from the victim's account to a second Italian account, where they were immediately transferred to an account in the Liechtenstein registry and then on to the UK registry. In the aftermath Holcim recuperated almost 70% of the stolen amount and other countries witnessed similar developments. Munich Re proposed an insurance product for protecting emitters from being victims of cybercrime on registries.

Table 1 shows the timeline of the theft, that involved countries and companies as well as the amount of stolen allowances, which amounted to 35 million dollars at the market prices. The fact that the attacks came in a cluster is a strong indication that they were coordinated and the cybercriminals had a good knowledge of the weaknesses of the system.

The carbon registry was a closed system and thus the allowances could not leave the confined cyberspace. Nevertheless the European investigations had a hard time tracking the allowances

TABLE 1 Timeline of the CO_2 Allowances Theft

Date	Public info	Company	Country	Stolen quantity	Transfers
16/10/2010	30/10/2010	Holcim	Romania	1,600,000	Lichtenstein, Italy
–	27/01/2011	CEZ	Czech Rep.	700,000	–
19/01/2011	40,577	–	Austria	488,141	Lichtenstein, Sweden
18/01/2011	30/01/2011	Halyps	Greece	300,000	–
24/11/2010	40,757	–	Italy	267,991	Lichtenstein, UK

Source: Frunza [1].

and identifying the criminals. First, the system did not have a centralized view of all accounts in order to identify the fluxes of allowances. In many cases, the 27 countries acted independently in their registries after the CO_2 was stolen. Second, the various European task forces did not have the right to interfere in the national investigations, thereby delaying the tracking of the criminals.

4 CYBERCRIME AS A SYSTEMIC RISK

With the continuous change of the economy from the physical to the digital domain, new risks, and challenges arose during this translation. Electronic transfers, electronic exchanges, e-commerce, and crypto-currencies are just some areas where the digital quasi-replaced the physical domain. This drift is even more pronounced in the financial industry. Currently the risks relate to cyber-security are included by organization in the field of operational risk, which accounts for almost 15% of their capital reserves in case of distress. Nevertheless almost the full infrastructure of a bank relies on the digital support, thereby exposing the institution at all levels to cyber-attacks.

Systemic risk became a real concern for financial institutions after the Long Term Capital Management default in 1998 and the Lehman default in 2008. Currently the industry's perception of systemic risk is related to the propagation of losses or distress across organizations. The likelihood of the systemic event being related to the cyber-security of banks is still underestimated.

4.1 Market Infrastructures and Cybercrime

The International Organization of Securities Commissions and World Federation of Exchanges published in 2013 an alarming survey [115] about cybercrime as a source of systemic risk for securities infrastructure.[8]

Among the exchanges that answered the survey more than 53% reported suffering a cyber-attack, which were a mixture of simplistic attacks like DoS or more sophisticated attacks including worms or Trojan horses. The survey pointed out that 89% of exchanges perceive cybercrime as a systemic risk and report having a formal plan/documentation addressing cyber-threats and 70% of exchanges share information with authorities, regulators, and other actors on a national basis.

Some of the publicly known examples of attacks include those targeting the exchange operators NASDAQ OMX Group and BATS

[8]Cyber crime, securities markets, and systemic risk, http://www.csrc.gov.cn/pub/csrc_en/affairs/AffairsIOSCO/201307/W020130719521960468495.pdf.

Global Markets which reported that in 2012 they were targeted with DoS attacks. In October 2011, NYSE Euronext's New York Stock Exchange website was inaccessible for 30 min, but the exchange managed to insure no interruption of service. In 2010, hackers managed to infiltrate NASDAQ's computer systems and to install malicious software that allowed them to spy on the directors of publicly held companies. Currently all these attacks against exchanges have had no impact on market integrity and efficiency.

Exchanges are nonsubstitutable infrastructures and they are heavily interconnected, thus any attack that is disruptive in nature can generate a systemic event across markets. The systemic nature of the cybercrime risk can occur as a consequence of the following scenarios [115]:

- *Disrupting exchanges activity*. Cyber-attacks can affect the trading activity over an exchange or affect the function of a clearing house to settle the trades. A cyber-attack can disrupt the trading also by targeting the electronic communication infrastructure of the exchange. The risk around centralized clearing counterparties will be developed further in the section.
- *Manipulating markets*. As presented in a previous section markets can be manipulated through takeover of accounts and placing unauthorized trades in those markets.
- *Data manipulation*. Exchanges are also originators of the financial information used by institutions for making investment and risk management decisions. Changing data like settlement prices or bid-asks and compromising the financial data integrity can be really disruptive.
- *Data theft*. Exchanges store highly confidential information about the finances and trades of various institutions. Going after insider information by placing viruses or worms can lead to further financial crimes.

4.2 Centralized Counterparties and Cybercrime: Scenario for a Systemic Risk

Following the financial crisis starting in 2008, the paradigm of "too big to fall" was reassessed by regulators. Therefore in 2009 the American Congress passed the Dodd-Frank bill which involved among other things the creation of centralized counterparties (CCPs), intended to be clearing entities for the massive positions on Over-the-Counter derivatives held by the big banks. The European Union passed a similar regulation later: European Market Infrastructure Regulation (EMIR).

By interposing themselves in transactions, CCPs help to manage counterparty risk for market members and facilitate the netting positions (Figure 2). Nevertheless CCPs are themselves exposed to various risks, the most important being the risk due to the propagation of losses from the default of one of its Clearing Members. In the case of a Clearing Member's default the loss will be amortized by the CCP, depending on the magnitude of the exposure at that time. If the loss cannot be amortized, the CCP enters into default. Nevertheless the Clearing Members start to observe losses before the technical default of the CCP.

Most transactions in the OTC derivatives market establish future financial obligations between counterparties. If one becomes insolvent (Figure 3), then these will most likely not be met. Such failures may lead to further insolvencies especially if the positions were important hedges.

To reduce the negative externality of the propagation of counterparty risk to the real economy, the Dodd-Frank bill and EMIR requires for example moving standardized swaps to swap execution facilities and central counterparties. The risk of a swap no longer depends upon the counterparty, it depends only on the CCP. Counterparties no longer face rising costs of executing large one-sided volumes through risk premiums. But CCPs deal with this by having concentration

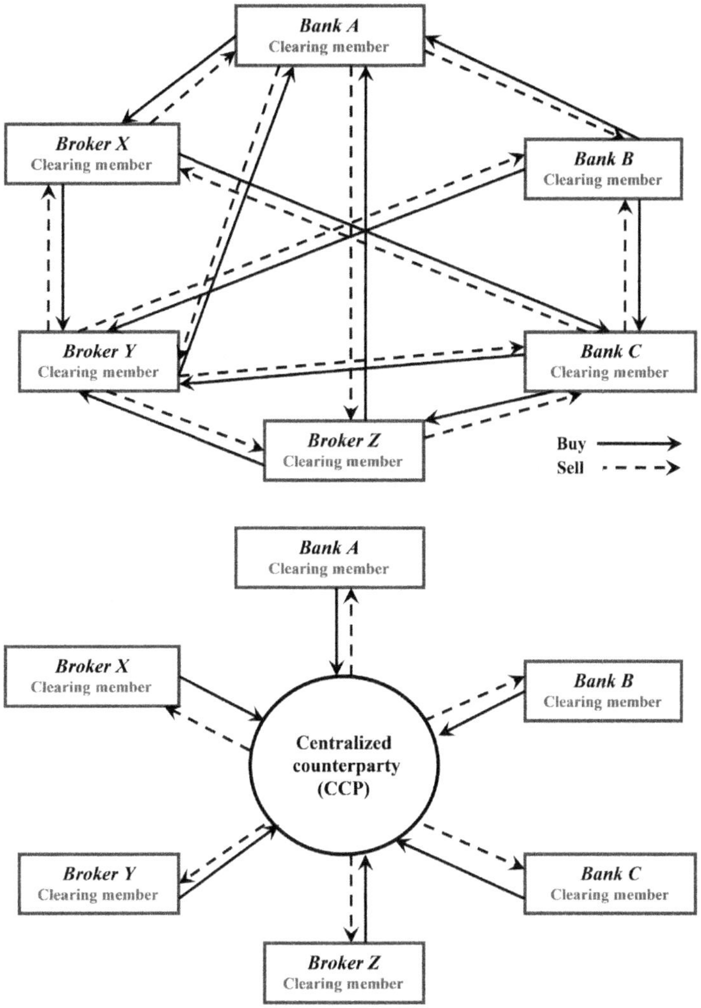

FIGURE 2 Derivatives clearing via bilateral trades (left) or CCP cleared trades (right).

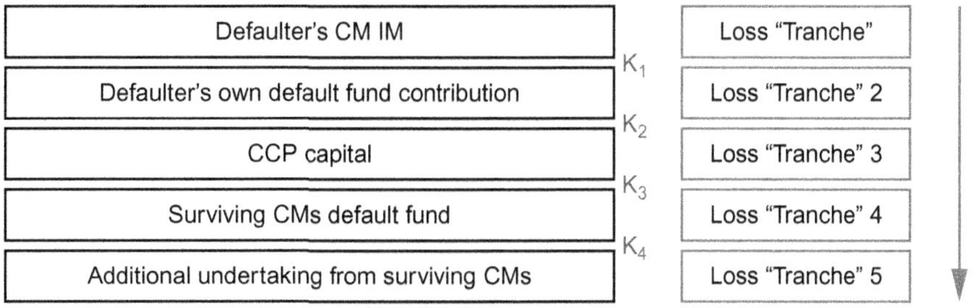

FIGURE 3 Classic structure of a CCP default waterfall.

limits and also creditworthiness-based margins [116–118]. A typical CCP has a multi-layer capital structure (CCP default waterfall) to protect itself and its members from losses due to member defaults. The CCP default waterfall is composed of the following elements listed in the order in which they are intended to cover the eventual losses:

- *Variation margin*: Variation margin is charged or credited daily to clearing member accounts to cover any portfolio mark-to-market changes.
- *Initial margin*: Initial margin is posted by clearing members to the CCP. This is to cover any losses incurred in the unwinding of a defaulting member's portfolio. Typically the margin is set to cover all losses up to a predefined confidence level in normal market conditions.
- *CCP equity*: A typical CCP will have an equity layer provided by shareholders. The position of the equity buyer in the capital structure can vary between CCPs.
- *Default fund (funded)*: Every member contributes to the clearing house default fund. This acts as a form of mutualized insurance for uncollateralized losses.
- *Default fund (unfunded)*: In addition to the default fund contributions that have been posted to the CCP, each clearing member is usually committed to providing further funds if necessary. The maximum amount of additional funds that can be called upon depends on the CCP. In some cases, the liability is uncapped.

By their nature CCPs are market and counterparty risk concentrators. In addition to those risks due to the high amounts involved CCPs could be easy targets for cyber-attacks. In the likelihood of a cyber-attack, the aim would be more related to a terrorist disruptive nature and less to a fraud. If a group of persons or a state intended to destabilize the financial system of a country, a region or at a global level, a CCP would be the perfect target for achieving this purpose. From the perspective of a scenario analysis it is crucial to understand how the safety cushions of a CCP are related to the absorption of financial losses.

The bottom line of this structure is that a CCP is not aimed to default. If one of the members experiences big losses that propagate to all layers of the waterfall, ultimately the remaining members should absorb the losses with their own reserves. Therefore, in the light of a cyber-attack, a CCP faces a direct and an indirect risk:

- A CCP can be the *direct* target of a cyber-attack involving DoS or worms that would affect the valuation or settlement of the trades.
- A CCP could suffer collateral damage in an *indirect* way if one of its members is the object of an attack and its losses propagate on the CCP. Experiments show that even small members can inflict big losses on the other members under certain market conditions.

The indirect risk is still underestimated, despite recent evidence showing how disruptive such an event can be. Figure 4 shows a potential scenario of a cyberattack able to disrupt the activity of a CCP.

The consequences of the Korean broker HanMag[9] constitute relevant evidence for this scenario. The Korea Exchange (KRX), Korea's sole securities exchange operator, faced in December 2013 the default of one of its members HanMag Securities, a small brokerage house specialize in futures. The Korean broker HanMag Securities allegedly confused calls with puts on the Korea Composite Stock Price Index. The losses occurred on HanMag's automated trading

[9]HanMag debacle hits brokerages, http://www.koreatimes.co.kr/www/news/biz/2013/12/488_148108.html.

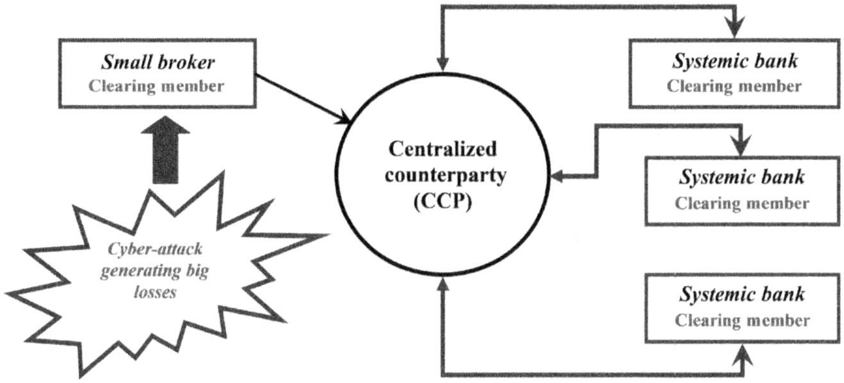

FIGURE 4 Cyber-attack scenario: a cybercriminal who is (or not) a client of a brokerage house can launch an attack against it. The attack can include DoS, hacking or even intrusion in the trading algorithm or scamming the order book. Such an attack can generate massive losses for the broker that could be transmitted to the CCP. If the waterfall structure cannot absorb the losses, bigger banks with a systemic loss would face the necessity of injecting funds in order to keep the CCP running. Thus a cyber-attack on a small clearing member can affect the CCP and its bigger members.

platform related to its proprietary trading desk, thereby executing the trades against unrealistic prices. They placed a program order right after market opening. HanMag Securities attributed the error to its computer network. There were a total of 36,100 trades associated with the incident involving 46 traders. The broker's exposure across the securities market was about 6.3 million dollars, and across the derivatives market 58.4 million dollars. For the derivatives exposure HanMag was able to pay only 1.4 million dollars, thus generating a loss of 57 million dollars. The losses generated by HanMag were three times bigger than their total equity of 19 million dollars.

After the turmoil HanMag, which was a privately held firm, requested the KRX for an Error Trade Bailout, but this was rejected as it did not meet the error trade requirements. The risk of a broker going into insolvency is covered by a dedicated Korean fund with a reserve of 350 million USD, financed by Korean brokers, but as there were no client losses in that event, KRX needed to take the loss on its own waterfall structure. This small broker generated such a big loss that the initial margin and the KRX's default funds were not sufficient. Therefore, all the other members of the CCP were required to inject liquidity to compensate for HanMag's problems.

In the cyber-attack scenario toward a CCP, a cybercriminal who is (or not) a client of a brokerage house can launch an attack against it. The attack can include DoS, hacking or even intrusion in the trading algorithm or scamming the order book. Such an attack can generate massive losses for the broker that can be transmitted to the CCP. The CCP has as members big banks with a systemic role, which are also contributors to the unfunded default fund. If the CCP's waterfall structure cannot absorb the losses, bigger banks with a systemic role would have to inject funds in order to keep the CCP running. Thus a cyber-attack on a small clearing member can affect the CCP and its bigger members.

5 OUTLOOK

Cybercrime is still an underrated threat in relation to securities markets. This tendency is currently changing and the concern about cyber-attacks on markets will gain more momentum and more solutions will be needed.

Cyber-attacks against markets or market infrastructure are not stand alone and are often linked to other financial crimes like market manipulation, insider trading, and money laundering. Cyber-security needs to be addressed in concert with the physical security and internal surveillance with institutions. Physical security within organizations is easier to assess than the informational security. Cyber-attacks can be linked to groups of individuals within an organization and this scenario would be difficult to track.

Systemic institutions like big investment banks, exchange, or centralized clearing houses can be targets for a foreseeable cyber-attack with systemic consequences. At the origin of those attacks can be found criminal organizations, terrorist groups, or governments.

Epilogue

The ontology of criminal behavior within the financial industry involves psychological and structural aspects of the sector. If the individuals using services provided by the industry are affected by ubiquitous crimes including credit card fraud or insurance scams the crime on financial markets has much more ramified and complex effects on the real economy.

First, offenses involving markets affect the investors and their confidence in the robustness of financial systems. Market manipulation or insider trading often leads to litigation from investors and investigations from regulatory bodies. Nevertheless in many cases criminal behavior within a market can produce a systemic effect resulting in general loss of confidence, withdrawal of liquidity, and a bearish tendency in that market. The example of the fraud on the CO_2 emissions market which led to the near dismissal of the scheme is relevant in that sense.

A second type of effect is the structural damage of the institution or group of institutions affected or harboring the offenders. The default of Barings is the best known example, but the effect can go further and an entire sector can lose confidence. The effect of misconduct in the credit derivatives market had a strong negative impact on the investment banking sector and reshaped seriously the entire financial arena after the financial crisis. The systemic effects of financial crime on the real economy are still underestimated and insufficiently studied.

The third consequence is linked to the concept of *fair value*, or even more precisely *unfair value*. Without dissecting the foundations of the concept, market prices are used directly or as proxies for financial instrument valuation. Prices in a market affected by fraud could obviously result in a misleading valuation of an asset or of a group of assets in a portfolio. For instance, the last allegation of FX market rigging could have effects way beyond the domain of buyers and sellers involved in the manipulation. A significant manipulation of the foreign exchange could have massive impacts on many firms or investments using the FX reference for business or accounting purposes.

The fourth dimension is the political one. We will not refer here to investments or speculations that are built around a particular political event. A good example in this sense is the speculation which led to a rise in volatility of agricultural markets. The *Arab Spring* is believed to have been generated among many things by the increase in the price of grains and scarce supply to the North African countries. One could easily imagine that altering the price of these commodities can have huge socio-political impact. On the same registry, we mention here the role of energy markets in the recent conflict in Donbass (Ukraine) or the strategies of hedge funds on distressed sovereign debt (i.e., Argentina). Integrity is a fragile topic for main markets like stocks, interest rates, or currency and one could imagine, in a *"what if" scenario*, the political outcome of market rigging on a market-sensitive region or country.

The financial literature is mainly oriented toward the assessment of markets' features, the construction of sound investment strategies, with reasonably mitigated risks. With few exceptions the main financial concepts of both quantitative and qualitative aspects do not include the occurrence of offenses in financial markets. Many researchers underlined over the past 20 years that markets have often counterintuitive behaviors with abnormal features very different from theoretical assumptions. And theories have also proposed solutions to address the valuation of financial instruments under these abnormal conditions. There is an abundance of pricing methods for derivatives in markets with abrupt variations and volatility clustering. Analyzing markets in the light of the likelihood of criminal behavior is a recent development.

The heterogeneity of offenses in the investment world requires a multi-disciplinary approach. The ethical mutations in society, the continual innovation in technology and markets amplified by an increasing speed of information flows are the main challenges in this process. On one hand, despite the heavy involvement of technology and automated processes in investment firms the human presence is still crucial in most operational decisions, thereby making it more vulnerable to potential errors, misconduct, or fraud. On the other hand, technology is intended to be a useful asset in mitigating risk but in many situations can and does creates disruptive situations for financial systems.

The recent crisis underlined the fact that the prudential framework of risk mitigation is at least one step behind the issues that can arise within organizations or markets. On the same note regulation addressing misconduct and crime in finance is one step behind current or previous issues and very far away from providing a prevention framework. Financial crime investigation should as a discipline or a set of techniques be overseeing the process of regulation and looking beyond it, from a more economic perspective.

Scenario analysis is popular in traditional risk management and is also used within organizations in crime intelligence units. In the context of financial crime, real-life scenarios are with some exceptions very different from what has actually happened, the reason being that organizations take action after a fraud is discovered. Thus scenarios analysis should be employed in an exploratory manner. An example could be in the technology industry, which uses white hat hackers to point out the weaknesses in the system.

Bibliography

[1] M.-C. Frunza, Fraud and Carbon Markets: The Carbon Connection, vol. 5, Routledge, Abingdon, 2013.

[2] B. Franklin, Advice to a Young Tradesman, vol. 1748, The Federal Edition, Philadelphia, PA, 1750.

[3] M. Van de Mieroop, Cuneiform Texts and the Writing of History, Routledge, London, 2005.

[4] E.J. Weber, A Short History of Derivative Security Markets, Springer, Berlin, 2009.

[5] E.J. Swan, Building the Global Market: A 4000 Year History of Derivatives, Kluwer Law International, The Hague, 2000.

[6] S. Zarlenga, A Brief History of Interest, American Monetary Institute, London, 2000.

[7] S. Kummer, C. Pauletto, The history of derivatives: a few milestones, in: EFTA Seminar on Regulation of Derivatives Markets, 2012.

[8] R.R. Wasendorf, P. Stahl, Commodities Trading: The Essential Primer, Irwin Professional Pub, Illinois, 1985.

[9] A.L. Slotsky, The bourse of Babylon, in: Market quotations in the Astronomical Diaries of Babylonia, vol. 57, 1997, pp. 493–495.

[10] P. Temin, Price behavior in ancient Babylon, Explor. Econ. Hist. 39 (1) (2002) 46–60.

[11] J.W. Gilbart, A. Michie, The History, Principles, and Practice of Banking, vol. 2, G. Bell and sons, London, 1901.

[12] K. Nayan Kabra, J. Shah, B. Rath, Back to the future: roots of commodity trade in India, Indian J. Agric. Econ. 65 (4) (2010) 803.

[13] P. Temin, Financial intermediation in the early Roman Empire, J. Econ. Hist. 64 (3) (2004) 705–733.

[14] U. Malmendier, Roman shares, in: Origins of Value: A Document History of France, Oxford University Press, New York, 2005, pp. 31–42.

[15] W.N. Goetzmann, K.G. Rouwenhorst, The Origins of Value: The Financial Innovations That Created Modern Capital Markets, Oxford University Press, New York, 2005.

[16] V.L. Hou, Derivatives and dialectics: the evolution of the Chinese futures market, NYUL Rev. 72 (1997) 175.

[17] G.W. Schwert, Indexes of US Stock Prices from 1802 to 1987, J. Bus. 63 (3) (1990) 399–426.

[18] J.J. Siegel, Stocks for the Long Run: The Definitive Guide to Financial Market Returns and Long-Term Investment Strategies, third ed., McGraw-Hill, New York, 2002.

[19] D. Marteau, P. Morand, Normes comptables et crise financière: Propositions Pour une réforme du système de régulation comptable, La Documentation française, 2010.

[20] J.P. de la Vega, Confusión de Confusiones re, John Wiley and Sons Inc, USA, 1668.

[21] P. Held, The confusion of confusions: between speculation and eschatology, Concentric Literary Cult. Stud. 32 (2) (2006) 111–144.

[22] R.G. Frehen, W.N. Goetzmann, K.G. Rouwenhorst, New evidence on the first financial bubble, J. Financ. Econ. 108 (3) (2013) 585–607.

[23] A. Dumas, The Count of Monte Cristo, 1844, NY Collier, New York, 1910, reprint.

[24] F. Allen, L. Litov, J. Mei, Large investors, price manipulation, and limits to arbitrage: an anatomy of market corners, Rev. Finance 10 (4) (2006) 645–693.

[25] W.D. Cohan, The Last Tycoons: The Secret History of Lazard Frères & Co, Anchor, USA, 2008.

[26] C.H. Bennett, G. Brassard, C. Crépeau, R. Jozsa, A. Peres, W.K. Wootters, Teleporting an unknown quantum state via dual classical and Einstein-Podolsky-Rosen channels, Phys. Rev. Lett. 70 (13) (1993) 1895.

[27] L.M. Adleman, Molecular computation of solutions to combinatorial problems, Science 266 (5187) (1994) 1021–1024.

[28] L.M. Adlemany, On Constructing a Molecular Computer, Citeseer, 1995.

[29] C. Moussu, A. Petit-Romec, ROE in banks: myth and reality, Financial Times, 2011.

[30] T. Philippon, Has the US finance industry become less efficient? On the theory and measurement of financial intermediation, Tech. Rep., National Bureau of Economic Research, 2012.

[31] A. Smith, The Wealth of Nations, vol. 2, Dent/Dutton, London/New York, 1971.

[32] P.R. Krugman, Increasing returns, monopolistic competition, and international trade, J. Int. Econ. 9 (4) (1979) 469–479.

[33] A.C. Pigou, The Economics of Welfare, 1920, McMillan & Co., London, 1932.

[34] P.A. Samuelson, W. Nordhaus, Economics, McGraw-Hill, New York, 1985.

[35] D. Begg, S. Fisher, R. Dornbusch, Economics, McGraw-Hill Publishing Company, England, 1994.

[36] R.C. Merton, On the pricing of corporate debt: the risk structure of interest rates, J. Finan. 29 (2) (1974) 449–470.

[37] F. Reserve, Supervisory Guidance on Model Risk Management, Board of Governors of the Federal Reserve System, Office of the Controller of the Currency, SR Letter, 2011, pp. 11–17.

[38] E. Derman, Model Risk: What Are the Assumptions Made in Using Models to Value Securities and What Are the Consequent Risks?, vol. 9, Risk Magazine Limited, London, 1996, pp. 34–38.

[39] R. Rebonato, Theory and practice of model risk management, in: Modern Risk Management: A History, Citeseer, RiskWaters Group, London.

[40] F. Black, M. Scholes, The pricing of options and corporate liabilities, J. Polit. Econ. 81 (1973) 637–654.

[41] H.U. Gerber, E.S. Shiu, Option pricing by Esscher transforms, Trans. Soc. Actuaries 46 (99) (1994) 140.

[42] E. Eberlein, K. Prause, The generalized hyperbolic model: financial derivatives and risk measures, in: Mathematical Finance Bachelier Congress 2000, Springer, 2002, pp. 245–267.

[43] S.L. Heston, S. Nandi, A closed form GARCH option valuation model, Rev. Financ. Stud. 13 (3) (2000) 585–625.

[44] C. Gourieroux, A. Monfort, Econometric specification of stochastic discount factor models, J. Econom. 136 (2) (2007) 509–530.

[45] J.V. Rosenberg, R.F. Engle, Empirical pricing kernels, J. Financ. Econ. 64 (3) (2002) 341–372.

[46] C. Chorro, D. Guégan, F. Ielpo, Option pricing for GARCH-type models with generalized hyperbolic innovations, Quant. Finan. 12 (7) (2012) 1079–1094.

[47] J.-C. Duan, G. Gauthier, J.-G. Simonato, An analytical approximation for the GARCH option pricing model, J. Comput. Finan. 2 (4) (1997) 75–116.

[48] J.-C. Duan, The GARCH option pricing model, Math. Finan. 5 (1) (1995) 13–32.

[49] G. Barone-Adesi, R.F. Engle, L. Mancini, A GARCH option pricing model with filtered historical simulation, Rev. Financ. Stud. 21 (2008) 1223–1258.

[50] L. Forsberg, A. Eriksson, The mean variance mixing GARCH(1, 1) model, in: Econometric Society 2004 Australasian Meetings (No. 323), Econometric Society, 2004, August.

[51] N.N. Taleb, Bleed or blowup? Why do we prefer asymmetric payoffs? J. Behav. Finan. 5 (1) (2004) 2–7.

[52] D.X. Li, On default correlation: a copula function approach, J. Fixed Income 9 (4) (2000) 43–54.

[53] P. Embrechts, F. Lindskog, A. McNeil, Modelling dependence with copulas and applications to risk management, in: Handbook of Heavy Tailed Distributions in Finance, vol. 8, 2003, pp. 329–384.

[54] J. de Kort, Modeling tail dependence using copulas-literature review, U. Delft, Netherlands. http://ta.tw.tudelft.nl/users/numanl/Kort-scriptie.pdf, 2007.

[55] R.T. Rockafellar, S. Uryasev, The fundamental risk quadrangle in risk management, optimization and statistical estimation, Surv. Oper. Res. Manag. Sci. 18 (1) (2013) 33–53.

[56] P. Artzner, F. Delbaen, J.-M. Eber, D. Heath, Coherent measures of risk, Math. Finan. 9 (3) (1999) 203–228.

[57] S. Emmer, M. Kratz, D. Tasche, What is the best risk measure in practice? A comparison of standard measures (2013), arXiv preprint arXiv:1312.1645.

[58] P.F. Christoffersen, Evaluating interval forecasts, Int. Econ. Rev. 39 (1998) 841–862.

[59] P.H. Kupiec, Techniques for verifying the accuracy of risk measurement models, J. Deriv. 3 (2) (1995) 73–84.

[60] T. Gneiting, A.E. Raftery, Strictly proper scoring rules, prediction, and estimation, J. Am. Stat. Assoc. 102 (477) (2007) 359–378.

[61] Basle Committee and Bank for International Settlements, International Convergence of Capital Measurement and Capital Standards: A Revised Framework, Lulu.com, 2004.

[62] T. Gneiting, Making and evaluating point forecasts, J. Am. Stat. Assoc. 106 (494) (2011) 746–762.

[63] D. Moss, E. Kingten, The Dojima Rice Market and the Origins of Futures Trading, Harvard Business School, Boston, MA, 2010.

[64] R. Cornwell, God's Banker, Dodd, Mead, 1984.

[65] R.T. Ainsworth, VoIP MTIC-VAT fraud in voice over Internet protocol, Tax Notes Int. 57 (2010) 1079–1094.

[66] M. Hellerman, T.C. Renner, Wall Street Swindler, Doubleday, Garden City, NY, 1977.

[67] R. Broadhurst, K.W. Lee, The transformation of triad "dark societies" in Hong Kong: the impact of law enforcement, socio-economic and political change, Secur. Challenges 5 (2009) 1–38.

[68] T.W. Lo, Beyond social capital: triad organized crime in Hong Kong and China, Br. J. Criminol. 50 (5) (2010) 851–872.

[69] P. Augustin, M. Brenner, M.G. Subrahmanyam, Informed options trading prior to M&A announcements: insider trading?, 2014, available at SSRN 2441606.

[70] M. Artzrouni, The mathematics of Ponzi schemes, Math. Soc. Sci. 58 (2) (2009) 190–201.

[71] M. Cunha, H. Valente, P.B. Vasconcelos, et al., Ponzi schemes: computer simulation, Tech. Rep., OBEGEF-Observatório de Economia e Gest ao de Fraude & OBEGEF Working Papers on Fraud and Corruption, 2013.

[72] B.R. Parodi, A Ponzi scheme exposed to volatile markets, (No. 60584), University Library of Munich, Germany, 2014.

[73] F. Allen, D. Gale, Stock-price manipulation, Rev. Financ. Stud. 5 (3) (1992) 503–529.

[74] R.K. Aggarwal, G. Wu, Stock market manipulations, J. Bus. 79 (4) (2006) 1915–1953.

[75] J.J. Angel, L.E. Harris, C.S. Spatt, Equity trading in the 21st century, Q. J. Finan. 1 (01) (2011) 1–53.

[76] M. Lewis, Flash Boys: A Wall Street Revolt, WW Norton & Company, USA, 2014.

[77] M. Gallmeyer, D. Seppi, Derivative security induced price manipulation (No. 2000-E41), Carnegie Mellon University, Tepper School of Business, 2000.

[78] G. Soros, Soros on Soros: Staying Ahead of the Curve, John Wiley & Sons, New York, 1995.

[79] U. Horst, F. Naujokat, Illiquidity and derivative valuation, 2008, arXiv preprint arXiv:0901.0091.

[80] H. Kraft, C. Kühn, Large traders and illiquid options: hedging vs. manipulation, J. Econ. Dyn. Control 35 (11) (2011) 1898–1915.

[81] T.Y. Wang, A. Winton, X. Yu, Corporate fraud and business conditions: evidence from IPOs, J. Finan. 65 (6) (2010) 2255–2292.

[82] P. Povel, R. Singh, A. Winton, Booms, busts, and fraud, Rev. Financ. Stud. 20 (4) (2007) 1219–1254.

[83] R.K. Aggarwal, A.K. Purnanandam, G. Wu, Underwriter manipulation in initial public offerings, 2005, available at SSRN 686252.

[84] M. Lowry, S. Shu, Litigation risk and IPO underpricing, J. Financ. Econ. 65 (3) (2002) 309–335.

[85] L. Chincarini, A. Etzkowitz, J. Kadish, The effects of laddering and spinning in underwriter manipulation of IPOs, Mich. J. Bus. 5 (2012) 43–59.

[86] M. Kenney, D. Patton, Firm database of emerging growth initial public offerings (IPOs), 1990–2010. http://hcd.ucdavis.edu/faculty/webpages/kenney/misc/Firm_IPO_Database_Guide.pdf, 2013.

[87] H. Schilit, Financial Shenanigans, Tata McGraw-Hill Education, New York, 2010.

[88] A. Brace, M. Musiela, et al., The market model of interest rate dynamics, Math. Finan. 7 (2) (1997) 127–155.

[89] R. Rebonato, Volatility and Correlation in the Pricing of Equity, FX, and Interest-Rate Options, John Wiley, Chichester, 1999.

[90] D.M. Dang, Modeling multi-factor financial derivatives by a partial differential equation approach with efficient implementation on graphics processing units, Ph.D. thesis, University of Toronto, 2011.

[91] X. Luo, P.V. Shevchenko, Pricing TARN using a finite difference method, 2013, available at SSRN.

[92] G. Pemberton, Money laundering through the securities market, The Money Laundering Bulletin, URL http://www.bcbqatar.com/English/Articles/LAUNDRY.pdf, Accessed 14.

[93] M. Levi, R.G. Smith, et al., Fraud Vulnerabilities and the Global Financial Crisis, Australian Institute of Criminology, Canberra, 2011.

[94] M. Levi, P. Reuter, Money laundering, Crime Justice 34 (1) (2006) 289–375.

[95] M. Levi, Controlling the international money trail: what lessons have been learned, in: Global Enforcement Regimes. Transnational Organized Crime, International Terrorism and Money Laundering, 2005.

[96] M. Himmel, M. Oliver, Do hedge funds really pose a money laundering threat? A decade of regulatory false starts raises questions, Hedge Fund Law Report, 2012.

[97] I. Ben-David, F. Franzoni, A. Landier, R. Moussawi, Do hedge funds manipulate stock prices? J. Finan. 68 (6) (2013) 2383–2434.

[98] G. Cici, A. Kempf, A. Puetz, Caught in the act: how hedge funds manipulate their equity positions, Tech. Rep., University of Cologne, Centre for Financial Research (CFR), 2010.

[99] W.F. Sharpe, The Sharpe ratio, in: Streetwise-the Best of the Journal of Portfolio Management, Princeton University Press, Princeton, NJ, 1998, pp. 169–185.

[100] W. Goetzmann, J. Ingersoll, M. Spiegel, I. Welch, Portfolio performance manipulation and manipulation-proof performance measures, Rev. Financ. Stud. 20 (5) (2007) 1503–1546.

[101] B. Liang, Hedge fund returns: auditing and accuracy, 2003, available at SSRN 968717.

[102] A. Abdulali, The Bias Ratio: Measuring the Shape of Fraud, Protégé Partners Quarterly Letter, 2006.

[103] S.G. Dimmock, W.C. Gerken, Regulatory oversight and return misreporting by hedge funds, 2014, available at SSRN 2260058.

[104] E. Zask, Finding financial fraudsters: quantitative and behavioural finance approaches, J. Secur. Oper. Custody 6 (4) (2014) 308–324.

[105] F. van Dyk, G. van Vuuren, A. Heymans, The bias ratio as a hedge fund fraud indicator: an empirical performance study under different economic conditions, Int. Bus. Econ. Res. J. (IBER) 13 (4) (2014) 867–896.

[106] D. Burgstahler, I. Dichev, Earnings management to avoid earnings decreases and losses, J. Account. Econ. 24 (1) (1997) 99–126.

[107] Y. Takeuchi, On a statistical method to detect discontinuity in the distribution function of reported earnings, Math. Comput. Simul. 64 (1) (2004) 103–111.

[108] N.P. Bollen, V.K. Pool, Predicting hedge fund fraud, Tech. Rep., Working Paper, 2009.

[109] S. Browna, M.-S. Kang, F. Inb, G. Lee, Resisting the manipulation of performance metrics: an empirical analysis of the manipulation-proof performance measure, SSRN eLibrary, 2010.

[110] M. Getmansky, A.W. Lo, I. Makarov, An econometric model of serial correlation and illiquidity in hedge fund returns, J. Financ. Econ. 74 (3) (2004) 529–609.

[111] D. Straumann, Measuring the quality of hedge fund data, J. Altern. Invest. 12 (2) (2009) 26–40.

[112] F. Benford, The law of anomalous numbers, Proc. Am. Philos. Soc. (1938) 551–572.

[113] S. Cohen, A. Schwartz, Privatization in Eastern Europe: the tunnel at the end of the light, Am. Prospect 4 (1993) 99–108.

[114] B.J. Field, A.N. Guiora, Using and abusing the financial markets: money laundering as the Achilles' heel of terrorism, J. Int. Econ. Law 29 (1) (2007) 59.

[115] R. Tendulkar, Cyber-crime, securities markets and systemic risk, CFA Digest 43 (4), CFA Institute (2013).

[116] R. Cont, Credit default swaps and financial stability, Financ. Stability Rev. 14 (2010) 35–43.

[117] V. Acharya, R. Engle, S. Figlewski, A. Lynch, M. Subrahmanyam, Centralized clearing for credit derivatives, Financ. Mark. Inst. Instrum. 18 (2) (2009) 168.

[118] D. Duffie, H. Zhu, Does a central clearing counterparty reduce counterparty risk? Rev. Asset Pricing Stud. 1 (1) (2011) 74–95.

Index

Note: page numbers followed by *f* indicate figures and *t* indicate tables.

T

U

V

W

Y

Printed in the United States
By Bookmasters